Funktion /Dysfunction
Function /Dysfunktion

/prospekt/

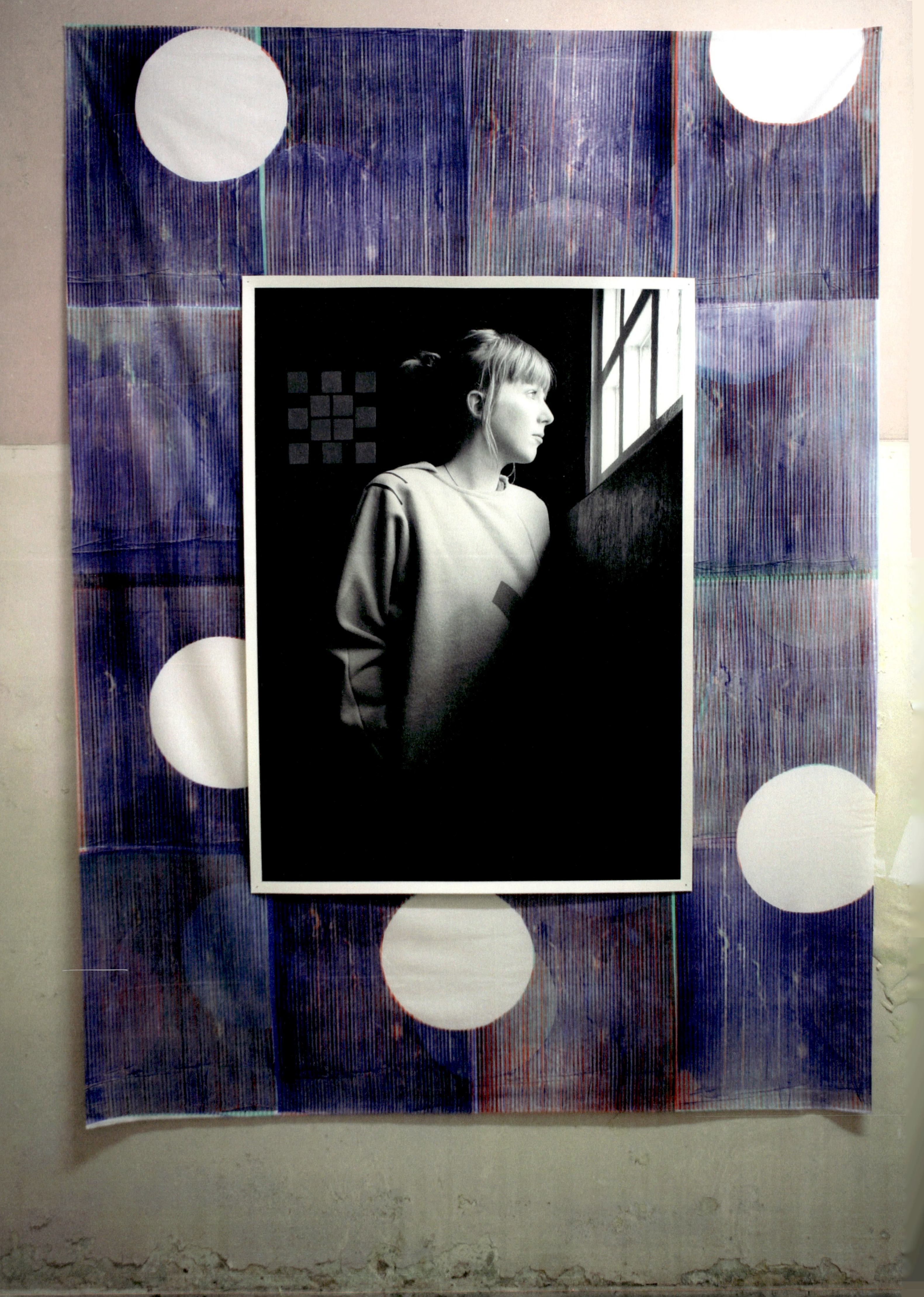

Funktion / *Dysfunction*
Function / Dysfunktion

Kunstzentrum
Contemporary Art from Glasgow

Claire Barclay
Martin Boyce
Nick Evans
Nicolas Party
Ciara Phillips
Mary Redmond

VERLAG *für* MODERNE KUNST

neues**museum**
Staatliches Museum für Kunst und Design in Nürnberg

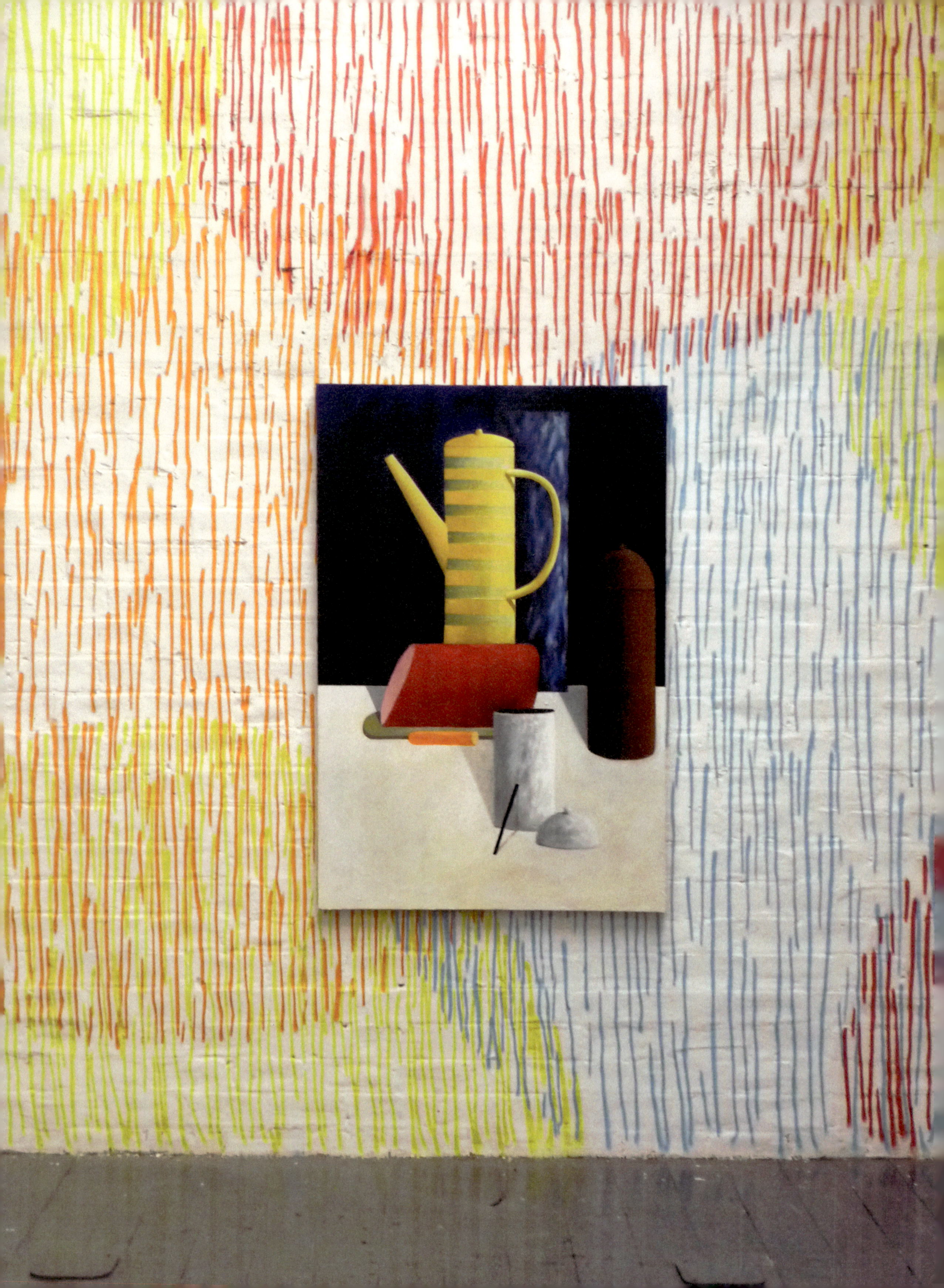

Grußwort

Foreword

Der British Council und Creative Scotland freuen sich über die überaus lebendige Partnerschaft zwischen Bayern und Schottland, die sich seit 2003 auf vielen kulturellen, wirtschaftlichen und gesellschaftlichen Ebenen manifestiert und zudem fest auf den zahlreichen städtepartnerschaftlichen Verbindungen basiert. Die Pflege von internationalen Kulturbeziehungen und der künstlerische Austausch stehen im Zentrum der Arbeit des British Councils und Creative Scotlands. Höhepunkt unserer kulturellen Zusammenarbeit mit Bayern waren eine Studienreise für Kuratoren nach Schottland im Jahre 2004 und im Anschluss ein großzügiges, von der bayerischen Staatsregierung finanziertes Stipendienprogramm für sechs schottische Künstler in der Villa Concordia Bamberg. Gerne erinnern wir uns aber auch an Einzelprojekte, wie die großartige Karla-Black-Skulpturenausstellung in der Kunsthalle Nürnberg im Jahre 2010.

Zur weiteren Stärkung der deutsch-schottischen Zusammenarbeit haben der British Council und Creative Scotland nun gemeinsam das *Creative Futures in Germany*-Programm aufgelegt, das Künstlern aus Schottland den Zugang zur Kunstszene in Deutschland mittels Projektförderung und Artist-in-Residencies erleichtern will. Wir sind glücklich, dass unsere Initiative bei Kunstvereinen und Ausstellungshäusern vielerorts auf fruchtbaren Boden gestoßen ist und insbesondere Künstlern aus Glasgow eine sichtbare Präsenz verliehen hat. Dave Sherry und Justin Carter, Professoren der Glasgow School of Art, haben mit ihren Studenten im Sommer das Projekt *Clyde meets Elbe* im Kunstverein Cuxhaven realisiert. Die renommierte Glasgower Kritikerin Sarah Lowndes kuratierte im September ein brillantes Porträt der frischen Glasgower Kunstszene an der Volksbühne Berlin.

Die Ausstellung *Funktion / Dysfunktion. Kunstzentrum Glasgow* im Staatlichen Museum für Kunst und Design in Nürnberg zeichnet nun anhand von sechs künstlerischen Positionen ein brandaktuelles wie auch in seiner einzigartigen Geschichte verwurzeltes Bild Glasgows als Zentrum für Kunst und Design. Längst ist Glasgow als kreativer Ort für Künstler international bekannt. Wir sind zuversichtlich, dass die von Melitta Kliege sorgfältig recherchierte Ausstellung die Attraktivität Glasgows noch mehr steigern und die partnerschaftlichen Beziehungen zwischen dem Freistaat Bayern und Schottland weiter stärken wird. Wir wünschen der Ausstellung viel Erfolg und großen Publikumszuspruch.

JOHN WHITEHEAD

British Council Germany

AMANDA CATTO

Creative Scotland

The British Council and Creative Scotland are delighted about the lively partnership between Scotland and Bavaria which, since 2003, has manifested itself on a number of cultural, economic and social levels and has been firmly anchored with several successful town twinnings. The nurturing of international cultural relations and artistic exchange are at the heart of the British Council's and Creative Scotland's work. A particular highlight of our cultural collaboration with Bavaria was a study visit of curators to Scotland in 2004, which was followed by a scholarship programme, very generously funded by the Bavarian State Government, for six Scottish artists at the Villa Concordia Bamberg. We also have fond memories of the many individual projects, such as the tremendous Karla Black sculpture exhibition at the Kunsthalle Nürnberg in 2010.

To strengthen the cooperation between Germany and Scotland further, the British Council and Creative Scotland have launched the initiative *Creative Futures in Germany*. The programme aims to give Scottish artists access to the German artistic scene through project support and artist-in-residence schemes. We are pleased to see that our initiative has met with an enthusiastic response from a number of art societies and exhibition spaces across Germany and has given Scottish artists, in particular Glaswegian artists, a strong visible presence. Professors Dave Sherry and Justin Carter of the Glasgow School of Art have, together with their students, created the project *Clyde meets Elbe* which could be seen at the Kunstverein Cuxhaven this summer. In September, the renowned Glasgow critic Sarah Lowndes curated an outstanding portrait of the current Glasgow art scene at the Volksbühne in Berlin.

The exhibition *Function / Dysfunction. Contemporary Art from Glasgow* at the State Museum for Art and Design in Nuremberg features six artistic perspectives portraying Glasgow as a centre of art and design, an image which is both highly topical today and rooted in the city's history. Glasgow has long been recognised, both nationally and internationally, as a creative space for artists. We are confident that the exhibition, which was thoroughly researched by Melitta Kliege, will further enhance Glasgow's position as a centre for art and design, and will strengthen the relationship between Scotland and the Free State of Bavaria. We wish the exhibition every success and hope that it is enjoyed by many visitors.

Grußwort

Foreword

Ein herzliches Willkommen den Künstlerinnen und Künstlern aus Glasgow in Nürnberg!

Glasgow ist eine faszinierende Stadt, ebenso reich an gegensätzlichen Traditionen wie an künstlerischer Vitalität. Seit Charles Rennie Mackintosh vor mehr als einhundert Jahren die Stadt Glasgow auf die Europakarte der modernen Kunst brachte – ubrigens mit engen Kontakten nach Deutschland und Österreich –, macht Glasgow immer wieder Kunstfreunde auf sich aufmerksam: Ich denke an die Glasgow School of Art, die Kelvingrove Art Gallery and Museum, die Burrell Collection und nicht zuletzt das House for an Art Lover, die zeitgenössische Umsetzung eines Originalentwurfs von Mackintosh.

In Nürnberg, der Partnerstadt Glasgows, kann man von Oktober 2013 bis Februar 2014 einigen Werken zeitgenössischer Künstlerinnen und Künstler aus Schottland begegnen. In manchen wird man das Spiel mit dem Design entdecken, in anderen die intensive Auseinandersetzung mit der Industriearchitektur, die Glasgow seit der industriellen Revolution geprägt hat.

Ich wünsche der Ausstellung viele aufgeschlossene Besucher. Mitten in Franken will sie uns zu einem Abstecher in das Schottland von heute einladen. Zugleich setzt sie damit ein sympathisches Signal für die gute Partnerschaft zwischen Schottland und Bayern, die heuer zehn Jahre alt wird und zwei starke, zukunftsorientierte europäische Regionen miteinander verbindet.

EMILIA MÜLLER

Staatsministerin für Bundes- und Europaangelegenheiten
in der Bayerischen Staatskanzlei
Bevollmächtigte des Freistaates Bayern beim Bund /
State Minister for Federal and European Affairs in the Bavarian State Chancellery
Plenipotentiary of the Free State of Bavaria to the Bundesrat

First of all, I would like to welcome the artists from Glasgow to the city of Nuremberg!

Glasgow is a fascinating city with a rich cultural and industrial heritage. Ever since Charles Rennie Mackintosh put it firmly on the European art map more than a century ago – with the help, incidentally, of some close links to Germany and Austria – Glasgow has attracted successive generations of artists and art lovers alike, offering outstanding institutions such as Glasgow School of Art, Kelvingrove Art Gallery and Museum, the Burrell Collection, and of course the House for an Art Lover, which was built in the 1990s to an original design by Mackintosh from 1901.

From October 2013 to February 2014, visitors to this new exhibition in Nuremberg – twinned with Glasgow since 1985 – have the opportunity to view works by contemporary artists who live and work in Scotland's largest city. These six young artists explore themes ranging from the interplay of art and design to the industrial architecture that has defined Glasgow since the Industrial Revolution.

I hope many people will visit and enjoy this highly interesting group show, which transports us from the centre of Franconia to the heart of Scotland. The exhibition is a further positive outcome of the ongoing partnership between Scotland and Bavaria, which celebrates its tenth anniversary in 2013 and unites two strong, forward-looking regions of Europe.

Grußwort

Foreword

Die Städtepartnerschaft mit Glasgow zählt zu den traditionsreichsten und am tiefsten verwurzelten Beziehungen unserer Stadt. Dies hat sicherlich seinen Grund nicht allein in der Dauer der Beziehung, die weit über den 1985 geschlossenen Partnerschaftsvertrag hinausreicht, sondern auch in den vielen Anknüpfungspunkten, die beide Städte besitzen. Beispielsweise müssen und mussten beide Städte den wirtschaftlichen Strukturwandel bewältigen, und hierbei – das verbindet sie erneut – spielen Bildungs- und Kulturinstitutionen eine wichtige Rolle. Gerade mit der Ernennung zur Kultur(haupt)stadt Europas* im Jahre 1990 wurde diese Schwerpunktsetzung Glasgows allgemein sichtbar.

Bei den Verbindungen zwischen beiden Städten auch langfristige Strukturen zu entwickeln, ist hierbei ein Anliegen. Der Austausch junger Musiker durch die existierende Partnerschaft zwischen zwei Rundfunksendern oder auch die nachhaltige Kooperation zwischen dem Nürnberger Menschenrechtsfilmfestival und dem Partnerfestival *Document* in Glasgow stehen hierfür als Beispiele.

Die Präsentation des Kunstzentrums Glasgow im Neuen Museum demonstriert uns dessen Vitalität und Bedeutung – mittlerweile auch im internationalen Maßstab. Es ist sicherlich kein Zufall, dass die in den Fassadenräumen des Neuen Museums ausgestellten sechs Positionen alle von in Glasgow lebenden Künstlerinnen und Künstlern stammen, die aber zur Hälfte über eine andere Herkunft (Kanada, Schweiz, England) verfügen. Regionalität erhält damit einen ganz neuen, den gesellschaftlichen Entwicklungen angemessenen Klang. Die vielfach implizierte Identität von Geburts- und Arbeitsort, wenn wir eine regionale Kulturlandschaft präsentieren, gehört mittlerweile der Vergangenheit an. Kunst und Kultur müssen auch in diesen Fragen Türen öffnen.

Auf unsere (Seh-)Gewohnheiten ein besonderes Augenmerk zu richten, ist ein direktes Ziel dieser Ausstellung, wenn Gegenstände, seien es Designprodukte oder Handwerksmaterialien, künstlerisch integriert werden und so einen anderen Bedeutungskontext erhalten. Der Ausstellung und den beteiligten Künstlerinnen und Künstlern wünsche ich viel Erfolg und uns allen vielfache Anregungen.

DR. ULRICH MALY

Oberbürgermeister der Stadt Nürnberg / Lord Mayor of the City of Nuremberg

The town twinning with Glasgow is one of the strongest and most deeply rooted relationships our city maintains. This is not only due to the length of the relationship – which dates back much further than the signing of the partnership agreement in 1985 – but also to the many links between Nuremberg and Glasgow. For example, both cities have had to cope with the effects of economic structural change, whereby educational and cultural institutions have played a key role in shaping the future. Above all, Glasgow's designation as European City* of Culture in 1990 was a clear signal of the city's commitment to the promotion of the arts.

The development of long-term initiatives is a crucial element in establishing and maintaining connections between the two cities. Examples of such initiatives include a partnership between two radio stations that organise an exchange programme for young musicians, and the long-standing cooperation between the Nuremberg International Human Rights Film Festival and its partner, the *Document* film festival in Glasgow.

The current presentation of contemporary art from Glasgow at the Neues Museum demonstrates the vitality and growing importance of this institution on an international scale. As the exhibition portrays aspects of the cultural landscape of the Scottish region, it is important to note that although the six featured artists are all based in Glasgow, three of them were born outside Scotland (in Canada, Switzerland and England, respectively). Regionalism has therefore taken on a new meaning, as the idea that a person's place of birth is identical to their place of work has become a thing of the past. Art and culture can lead the way in responding to such important social developments, as this exhibition effectively shows.

Function / Dysfunction. Contemporary Art from Glasgow examines our customary viewing habits by exploring how elements of applied art such as design products or craft materials are incorporated into fine art and gain new meaning in this context. I am certain that the exhibition will provide stimulating insights into this topic, and I wish the organisers and the participating artists every success.

---

* Bis 1998 trug die Kulturhauptstadt Europas die Bezeichnung Kulturstadt Europas.

* Until 1998 the European Capital of Culture was called the European City of Culture.

Vorwort
Preface

Die diesjährige Ausstellung in der Reihe */prospekt/* widmet sich dem schottischen Kunstzentrum Glasgow. Anhand von sechs künstlerischen Positionen untersucht die Ausstellung, wie Motive und Formen, die ursprünglich aus dem Bereich des Angewandten stammen, in vor allem raumgreifende Installationen Eingang gefunden haben. Längst hat die zeitgenössische Kunst die Grenzen zwischen den Disziplinen überwunden, und so ist es auch in der Rezeption nicht (mehr) sinnvoll, diese Grenzen zu suchen. Doch erscheint es lohnenswert, der Semantik der verschiedenen Bereiche nachzuspüren, um die Bedeutung von Artefakten umfänglich zu verstehen. Auf die ursprüngliche Dichotomie von angewandter Kunst respektive Design und bildender Kunst sowie der beidseitigen Strategien von Zweckzuordnung und Zweckentfremdung verweist der Titel der Ausstellung *Funktion / Dysfunktion*.

Claire Barclay, Martin Boyce, Nick Evans, Nicolas Party, Ciara Phillips und Mary Redmond sind eingeladen, jeweils einen der insgesamt sechs Fassadenräume des Neuen Museums zu gestalten. Die in den 1960er, 70er und 80er Jahren geborenen Künstlerinnen und Künstler können für drei „Generationen" schottischer Kunst stehen. Ihnen gemeinsam sind ein Interesse und eine Haltung, die traditionellen Bereiche des Freien und des Angewandten in Material und Technik zu neuen Aussagen zu führen.

Funktion / Dysfunktion. Kunstzentrum Glasgow ist der fünfte Auftritt innerhalb der Ausstellungsreihe */prospekt/*. Das Neue Museum hat sich die in der Architektur angelegte Transparenz und Offenheit des Gebäudes zur Programmatik gemacht, indem es im Jahr 2009 ein neues Ausstellungsformat mit dem Titel */prospekt/* startete. Ungewöhnlicher Ort dieser Ausstellungsreihe sind die sechs vom Klarissenplatz aus einsehbaren Fassadenräume auf zwei Etagen, die sich wie Schaufenster zum Außenraum hin öffnen und auch über die Öffnungszeiten hinaus das Museum nach außen präsentieren. Zeigt sich traditionell eine Ausstellung in der horizontalen Fläche in einem geschlossenen Raum, so bieten die auf zwei Etagen übereinanderliegenden sechs Fassadenräume die Möglichkeit, eine in die Vertikale gelegte Fläche zu bespielen und gleichzeitig – das Museum als Vitrine – den Betrachterstandort vom Innen- in den Außenraum zu verlegen.

Nach den monografischen Ausstellungen von Katharina Grosse (Malerei), Gerhard Mayer (Zeichnung) sowie Martin Wöhrl (Installation) widmete sich die Reihe */prospekt/* im letzten Jahr mit einer thematischen Ausstellung der aktuellen Kunstproduktion der Akademie der Bildenden Künste in Nürnberg.

This year's exhibition in the */prospekt/* series focuses on the Scottish city of Glasgow as a thriving centre of contemporary art. Featuring six Glasgow-based artists, it explores how forms and subject matter derived from applied art and design have found their way into works of fine art, often in the context of expansive installations. Contemporary visual art has long since blurred the boundaries between conventional disciplines, so that we no longer need to seek such distinctions when viewing works, but exploring the semantics of the different realms can nevertheless help us to understand the meaning of artefacts. The exhibition title – *Function / Dysfunction* – refers to the traditional dichotomy between applied art (or design) and fine art, as well as between the concepts of function and non-function.

Claire Barclay, Martin Boyce, Nick Evans, Nicolas Party, Ciara Phillips and Mary Redmond were each invited to create a work for one of the Neues Museum's facade spaces. Born in the 1960s, 70s or 80s, they represent three 'generations' of Scottish art and share an interest in creating new forms of expression by combining materials and processes from the realms of fine and applied art.

Function / Dysfunction. Contemporary Art from Glasgow is the fifth exhibition in the */prospekt/* series. With this new exhibition format, which was launched in 2009, the Neues Museum has developed a programmatic concept based on the transparency and openness of its architecture. The spaces directly behind the museum's glass facade provide the unusual location for these exhibitions: facing onto Klarissenplatz, they can be viewed from outside like shop windows and act as an interface between the museum and the external surroundings, even outside opening hours. Whereas a conventional exhibition is presented as a horizontal display in an enclosed space, here the six spaces extend over two storeys, making it possible to create a vertically oriented display and transforming the museum itself into a vitrine by shifting the viewer's perspective to outside the building.

Following monographic exhibitions by Katharina Grosse (painting), Gerhard Mayer (drawing) and Martin Wöhrl (installation), last year's exhibition in the */prospekt/* series focussed on contemporary practice at the Academy of Fine Arts in Nuremberg. The current exhibition impressively demonstrates the important role played by art schools in the development of a strong art scene. All six artists graduated with Bachelor and/or Master of Fine Art degrees from Glasgow School of Art. Founded in 1845

Welche Bedeutung Akademien für die Entwicklung eines Kunstzentrums besitzen, belegt nun eindrucksvoll die aktuelle Ausstellung. Alle sechs Künstlerinnen und Künstler haben die renommierte Glasgow School of Art besucht. Diese Mitte des 19. Jahrhunderts als „School of Design" gegründete Hochschule gilt heute als eine der international renommiertesten Akademien für bildende Kunst und Design. Das hier verortete Neben- und Miteinander von Disziplinen hat sicherlich zu einer Atmosphäre beigetragen, die sich durch Offenheit und Medienvielfalt auszeichnet, aber auch Stringenz und Qualität der individuellen künstlerischen Positionen fördert.

Dr. Melitta Kliege hat die Ausstellung *Funktion / Dysfunktion* initiiert und kuratiert sowie den begleitenden Katalog konzipiert. Herzlich möchte ich ihr für die verantwortliche Tätigkeit und ihren großen Einsatz einen besonderen Dank aussprechen. Ein großer Dank geht ebenfalls an die Registrarin Susanne Teichmann für die Logistik des Leihverkehrs sowie an alle Mitarbeiterinnen und Mitarbeiter, die zum guten Gelingen der Ausstellung beigetragen haben.

Wir freuen uns, dass diese Publikation im Verlag für moderne Kunst Nürnberg erscheinen kann und danken für die bewährte und gute Kooperation. Ein herzlicher Dank geht an Lena Mozer und Ernst Georg Kühle für die ausgezeichnete grafische Gestaltung der Publikation.

Sehr herzlich möchte ich, auch im Namen von Dr. Melitta Kliege, den Autorinnen und Autoren Dank sagen für ihre kenntnisreichen Texte, die sie als Spezialisten der schottischen Kunstszene verfasst haben: Dr. Katrina Brown, Direktorin The Common Guild und Co-Kuratorin des schottischen Beitrags auf der diesjährigen Biennale in Venedig, Dr. Fiona Bradley, Direktorin The Fruitmarket Gallery, den Kunstkritikern und Autoren Kitty Anderson, Oliver Basciano, Stephen Feeke und Fiona Jardine sowie Dr. Sarah Lowndes, an der Glasgow School of Art lehrend und bekannt durch ihre Publikationen zur Kunst in Glasgow.

Ein Ausstellungsprojekt in dieser Größe wäre ohne die Unterstützung von dritter Seite nicht möglich. So möchte ich einen sehr herzlichen Dank für ihre großzügige Unterstützung sagen: dem British Council Germany und Creative Scotland, der Staatsregierung Bayern und dem Bayerischen Staatsministerium für Wissenschaft, Forschung und Kunst sowie der Stadt Nürnberg.

Der größte Dank schließlich geht an Claire Barclay, Martin Boyce, Nick Evans, Nicolas Party, Ciara Phillips und Mary Redmond für ihre Teilnahme an der Ausstellung und ihren großen Einsatz.

ANGELIKA NOLLERT

Direktorin / Director, Neues Museum – Staatliches Museum für Kunst und Design in Nürnberg

as a Government School of Design, GSA is internationally recognised as a leading college of fine art, design and architecture. The scope and intersection of its academic courses creates an atmosphere of openness – above all towards the use of media – while promoting intellectual rigour and artistic depth in the development of individual approaches.

Dr Melitta Kliege initiated and curated the exhibition *Function / Dysfunction*, and also edited this publication – my sincere thanks to her for all her work and her dedicated commitment to the project. Thanks are also due to our registrar Susanne Teichmann for arranging the loans, as well as to all the other members of the Neues Museum staff who have contributed to the success of the exhibition.

We are very grateful to Verlag für moderne Kunst Nürnberg for publishing the catalogue and for their continued support and cooperation. Sincere thanks also to Lena Mozer and Ernst Georg Kühle for their excellent graphic design.

Dr Melitta Kliege and I would like to thank the authors for the valuable insights they have provided as experts on the Scottish art scene: Dr Katrina Brown, Director of The Common Guild and co-curator of the Scottish contribution to this year's Venice Biennale; Dr Fiona Bradley, Director of The Fruitmarket Gallery; art critics and writers Kitty Anderson, Oliver Basciano, Stephen Feeke and Fiona Jardine; and special thanks to Dr Sarah Lowndes, who lectures at Glasgow School of Art and has written an excellent book on the rise of the Glasgow art scene.

An exhibition on this scale would not be possible without third-party assistance, and I would like to take this opportunity to thank the British Council Germany; Creative Scotland; the Bavarian State Government; the Bavarian State Ministry of Sciences, Research and the Arts; and the City of Nuremberg for their generous support.

Finally, our most sincere thanks are due to Claire Barclay, Martin Boyce, Nick Evans, Nicolas Party, Ciara Phillips and Mary Redmond for agreeing to take part in the exhibition and creating such impressive and interesting works.

Funktion / Dysfunktion
Kunstzentrum Glasgow

Claire Barclay, Martin Boyce, Nick Evans, Nicolas Party, Ciara Phillips und Mary Redmond

„Kompromisse gehen nicht. Als ich jetzt nach Edinburgh fuhr, hatte ich eigentlich überhaupt nichts. Nur das Bewußtsein, ich mache dort ein Konzert. Ich hatte Filme bestellt, ein Klavier und vieles andere. Ich wußte nicht, was kam. Ich wußte nur, ich mache das Konzert. Innerlich bereitete ich mich vor. Als ich hinkam, stand dort ein alter Stock. Es stellte sich heraus, daß der wichtig war. Den brauchte ich. Unterwegs sah ich in einem Geschäft eine Axt. Die kaufte ich, denn unter Umständen konnte ich sie gebrauchen. Die hab ich hingestellt und doch nicht gebraucht, aber es war gut, daß sie da stand. Dann fing ich an, sah mich im Raum um und fing an, alles ein bißchen abzutasten und die entsprechenden Zeichen zu entwickeln; einen Zeitplan zu entwerfen, dann kam Henning Christiansen dazu. Wir fingen einfach an. [...] Der Ort ist wichtig. Denn ich sage, wir leben nun mal auf diesem Planeten, und wenn man den als einen Organismus betrachtet, der lebt, so spielt der Ort eine Rolle. Einfach erst als Frage. Was ist das hier in Schottland? Was ist das hier?"[1] Joseph Beuys kam 1970 erstmals nach Schottland, um dort an einer Ausstellung teilzunehmen und seine Aktion *Celtic (Kinloch Rannoch) Schottische Symphonie* [**Abb. 1**] durchzuführen, von deren Vorbereitungen er hier in einem Gespräch gegenüber Hagen Lieberknecht berichtet. Anlässlich des Edinburgh International Festival hatte der Galerist Richard Demarco gemeinsam mit der Kunsthalle Düsseldorf zu einer Ausstellung eingeladen, welche die aktuelle Kunstproduktion aus Düsseldorf vorstellen sollte. Insgesamt 35 Künstler zeigten ihre Werke in der Ausstellung *Strategy: Get Arts* im Edinburgh College of Art. Der Kunsthallenleiter Karl Ruhrberg hatte Akademieprofessoren wie Joseph Beuys und damals bereits arrivierte Künstler der Düsseldorfer Szene wie Adolf Luther, Ferdinand Kriwet, Erwin Heerich, Konrad Klapheck, Heinz Mack oder Günther Uecker ausgewählt, aber auch junge Absolventen der Kunstakademie einbezogen wie Sigmar Polke, Gerhard Richter oder Blinky Palermo.

Düsseldorf war damals innerhalb des Rheinlandes ein sich gerade etablierendes Kunstzentrum. Mit einem Bildungsauftrag nach innen, also internationale Kunst vor Ort vorzustellen, war die Region damals Anlaufstelle im internatio-

Function / Dysfunction
Contemporary Art from Glasgow

Claire Barclay, Martin Boyce, Nick Evans, Nicolas Party, Ciara Phillips and Mary Redmond

"There can be no compromises. When I went to Edinburgh I really had nothing at all. Just the idea of doing a concert there. I had ordered films, a piano and lots of other things. I didn't know what was going to happen. I only knew I would do the concert. I prepared myself inwardly. When I got there I found an old staff. It turned out to be important. I needed it. When I was out and about in town I spotted an axe in a shop. I bought it because I thought I might need it. I put the axe in place and in the end I didn't use it, but it was good to have it there. Then I got started. I had a look around the space and began to get a feeling for it all, to develop the corresponding symbols and draw up a schedule, and then I was joined by Henning Christiansen. We just got started. [...] The place is important. Because after all, I say, we live on this planet, and if you think of it as a living organism then the place plays a part, first of all simply as a question. What is this here in Scotland? What is this?"[1] Joseph Beuys visited Scotland for the first time in 1970 to take part in an exhibition and perform his "action" *Celtic (Kinloch Rannoch) Scottish Symphony* [fig. 1], the preparations for which he is describing in the above excerpt from an interview with Hagen Lieberknecht. The exhibition *Strategy: Get Arts* was organised by the Edinburgh-based gallerist Richard Demarco in collaboration with the Kunsthalle Düsseldorf, and focussed on contemporary art from Düsseldorf. Thirty-five artists presented their work in the show, which was held at Edinburgh College of Art as part of the Edinburgh International Festival. Among those invited to take part by Karl Ruhrberg, the director of the Kunsthalle Düsseldorf, were professors from the Kunstakademie Düsseldorf such as Beuys, other established figures from the city's art scene including Adolf Luther, Ferdinand Kriwet, Erwin Heerich, Konrad Klapheck, Heinz Mack and Günther Uecker, but also a number of young graduates from the Kunstakademie such as Sigmar Polke, Gerhard Richter and Blinky Palermo.

At that time, Düsseldorf was in the process of establishing itself as an art centre within the Rhineland. As part of a cultural initiative aimed at introducing

nalen Kunstgeschehen. In Düsseldorf zeigte die Kunsthalle beispielweise Künstler wie Gilbert & George, Marcel Broodthaers oder Ad Reinhardt. Die seit 1967 existierende Galerie von Konrad Fischer präsentierte Carl Andre, Sol LeWitt, Bruce Nauman oder Robert Smithson, und Alfred Schmela stellte bereits seit Ende der fünfziger Jahre internationale Positionen vor wie Antoni Tàpies, Yves Klein oder Robert Morris. In Köln war 1967 der „Kunstmarkt" als erste Kunstmesse entstanden und zu den umliegenden Hot Spots gehörten beispielsweise das Stedelijk Van Abbemuseum in Eindhoven, das Museum Haus Lange in Krefeld, das Städtische Museum in Leverkusen – Schloss Morsbroich, das Städtische Museum in Mönchengladbach, das Rijksmuseum Kröller-Müller in Otterloo oder die Wide White Space Gallery in Antwerpen.

local audiences to international art, efforts had been made to transform the region into a global art destination. The Kunsthalle Düsseldorf, for example, mounted exhibitions with artists such as Gilbert & George, Marcel Broodthaers and Ad Reinhardt. Konrad Fischer presented work by Carl Andre, Sol LeWitt, Bruce Nauman and Robert Smithson, among others, in the gallery he had set up in 1967, while Alfred Schmela had been showing international artists such as Antoni Tàpies, Yves Klein and Robert Morris since the late 1950s. The "Kölner Kunstmarkt", established in Cologne in 1967, was the world's first contemporary art fair, and among the popular meeting places in the surrounding area were the Stedelijk Van Abbemuseum in Eindhoven, Museum Haus Lange in Krefeld, the Städtisches Museum Schloss Morsbroich in Leverkusen, the Städtisches

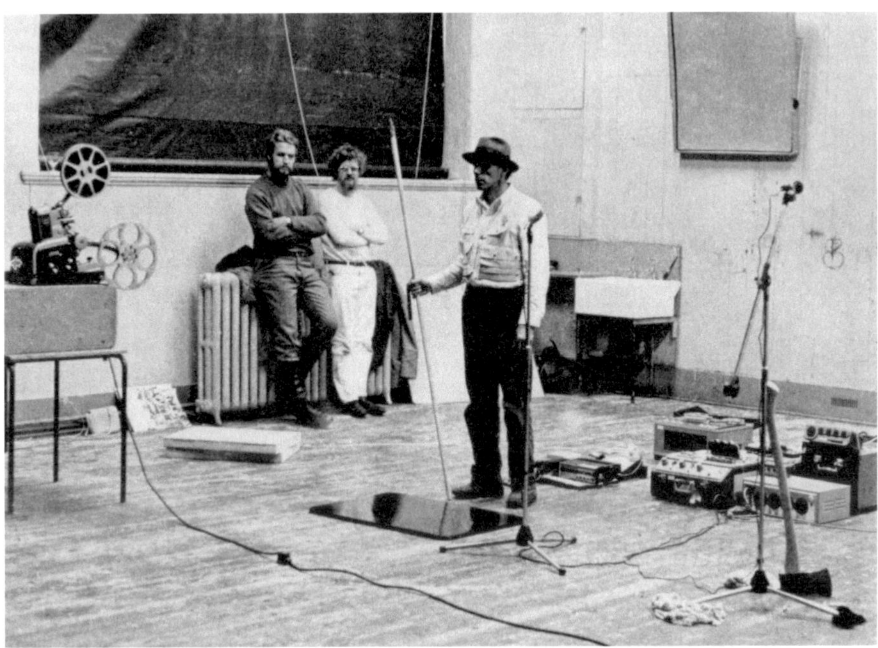

1 Joseph Beuys, Aktion *Celtic (Kinloch Rannoch) Schottische Symphonie*, 1970, Edinburgh College of Art, Edinburgh

Beuys führte in einer Klasse im Erdgeschoss des Edinburgh College of Art seine dreieinhalbstündige Aktion ab dem Eröffnungstag dieser Ausstellung zur Düsseldorfer Szene am 23. August 1970 an acht aufeinander folgenden Tagen insgesamt zwölf Mal durch.[2] Im Titel seiner Aktion bezieht er sich auf den Ort, indem er auf ein Dorf im schottischen Hochland verweist und auf den deutschen Komponisten Felix Mendelssohn, der 1829 die schottischen Highlands bereiste, um „Anzeichen der Ursprünge der keltischen Kultur in dieser Landschaft zu suchen"[3].

Rein formal gesehen, präsentierte Beuys mit seiner Aktion 1970 in Edinburgh einen Kunstbegriff, bei dem die eingesetzten Materialien Kontexte erschließen zum Ort des Geschehens selbst und zu allgemeinen Handlungen. Die Elemente seiner Aktion, beispielsweise das Klavier, die Ton- und Film-

Museum in Mönchengladbach, the Rijksmuseum Kröller-Müller in Otterloo and the Wide White Space Gallery in Antwerp.

Beginning on 23 August 1970, the first day of the exhibition on the Düsseldorf art scene, Joseph Beuys performed his three-and-a-half-hour-long action a total of 12 times over eight consecutive days in a classroom on the ground floor of Edinburgh College of Art.[2] The title of the piece contains references to the Scottish location, including the name of a village in the Scottish Highlands, as well as to the German composer Felix Mendelssohn, who explored the region in 1829, "looking for traces of the origins of Celtic culture in this landscape"[3].

From a purely formal perspective, Beuys' action in Edinburgh in 1970 presented a

medien, der Stock, die Axt, die Schiefertafel und die Kreide, das beschriebene Papier oder die Gelatine, eröffnen Gedankenzusammenhänge zu Tätigkeitsfeldern, wie dem Schreiben, dem Musizieren, dem Stimmen des Instrumentes, dem Filmen beziehungsweise dem Konservieren und Übertragen von Ton und Bild, aber auch zu nützlichen Tätigkeiten des Alltags wie dem Holzhacken. Der Akademieprofessor der Düsseldorfer Bildhauerklasse demonstriert so einen Skulpturbegriff, bei dem alltägliche Dinge und Materialien zunächst an einem Ort räumlich verbunden werden, um so in gänzlich verschiedene Richtungen Kontexte herzustellen, sei es hin zur Musik, zu archaischer Kultur, zur Kunst, zu regionalen Aspekten, zum Handwerk oder zum spirituellen Leben. Wenn Beuys künstlerisch auch andere Ziele verfolgt hat, so ist diese kontextualisierende Strategie doch durch die Ansätze der Fluxus-Künstler beeinflusst, die beabsichtigten, in ihren Aktionen kurze Alltagsmomente aufscheinen zu lassen, wie *Exit* von George Brecht, *Music while you work* von Arthur Koepcke oder Nam June Paiks *Simple* als Beispiele zeigen.

Als die Idee entstand, im Neuen Museum in Nürnberg in der Reihe */prospekt/* die künstlerische Produktion Schottlands vorzustellen, konzentrierte sich die Auswahl der Künstler bald auf die Kunstmetropole Glasgow. Kunst aus Schottland ist in den Blickpunkt internationaler Aufmerksamkeit gerückt, wie Katrina Brown und Rob Tufnell schon 2001 in ihrem Vorwort zur Ausstellung *Here + Now* festgestellt hatten, dem gewichtigen Überblick zur schottischen Kunst mit über sechzig Künstlern im DCA – Dundee Contemporary Arts in Dundee.[4] Schottland leistet sich eine ganze Reihe Hochschulen für Kunst wie das Edinburgh College of Art in Edinburgh, das Duncan of Jordanstone College of Art & Design (DJCAD) in Dundee, die Gray's School of Art in Aberdeen oder die Glasgow School of Art (GSA) in Glasgow. Hinzu kommen künstlerische Werkstätten, wie das DCA Print Studio in Dundee oder Peacock Visual Arts in Aberdeen. Immerhin hatten rund fünfzig der in Dundee eingeladenen Künstler, so stellt John Calcutt im Katalog zur Ausstellung heraus, zu dem einen oder anderen Zeitpunkt die Akademie in Glasgow besucht. Glasgow hatte sich mit der traditionsreichen Glasgow School of Art (GSA) in dem eindrucksvollen Gebäude von Charles Rennie Mackintosh zum Zentrum einer sich international etablierenden Kunstszene entwickelt. Der in Glasgow tätige Künstler Douglas Gordon hatte bereits 1996 den von der Tate Britain ausgelobten renommierten Turner Prize gewonnen, 2005 sollten noch Simon Starling, 2010 Richard Wright und 2011 Martin Boyce folgen.

concept of creating art whereby the materials used by the artist open up new contexts in relation to a place, and also to more general, universal activities. The various components of his artistic "action" – for example the piano, the sound- and film-based media, the wooden staff, the axe, the blackboard and chalk, the paper with writing on it and the gelatine – evoke associations with activities such as writing, playing music, tuning instruments, making films, or preserving and broadcasting sounds and images, but also with productive everyday activities such as chopping wood. Beuys, who was a professor of sculpture at the Kunstakademie Düsseldorf, thus demonstrated a form of sculptural practice in which everyday objects and materials are first of all connected to a particular site and from there forge links in many different directions, whether it is to music, archaic culture, art, regional aspects, craft-based activities or spirituality. While Beuys also pursued other artistic objectives, this contextualising strategy is influenced by the Fluxus artists' aim of incorporating elements of everyday life into their "actions" – as seen, for example, in George Brecht's work *Exit*, Arthur Koepcke's *Music while you work* or Nam June Paik's *Simple*.

When the idea emerged of presenting contemporary art from Scotland at the Neues Museum in Nuremberg as part of our */prospekt/* series, the selection of artists soon became focussed on the city of Glasgow as a leading art centre. Scottish art is increasingly gaining international attention, as Katrina Brown and Rob Tufnell already observed in 2001 in the catalogue to accompany the exhibition *Here + Now*, an extensive survey of contemporary artistic practice in Scotland – involving more than 60 artists – that was presented at Dundee Contemporary Arts (DCA).[4] Scotland has a relatively large number of art colleges, including Edinburgh College of Art, Duncan of Jordanstone College of Art & Design (DJCAD) in Dundee, Gray's School of Art in Aberdeen and Glasgow School of Art (GSA). Facilities for making and showing art are also provided by artists' workshops such as DCA Print Studio in Dundee or Peacock Visual Arts in Aberdeen. It is worth noting, however, as John Calcutt writes in the above-mentioned catalogue, that around 50 of the artists on show in Dundee had studied at Glasgow School of Art at one time or another. This long-established art school, housed in an impressive building designed by Charles Rennie Mackintosh, undoubtedly helped Glasgow to become the centre of an emerging international art scene. One of its graduates, Douglas Gordon, won the Turner Prize – the

Die Kulturpolitik und das Bereitstellen von Mitteln aus öffentlicher Hand spielten keine unerhebliche Rolle, um die künstlerischen und kulturellen Ambitionen einer jungen Generation zu unterstützen und ihr zum internationalen Durchbruch zu verhelfen. Denn dieser Aufstieg hatte ohne einen regional vorhandenen Kunstmarkt stattfinden können. Über sehr verschiedene Programme unterstützte der (1967 unter der Labour Regierung durch die damalige Kultusministerin Jennie Lee gegründete) Scottish Arts Council (heute: Creative Scotland) die Kulturschaffenden und vergab etwa Reisestipendien an Künstler, beispielsweise zur Biennale nach Venedig oder zur Art Basel, oder mit den Creative Scotland Awards sogar gewichtige Produktionsstipendien, mit denen Künstler aller Sparten neue Werke schaffen konnten. Seit 1995 wurden zudem Mittel aus dem National Lottery Capital Fund für Gebäude bereitgestellt, wie für den Neubau des 1999 eröffneten Kunstmuseums DCA oder für die Renovierung vorhandener Institutionen wie des Centre for Contemporary Arts (CCA) und der Ausstellungshalle Tramway in Glasgow. Als Schottland 2003 nach der Einrichtung eines eigenen Parlaments eine Regionalpartnerschaft mit Bayern einging, luden das British Council und das Scottish Arts Council im Folgejahr Kuratoren aus Bayern zu einer Studienreise nach Schottland ein, was schließlich auch den Grundstein zu diesem Ausstellungsprojekt in Nürnberg legte.

Creating Our Future … Minding Our Past. Scotland's National Cultural Strategy – in einer neuen Liaison von Politik und Kultur hatte die Regierung im Jahr 2000 ein aktuelles Strategiepapier zur Förderung der Kultur verfasst. Anlässlich der Einweihung des DCA in Dundee hatte der Staatssekretär Donald Dewar 1999 eine Verbindung zwischen der neuen selbstbewussten Kraft der schottischen Politik und der schottischen Kunst vorgeschlagen und so der Kulturpolitik eine zentrale Funktion für die regionale Selbstbehauptung zugewiesen. Zeitgenössische Kunst wird als ein identitätsstiftendes Element der Gesellschaft erkannt und genutzt. In der Folge sollte Schottland ab 2003 unter dem Signet „Scotland and Venice" einen eigenen nationalen Beitrag zur Biennale in Venedig beisteuern. Bei den vergangenen sechs Biennalen wurden so insgesamt 17 Künstler in Venedig vorgestellt, unter ihnen auch Claire Barclay 2003 und Martin Boyce 2009. Die Stadt Glasgow richtet zudem seit 2004 das zweijährlich stattfindende Glasgow International Festival of Visual Art aus, bei dem 2006 zunächst nicht sicher war, ob es weitergeführt werden sollte. Doch als die Stadt durch eine Studie herausfand, dass mit dem Festival auch ein wirtschaftlicher Erfolg verbunden war und für

prestigious art prize awarded annually by Tate Britain – in 1996, and he was to be followed by Simon Starling in 2005, Richard Wright in 2010 and Martin Boyce in 2011.

State cultural policy and public funding played a not inconsiderable role in furthering the creative and cultural ambitions of a generation of young artists and helping them to break into the international scene. This factor is all the more significant because Scottish art rose to prominence in the relative absence of a market for contemporary art in the country. The Scottish Arts Council (SAC – now Creative Scotland), which was set up in 1967 by Jennie Lee, the Minister for the Arts under the then Labour government, provided valuable support to visual artists and other creative professionals through a wide range of programmes. These included travel grants that enabled artists to visit the Venice Biennale or Art Basel and, in the form of Creative Scotland Awards, substantial production grants with which artists from all disciplines could create new works. From 1995 onwards, the National Lottery Capital Fund provided financial support for new building projects such as the construction of DCA in Dundee, which opened in 1999, as well as for the refurbishment of existing institutions, such as the Centre for Contemporary Arts (CCA) and the Tramway exhibition space in Glasgow. Following the establishment of the devolved Scottish parliament, Scotland entered into a regional partnership with the German state of Bavaria in 2003. The following year, the British Council and the Scottish Arts Council invited curators from Bavaria to make a study visit to Scotland, which also laid the foundations for the current exhibition project in Nuremberg.

Creating Our Future … Minding Our Past. Scotland's National Cultural Strategy – in 2000 the Scottish Executive published its strategy for the promotion of culture in Scotland, reflecting a new liaison between politics and culture. On the occasion of the opening of DCA in Dundee in 1999, Donald Dewar – at that time the Secretary of State for Scotland – had proposed that the assertiveness of the country's new political identity should be reflected in its art, and thus assigned cultural policy a key role in the development and projection of Scotland's self-image. Contemporary art was thereby recognised and used as a key element in the construction of social identity. To this end, it was decided that from 2003 onwards, Scotland would make its own national contribution to the Venice Biennale under the heading "Scotland and Venice". A total of 17

jedes ausgegebene Pfund gleich neun zurückkommen würden, erhöhte sie das Budget sprunghaft von 70.000 Pfund 2006 auf 400.000 Pfund 2008.[5]

Social Sculpture betitelt Sarah Lowndes frei nach Beuys ihre aufschlussreiche sozialgeschichtliche Studie zum Aufstieg der Glasgower Kunstszene.[6] Sie beschreibt im Hinblick auf bildende Kunst, Literatur und Musik die Entwicklung einer sich bis 2002 herausbildenden und sich dann international etablierenden Kunstmetropole. Ihre Darstellung konzentriert sich neben den öffentlichen Institutionen, wie etwa The Fruitmarket Gallery in Edinburgh oder CCA und Tramway in Glasgow, besonders auf das Programm und die Entwicklung der zahlreichen Künstlerinitiativen, allen voran von Transmission in Glasgow. Die 1983 gegründete Produzentengalerie hat mit ihrer basisdemokratischen Struktur bis heute eine beeindruckende Kontinuität als Treffpunkt inne. Die Stärke dieser Institution scheint gerade in der Programmatik eines stets wechselnden Künstlergremiums (Committee for the Visual Arts – CVA) zu liegen, mit seinen sich jeweils verändernden und immer aktuellen künstlerischen Fragestellungen und Herangehensweisen. So hatte Transmission in den achtziger Jahren ein eher linkspolitisches Profil und trat zu Beginn mit den damals aktuellen expressiven Malereipositionen des New Image Painting um Steven Campbell (1953–2007) und Adrian Wiszniewski (geb. 1958) in Erscheinung.[7] Mit Glasgow als europäischer Kulturhauptstadt entwickelte sich Transmission dann ab 1990 zu einer sich öffnenden Institution; internationale Künstler wurden im Programm berücksichtigt. *Installation Work* nannte sich die Ausstellung zum Hauptstadtjahr, auf deren Einladungskarte die Do-It-Yourself-Mentalität der mit diesem Ausstellungsraum verbundenen Künstler hervorgehoben wurde. Martin Boyce, der damals gerade die Hochschule absolviert hatte und später auch zum Gremium von Transmission gehörte, erinnert sich: „Transmission schien damals nicht nur der Mittelpunkt der Arbeit, sondern einer gesamten Haltung zu sein. Es war eine Art soziales Zentrum und ein Brennpunkt – es war die erste Anlaufstation für Freunde, die zu Besuch kamen. Ich weiß noch, dass ich als Aufsicht dort war, bevor ich Gremiumsmitglied wurde, und die Leute stiegen aus dem Londoner Zug und gingen direkt dorthin, weil sie wussten, sie könnten dort jemanden treffen und einen Drink nehmen. Keiner von uns hatte ein Atelier, also war dies der Ort, um abzuhängen oder mit jemandem zu reden."[8]

Für die bildende Kunst bedeutete das große kulturpolitische Engagement Schottlands zwischenzeitlich aber auch einen Rückschlag, als 1998/99 gleich zwei Institutionen, das

artists based in Scotland have presented their work at the last six editions of the Biennale, including Claire Barclay in 2003 and Martin Boyce in 2009. Since 2004, the city of Glasgow has organised the biennial Glasgow International Festival of Visual Art (GI). In 2006 there was uncertainty as to whether the festival would be continued, but a study carried out by the city authorities soon revealed its economic benefits: for every pound spent on its organisation, nine pounds were earned for the local economy. The budget for the project was sharply increased as a result – from £ 70,000 in 2006 to £ 400,000 in 2008.[5]

Sarah Lowndes' enlightening study[6] into the rise of the Glasgow art scene is entitled *Social Sculpture*, a term coined by Joseph Beuys. In the two editions of her book, conceived as a social history of the city with reference to visual art, literature and music, Lowndes describes Glasgow's development from an emergent art scene in the period up to 2002 to an established international art centre as it is now. While it covers the work of public art institutions such as the Fruitmarket Gallery in Edinburgh or CCA and Tramway in Glasgow, her study focuses above all on the development and programming concepts of the numerous artists' initiatives in the region, with particular emphasis on Transmission in Glasgow. Founded in 1983, this artist-led gallery with its grassroots democratic structure has shown impressive continuity and is still a place where artists gather and create. Its strength appears to lie in the principle of putting a rotating artistic committee (Committee for the Visual Arts – CVA) in charge of programming, resulting in a wide variety of approaches to current artistic issues. In the 1980s, Transmission had a politically left-wing profile and became known for exhibitions of expressive figurative painting by the New Image artists around Steven Campbell (1953–2007) and Adrian Wiszniewski (b. 1958), who came to prominence during that decade.[7] From around 1990 onwards, when Glasgow was designated European City of Culture, Transmission developed a more open approach and began to include international artists in its exhibition programme. *Installation Work* was the title of Transmission's show to mark the Year of Culture, and the invitation card emphasised the do-it-yourself mentality of the artists associated with this exhibition space. Martin Boyce, who had then just graduated from Glasgow College of Art and later served on the Transmission committee, recalls: "At that time Transmission seemed really central to not just the work but a complete attitude. It was kind of a central place socially and was a focus – it was the first

CCA und das Tramway, wegen Renovierungen geschlossen wurden. Denn als das Tramway im Jahr 2000 und das CCA im Oktober 2001 wieder öffneten, bestand die berechtigte Kritik wohl darin, dass der Handlungsspielraum gerade für die bildende Kunst in diesen bestehenden Instituten zugunsten einer Konzeption von spartenübergreifenden Kulturzentren oder Kulturmaschinen zurückgedrängt worden war und praktisch der Raum, das Personal und die finanziellen Mittel ausgerechnet für diese Sparte fehlten. Als Lowndes 2010 ihre 2003 veröffentlichte Studie in erweiterter Form herausgab, konnte sie mit Rücksicht auf die Entwicklungen im ersten Jahrzehnt jedoch zu dem Fazit gelangen, dass mit Blick auf die Glasgower Szene inzwischen nicht mehr nur von einer entstehenden, sondern eben von einer etablierten Kunstszene gesprochen werden kann: „Seit den '90ern hat sich die Glasgower Kunstszene innerhalb der Stadtlandschaft vom Rand in den Mittelpunkt bewegt und ist zu einem geschätzten und wichtigen Teil der Glasgower Identität und Gesamtwirtschaft geworden.“[9]

Zu den Bedingungen, die diese Entwicklung gerade von Glasgow zu einem Zentrum der bildenden Kunst beförderte, gehörte vor allem die Einrichtung eines neuen Fachbereichs an der Glasgow School of Art. 1986 wurde dort die Abteilung Environmental Art unter der Leitung von David Harding eingerichtet. Harding, der am Dartington College of Arts in Devon den Kurs „Art and Social Context“ entwickelt und geleitet hatte, verwandelte das frühere Murals and Stained Glass Department gemeinsam mit den Studenten in einen zukunftsweisenden und herausfordernden neuen Fachbereich. Dieser Kurs bot den Akademiestudenten (vor dem Hintergrund aktueller Entwicklungen in der Kunst) eine Alternative zu den bestehenden Sparten Malerei, Bildhauerei und Grafik. Untergebracht war der neue Fachbereich in einer Außenstelle, der alten Girls' High School, und befand sich damit isoliert von den anderen Abteilungen. 1987 wurde dort zudem der Masterstudiengang (Master of Fine Art – MFA) neu eingerichtet, dessen Leitung Sam Ainsley, bis dahin Tutorin von Harding im Fachbereich Environmental Art, übernahm. Das MFA bot eine Plattform für rechercheorientiertes Arbeiten und zog rasch vor allem auch Studenten anderer, auch internationaler Hochschulen an.

Die Auswahl der Künstler zu dieser Ausstellung mit **Claire Barclay**, **Martin Boyce**, **Nick Evans**, **Nicolas Party**, **Ciara Phillips** und **Mary Redmond** reflektiert in ihrer durch die räumliche Vorgabe der Fassadenräume notwendigen Konzentration auf sechs Positionen sowohl diese Entwicklung

port of call for friends coming up to visit. I remember being there invigilating before I was on the committee and people would come off the train from London and go straight there because they knew they could meet somebody there and go for a drink. No-one had studios so it was the place to go to hang out or to talk to someone.“[8]

At times, however, Scotland's cultural policy has also resulted in setbacks for visual art and its practitioners, such as when two art institutions – Tramway and the CCA – were closed for renovation in 1998/99. When they reopened – Tramway in 2000 and the CCA in October 2001 – there was justified criticism that the area of visual art in these institutions had been reduced in favour of a new concept of cross-genre cultural centres or 'cultural machines', and that in practical terms there was now insufficient space, staff and funding available for visual art. Nevertheless, when Lowndes published the expanded edition of her study in 2010, she was able to report that "[s]ince the '90s, the Glasgow art scene has shifted from a marginal to a central position within the landscape of the city, becoming a valued and important part of Glasgow's identity and overall economy."[9]

One of the key factors that led to Glasgow becoming a centre of visual art was the establishment of a new department at Glasgow School of Art. The Environmental Art Department was set up in 1986, with David Harding at its head. Together with his colleagues and students, Harding – who had previously developed and run the "Art and Social Context" course at Dartington College of Arts in Devon – transformed the former Murals and Stained Glass Department into a challenging new course with a progressive, interdisciplinary outlook. Reflecting current developments in art and critical theory, it offered students an alternative to the existing disciplines of painting, sculpture and printmaking. The new department was housed in an auxiliary building – a former Girls' High School – and thus isolated from the other departments. In 1987 a new postgraduate course, Master of Fine Art (MFA), was set up at the college and placed under the direction of Sam Ainsley, who until then had been a tutor in the Environmental Art Department. The MFA provided a platform for research-based work and soon became very popular, attracting graduates from other national and international art schools as well as from the School of Art itself.

The selection of artists for the exhibition – **Claire Barclay**, **Martin Boyce**, **Nick Evans**, **Nicolas Party**, **Ciara Phillips** and **Mary Redmond** – which was limited to

eines starken schottischen Kunstzentrums über mehrere Generationen hinweg als auch die internationale Durchmischung sowie den ausgeglichenen Anteil von Künstlerinnen und Künstlern der inzwischen in Glasgow ansässig gewordenen Künstlerschaft. Als Mary Redmond 1990 ihr Studium an der Glasgow School of Art begann, verließen Martin Boyce und Claire Barclay gerade als Absolventen die Akademie. Einige Jahrgänge später schloss im Jahr 2000 Nick Evans aus England sein Studium ab, die Kanadierin Ciara Phillips absolvierte den Masterstudiengang (MFA) im Jahr 2004 und 2009 graduierte dort Nicolas Party aus der französischen Schweiz. Alle Künstler leben und arbeiten seit ihrer Studienzeit weiterhin in Glasgow.

Der Titel *Funktion / Dysfunktion* verweist auf die inhaltliche Fragestellung dieser Ausstellung. Anhand der sechs Positionen aus Glasgow diskutiert sie neben der Kunstlandschaft Glasgow zugleich das seit den neunziger Jahren international sichtbar gewordene künstlerische Phänomen, dass Formen des Angewandten in die Kunst einfließen. Kunst und Design gehen Verbindungen ein. Die Vorgehensweisen sind weit gefächert, sei es, dass auf Designobjekte konkret Bezug genommen wird, sei es, dass Dinge des alltäglichen Gebrauchs wie Mobiliar oder Hausrat integriert oder aber mit den Werken motivisch abgestimmt werden, sei es, dass Materialien aus industrieller Fertigung, etwa Baustoffe oder Textilien, eingesetzt oder dass schließlich Techniken und Verfahren des Handwerks, der Industrie oder des Kunsthandwerks genutzt werden.

/prospekt/ – der Reihentitel informiert über den Ort dieser Ausstellung in den Räumen an der Fassade des Neuen Museums. Er rückt dabei nicht das architektonische Moment des spektakulären Fassadenschnittes von Volker Staab in den Vordergrund, sondern dessen situatives Potenzial einer Verschränkung verschiedener Blicke: die Blicke nach innen und nach außen wie auf einen Bühnen- oder in einen Landschaftsprospekt sowie eine Vorausschau auf die Gegenwart und die nahe Zukunft. Im Neuen Museum als einem Museum für Kunst und Design beschäftigt sich dieses Porträt einer Kunstlandschaft insbesondere mit der Frage, wie der Dialog und diese Verbindungen von Kunst und Design jeweils beschaffen sind und mit welcher Intention überhaupt Formen des Angewandten in der Kunst eingesetzt werden.

Bereits mit den neuen Zielsetzungen in der Kunst der sechziger und siebziger Jahre, beispielsweise mit der Forderung nach Teilbarkeit und Unmittelbarkeit, öffneten sich die künstlerischen Arbeiten, um durch bestimmte Strategien Aspekte des Alltäglichen und des Designs aufzunehmen und

six participants in accordance with the spaces available behind the museum's facade, reflects not only the emergence of this major Scottish art centre over several generations, but also the blend of nationalities and balance of male and female artists among those who have chosen to base themselves in Glasgow. When Mary Redmond started studying at Glasgow School of Art in 1990, Martin Boyce and Claire Barclay had just finished their Bachelor degrees. Nick Evans from England was a few classes behind them, gaining his degree in 2000. The Canadian artist Ciara Phillips completed her MFA in 2004 and Nicolas Party, who was born in French-speaking Switzerland, gained his Master's degree in 2009. All of these artists have continued to live and work in Glasgow since leaving the School of Art.

The title of the exhibition, *Function / Dysfunction,* refers to its thematic focus. In addition to portraying aspects of the Glaswegian art landscape, this presentation of work by six of the city's contemporary artists highlights a noticeable international trend in art since the 1990s to incorporate or reference applied forms of art. Connections are established between art and design in a wide range of ways, whether it is by making specific reference to design objects, integrating or evoking everyday items such as pieces of furniture or household articles, incorporating industrially produced elements such as building materials or textiles, or employing craft-based, industrial or artisanal techniques and processes to produce artworks.

/prospekt/ – the series title indicates the site of this exhibition, directly behind the glass facade of the Neues Museum. The emphasis here is less on the architectural qualities of this spectacular building front, which was designed by Volker Staab, and more on the opportunity to compare and contrast different perspectives that this situation provides: a combination of outward and inward views, reminiscent of a stage set or a landscape prospect, and a simultaneous projection of the present and the near future. In line with the Neues Museum's mission as a museum of both art and design, this portrait of the Scottish art landscape also explores the connections and dialogue between the two realms, and considers the specific intentions behind the use of applied forms in fine art.

With the new artistic concerns that emerged in the 1960s and 70s, such as the demands for participation and immediacy, art began to open up and strategically include elements of everyday life and design. The artistic practice

einfließen zu lassen. Die Werke von Richard Artschwager (1923–2013) sind hier ein Beispiel [Abb. 2]. Ausgebildet als Schreiner, zimmert Artschwager ab 1963 einfache Kuben, die er durch Einsatz von Resopalfurnier unweigerlich in Tische und Stühle verwandelt. Seine Arbeiten sind im Schreinerhandwerk ausgeführt, mit dem fototechnisch erzeugten Resopal und dem Holz kommen Materialien industrieller Produktion zum Einsatz, und als ein Motiv sind Möbel entstanden. Dass diese Möbel jedoch nicht dem Design, sondern der Kunst zuzuordnen sind, ist an ihrem künstlerischen Zweck erkennbar. Artschwagers Werke sind situative Kunstobjekte. Die Möbel und *blps* der sechziger, die Bilder der siebziger oder die *Crates* der neunziger Jahre folgen dabei insgesamt demselben Ziel. Die Werke thematisieren und inszenieren verschiedene Blicke des Menschen auf seine Umwelt mit dessen jeweils eigenen inneren Haltungen. Artschwager macht diese durch seine Arbeiten in der Konfrontation vor dem Objekt – sei es ein Möbelstück, ein Bild, ein Spiegel, der blinde Fleck eines *blps* oder eine Transportkiste – jeweils unmittelbar erfahrbar. Liegt den Arbeiten Artschwagers hier ein wahrnehmungspsychologisches und erkenntnisorientiertes Kunstverständnis zugrunde, so ist der Einsatz alltäglicher Gegenstände beispielsweise bei den Installationen von Marcel Broodthaers (1924–1976) [Abb. 3] anders gelagert. Bei einer Arbeit wie *Musée d'Art Moderne, Département des Aigles, Section XVIIe Siècle*, 1969 in Antwerpen oder 1972 in der Kunsthalle Düsseldorf gezeigt, oder bei anderen seiner fiktiven Museumskonzeptionen, die er in Ausstellungen realisierte, werden die Bestandteile einer Installation zu bestimmten Raumatmosphären oder Raum-

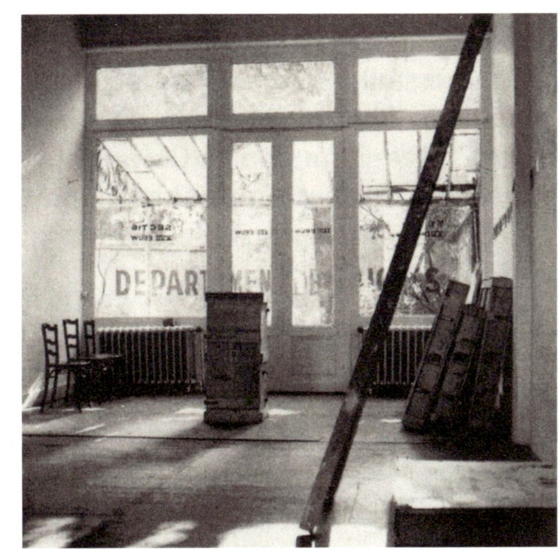

3 Marcel Broodthaers, *Musée d'Art Moderne, Département des Aigles, Section XVIIe Siècle*, 1969, Wide White Space Gallery, Antwerpen / Antwerp

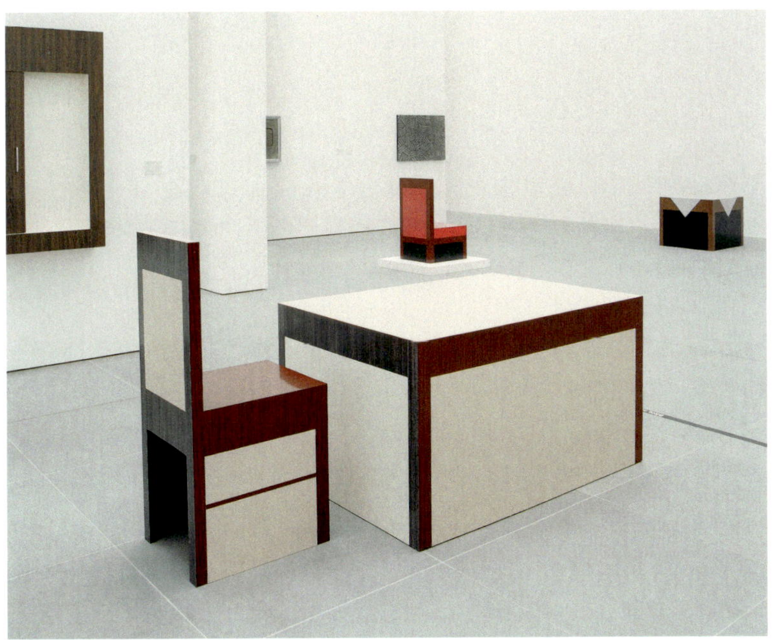

2 Richard Artschwager, *Table and Chair*, 1963/64, Installationsansicht / Installation view *Richard Artschwager. Up and Across*, Neues Museum – Staatliches Museum für Kunst und Design in Nürnberg / Nuremberg 2001

of Richard Artschwager (1923–2013) serves as a good example of this development [fig. 2]. In 1963, after training as a carpenter, Artschwager started producing simple blocks made of wood and Formica that inevitably evoked the forms of tables and chairs. His works were therefore executed with a carpenter's skills, involved the use of industrially produced materials – Formica is created with the aid of photo technology – as well as wood, and the resulting objects resemble pieces of furniture. The fact that they are nevertheless to be categorised as art rather than design objects is determined by their artistic intention. Artschwager's works are situational art objects. The furniture and *blps* he created in the 1960s, the paintings from the 1970s and the *Crates* from the 1990s all pursue the same objective: they represent different ways in which people view their surroundings and examine how this perception is shaped by subjective cognitive processes. Artschwager allows the viewer to experience these processes through direct confrontation with an object – whether it is a piece of furniture, a painting, a mirror, the blind spot of a *blp* or a shipping crate. While Artschwager's works derive from a cognition-oriented understanding of art that has its roots in perceptual psychology, the use of everyday objects in, say, the installations of Marcel Broodthaers (1924–1976) [fig. 3] has an entirely different intention. In a work such as *Musée d'Art Moderne, Département des Aigles, Section XVIIe Siècle*, which Broodthaers presented in Antwerp in 1969 and at the Kunsthalle Düsseldorf in 1972, or in other fictitious museums he realised in the context of exhibitions, the various components of the installation have been combined to create a specific atmosphere or spatial quality, while their arrangement depicts a particular scenario. In the 1980s, this kind of

19

qualitäten zusammengefügt. Die Arrangements illustrieren dabei bildhaft eine bestimmte Szenerie. Eine solche kontextualisierende Vorgehensweise, bei der die Betrachter komplett in eine Situation einbezogen werden, hat der Belgier Guillaume Bijl (geb. 1946) dann in den achtziger Jahren in dem Konzept eines radikalen Readymade-Environments, in den *Transformation Installations*, zu seinem Markenzeichen gemacht und Ausstellungsräume vollständig in Waschsalons, Fitnesscenter, Herrenausstatter oder Konferenzräume umgewandelt.

Donald Judd (1928–1994) produzierte seit den siebziger Jahren Möbel, die dann allerdings *neben* seiner Kunst eher als Accessoire eines Lifestyles, eines vermeintlich kunstbezogenen Lebensstils, Bestand hatten. Wiebke Siem (geb. 1954) hingegen setzte den Anspruch der siebziger Jahre nach Beteiligung des Betrachters und nach einer funktionalen oder nützlichen Kunst Anfang der achtziger Jahre konsequent um. Mit ihren Kleidungsobjekten und den Wandgestaltungen [**Abb. 4**] hat sie Werke geschaffen, die vollständig im gesellschaftlichen Raum aufgingen, mit eben all den damit verbundenen Tücken einer Kunst, die in den öffentlichen Raum eintaucht und sich so unsichtbar macht.

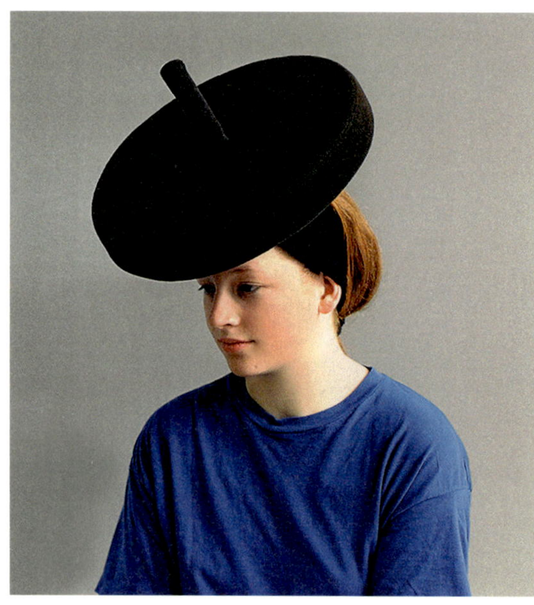

4 Wiebke Siem, *Hut / Hat*, 1987

Ab den neunziger Jahren wird eine „zunehmende Auflösung der abgesteckten Grenzen zwischen Kunst und Design"[10] beobachtet. Dabei sind die Herangehensweisen sehr unterschiedlich, mit welchen Fragestellungen Gegenstände des Gebrauchs, Designobjekte, Materialien industrieller Fertigung oder Techniken des Handwerks in die Kunst einfließen. Einer der Ansätze folgt der konzeptuellen Strategie, ein Werk aufgrund von vorab festgelegten Handlungsentwürfen entstehen zu lassen. Beispiele sind die (zwar zunächst) parti-

contexualising approach, whereby the viewer is completely drawn into a specially designed situation or fabricated reality, became the trademark of the Belgian artist Guillaume Bijl (b. 1946), whose radical concept of the 'ready-made environment' completely transformed exhibition spaces into launderettes, fitness centres, menswear stores or conference rooms, in a series of works he calls *Transformation Installations*.

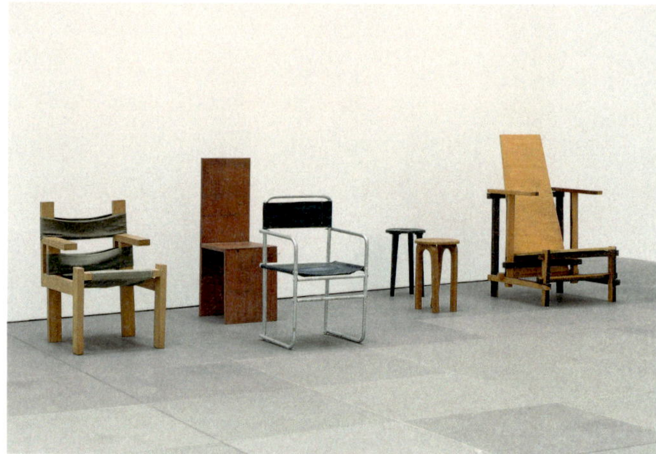

5 Tobias Rehberger, *Peuè Seè e Faàgck Sunday Paàe*, 1994, Installationsansicht / Installation view *70/90. Engagierte Kunst*, Neues Museum – Staatliches Museum für Kunst und Design in Nürnberg / Nuremberg 2004

From the 1970s onwards, the American artist Donald Judd (1928–1994) designed and produced pieces of furniture; these existed, however, *alongside* his art and appear more reminiscent of accessories to an art-oriented lifestyle. Wiebke Siem (b. 1954), on the other hand, rigorously implemented the demand for viewer participation as well as for functional, useful art that emerged in the 1970s. In the early 1980s she began creating clothing objects and designs for wall surfaces [fig. 4] that blend into their social environment – with all the pitfalls of art that is so immersed in public space it can ultimately become invisible.

An "increasing dissolution of the established borders between art and design"[10] could be observed from the 1990s onwards, whereby the incorporation of utilitarian items, design objects, industrially produced materials or craft-based techniques into art reflected a variety of artistic concerns, concepts and working methods. One conceptual strategy involved producing an artwork by carrying out a predetermined plan of action. Examples of this method are Tobias Rehberger's (b. 1966) works from the early 1990s, which initially appear aimed at a participatory, communicative form of engagement, but prove to be much more conceptually and aesthetically oriented. In 1994, for example, Rehberger had classic chair designs reconstructed by craftsmen in Cameroon, with all the inconsistencies that inevitably arise

zipatorisch und kommunikativ anmutenden, dann jedoch vielmehr konzeptuell begründeten, ästhetischen Arbeiten der frühen neunziger Jahre von Tobias Rehberger (geb. 1966). Rehberger lässt beispielsweise 1994 in Kamerun Klassiker des Stuhldesigns von afrikanischen Handwerkern nachbauen mit all den Unzulänglichkeiten, die durch die Skizzierung der Möbel aus der Erinnerung (durch den Künstler) einerseits und mit der Übersetzung dieser Bauvorlagen in einen fertigen Stuhl (durch die Handwerker) andererseits entstehen. Als Methode seiner skulpturalen Werke[11] [Abb. 5] adaptiert Rehberger hier eine konzeptuelle Herangehensweise der siebziger Jahre – etwa die Kooperationsmodelle eines Alighiero Boetti (1940–1994).

Simon Starling (geb. 1967) und Florian Slotawa (geb. 1972) gehen ähnlich konzeptuell vor. Beide entwickeln Arbeiten aus dem jeweiligen Umfeld von Ausstellungen. 1997 zu einem Beitrag in einem Londoner Ausstellungsraum eingeladen, nahm Starling den Eames-Stapelstuhl aus dem dort in der Nähe gelegenen Designmuseum als Vorbild für zunächst 12 Stuhlnachbauten. Das Selbermachen, die Idee vom Heimwerkern oder das Kopieren gehören hier zu den Handlungskonzepten. Das Projekt *Home made Eames* wird 2001 noch durch die Arbeit *Black Stack* – eine zweite Version mit 32 Stuhlkopien – erweitert sowie 2002 durch *Formers, Jigs & Molds*, dies sind schließlich die Produktionsmittel selbst, die Starling für die Herstellung der Stuhlkopien angefertigt und verwendet hatte [Abb. 6]. Auch das Prinzip von Slotawa ist es, mit (an einem Ausstellungsort) vorgefundenen Materialien zu arbeiten und daraus oft nur temporäre Werke zu schaffen. Die Arbeit *Kieler Sockel* ist beispielsweise 2004 für eine Ausstellung in der Kunsthalle Kiel aus Einrichtungs-

when original designs are sketched from memory (by the artist) and the construction designs are then translated into finished chairs (by the craftsmen). Rehberger's method of producing sculptural works[11] [fig. 5] is an adaptation of conceptual approaches that emerged in the 1970s – parallels can be seen, for example, to the collaborative models developed by Alighiero Boetti (1940–1994).

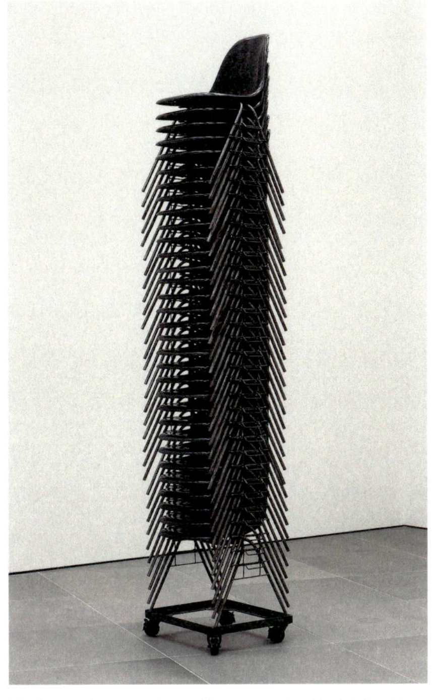

6 Simon Starling, *Black Stack*, 2001, Installationsansicht / Installation view *Wenn Handlungen Form werden*, Neues Museum – Staatliches Museum für Kunst und Design in Nürnberg / Nuremberg 2007

Simon Starling (b. 1967) and Florian Slotawa (b. 1972) pursue similarly conceptual approaches. Both artists develop works in relation to the respective exhibition context, often incorporating and transforming existing or found elements. Having been invited to take part in an exhibition in London in 1997, for example, Starling produced 12 replicas of a stackable chair – a modern classic designed by Charles Eames – which was on display in the nearby Design Museum. Do-it-yourself, craft and replication techniques are here employed as means of artistic production. Starling's *Homemade Eames* project was extended to include *Black Stack*, 2001 – a second version with 32 replica chairs in a single stack – and *Home-made Eames (Formers, Jigs & Molds),* 2002, which features the tools and gadgets he had used to create the replica chairs [fig. 6]. Employing the same principle of working with existing materials, Florian Slotawa transforms elements found in the venues hosting his exhibitions into what are often temporary artworks. *Kieler Sockel*, for example, was created in 2004 for an exhibition at the Kunsthalle Kiel using furnishings and everyday items from the museum itself; Slotawa transformed

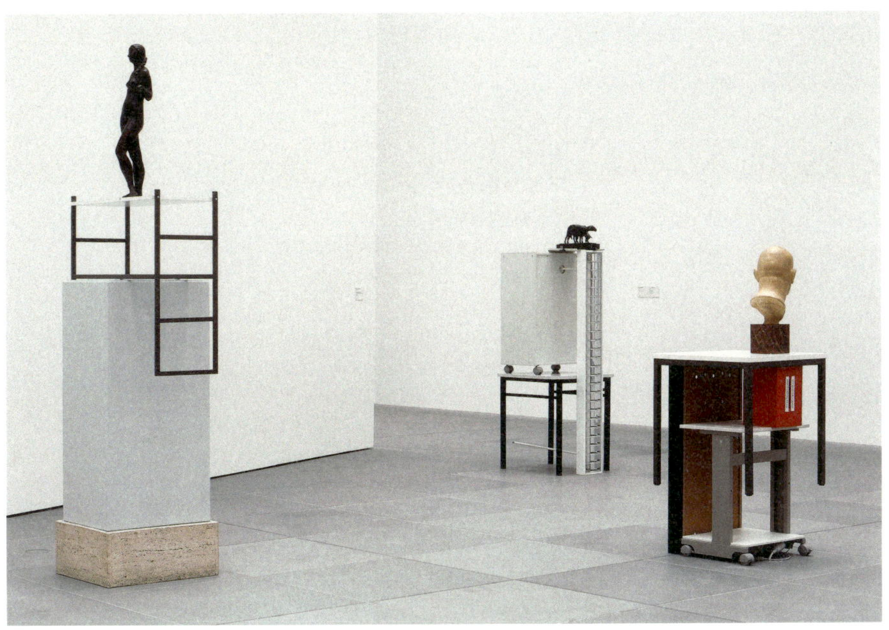

7 Florian Slotawa, *Kieler Sockel*, 2004/2007, Installationsansicht / Installation view *Wenn Handlungen Form werden*, Neues Museum – Staatliches Museum für Kunst und Design in Nürnberg / Nuremberg 2007

gegenständen des Museums entstanden, die er zunächst temporär als Sockel für ausgewählte Skulpturen der Sammlung nutzte [Abb. 7]. Ein solcher Kunstbegriff, bei dem fest umrissene Handlungskonzepte der Konstitution von Werken zugrunde liegen, geht letztlich auf die konsequent konzeptuelle Vorgehensweise der Nouveaux Réalistes zurück, die einfache Handlungsanweisungen wie das Verpacken (von Dingen) oder das Sammeln (von Gebrauchsgegenständen) als Grundlage für die Werkentstehung nahmen.[12]

Neben solchen, konzeptuell begründeten Herangehensweisen ist die Verbindung von Kunst mit einem nützlichen oder funktionalen Gegenstand ein weiterer Ansatz, um Kunst und Design einander anzunähern. Der Mehrwert für die künstlerische Arbeit als ein für die Gesellschaft gewollt sinnvolles Element ist bei dieser Strategie offensichtlich. Sobald ein Ding eine Funktion oder einen Zweck für den Menschen erfüllt, zum Beispiel Möbel wie ein Stuhl zum Sitzen oder Gebrauchsgegenstände wie Lampen, hat es zugleich von sich aus eine partizipatorische, also das Publikum beteiligende Kraft. Dies ist auch die Vorgehensweise des dänischen Künstlers Jeppe Hein (geb. 1974), der von Beginn seiner künstlerischen Laufbahn an Bänke, Lampen oder Stühle als künstlerische Formen entwickelt und damit sofort und unmittelbar einen Dialog mit seinem Publikum aufbaut. Waren die Werke anfangs tatsächlich Gebrauchsgegenstände, wie bei seinem Beitrag *Stage. Design of meeting point for interviews and discussions* 2001 in Venedig, als er flexibles Mobiliar für Veranstaltungen konzipierte, so nahmen seine Werke im Laufe der Zeit stärker einen Dialog zur Kunstgeschichte auf. Bis heute handelt Hein nach dieser Idee, bei der er seine „Kunst als ein Werkzeug für Kommunikation und Dialog"[13] versteht.

Als in Glasgow 1986 der neue Studiengang Environmental Art eingerichtet wurde, war dieser gekennzeichnet durch einen offenen Medienbegriff, durch ortsbezogene und installative künstlerische Ansätze. Schon mit dem ungewöhnlichen Namen dieses Fachbereichs, der weder allein eine Kunst im öffentlichen Raum bezeichnet noch den bei uns gebräuchlichen Begriff des Environments meint, scheint vielmehr eine Idee von Kunst anzuklingen, die sich auf die soziale Umwelt und den gesellschaftlichen Raum ganz allgemein bezieht. In diesem rechercheorientierten Fachbereich entsteht bei den Werken der Studierenden zumindest schnell ein Dialog zwischen den Sparten Architektur, Kunst und Design, wie dies um 1990 bereits an Werken von Nathan Coley (geb. 1967), Martin Boyce, Andrew Miller (geb. 1969) oder Simon Starling sichtbar wird. „Der Kontext ist das halbe Werk"[14] war

these into (initially) temporary plinths on which he presented a selection of works from the Kunsthalle's sculpture collection [fig. 7]. This kind of artistic method, whereby works are created according to a roughly defined plan of action, can ultimately be traced back to the rigorously conceptual approach of the Nouveaux Réalistes, who used actions such as wrapping (things) or collecting (utilitarian objects) to create artworks.[12]

Besides such conceptually oriented approaches, another method of combining art and design is to establish an association between artworks and utilitarian or functional objects. The value that is added to an artwork intended to serve a meaningful social purpose becomes apparent here. When an object serves a human purpose or performs a useful function – a chair to sit on, perhaps, or a utility item such as a lamp – it has an inherently participatory dimension due to the fact that it involves the audience. This strategy has been adopted by the Danish artist Jeppe Hein (b. 1974), who throughout his career has created benches, lamps and chairs as artistic forms and thus engaged in direct dialogue with his audience. While his early works were genuinely utilitarian objects – as in *Stage. Design of meeting point for interviews and discussions*, a set of flexible furnishing elements he designed for communicative events and presented in Venice in 2001 – over time his works have increasingly entered into a dialogue with the history of art itself. Nevertheless, Hein still operates according to the principle of employing "art as a tool for communication and dialogue"[13].

The new Environmental Art course that was established at Glasgow School of Art in 1986 was characterised by its openness to the exploration of different media, as well as its encouragement of site-specific and installation-based artistic practices. The very name of the course, which refers neither exclusively to public art nor to what is commonly understood by the term 'environment', alludes to a notion of art that relates to social contexts and the broader societal realm. It certainly did not take long for a dialogue to be established between architecture, art and design in the output of students on this research-based course, as can be seen in works by the likes of Nathan Coley (b. 1967), Martin Boyce, Andrew Miller (b. 1969) or Simon Starling from around 1990. "Context is half the work"[14] became the (unofficial) motto underlying this progressive approach, which Boyce later described as follows: "In Environmental Art it was accepted that painting, sculpture, photography, performance and wall painting were all just options in making an art-

das Motto dieser aktuellen Herangehensweise, die Boyce später so beschrieben hat: „In Environmental Art wurde anerkannt, dass sowohl Malerei und Bildhauerei als auch Fotografie, Performance und Wandmalerei nur Optionen darstellten, um ein Kunstwerk zu schaffen – sie alle waren Strategien oder Möglichkeiten und eben kein vorherrschendes Medium oder Verfahren."[15] Mit diesem neuen Ansatz nahm die junge Künstlergeneration die damals prominenten Maler des New Image Painting immer weniger als Bezugsquelle.[16] Es ging vielmehr darum, sich abzugrenzen und eine eigene Identität dieses Studienganges herzustellen. Mit dieser medienoffenen und kontextbezogenen Auffassung entstand zugleich ein Kampfbegriff sowohl innerhalb der Hochschule gegenüber der expressiven Malereiposition, die in den achtziger Jahren internationale Anerkennung erlangt hatte, als vor allem auch, um sich schließlich international zu positionieren und zu behaupten.

Bei den Arbeiten von **Martin Boyce** (geb. 1967) ist eine Verbindung von Kunst und Design offensichtlich. Seit den neunziger Jahren bezieht sich der Künstler mit seinen Werken

work – they were all strategies or possibilities rather than there being a dominant medium or approach."[15] For the young generation of students who had been introduced to this new approach to making work, New Image painting no longer provided the main reference point.[16] It was more a matter of differentiating themselves and developing a specific identity for the Environmental Art course. Pursuing this non-media-specific, context-based approach not only enabled the emerging artists to set themselves apart from the expressionist mode of painting at Glasgow School of Art that had gained international recognition in the 1980s, but also and above all it encouraged them to develop and assert their own positions in the international arena.

A combination of art and design is clearly evident in the work of **Martin Boyce** (b. 1967). Since the 1990s, Boyce has not only referenced the work of acclaimed modernist designers such as Charles and Ray Eames, Arne Jacobsen, Jean Prouvé and Charlotte Perriand; he has also recast classic design objects and incorporated elements of these pieces into his own artworks: the Eames

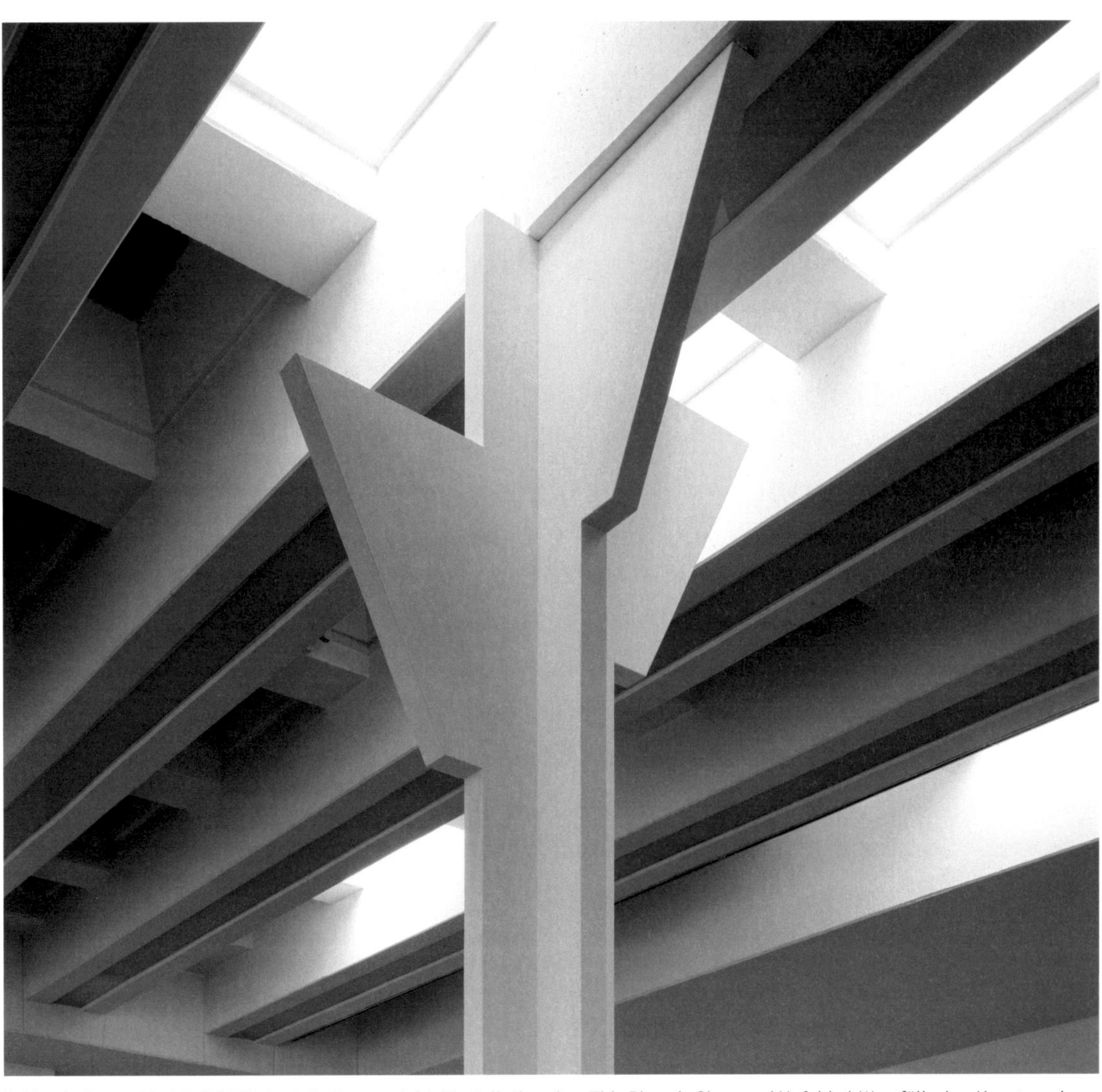

8 Martin Boyce, *Untitled*, 2008, Installationsansicht / Installation view *This Place is Close and Unfolded*, Westfälischer Kunstverein, Münster 2008

nicht nur auf Klassiker des Designs, wie Charles und Ray Eames, Arne Jacobsen, Jean Prouvé oder Charlotte Perriand. Der Künstler fertigt selbst neu interpretierte Nachbauten an oder integriert Originalteile von Designobjekten in seine Arbeiten: Die *Eames Storage Units* erfahren eine Neufassung, ausrangierte Sitzschalen von Jacobsen-Stühlen bilden ein Mobile, wieder andere Stuhlrelikte des Designers begründen das Werk einer an ethnografische Sammelstücke erinnernden Maske. *No Reflections* ist der Titel seiner Installation im Palazzo Pisani 2009 für die Biennale in Venedig. Boyce zeigt dort eine durch sieben Räume sich erstreckende Arbeit, die sich auf Jan und Joël Martel bezieht. „Seit 2005 beschäftige ich mich fast ausschließlich mit einem Werkzyklus, der sich auf ein historisches Bild mit vier Betonbäumen von Jan und Joël Martel bezieht, die 1925 für eine Ausstellung in Paris hergestellt wurden", erläutert Boyce [**Abb. 8**]. „Ich habe mich sehr dafür interessiert, wie in diesen ‚Bäumen' Architektur und Natur zusammenfallen. Die erste Arbeit, die sich auf diese Objekte bezog, war eine fotografische: *Concrete Autumn (Phantom Tree)*. Mein Wunsch war es nicht, den ‚Baum' selbst wieder aufzugreifen, sondern ihn vielmehr als Phantom wieder erscheinen zu lassen. Ich begann also, Modelle dieser Bäume zu bauen, um ihr Konstruktionssystem zu verstehen. Dabei wurden die einzelnen Formen, aus denen die Objekte zusammengesetzt sind, langsam zu einer Art Lexikon für mich, ein modulares System wie eine Sprache, aus der sich dann einige skulpturale Arbeiten entwickelten. Aus den Umrissen und Formen des Baumes entwickelte ich ein lineares, wiederholbares Muster, einen ‚grafischen Wald' aus ‚abstrakten Bäumen'. Auch hier bildeten sich aus den grafischen Elementen allmählich und mit der Zeit Buchstaben des Alphabetes heraus, und auf diese Weise entstand eine Typografie aus der gefundenen Form."[17] Nach dem vorgefundenen Foto rekonstruierte Boyce zunächst den abgebildeten, dreidimensionalen Betonbaum, um ihn anschließend wieder in einzelne Formen zu zerlegen. Diese durch die Dekonstruktion des Vorbilds erhaltenen Formen bilden seit 2005 ein ausgedehntes Vokabular, aus dem wiederum dem Motiv nach entfernt an Möbelstücke oder Gebrauchsgegenstände erinnernde Objekte entstehen, wie Bett, Bank, Trittsteine, Telefonzelle, Raumteiler, Tischtennisplatte, Papierkorb, Lampen oder eben auch ein Alphabet. Diese Elemente bilden dann nicht vereinzelte Werkstücke, sondern werden in den Installationen des Künstlers zu Raumatmosphären zusammengeführt, die Innen- und Außenräume miteinander verschränken. Solchen künstlerischen Gebrauchsgegenständen ist durch die Formulierung jedoch stets vollständig die

storage units have been given a new interpretation, discarded sections of Jacobsen-designed chairs have been reassembled into a mobile, while other parts have been used to create a mask that recalls a piece from a collection of ethnographic objects.

No Reflections was the title of Boyce's installation at Palazzo Pisani in 2009, his contribution to that year's Venice Biennale. Installed across seven interconnected rooms of the palazzo, it related specifically to the French sculptors and designers Jan and Joël Martel: "Since 2005 I have been working almost exclusively with a body of work that refers back to a source image that shows four concrete trees that were made by Jan and Joël Martel for an exhibition in Paris in 1925 [fig. 8]. I was very interested in how they represented this collapse of architecture and nature. The first piece I made in relation to the Martel tree was the photographic piece *Concrete Autumn (Phantom Tree)*. My desire was not to revisit the tree, but that the tree was now reappearing as a phantom. I started to make models of the trees in order to understand their system of construction, and the component shapes of the trees slowly became a lexicon, a modular system or a language from which sculptural works developed. From the shapes and forms of the trees I also developed a linear repeat pattern, a graphic forest of abstract trees. Again, slowly and over time, letters of the alphabet began to emerge from the lines of the repeat and so a typography appeared from these found forms."[17] On the basis of the found photograph, therefore, Boyce reconstructed the depicted concrete tree as a three-dimensional model and then broke this down into its constituent forms. Since 2005, the shapes he created by deconstructing the source image in this way have evolved into an extensive vocabulary of forms; these are used by Boyce to create objects that vaguely recall pieces of furniture or utilitarian items such as a bed, a bench, stepping stones, a telephone box, room dividers, a ping-pong table, a dustbin, lamps or an alphabet. These elements do not constitute individual artworks, however, but are assembled into atmospheric installations that conflate interior and exterior spaces. As a result of their artistic transformation, however, the functional dimension of such utilitarian items is completely removed. For Boyce, therefore, they are not connected to a purpose or use but to an idea.[18] Here, the motivation for establishing a link between art and design is that direct reference can be made to recollected real-world contexts through the elements of the artwork. Its different components and the relations between them

Funktion entzogen. Dadurch knüpfen sie bei Boyce eben nicht beim Gebrauch oder Nutzen, sondern beim Gedanken an.[18] Der Sinn einer Verbindung von Kunst und Design liegt hier darin begründet, dass mit den Elementen der Arbeit unmittelbar Erinnerungsbezüge zur realen Umwelt möglich sind. Die Werkbestandteile und deren Relation untereinander bilden die durch den Menschen geschaffene Realität und deren Unzulänglichkeiten modellhaft in abbrevierter, abstrahierter und formalisierter Weise nach und ermöglichen so einen distanzierten Blick auf die eigene Lebenswelt. Der Grund dieser oft als Grenzüberschreitung beschriebenen Verbindung von Kunst und Design liegt somit vor allem darin, dass in der Kunst auf diese Weise an normale, alltägliche Erfahrungen unserer Gesellschaft angeknüpft werden kann. Durch diese Methode entsteht ein Zugang zum konkreten Erfahrungspotenzial. Boyce' Nachbildungen schaffen so als Effekt eine Distanz zur realen Umwelt.

„Nun, ich vermute, die herkömmliche Betrachtungsweise des Kunsthandwerks ist die, dass es eine praktische Funktion hat, entweder eine eher buchstäbliche Funktion, wie eine Schale, aus der man isst, oder eine symbolische Funk-

9 Claire Barclay, *Flat Peach*, 2010, Installationsansicht / Installation view *Flat Peach*, Stephen Friedman Gallery, London 2010

reconstruct reality as shaped by man – with all its flaws – in the form of an abbreviated, abstracted and formalised model, and thus enable a detached perspective upon one's own life-world. The combination of art and design, which is often interpreted as overstepping a boundary, is here motivated above all by the fact that art can be linked to normal, everyday experiences in our society, tapping into the potential of concrete personal experience. To this end, Boyce's reconstructions create a heightened sense of detachment from reality.

"Well I suppose the conventional way of seeing craft is that it has a practical function, either a more literal function, like a bowl for eating out of, or a symbolic function like a lot of decorative art. I suppose I'm interested in disrupting the logic of function, playing with the balance between function and dysfunction, and consciously trying to make objects that are pivotal in that way; they attempt to masquerade as functional everyday things, but do not fit any identified mould."[19] **Claire Barclay**'s (b. 1968) sculptural works draw upon traditional craft and industrial processes. Rather than working with found objects, Barclay employs conventional craft techniques to handcraft the extremely diverse materials employed in her sculptural objects, which are assembled into installations. She combines metal, textiles and wood with elements drawn from the clothing industry, mechanical engineering or furniture construction, but also from the realm of arts and crafts [fig. 9]. The corresponding processing techniques – commonly used by carpenters, metalworkers, coopers, tailors or potters, for example – are likewise integrated to produce the various components of her contextualising installations. Approaching these production methods as an amateur, Barclay appropriates them and incorporates her acquired knowledge of the respective processes into her own artistic practice. The background to her choice of materials and adoption of traditional craft techniques also serves as the point of access to her work. The use of familiar materials and techniques to produce the incorporated elements facilitates their reception by encouraging viewers to connect with them on a mental or emotional level. Choosing to work with media that are not usually associated with fine art but reflect everyday experience is what enables Barclay to create a proximity between the art and the audience, thereby triggering a process of reflection. In her installations, the different elements of her works are contextualised in relation to one another and to the surrounding space, and thus enter into a dialogue. "It's often quite difficult for me to decipher within the

tion, wie ein Gutteil der angewandten Kunst. Ich glaube, ich interessiere mich dafür, die Logik der Funktion zu durchbrechen, mit dem Gleichgewicht von Funktion und Dysfunktion zu spielen und bewusst zu versuchen, Objekte zu schaffen, die in dieser Hinsicht grundlegend sind; sie bemühen sich, als funktionale Alltagsgegenstände durchzugehen, aber passen in keine bekannte Form."[19] Die skulpturalen Werke von **Claire Barclay** (geb. 1968) beruhen auf dem Einsatz von traditionellen Verfahren des Handwerks und des Kunsthandwerks. In ihren Installationen setzt die Künstlerin keine Gegenstände ein, die sie gefunden hat. Die stark divergierenden Materialien, die verwendet werden, bearbeitet sie selbst in herkömmlichen Handwerkstechniken und stellt so ihre Objekte her. Sie arbeitet mit Metall, mit Stoff, mit Holz oder mit Elementen der Kleiderindustrie, des Maschinenbaus, des Möbelbaus, aber auch des Kunsthandwerks [**Abb. 9**]. Die den Materialien entsprechenden Techniken des Schlossers, des Schreiners, der Metallbearbeitung, des Büttners, des Schneiders oder des Töpfers werden bei der Herstellung der verschiedenartigen Werkbestandteile ihrer kontextualisierenden Installationen einbezogen. Mit ihrer amateurhaften Herangehensweise an diese Fertigungstechniken eignet sie sich diese an und bezieht dabei ihr Verständnis der Herstellungsprozesse jeweils mit in die eigene Arbeit ein. Der Hintergrund von Barclays Materialentscheidung sowie ihres Bezugs auf traditionelle handwerkliche Herstellungsverfahren ist wieder der Zugang. Die eingesetzten Werkelemente erleichtern den Einstieg für die Betrachtung. Denn über diese jedem vertrauten Materialien und Techniken lassen sich schnell gedankliche oder emotionale Anknüpfungspunkte finden. Gerade durch kunstferne, aber der alltäglichen Erfahrung entsprechende Medien wird eine Nähe zum Publikum hergestellt und so ein Reflexionsprozess in Gang gesetzt. Die Bestandteile von Barclays Arbeiten werden dann in den Installationen sowohl untereinander als auch im Bezug zum jeweiligen Raum kontextualisiert und so in einen Dialog gebracht. „Es ist oft ziemlich schwierig für mich, in der fertigen Installation zu entziffern, inwieweit der Kontext das Werk geformt hat. Auch weil die Installationen teilweise an Ort und Stelle entstehen, wird ihre Platzierung im Raum zum Teil des Werks; die Art, wie etwas den Boden berührt oder auf die Wand trifft, oder die Art, wie das Tageslicht auf seiner Oberfläche spielt, wirken sich alle auf die Art und Weise aus, wie das Werk wahrgenommen wird."[20] In den ausgreifenden Installationen werden die einzelnen skulpturalen Fragmente dann aber von Barclay in eher ungewöhnliche und unerwartete Konstellationen gebracht, sodass

finished installation to what extent the context has moulded the work. Also, because the installations are partially made *in situ*, their placement in the space becomes part of the work; the way something touches the floor or joins the wall or the way the daylight plays on its surface all have an effect on the way the work is perceived."[20] In Barclay's expansive sculptural environments, however, the individual fragments are assembled into unusual or unexpected configurations and create overlapping, often contradictory impressions: a perceived or expected functionality proves to be the opposite; interior and exterior spatial features are interwoven; utilitarian craft and decorative art merge as opposing qualities – hard and soft, pointed and round, light and heavy – are set off against one another. Many different forces are simultaneously exerted upon the materials, with the result that the works exist in a tense and often precariously balanced state. "Sculpture as event"[21] is how Claire Doherty describes Barclay's practice, and the artist herself says: "Sometimes, I wonder if my attitude is too vague, but what I really enjoy about making art is attempting to reach a point of ambiguity where two different processes, thinking and making, come together. I want to find this point because there lies the tension, at the point of balance between two opposing things."[22]

Contemporary building materials and everyday objects that are used by man to structure his environment provide the starting point for the sculptural works and installations of **Mary Redmond** (b. 1973). Corrugated sheet iron, metal rods, reinforcing steel, wire mesh, metal fencing, cable, bricks, nails, insulating materials, breeze blocks, blinds, beams and plastic twine are easily acquired, recognisable construction elements [fig. 10]. With their unappealing and occasionally garish colouring, their often inferior quality (reflecting the implementation of tightly budgeted manufacturing concepts), and their purely functional structural design, such materials present a less than attractive image of the quality and style of materials used in the built environment that surrounds us. Redmond often employs these kinds of materials, which derive their shape and properties from a mode of production based solely on utility and expediency. As they usually vanish inside the core of a building and are thus rendered invisible, these materials are not normally subject to individual design criteria, but often follow the design principles of a particular manufacturer or reflect regional taste. In her installation-based works, however, Redmond so effectively transforms these rather unappealing

sich dabei widersprüchliche Eindrücke verschränken. Die erwartete Funktionalität verkehrt sich in eine tatsächliche Funktionslosigkeit. Merkmale des Innenraumes und des Außenraumes sind verwoben. Nützliches Handwerk und schmückendes Kunsthandwerk gehen Verbindungen ein. Eigenschaften wie hart und weich, spitz und rund, schwer und leicht treffen aufeinander. Auf die Materialien wirken Kräfte ein. Sie stehen unter Spannung oder sind oftmals in ein labiles Gleichgewicht gebracht. „Skulptur wird zum Ereignis"[21], beschreibt Claire Doherty diese Werkkonstellation, und die Künstlerin selbst fasst zusammen: „Manchmal frage ich mich, ob meine Einstellung zu vage ist, aber was ich am Kunstschaffen wirklich genieße, ist der Versuch, einen Punkt der Mehrdeutigkeit zu erreichen, an dem zwei unterschiedliche Prozesse, das Denken und das Machen, zusammenkommen. Ich will diesen Punkt finden, weil da die Spannung liegt, im perfekten Gleichgewicht zweier gegensätzlicher Dinge."[22]

Heutige Baustoffe und alltägliche Materialien, mit denen der Mensch seine Umwelt strukturiert, sind der Ausgangspunkt der skulpturalen Arbeiten und Installationen von **Mary Redmond** (geb. 1973). Wellblech, Metallstäbe, Bewehrungsstahl, Verstärkungsnetze, Maschendraht, Kabel, Ziegelsteine, Nägel, Dämmstoffe, Ytong-Steine, Jalousien, Balken oder Kunststoffschnüre sind gut erreichbare und einfach zu beschaffende Materialien [**Abb. 10**]. In ihrer manchmal auf-

materials into pictorial scenarios that one quickly loses sight of the individual components. She does this on the one hand by combining divergent materials, enabling her to shift the scale of her sculptures and create, for example, miniature landscapes or fragmentary images. On the other, she treats the assembled materials in an unconventional manner that includes bending, folding and buckling them, and thus transforms them. An oven grille becomes a flying element, for example, while a black-painted venetian blind is made to resemble a storm breaking over islands in the sea. Redmond incorporates a range of creative processes into her practice, but above all she employs cultural skills and artistic methods borrowed from other cultures, such as Japanese folding or knotting techniques. At the same time she draws upon the aesthetic concepts underlying these techniques, such as the principle of non-literalness that determines the use of materials in a Japanese garden. *Seven Split Overglide* is the title of an installation Redmond made on the seventh floor of a disused multi-storey car park in London in 2012. Using a limited vocabulary of industrial and organic materials – sheets of corrugated metal, paving slabs and bamboo canes, among others – and only a few technical measures, she transformed these raw materials into an image of nature within the enclosed space of this brutalist architecture. The finished piece recalls an autumnal landscape with floating, wilting leaves, ascending plant shoots and expanses

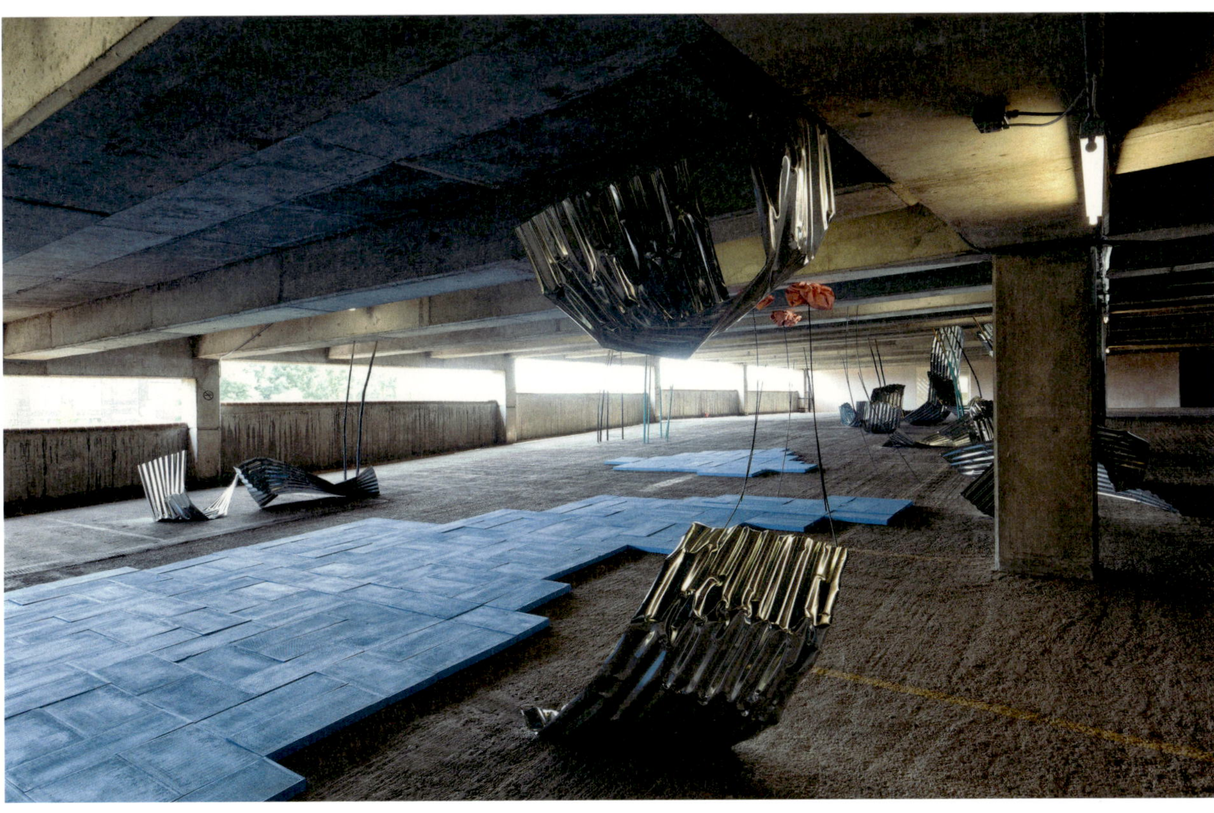

10 Mary Redmond, *Seven Split Overglide*, 2012, Installationsansicht / Installation view *Bold Tendencies Sculpture Project 6*, Peckham multi-storey car park, London 2012

dringlichen Farbigkeit, in der oft minderen Ausführung einer gut kalkulierten Produktion und in der auf ihre Funktion reduzierten Strukturierung zeichnen solche Mittel ein recht uncharmantes Bild von der Qualität und Machart der Baustoffe, die uns heute umgeben. Gerade solche Baustoffe zieht Redmond oftmals heran, die ihre Formen und ihre Eigenschaften durch einen ausschließlich vom Nutzen und von der Zweckdienlichkeit geprägten Produktionsgedanken erhalten haben. Da diese Materialien in der Regel im Bau verschwinden und dann unsichtbar sind, unterliegen sie meist selbst keinen speziellen Gestaltungsmerkmalen; häufig entsprechen sie dennoch einer durch den Hersteller oder den regionalen Geschmack geprägten Formgebung. Solche eigentlich abweisenden Materialien transformiert Redmond in ihren installativen Arbeiten dann aber in bildhafte Szenerien, welche die einzelnen Bestandteile bald gänzlich in Vergessenheit geraten lassen. Sie erreicht dies zum einen durch die Kombination verschiedener Materialien, womit sie ihren Skulpturen schnell den Maßstab entzieht und so etwa miniaturhafte Landschaften oder ausschnitthafte Szenerien entstehen können. Zum anderen bearbeitet sie die erworbenen Materialien gerade sinnwidrig, indem sie diese mit Knicken versieht, sie biegt und faltet und so umformt. Aus einer Art Backofenrost wird so beispielsweise ein fliegendes Element oder aus einer schwarzen Jalousie ein Unwetter, das auf Inseln im Meer niedergeht. In ihre Gestaltung bezieht Redmond sehr unterschiedliche Bearbeitungsverfahren ein, aber vor allem auch fremde Kulturtechniken oder künstlerische Methoden, wie Falt- oder Knotentechniken der japanischen Kultur, sowie deren ästhetische Konzepte, wie der auf dem Prinzip der Uneigentlichkeit basierende Einsatz von Materialien im japanischen Zengarten. *Seven Split Overglide* ist eine Installation, die Redmond 2012 in einer Etage eines brutalistisch anmutenden Parkhauses in London ausführte. Sie verwandte mit Wellblech, Gehwegplatten oder Bambusstangen ein umgrenztes Vokabular an Materialien. Diese rohen Baumaterialien wandelte sie in diesem geschlossenen Raum durch nur wenige technische Eingriffe in ein Bild der Natur um, in eine Art Herbstlandschaft mit wehenden, welken Blättern, sich emporpressenden Pflanzenstäben und Wasserflächen. Wieder ist der Maßstab – hier eine Überdimensionierung im Verhältnis zum Menschen – ein zentrales Moment ihrer Inszenierung einer abbrevierten, abstrakten Naturerfahrung.

Auch **Ciara Phillips** (geb. 1976) wendet sich in ihren Arbeiten einem traditionellen analogen Herstellungsverfahren zu,

of water. Here, too, the question of scale – in this case the elements are oversized in relation to human dimensions – is a central element of Redmond's staged presentation of an abbreviated, abstract experience of nature.

Ciara Phillips (b. 1976) also employs a traditional analogue technique – the art of printmaking [fig. 11]. The Canadian-born artist combines silkscreen printing with painting in her artworks, which are created on a variety of surfaces and supports. She works directly on walls and paper, but also on fabrics, with the result that her installations have an artisanal quality. The patterns on her printed fabrics occasionally create the impression of three-dimensionality, while the ornamentation often obeys a serial principle that allows them to be endlessly repeated or reproduced as fragments. Through the works created directly on the wall, the site of Phillips' printmaking is regularly shifted into the exhibition space itself, as "a way of emphasising the principles of serial work executed by hand and experienced in practical terms"[23]. Phillips places printmaking at the centre of her practice; her works reference and explore the history of this reproductive technique from two different perspectives: on the one hand as a medium of communication that facilitates the dissemination of visual or textual information, and on the other

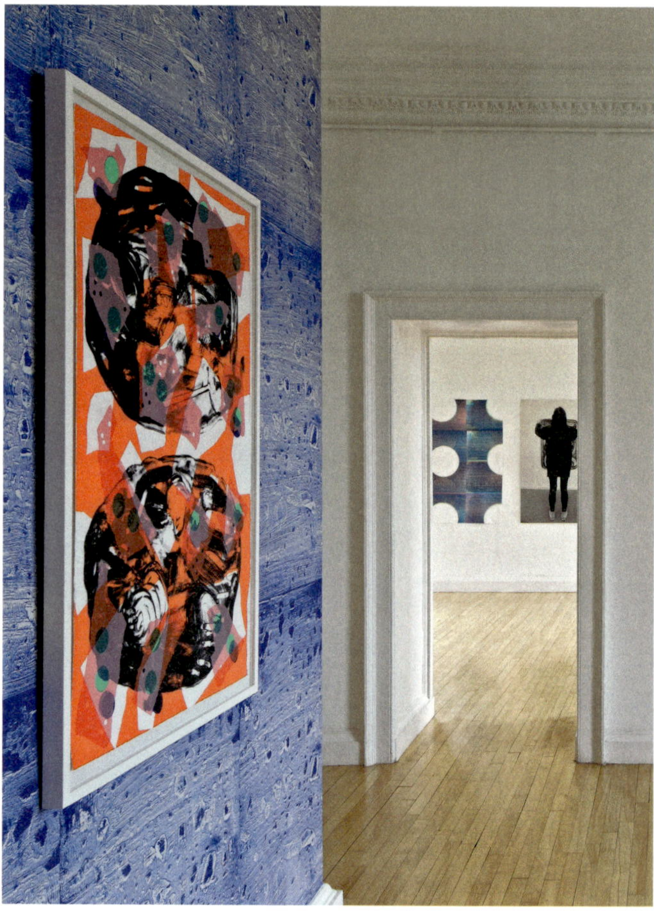

11 Ciara Phillips, Installationsansicht / Installation view *And more*, Inverleith House, Edinburgh 2013

der Drucktechnik [**Abb. 11**]. Die in Kanada geborene Künstlerin kombiniert in ihren Werken Malerei und Siebdruck-
technik, die auf unterschiedlichen Trägern zum Einsatz
kommen. Sie arbeitet direkt auf der Wand und auf Papier,
aber eben auch auf Stoffen. Auf diese Weise erhalten ihre Installationen einen kunsthandwerklichen, kunstgewerblichen
Charakter. Ihre Stoffe bedruckt Phillips in Mustern mit teils
tiefenräumlich wirkenden Rapports. Das Prinzip der Seriali-
tät ist den Ornamenten oft eigen, so lassen sie sich unendlich
fortsetzen oder in einem Fragment wiedergeben. Mit den
Wandarbeiten verlagert sich der Ort ihrer Druckproduktion
zuweilen direkt in den Ausstellungsraum. Dadurch wird „das
Prinzip einer handwerklich-seriellen, physisch ausgeführten
und praktisch erlebbaren Arbeit betont".[23] Phillips stellt das
Verfahren der Drucktechnik ins Zentrum ihrer künstlerischen Überlegungen. Damit öffnen sich ihre Arbeiten inhaltlich der Geschichte dieser Reproduktionstechnik, und dies in
zwei Richtungen, einerseits als Kommunikationsmedium
mit den Möglichkeiten der Verbreitung von Bild- und Text-
informationen und andererseits als Gestaltungsmedium mit
der Möglichkeit der Herstellung von Dekor oder Raumschmuck. In der Konzentration auf diese analoge Bildtech-
nik wie deren Geschichte und deren Anwendungen entstehen Installationen, die beides verbinden: künstlerische und
kunsthandwerkliche Verfahren. Durch diese Entscheidung
für ein Verfahren fließen in die Inszenierungen vielfältige
Gesichtspunkte ein: der Bezug von räumlicher Darstellung
im Flächenmuster und der realen Räumlichkeit; das Verhältnis von (durch die Malerei) direktem und (durch die
Drucktechnik) indirektem künstlerischem Verfahren; der
Wechsel von abstrakten Gestaltungsformen im Muster und
der Wiedergabe von Realität in der reproduzierten Fotografie; die Beziehung des Gebrauchs von Mustern und von
Grafik im Design einerseits und in der Kunst andererseits.

Die Idee eines kontextualisierenden Kunstbegriffs hat in der
Kunst zu Werken geführt, die auf das gesamte Spektrum der
Gesellschaft reagieren und der Form nach kunstnahe Erken-
nungsmerkmale eher ablegen. Materialien aus industrieller
Produktion, nützliche und funktionale Dinge des täglichen
Lebens, Gestaltungselemente der Umwelt oder Herstel-
lungstechniken aus dem Handwerk oder dem Kunsthand-
werk fließen ein. Dies geschieht mit dem Ziel, sich inhaltlich
zur Gesellschaft hin öffnen zu können. Doch in der jüngeren
Generation ist die Tendenz zu beobachten, über die Idee der
Möblierung doch wieder klassische Formen der Kunst in
Installationen zuzulassen und damit durch die Hintertür

as a creative medium that can be used to
produce functional or decorative objects
and designs. By focussing on this analogue technique, its history and its appli-
cations, Phillips creates installations
that combine artistic and craft-based
processes. Her choice of medium means
that many different aspects are incorporated into the staged environments: the
relationship between three-dimensional
representation in a fill pattern and the
real space of a chosen site; the connection between direct (painting) and indir-
ect (printmaking) working methods; the
switch from abstract forms in the patterns to reality depicted in the reproduced photographs; the use of pattern
and graphic design in the realm of fine
and applied art.

The concept of contextualising art has
led to the creation of works that respond
to a wide range of social realities and
generally avoid typically 'artistic' forms.
Instead they incorporate industrially
produced materials, utilitarian objects
or functional everyday items, draw on
design elements encountered in their
surroundings or employ production techniques that are traditionally associated
with craft-based, applied or decorative
arts. Often this is done in an attempt to
open up to society in terms of thematic
orientation. Among the younger generation of artists, however, a trend can be
observed of reintroducing classical
forms of art through the idea of 'furnishing' installations – allowing traditional
forms to re-enter through the back door,
as it were, and thus heading back in the
direction of the autonomous artwork.
In this case, the autonomous work of art
itself becomes a constituent element of
a spatial design. Recalling the conceptual approach of the Russian artist Ilya
Kabakov, the installation thus provides
the setting and the context for autonomous paintings or sculptures. The
staged environments created by Nick
Evans and Nicolas Party are good examples of this development. While Evans
demonstrates a contemporary approach
to abstract sculpture, Party arranges
autonomous paintings like furnishing
elements in the context of his installations. Figurative and abstract motifs are
incorporated into the work of both
artists, and both combine entertaining,
decorative elements with art-historical
references. **Nick Evans'** (b. 1976) plaster
sculptures have all the characteristics
expected of contemporary sculptural
practice. While formally reminiscent of
the abstract works of Henry Moore, they
are in fact created according to a modular system, assembled in an additive way
from plaster casts of a small number of
moulded clay forms; as such they reflect
the production process [fig. 12]. The
mode of display – the sculptures are

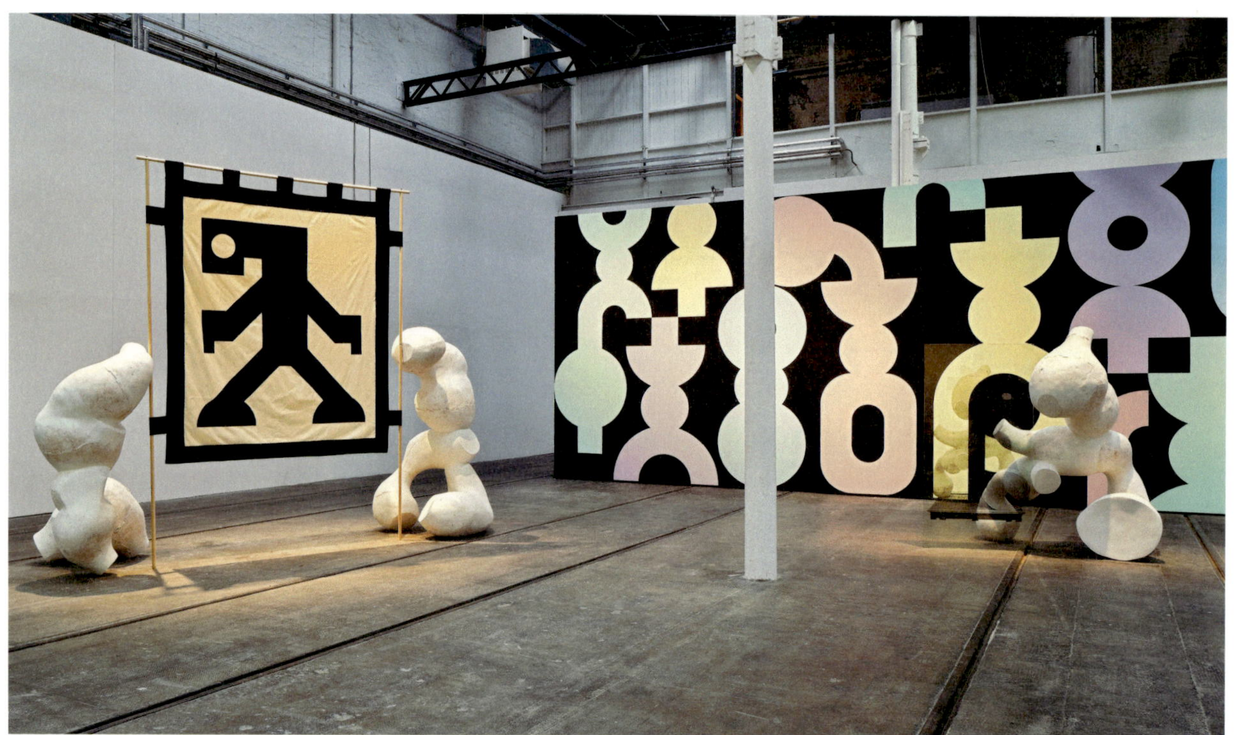

12 Nick Evans, Installationsansicht / Installation view *Solar Eyes*, Tramway, Glasgow 2013

wieder auf das autonome Werk zuzusteuern. Das autonome Werk wird hier zunächst selbst als Gestaltungselement in die Raumstruktur integriert. An die Werkauffassung des russischen Konzeptualisten Ilya Kabakov erinnernd, bildet eine Installation so erst den Kontext für autonome Gemälde oder Skulpturen. Beispiele dafür sind die Inszenierungen von Nick Evans und Nicolas Party. Während Nick Evans auf die abstrakte Skulptur zugeht, sind es bei Nicolas Party autonome Gemälde, die wie Ausstattungsstücke im Kontext einer Installation eingesetzt werden. Bei beiden gibt es Anlehnungen sowohl an figürliche wie an abstrakte Motive, unterhaltsame, dekorative Elemente sind ebenso vorhanden wie Bezüge zur Kunstgeschichte. Die Gipsskulpturen von **Nick Evans** (geb. 1976) weisen alles auf, was ein zeitgemäßer Skulpturbegriff heute beinhalten muss. Formal an die abstrakten Werke von Henry Moore erinnernd, sind sie jedoch nach einem Baukasten- oder Modulsystem entstanden und aus einzelnen Gussformen additiv zusammengesetzt; darin reflektieren sie den Produktionsprozess [**Abb. 12**]. Die Art der Aufstellung auf Eichenschemeln oder Hockern, auf gestuftem, ornamentiertem Sockel, auf einer Plattform, auf rotierender Stele oder direkt auf dem Fußboden diskutiert spielerisch den so problematischen Sockelbegriff und die vielen Funktionsweisen, die der Skulptur als Monument und Denkmal, als autonomem Objekt, als Raumschmuck oder als volkskundlichem Fetisch zugewiesen werden. Doch zudem personifiziert Evans seine abstrakten Objekte und weist ihnen ähnlich wie Staffagefiguren verschiedene Funktionen zu, wie – als nur ein Beispiel – die Rolle eines Fahnenträgers.

placed on oak bases and stools, tiered and ornamented plinths, a platform, rotating stelae or directly on the floor – playfully addresses not only the problematic issue of the pedestal but also the multiple roles played by sculpture, which can serve as a monument or memorial, an autonomous object, an element of interior decoration or a folkloristic fetish. At the same time, however, Evans personifies his abstract objects and has them perform different functions, similar to staffage figures – one is assigned the role of standard-bearer, for example. As 'performers' within a spatial constellation, these individualised objects on the one hand convey aspects of outdoor space, such as a picnic or a monument on a public square, but on the other recall indoor situations such as a display of artefacts in an ethnological museum or modern art collection. Evans structures the exhibition space with wall- and floor-based pieces made of printed wallpaper, featuring ornamental strips of repeated folkloristic motifs and abstract designs that recall 1950s décor in terms of their colouring and form.

Nicolas Party (b. 1980) likewise creates repetitive patterns for his wall works, but in his case the walls are hand-painted using three different techniques [fig. 13]. "What is interesting to me about the wall works is how the various materials react when applied to the same surface. I use three techniques on the wall: charcoal, spray paint and gold leaf. Each substance reacts in a unique way and reveals different aspects of the wall's surface. Charcoal is very sensitive and fragile. It registers every imperfection,

Als Personal in einem Raumprogramm platziert, vermitteln diese individualisierten Objekte einerseits Momente des Außenraumes, wie ein Picknick im Freien oder das Monument eines Platzes, aber andererseits auch Situationen des Innenraumes wie Artefakte in einem Museum für Volkskunde oder für moderne Kunst. Den Ausstellungsraum strukturiert Evans mit Wand- und Bodenarbeiten aus bedruckter Tapete. Diese zeigt Ornamentbänder sich im Rapport immer wiederholender volkskundlicher Motive oder eine abstrakte Ornamentik, die in Farbigkeit und Form an ein Dekor der fünfziger Jahre erinnert.

Auch **Nicolas Party** (geb. 1980) entwickelt fortlaufende Muster für seine Wandarbeiten. Er bemalt jedoch seine Wände eigenhändig in drei verschiedenen Techniken [**Abb. 13**]. „Was mich an den Wandarbeiten interessiert, ist, wie sich die verschiedenen Materialien verhalten, wenn sie auf dieselbe Oberfläche aufgebracht werden. Ich verwende an der Wand drei Techniken: Kohle, Sprühfarbe und Blattgold. Jede Substanz reagiert auf ihre eigene Weise und bringt unterschiedliche Aspekte der Wandoberfläche zum Vorschein. Kohle ist sehr empfindlich und fragil. Sie erfasst jede Unvollkommenheit und verrät so die Geschichte der Wand. Wenn es in der Wandfarbe einen Kratzer oder irgendeine Unebenheit gibt, wird man dies sehr viel deutlicher erkennen, sobald ich die Kohle auftrage. Die Sprühfarbe dagegen kaschiert die Wand perfekt. Sie erzeugt eine ‚zweite Haut‘, welche die Original-

revealing the history of the wall. If there is a scratch or any unevenness in the wall paint, you will see this much more clearly after I apply the charcoal. By contrast, the spray paint glosses over the wall perfectly. The spray paint creates a 'second skin' that masks the wall's original surface and thereby flattens it. The acrylic-based spray paint has a very even color; it does not play off the wall's surface. Finally there is the gold leaf. Like the charcoal, it augments any flaws in the wall."[24] While he uses acrylic paint to cover the surface of walls with brightly coloured repeat patterns, Party chooses charcoal to create black-and-white drawings directly on the walls. In this way he transforms the exhibition space into an atmospheric environment that serves as a kind of backdrop or stage for his oil paintings – because Nicolas Party is first and foremost a painter. In contrast to his ornamental designs, which have a light-handed, playful dimension, his oil paintings are created over a period of many months and appear curiously enigmatic and intriguing. Although the painted images can quickly be identified as still lifes of jugs, pots, flowers, fruit or vegetables, something about them still manages to trap the gaze. There is an improbability to the motifs – a skewed relationship between body and space, object and geometry, surface and volume – that confounds the gaze, which remains caught up in the process of trying to understand until Party's subtle humour (in the form of an olive or an apple core, for example) breaks through and

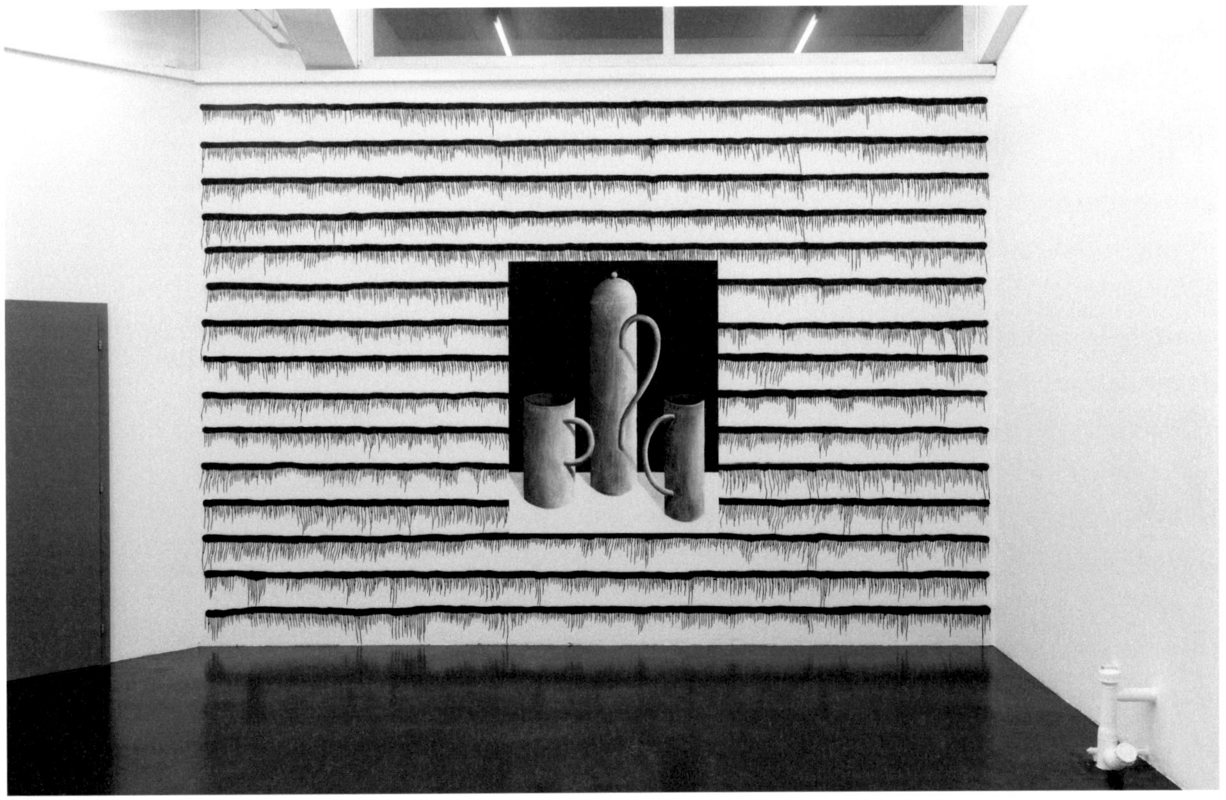

13 Nicolas Party, *Decorative Pattern*, 2012, Installationsansicht / Installation view *Still Lifes and Big Naked Women*, Gregor Staiger, Zürich / Zurich 2012

oberfläche der Wand abdeckt und sie dabei glättet. Sprühfarbe auf Acrylbasis ist ein sehr ebenmäßiges Farbmaterial; es hebt die Wandoberfläche nicht hervor. Und schließlich ist da das Blattgold. Wie die Kohle verstärkt es jeden Fehler in der Wand."[24] Mit der Acrylfarbe legt Party fortlaufende farbige Muster an, während er mit der Kohle schwarzweiße Bilder auf die Wand setzt. Er verwandelt so den Ausstellungsraum in ein Ambiente, eine Art Bühne für seine Ölbilder. Denn Nicolas Party ist vor allem Maler. Sind die Ornamente leicht und spielerisch, so stehen seine Ölgemälde dazu im Gegensatz. Er arbeitet langsam an diesen, sie haben auch einen rätselhaften, enigmatischen Charakter. Zwar sind die Bilder unmittelbar als Stillleben zu identifizieren mit Gefäßen, Blumen, Obst oder Gemüse, doch bleibt der Blick in ihnen gefangen. Denn die Motive lösen sich nicht ein. Körper und Raum, Objekt und Geometrie, Fläche und Volumen sind ineinander verdreht. So wird der Blick letztlich ins Leere geleitet und bleibt mit dem Prozess des Verstehenwollens im Bild gefangen, bis der stille Humor von Party in Form einer Olive oder einer Apfelkitsche sich Bahn bricht und wieder aus dem Bild herausleitet. Während Evans seine Skulpturen um das Zweidimensionale erweitert, führt Party das durch seine zehnjährige Graffiti-Erfahrung vorhandene Interesse an unterschiedlichen Trägern für Bildmotive hin zum Objekt. Mit dem Motiv des Elefanten bemalt er Sockel, die bald die Form von Sitzgelegenheiten annehmen, sowie in seriellen Mustern dann auch Tische, an denen zu Tischgesellschaften eingeladen wird. Für diese Einladungen konzipiert Party auch Teller und übernimmt das dazugehörige Fooddesign; sein malerisches Konzept bestimmt das Leben.

In zeitgenössischer Kunst ist eine Berührung und Durchmischung von Formen der Architektur, von Kunst und von Design unübersehbar. Doch hebt diese angesprochene Verbindung letztlich die Verschiedenartigkeit in den Zielsetzungen der Sparten Kunst, Design und Architektur doch nur hervor. Denn ebenso deutlich ist, dass die bildende Kunst eigenen Fragestellungen folgt. Elemente von Architektur und Design dienen ihr zwar als Einstieg, um einen Dialog zum Publikum zu initiieren und ganz reale Erfahrungen ansprechen zu können. Doch erst durch eine Umwandlung des Funktionalen gerade in eine Funktionslosigkeit treten die jeweils eigenen Themen dann zutage. Bildende Kunst hat allein Fragen zur Mentalität des Menschen zum Gegenstand und muss darüber hinaus keinem Zwecke dienen.

draws us back out of the image. While Evans has expanded his sculptures to include two-dimensionality, Party's interest in creating pictorial forms on different surfaces and supports, sparked by a decade of experience as a graffiti artist, has led him to the object. He paints an elephant motif around plinths, which quickly become transformed into seats, then extends these serial patterns to tables and invites us to gather around them. For these events he also takes on the task of designing the plates and even the food: Party's painting concept pervades all aspects of life.

The incorporation and combination of forms derived from architecture, art and design in works of contemporary art cannot be overlooked. Ultimately, however, they only serve to emphasise the different aims pursued by the various disciplines, as it is equally evident that visual art has questions of its own to address. While architectural and design elements can provide artists with a means of access, enabling them to initiate a dialogue with the audience and address real-life experiences, it is only by transforming the functional into the dysfunctional that their individual artistic concerns are brought to light. Visual art addresses issues related to human mentality and perception, and need serve no purpose beyond that.

1 Joseph Beuys in: „Auszüge aus einem längeren Tonbandinterview vom 29. September 1970 zwischen Joseph Beuys und Hagen Lieberknecht", in: *Joseph Beuys. Zeichnungen aus der Sammlung Schirmer*, Ausst.-Kat. Kunsthalle St. Gallen, 1970, S. 13.

2 In der Ausstellung *Strategy: Get Arts* zeigte Beuys zudem seine Arbeiten *the pack (das Rudel)* und *Arena*.

3 Mario Kramer, zit. nach: Uwe M. Schneede, *Joseph Beuys. Die Aktionen*, Ostfildern-Ruit, 1994, S. 268.

4 Ausstellungen zur schottischen Kunst fanden zuvor 1982 in der SAC Gallery in Edinburgh (*Scottish Art Now*), 1987 in der Scottish National Gallery of Modern Art in Edinburgh (*The Vigorous Imagination*), 1992 im Irish Museum of Modern Art in Dublin (*Guilt by Association*) und 1993/94 im CCA in Glasgow (*New Art in Scotland I, II, III*) statt. Kunst aus Glasgow wurde 1997 in der Kunsthalle Bern (*Glasgow*), 1998 im Museet vor Samtidskunst in Oslo (*Nettverk Glasgow*) und 2004 im Kunstraum B/2 in Leipzig (*Synth – 10 Artists from Glasgow*) gezeigt.

5 Vgl. Sarah Lowndes, *Social Sculpture: The Rise of the Glasgow Art Scene*, Edinburgh, 2010, S. 397.

6 Lowndes 2010.

7 Vgl. Lowndes 2010, S. 67.

8 Boyce, zit. nach: Lowndes 2010, S. 127.

9 Lowndes 2010, S. 412.

10 Jörg Huber und Heike Munder, „Geleitwort", in: *It's Not a Garden Table. Kunst und Design im erweiterten Feld*, hrsg. von Jörg Huber, Burkhard Meltzer, Heike Munder, Tido von Oppeln, Institut für Theorie, Zürcher Hochschule der Künste, Migros Museum für Gegenwartskunst, Zürich, 2011, S. 7.

11 Tobias Rehberger, *Peuè Seè e Faàgck Sunday Paàe*, 1994, Installation 2004 im Neuen Museum in Nürnberg.

12 Vgl. dazu *Wenn Handlungen Form werden*, Ausst.-Kat. Neues Museum in Nürnberg, 2007.

13 Hein, zit. nach: Birgit Ruf, „Die Welt steht Kopf im Spiegelkabinett", in Nürnberger Nachrichten, 22. Oktober 2010, S. 5.

14 Zit. nach: Lowndes 2010, S. 87.

15 Boyce, zit. nach: Lowndes 2010, S. 88.

16 Vgl. Gordon, zit. nach: Lowndes 2010, S. 87.

17 Boyce, zit. nach: „Max Borka, Martin Boyce, Frédéric Dedelley: Ist Kunst ein experimenteller Kontext für Design?" (öffentliches Gespräch) in: Huber, Meltzer, Munder, Oppeln, 2011, S. 271f.

18 Nützlichkeit ist für Boyce kein Ansatzpunkt einer Verbindung von Kunst und Design, wie er Burkhard Meltzer mitteilt: „Die Idee des sozialisierten Ausstellungsraumes, in dem man Leuten erlaubt, dort zu schlafen, zu musizieren oder zu essen, also das, was sie normalerweise dort nicht tun, war nie mein Hauptinteresse. Ich mag es, mir eine Ausstellung als eine Art gefrorenes Bild vorzustellen, durch das man hindurchlaufen kann oder, wo es möglich ist, einen Moment hineinzutreten, um eine Intimität und auch eine Distanz zu erleben." In: „Concrete Autumn – Martin Boyce", in: Huber, Meltzer, Munder, Oppeln, 2011, S. 114.

19 Barclay, zit. nach: „In conversation. Francis McKee and Claire Barclay", in: *Claire Barclay. Openwide*, Ausst.-Kat. The Fruitmarket Gallery, Edinburgh, 2009, S. 142.

20 Ebenda, S. 140f.

21 Claire Doherty, „Sculpture as Event", in: *Claire Barclay. Openwide*, S. 132.

22 Barclay, zit. nach: „In conversation. Francis McKee and Claire Barclay", in: *Claire Barclay. Openwide*, S. 144.

23 Gabrielle Schaad, in *frieze d/e*, No 6, Herbst / Autumn 2012, S. 142.

24 „Five Questions for Nicolas Party", Interview von Mara Hoberman anlässlich der Ausstellung *Still Life, Stones, and Elephants* im Swiss Institute, New York, Februar 2012. Veröffentlicht in: *Swiss Institute Contemporary Art*, Issue No. 1, March 2012, S. 24f.

1 Joseph Beuys, in 'Auszüge aus einem längeren Tonbandinterview vom 29. September 1970 zwischen Joseph Beuys und Hagen Lieberknecht', in *Joseph Beuys. Zeichnungen aus der Sammlung Schirmer*, exh. cat. (St. Gallen: Kunsthalle St. Gallen, 1970), p. 13.

2 Beuys also showed his works *the pack (das Rudel)* and *Arena* in the exhibition *Strategy: Get Arts*.

3 Mario Kramer, quoted in Uwe M. Schneede, *Joseph Beuys. Die Aktionen* (Ostfildern-Ruit: Verlag Gerd Hatje, 1994), p. 268.

4 Exhibitions on the subject of Scottish Art had previously been held at Edinburgh's SAC Gallery in 1982 (*Scottish Art Now*); at the Scottish National Gallery of Modern Art, also in Edinburgh, in 1987 (*The Vigorous Imagination*); at the Irish Museum of Modern Art in Dublin in 1992 (*Guilt by Association*); and at Glasgow's CCA in 1993/94 (*New Art in Scotland I, II, III*). Contemporary art from Glasgow was shown at the Kunsthalle Bern in 1997 (*Glasgow*), at the Museet vor Samtidskunst in Oslo in 1998 (*Nettverk Glasgow*) and at Kunstraum B/2 in Leipzig in 2004 (*Synth – 10 Artists from Glasgow*).

5 Cf. Sarah Lowndes, *Social Sculpture: The Rise of the Glasgow Art Scene* (Edinburgh: Luath Press, 2010), p. 397.

6 Sarah Lowndes, *Social Sculpture*. The Luath Press publication is a revised and expanded edition of Lowndes' original study, entitled *Social Sculpture: Art, Performance and Music in Glasgow. A Social History of Independent Practice, Exhibitions and Events since 1971*, which was published by STOPSTOP in 2003.

7 Lowndes, *Social Sculpture* (2010), p. 67.

8 Martin Boyce, quoted ibid., p. 127.

9 Ibid., p. 412.

10 Jörg Huber and Heike Munder, 'Preface', in Jörg Huber et al. (eds.), *It's Not a Garden Table: Art and Design in the Expanded Field* (Zurich: JRP|Ringier, 2011), p. 7.

11 Tobias Rehberger, *Peuè Seè e Faàgck Sunday Paàe*, 1994, installation at the Neues Museum in Nuremberg in 2004.

12 Cf. *Wenn Handlungen Form werden*, exh. cat. Neues Museum in Nürnberg (Nuremberg: Verlag für moderne Kunst, 2007).

13 Hein, quoted in Birgit Ruf, 'Die Welt steht Kopf im Spiegelkabinett', *Nürnberger Nachrichten*, 22 October 2010, p. 5.

14 Lowndes, *Social Sculpture* (2010), p. 87.

15 Boyce, quoted ibid., p. 88.

16 Cf. Gordon, quoted ibid., p. 87.

17 Boyce, quoted in 'Is the work of art an experimental context for design? Max Borka, Martin Boyce, Frédéric Dedelley', in Huber et al. (eds.), *It's Not a Garden Table*, p. 257.

18 For Boyce, utility is not the starting point for his combination of art and design, as he tells Burkhard Meltzer: "the idea of socializing the exhibition space and allowing people to do things that they don't normally do in exhibition spaces, like sleeping, make music, eating or so on – that has never been a priority of my interests. I like to think of the exhibition as a kind of a frozen image you can walk through, to be able to step inside a glimpse, so you have this intimacy and also a distance." In 'Concrete Autumn – Martin Boyce', ibid., p. 68.

19 Barclay, in 'In conversation. Francis McKee and Claire Barclay', in *Claire Barclay. Openwide*, exh. cat. (Edinburgh: Fruitmarket Gallery, 2009), p. 142.

20 Ibid., pp. 140 f.

21 Claire Doherty, 'Sculpture as Event', ibid., p. 132.

22 Barclay, in 'In conversation', ibid., p. 144.

23 Gabrielle Schaad, 'Ciara Phillips', *frieze d/e*, Issue 6, Herbst / Autumn 2012, p. 142.

24 'Five Questions for Nicolas Party', interview by Mara Hoberman in connection with his exhibition *Still Life, Stones, and Elephants*, held at the Swiss Institute, New York, in February 2012. Published in *Swiss Institute Contemporary Art*, Issue No. 1, March 2012, pp. 24 f.

Schaufensterbummel: Kunst aus Glasgow und die Politik der Präsentation

Window-shopping: Glasgow art and the politics of display

„Ich stieg in eine Straßenbahn. Sobald ich mich hingesetzt hatte, steckte ich meine Hand in die Tasche, um nachzusehen, ob mein Geld noch da war. Natürlich war es noch da. Ich lächelte mein fast transparentes Spiegelbild im Fenster an, blickte hinaus und sah dahinter, wie bei einer Erinnerung, die meinen Kopf verlassen hatte, eine junge Frau in einem rosa Mantel vor einem Schaufenster stehen, erhaschte einen Blick auf ihre Beine, die unter dem Mantelsaum blass und sonnenverbrannt wie Cathies waren, und ich fragte mich, ob ich unter anderen Voraussetzungen den Mut aufgebracht hätte, auszusteigen und mich bekannt zu machen. Die Straßenbahn fuhr weiter, eine Insel aus Fenstern."[1]

Die Aktivität des Schaufensterbummels, das Betrachten von Auslagen ohne Kaufabsicht, erhält in dieser Szene aus Alexander Trocchis Roman *Wasserläufe* von 1954 eine besondere Bedeutung. Trocchis Buch, angesiedelt rund um den Fluss Clyde während der Nachkriegsjahre, beschreibt ausführlich die Sehnsüchte und Entbehrungen der arbeitenden Bevölkerung in einer Phase, da der langsame Niedergang der traditionellen Glasgower Industriezweige Schiffbau, Stahl und Maschinenbau begonnen hatte. Doch Trocchis Szenario ist auch ein Prisma, durch das wir in die Zukunft dieser Stadt blicken können. Tatsächlich sollte sich Glasgow bis Mitte der 1990er Jahre in eine „Reisestadt" verwandeln und einen Wiederaufstieg erleben, der durch öffentliche Investitionen in Handel und Dienstleistung angetrieben wurde – und auch durch die Kunstszene der Stadt, eine Szene, die auf alternativen Werten und der Aktivität des Schauens, ohne zu kaufen, aufbaut. Fast sechzig Jahre nach Erscheinen der *Wasserläufe*, im Herbst 2013, werden die Positionen von sechs Glasgower Künstlern in der Ausstellung *Funktion / Dysfunktion. Kunstzentrum Glasgow* hinter der eindrucksvollen Glasfassade des Neuen Museums in Nürnberg zu sehen sein. Gezeigt werden die Arbeiten von Martin Boyce, Claire Barclay, Mary Redmond, Ciara Phillips, Nick Evans und Nicolas Party in sechs Räumen auf zwei Etagen, die von außen wie eine Ladenfront eingesehen werden können.

Die Industrieproduktion Glasgows ging zwischen 1978 und 1983 um 30 Prozent zurück.[2] Ein deutlicher Zuwachs

"I boarded a tram. As soon as I was seated I found myself putting my hand in my pocket to make sure my money was still there. Of course it was. I smiled at the almost transparent reflection of myself in the window and saw beyond it, like a memory walking out of my head, a girl in a pink coat who stood looking in a shop window, a glimpse of legs which under the hem of the coat were pale and sunburned as Cathie's had been, and I wondered whether under different circumstances I would have had the courage to get off and introduce myself. The tram moved on, an island of windows."[1]

'Window-shopping', or looking without the intention of buying, is an activity loaded with significance in this scene from Alexander Trocchi's 1954 novel, *Young Adam*. Trocchi's book, set in and around Glasgow's river Clyde in the postwar years, details the aspirations and deprivations of working people as the slow decline of the city's traditional industries of shipbuilding, steel and engineering began. Yet Trocchi's paragraph is also a prism through which we can glimpse Glasgow's future. Indeed, by the mid-1990s, Glasgow had transformed itself into a 'destination city': a re-ascent fuelled by public investment in shopping and services – and by the city's art scene, a scene predicated upon alternative values and the activity of looking without buying. Almost 60 years after the publication of *Young Adam*, in the autumn of 2013, the work of six Glasgow-based artists will be shown in the exhibition *Function / Dysfunction. Contemporary Art from Glasgow*, behind the impressive glass facade of the Neues Museum in Nuremberg. The work of Martin Boyce, Claire Barclay, Mary Redmond, Ciara Phillips, Nick Evans and Nicolas Party will be shown in six exhibition spaces on two storeys that can be viewed from outside like a shopfront.

Manufacturing in Glasgow contracted by 30 per cent between 1978 and 1983.[2] A marked rise in transport by air added to the problems of the beleaguered shipbuilding industry, and by 1983 the Clyde Port Authority reported a loss for the second year in succession. Of that year's deficit of £1.4m, £1.06m was made up of

beim Lufttransport verschärfte die Krise der angeschlagenen Schiffbauindustrie, sodass die Clyde Port Authority im Jahr 1983 zum zweiten Mal in Folge einen Verlust vermeldete. Das damalige Defizit von 1,4 Millionen Pfund bestand mit 1,06 Millionen Pfund zum größten Teil aus Abfindungen. Der düsteren Statistik zum Trotz begann im selben Jahr der Versuch, Glasgows Ansehen in der Öffentlichkeit zu verbessern, und zwar als gemeinsame Initiative des Glasgower Stadtrats und der Scottish Development Agency SDA. Beide sahen einzig und allein im Dienstleistungssektor realistische Chancen für ein Beschäftigungswachstum. Die Fremdenverkehrskampagne „Glasgow's Miles Better" (Glasgow ist um Meilen besser), die der Stadt mithilfe der Comicfigur Unser

redundancy payments. Despite these grim statistics, this was the year that the attempt began to change Glasgow's public profile, a joint initiative by Glasgow City Council and the Scottish Development Agency (SDA), both of which viewed the service sector as the only realistic area for growth in employment. 1983 saw the launch of the tourist campaign "Glasgow's Miles Better", which attempted to rebrand the city as a friendly place, with the aid of the Mr. Men cartoon character Mr. Happy. By the late 1980s, Glasgow City Council's new focus on tourism and retail had begun to regenerate the city's public profile through developments and projects like the £23m luxury shopping centre Princes Square, which opened in 1987, the

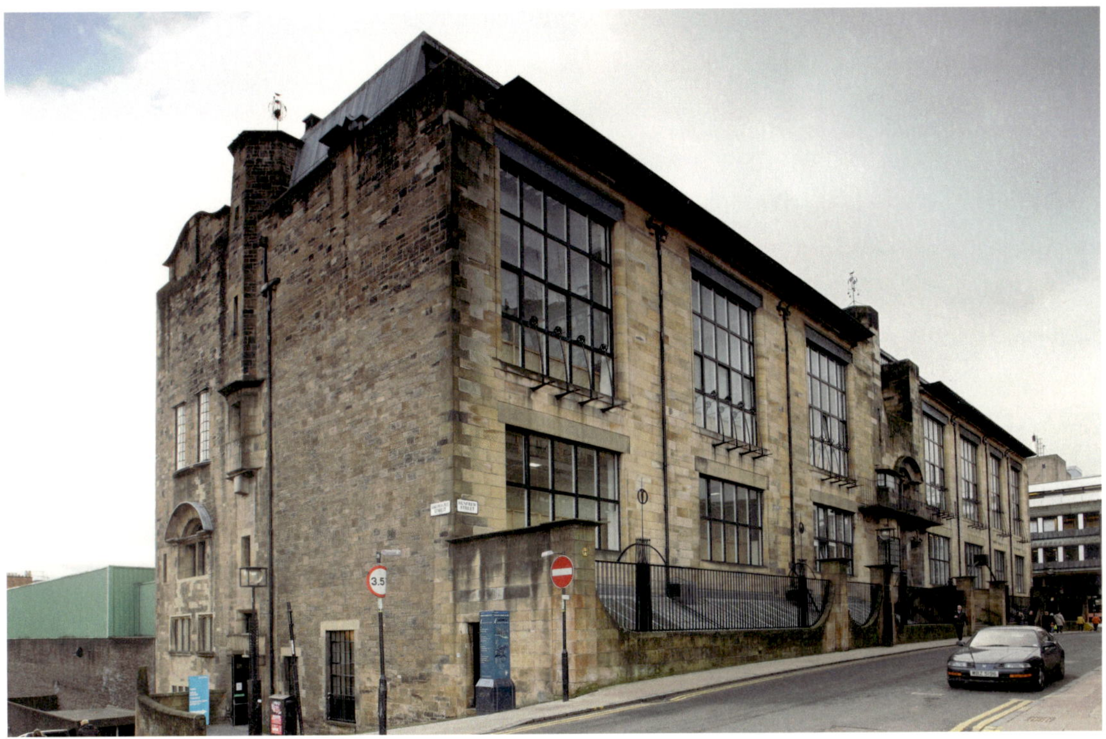

1 Glasgow School of Art (Mackintosh Gebäude / Mackintosh building)

Herr Glücklich aus der Kinderbuchreihe *Unsere kleinen Damen und Herren* ein neues Image als freundliche Metropole geben sollte, entstand 1983. Ende der 1980er Jahre zeigte der neue Fokus des Stadtrats auf Tourismus und Einzelhandel zunehmend Wirkung: Glasgow erhielt ein neues öffentliches Gesicht. Städtebauliche Entwicklungen und Projekte wie das 1987 eröffnete, 23 Millionen Pfund teure Luxusshoppingcenter Princes Square, das Glasgow Garden Festival (1988) und das bevorstehende Jahr als Kulturhauptstadt Europas (1990) trugen mit dazu bei, Glasgow als wettbewerbsfähiges Touristenziel zu etablieren.

Die eigentliche und bis heute andauernde Verwandlung Glasgows seit den 1980er Jahren aber ist größtenteils der Kunstszene der Stadt zuzuschreiben, die seit jener Zeit durch Generationen von Absolventen der Glasgow School of Art

Glasgow Garden Festival (1988) and the approaching European Year of Culture (1990), all of which played their role in re-establishing Glasgow as a viable tourist destination.

However, the real and ongoing transformation of Glasgow since the 1980s can largely be attributed to the city's art scene, which has been sustained since that time by successive generations of graduates emerging from Glasgow School of Art [fig. 1]. In the same year that Mr. Happy appeared on billboard hoardings and buses across Europe, urging tourists to consider Glasgow for their next holiday, the 'do-it-yourself' activities of young artists in the city were also finding public expression. However, in contrast to the emphasis upon shopping and services found in the official visioning of Glasgow, the artist-led activity

 getragen wird. Im selben Jahr, als Unser Herr Glücklich auf Plakatwänden und Bussen in ganz Europa auftauchte und Touristen ermunterte, Glasgow als Urlaubsziel zu wählen, fanden auch die Do-it-yourself-Aktivitäten von jungen Künstlern in der Stadt erstmals öffentlich Ausdruck. Doch im Gegensatz zu der offiziellen Außendarstellung Glasgows, in der Handel und Dienstleistung betont wurden, waren die von Künstlern initiierten und durchgeführten Aktionen prozessbezogen, wurzelten in gesellschaftlicher Beteiligung und wurden oft mit knappen Mitteln und Materialien realisiert. Im Winter 1983 nahm eine Gruppe von Malereiabsolventen der Glasgow School of Art in der Chisholm Street nahe der Trongate, einer der ältesten Straßen der Stadt, ein verfallenes Ladenlokal in Besitz und eröffnete Tür an Tür mit Terry's Tattoo Parlour Glasgows erste nicht gewinnorientierte Produzentengalerie: Transmission. Cathy Wilkes, die in den 1980er und 1990er Jahren an zahlreichen Non-Profit-Organisationen in der Stadt beteiligt war, so auch an der Frauenbibliothek, an Transmission und an einer Galerie in ihrer eigenen Wohnung, stellte fest: „Es erfordert eine Menge Kraft und Anstrengung, innerhalb eines Systems ein völlig anderes System aufzubauen. [...] Veranstaltungen und Klubs schießen aus dem Boden und bleiben eine Weile bestehen; sie sind Teil eines Wirtschaftssystems, das auf einer anderen Grundlage funktioniert als die Tauschwirtschaft, denn die Leute verdienen kein Geld damit und machen das einfach nur aus Liebe zur Sache."[3]

Mit der Ernennung von David Harding zum Fachbereichsleiter wurde 1985 an der Glasgow School of Art der neue Fachbereich Environmental Art offiziell ins Leben gerufen. Harding hatte zuvor zehn Jahre als Stadtkünstler in der schottischen Planstadt Glenrothes gewirkt und dann für acht Jahre am Dartington College of Arts im südenglischen Totnes den Kurs „Art and Social Context" geleitet, den er auch entwickelt hatte. Der neue Fachbereich bot den Studierenden eine Alternative zu den bestehenden Kategorien der bildenden Kunst – Malerei, Bildhauerei und Druckgrafik – und war beeinflusst von den Schriften zur New Genre Public Art von Suzanne Lacy und Lucy R. Lippard.[4] Später verfasste Harding ein Buch mit dem Titel *Decadent* (1995), in dem er einige seiner Gedanken zur Kunst im öffentlichen Raum skizzierte. Dort heißt es: „Um ein Vorwort zu Michel de Certeaus Essay ‚Gehen in der Stadt' zu paraphrasieren, verleiht Kunst im öffentlichen Raum dem Gehen eine zusätzliche Bedeutung und unterscheidet es vom Formellen, vom Alltagsleben, und zwar auf dieselbe Weise, wie die Dichtkunst sich von einem Planungshandbuch unterscheidet. Sie

that was taking place during the same period was process-based, rooted in social cooperation and often realised with an economy of means and materials. In the winter of 1983, a group of painting graduates from Glasgow School of Art took possession of a derelict Trongate shop premises on Chisholm Street, next door to Terry's Tattoo Parlour, where they set up the city's first nonprofit-making artist-run gallery, Transmission. Cathy Wilkes, who was involved in many of the city's non-profit organisations in the 1980s and 1990s, including the Women's Library, Transmission and running her own flat gallery, observed: "It takes a great deal of force and effort, within one system to create a whole other system. [...] There are events and clubs that spring up and last for a while, and they are part of that economy that works on a different basis from exchange economy, because people don't make money out of them, and they just do it for the love of it."[3]

In 1985, the new Environmental Art Department at Glasgow School of Art was formalised by the appointment of David Harding as the Head of Department. Harding had previously spent a decade as the town artist in the new town of Glenrothes, and worked for eight years as the developer of the 'Art and Social Context' course at Dartington College of Arts in Devon. Harding's course offered students at the school an alternative to the existing fine art categories of Painting, Printmaking and Sculpture, and was influenced by the "new genre public art" writings of Suzanne Lacy and Lucy R. Lippard.[4] Harding later penned a book entitled *Decadent: Public Art, Contentious Term and Contested Practice* (1997) in which he summarised some of his thoughts on the importance of public art. He wrote: "To paraphrase a preface to Michel de Certeau's essay, 'Walking in the City', public art gives to walking that extra meaning and makes it different to the official, from the business of life, in the way that poetry is different from a planning manual. It slows down the pace and increases perception. It grants to the twentieth-century urban experience a kind of drifting and the glamour that Walter Benjamin found in the nineteenth-century 'leisured observer'. Everyday life has a special value when it takes place in the gaps of the larger power structures."[5]

Under Harding's guidance, students were encouraged to invest in a kind of philosophical window-shopping, which often found concrete expression in exhibitions of site-specific and installation work staged in the city's numerous postindustrial gap sites: waste ground,

verlangsamt den Schritt und erhöht die Wahrnehmung. Sie beschert der urbanen Erfahrung des 20. Jahrhunderts eine Art Dahintreiben und einen Glanz, den Walter Benjamin im Flaneur des 19. Jahrhunderts fand. Der Alltag bekommt einen besonderen Wert, wenn er in den Leerstellen größerer Machtstrukturen stattfindet."[5]

Unter Hardings Anleitung wurden die Studierenden zu einer Art philosophischem Schaufensterbummel ermutigt, der seinen konkreten Ausdruck in Ausstellungen von ortsspezifischen Werken und Installationen erhielt, die in den unzähligen postindustriellen Baulücken der Stadt, den Brachflächen, den aufgegebenen Gebäuden oder leer stehenden Ladenlokalen stattfanden. Ende der 1980er, Anfang der 1990er Jahre studierten unter anderem Christine Borland, Claire Barclay, Douglas Gordon, Nathan Coley und Martin Boyce am Fachbereich. Sie alle wurden angespornt, umfangreiche Recherchen anzustellen und Kunst außerhalb der Ateliers und Galerien („mit oder durch Menschen") zu produzieren. Ab dem zweiten Studienjahr wurde gefordert, einmal jährlich ein Kunstwerk im öffentlichen Raum zu erschaffen und aufzustellen. Die damalige Tutorin des Fach-

derelict buildings and empty shop units. In the late 1980s and early 1990s, the department's students included Christine Borland, Claire Barclay, Douglas Gordon, Nathan Coley and Martin Boyce, all of whom were encouraged to undertake comprehensive research, to produce art outside studios and galleries ('with or through people') and were required to produce and site a piece of public art every year from second year onwards. Environmental Art tutor Sam Ainsley recalls: "Quite often in the department people had to persuade people who either didn't know anything about art or even actively hated it, to allow them to site a work. Those powers of persuasion, negotiation and sheer stubbornness in terms of making projects happen did differentiate the students in the department from students in other departments where their only context was the gallery."[6]

Meanwhile, the regeneration of the city centre under the guidance of Glasgow City Council and the Scottish Development Agency continued apace. Kirsty Milne wrote, in an article entitled 'Inside the Glasgow Glass Envelope' (1986): "To this end there's been a lot of em-

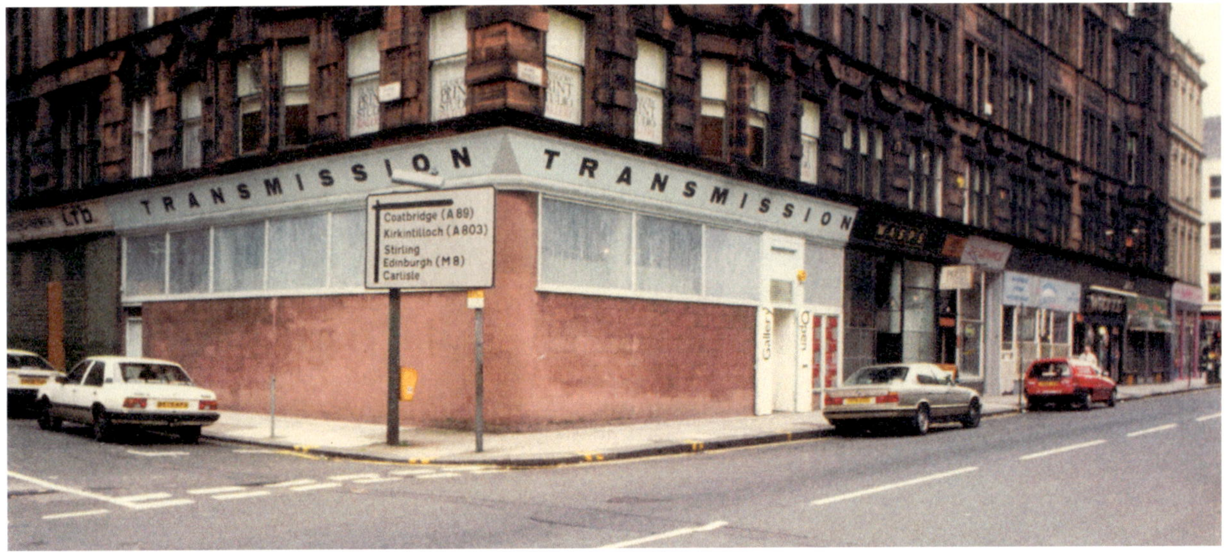

2 Transmission, neues Gebäude in der King Street Nr. 28, Sommer 1989 / Transmission, new space at 28 King Street, summer 1989

bereiches, Sam Ainsley, erinnert sich: „Ziemlich oft mussten Studierende aus dem Fachbereich andere Leute, die entweder keine Ahnung von Kunst hatten oder sie sogar lebhaft verabscheuten, dazu überreden, ihnen die Errichtung eines Werks zu genehmigen. Solche Überredungskünste, ein Verhandlungsgeschick und die absolute Hartnäckigkeit bei der Verwirklichung von Projekten unterschied die Studierenden dieses Fachbereichs von jenen anderer Fachbereiche, die als ihren Kontext nur die Galerie kannten."[6]

Inzwischen schritt die Umstrukturierung der Innenstadt unter Führung des Glasgower Stadtrats und der Scottish

phasis on improving the quality of the city centre, which is visibly in the process of turning itself inside out. The whole area known as Merchant City, with its extravagant Victorian facades, is being redeveloped to provide shops, offices and up to 2,000 homes as bait for Glasgow yuppies. South of Argyle St a huge site awaits a glass envelope which will protect a shopping centre, an ice rink and a multi-storey car park from the incessant Scottish rain in the £62m St Enoch's development. Even the old fish market, the Briggait, has been turned into a glossy umbrella for stalls and specialist shops …"[7]

Development Agency rasch voran. In einem Artikel mit dem Titel „Inside the Glasgow Glass Envelope" (1986) schrieb Kirsty Milne: „Zu diesem Zweck wurde viel Wert darauf gelegt, die Qualität des Stadtzentrums zu verbessern, das derzeit zusehends umgekrempelt wird. Der gesamte Bereich, der als Merchant City bekannt ist, mit seinen verschwenderischen viktorianischen Fassaden wird saniert, um dort Geschäfte, Büros und bis zu 2.000 Wohnungen als Köder für Glasgower Yuppies unterzubringen. Südlich der Argyle Street wartet die riesige Baustelle des 62 Millionen Pfund teuren St-Enoch-Komplexes auf eine gläserne Hülle, die ein Einkaufszentrum, eine Eislaufbahn und ein mehrgeschossiges Parkhaus vor dem permanenten schottischen Regen schützen soll. Selbst The Briggait, der alte Fischmarkt, wurde unter einem glitzernden Schirm zu einer Halle mit Verkaufsständen und Fachgeschäften umgewandelt ..."[7]

Auch das Künstlergremium von Transmission rüstete auf. 1988 zog die Galerie aus dem winzigen, rattenverseuchten Quartier in der Chisholm Street in die größeren Räume eines leer stehenden Geschäftes in der King Street. Der Glasgower Stadtrat, der in dem Projekt einen Schritt in Richtung Neugestaltung der Merchant City [Abb. 2] gesehen haben mag, unterstützte den Umzug finanziell. Douglas Gordon erinnert sich noch, wie er gemeinsam mit anderen ortsansässigen Künstlern, darunter Martin Boyce, die neuen Räume hergerichtet hat: „Ich war damit beschäftigt, Wände aufzustellen und Fußböden zu schleifen und all so'n Zeug, und ich habe das Transmission-Schild gemalt. Dies alles war für mich eine wirklich große, wichtige Sache, also war ich sowohl körperlich als auch geistig engagiert."[8] Die neue Transmission-Galerie war eine Art White Cube mit weißen Wänden und grauen Dielen; doch das war nicht alles, erinnert sich die Kuratorin und Autorin Nicola White: „Bislang hatte sich die Galerie bewusst außerhalb des kulturellen Mainstreams positioniert. In den frühen 1990er Jahren wurde Transmission zwar nicht Mainstream, aber rückte auf alle Fälle näher an die internationale Kunstszene heran. Wer die geradlinigen Räume betrat, hätte meinen können, sich in jeder beliebigen Stadt Europas zu befinden. Es kam zu Kooperationen und zum Austausch mit gleichgesinnten Künstlern und Galerien in Städten wie Belfast, London, Chicago und Köln. Die Galerie gewann außerhalb Schottlands zunehmend an Anerkennung und wurde in der Kunstpresse immer häufiger besprochen."[9]

Für die wachsende Internationalisierung der Glasgower Kunstszene kann auch die 1987 erfolgte Einführung eines Master of Fine Art (MFA) an der Glasgow School of Art ver-

The Transmission committee was also upgrading. In 1988, they moved from their tiny, rat-infested premises on Chisholm Street to larger premises in a vacant shop on King Street, a move that was lent financial support by Glasgow City Council, who may have viewed the project as a step towards the redevelopment of the Merchant City area [fig. 2]. Douglas Gordon remembers working with other local artists, including Martin Boyce, to get the new space ready. He recalls: "I got involved with banging up walls and sanding floors and all that stuff, and I painted the Transmission sign, so for me that was a really big important thing, so I had a kind of physical investment as well as a spiritual one."[8] The new Transmission was a 'white cube' gallery space with white walls and grey floorboards and, as curator and writer Nicola White remembers: "Previously the gallery had deliberately positioned itself outside the cultural mainstream. In the early 1990s Transmission became, not mainstream, but certainly more allied to the international art scene. Entering the clean-lined space, one could have been in any city in Europe. Alliances and exchanges were made with like-minded artists and galleries in such places as Belfast, London, Chicago and Cologne. The gallery became increasingly recognised outside of Scotland, and increasingly reviewed in the art press."[9]

The growing internationalism of the Glasgow art scene can also be attributed to the inception of the Master of Fine Art course at Glasgow School of Art in 1987, which was directed by former Environmental Art tutor Sam Ainsley from the late 1980s until 2006. The MFA attracted graduates who had studied at art schools elsewhere, including future Turner Prize winners Simon Starling and Richard Wright. Starling, Wright and their peers brought an important range of different approaches and experiences to the school, which widened the style of work being made within the city throughout the late 1980s and 1990s. Wright remembers: "Douglas Gordon and Christine Borland's generation were all growing up around the time of the Miner's Strike, this point of great political change in Britain. There was still a strong awareness of the Labour movement in their work. The younger generation is not unaware of that, but they are less concerned with it; it's less a part of their identity and sense of being connected. The first new wave of artists in the early 1990s was very Glasgow-based and they looked to people with similar political consciousness, but as Glasgow emerged more as a scene people have come here for different reasons and with different backgrounds. It's not just that they are younger, but their influences are differ-

antwortlich gemacht werden. Die Leitung dieses Studiengangs hatte von den späten 1980er Jahren bis 2006 die frühere Tutorin für Environmental Art, Sam Ainsley, inne. Der MFA zog Absolventen an, die an anderen Hochschulen Kunst studiert hatten, wie die Turner-Preisträger Simon Starling und Richard Wright. Starling, Wright und ihre Kollegen brachten eine bedeutende Bandbreite von unterschiedlichen Denkansätzen und Erfahrungen an die Schule, was dazu führte, dass der Stil der Arbeiten, die in den späten 1980er Jahren sowie in den 1990er Jahren in der Stadt entstanden, vielfältiger wurde. Wright sagt rückblickend: „Die Generation von Douglas Gordon und Christine Borland wuchs zur Zeit des großen Bergarbeiterstreiks auf, jenes bedeutenden Wendepunkts in der britischen Politik. In deren Werk spiegelte sich noch das Bewusstsein über diese Arbeiterbewegung. Die jüngere Generation ist sich dessen zwar nicht unbewusst, sie beschäftigt sich nur weniger damit; für ihre Identität und das Gefühl der Verbundenheit ist diese Zeit nicht so wichtig. Die erste Welle junger Künstler Anfang der 1990er Jahre war sehr vom Glasgow-Bezug getragen und orientierte sich an Leuten mit ähnlichem politischem Bewusstsein, doch seitdem Glasgow als Szene mehr hervorgetreten ist, kommen Menschen aus verschiedenen Gründen und unterschiedlicher Herkunft hierher. Sie sind nicht nur jünger, sondern sind auch anders beeinflusst, was zu einer neueren, einer anderen Art von Kunst beigetragen hat. Die Werke haben sowohl spielerische, Pop-Komponenten als ent and that has seeped into a newer, different kind of work. There is a playful, pop element, but also a tactile element to the work, that has to do with a re-instatement of a concern with material and its poetry, still done in a stripped-down way. The influence of Environmental Art has stayed strong, but the work is now much more gentle and open."[10]

The international alliances of the Glasgow art scene proliferated further during 1990, when Glasgow took the mantle of European City of Culture. As part of the cultural programme for that year, a former tram depot on the city's south side was relaunched as the largest visual arts exhibition space in Europe, with Nicola White as curator. She recalls: "It felt very international and fresh and I remember Douglas [Gordon] saying: 'It doesn't feel like Glasgow anymore'. That was to do with being able to do things on a large scale, or in a speculative kind of way, bringing artists over from abroad."[11] That year, the generation of Glasgow-based neo-conceptual artists that included Douglas Gordon, Christine Borland, Claire Barclay, Nathan Coley and Martin Boyce remained involved in or around Transmission, whilst also busy plotting shows such as *Windfall '91* [fig. 3], held in a disused Seamen's Mission on the Clyde, and later acclaimed in the first edition of *frieze* magazine. Claire Barclay [fig. 4] reflected recently: "My experience of art school was that it instilled in artists a desire for collaboration, generosity, improvisation and inclusion which helped establish a supportive art

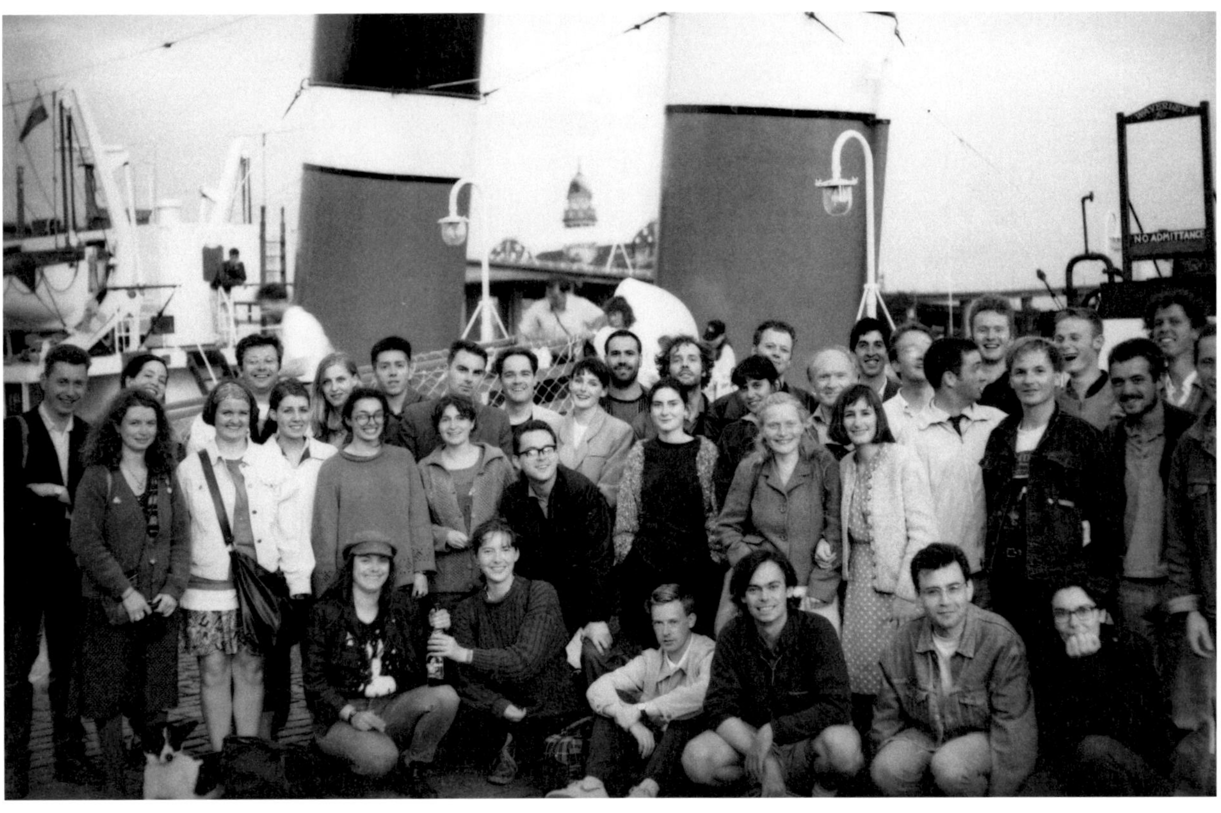

3 Teilnehmende Künstler von *Windfall* und Freunde, Sommer 1991 / Artists participating in *Windfall* and friends, summer 1991. In der Gruppe / Group includes Katrina Brown, Claire Barclay, Douglas Gordon und / and Nathan Coley.

auch haptische Vorlieben; dies hat mit einem Wiederaufleben eines Interesses am Material – und dessen Poesie – zu tun, das weiterhin geradeheraus eingesetzt wird. Der Einfluss des Fachbereichs Environmental Art ist nach wie vor stark, doch die Werke sind heute viel sanfter und offener.“[10]

Als Glasgow 1990 Europäische Kulturhauptstadt wurde, weiteten sich die internationalen Kontakte der Glasgower Kunstszene weiter aus. Teil des damaligen Kulturprogramms war die neue Nutzung eines ehemaligen Straßenbahndepots im Süden der Stadt als größte Ausstellungsfläche für bildende Kunst in Europa, mit Nicola White als Kuratorin. Sie berichtet: „Alles wirkte international und erfrischend, und ich weiß noch, wie Douglas Gordon meinte: ‚Es kommt mir überhaupt nicht mehr wie Glasgow vor.‘ Wir konnten Dinge in großem Maßstab konzipieren oder neue Ideen verwirklichen und auch Künstler aus dem Ausland einladen.“[11] Die Generation der in Glasgow lebenden neokonzeptuellen Künstler, darunter Douglas Gordon, Christine Borland, Claire Barclay, Nathan Coley und Martin Boyce, war in diesem Jahr weiterhin bei Transmission oder im Umfeld dieser Galerie aktiv und gleichzeitig damit beschäftigt, Ausstellungen wie *Windfall ’91* [Abb. 3] zu planen, die in einer stillgelegten Seemannsmission am Fluss Clyde stattfand und später in der ersten Ausgabe der Kunstzeitschrift *frieze* gefeiert wurde. Claire Barclay [Abb. 4] schrieb kürzlich: „Meine Erfahrung mit der Kunsthochschule war, dass sie uns Künstlern den Wunsch nach Zusammenarbeit, Großzügigkeit, Improvisation und Einbeziehung vermittelte, was dann dazu führte, dass sich in der Stadt eine Kunstszene bildete, die zusammenhielt. Künstlerinitiativen und Arbeiten, die außerhalb der Institutionen und auf freiwilliger Basis entstanden waren, sind sicher immer noch der Kern für die Dynamik und die Stärke der Glasgower Szene. Genauso wichtig ist das Einbringen von künstlerischen Aktivitäten in die Gesellschaft, was dem Einsatz einzelner Personen zu verdanken ist, sich mit neuen und unkonventionellen Ansätzen für eine Kunst im öffentlichen Raum und für ortsbezogene Arbeiten einzusetzen und den Kontext in den Mittelpunkt der künstlerischen Arbeit zu stellen.“[12]

2001 war Glasgow nach London zur zweitgrößten Einkaufsmeile Großbritanniens aufgestiegen. Die Wirtschaft der Stadt pulsierte wie seit zwanzig Jahren nicht mehr, gestützt durch einen starken Einzelhandel, den Finanzsektor und neu gegründete Unternehmen. Obwohl die Arbeitslosenquote mit 4,5 Prozent über dem Landesdurchschnitt lag, hatte Glasgow in den vergangenen drei Jahren ein Wirtschaftswachstum von 3,6 Prozent erzielt und damit den

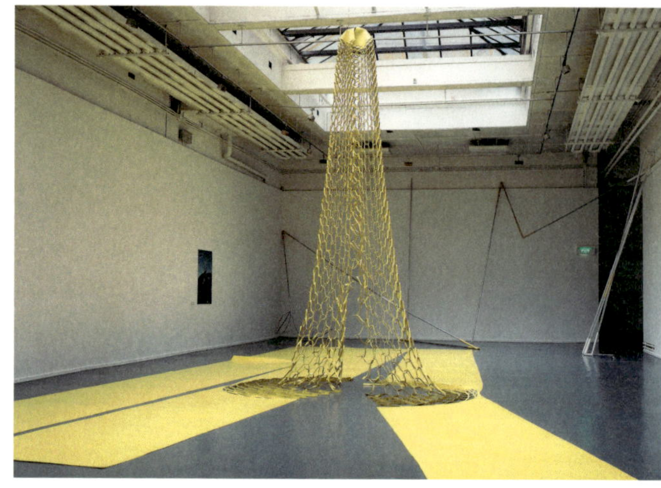

4 Claire Barclay, *Out of the Woods*, Centre for Contemporary Arts (CCA), Glasgow 1997

community in the city. Artists' initiatives and work made outwith the institutions and often through voluntary effort, are surely still the core strength and vibrancy of Glasgow's artistic scene. As is a strong network of artistic involvement within communities thanks to individuals working to find innovative, unconventional approaches to public art and site-specific projects, and helping to put context at the centre of art practice."[12]

By 2001 Glasgow had become the UK's biggest shopping centre after London. The city's economy was stronger than it had been for 20 years, buoyed by strong high street spending, the financial sector and new economic companies. Although unemployment at 4.5% was higher than the national average, the city had achieved economic growth of 3.6% over the past three years, ahead of the Scottish average of 2%. During the 1990s, £25m had been spent on streetscaping in central Glasgow, contributing to an affluent atmosphere in the city centre, especially in the Buchanan Street precinct, which was punctuated with saplings, polished stone benches and blue floodlights around the new Buchanan Galleries shopping development. John Calcutt, who took over the role of director of Glasgow School of Art's MFA course in 2006, commented: "I think Glasgow has become much more 'spectacularised' recently with the facelift of Buchanan Street – there are different kinds of shops, different kinds of bars, different kinds of restaurants. It's become much more self-consciously stylish... particularly in terms of bars. Sometimes you say the name of a bar to a taxi driver and he doesn't know it so you say, well it used to be such and such, and if he still doesn't know it you say, well before that it was called this... This constant building, that is inseparable for me from the rise of Douglas Gordon and Christine Borland. The city has become inseparably connected with those things too."[13]

schottischen Durchschnitt von 2 Prozent deutlich übertroffen. In den 1990er Jahren waren 25 Millionen Pfund in das Straßenbild des Stadtzentrums geflossen und hatten dazu beigetragen, in der Innenstadt eine Atmosphäre des Wohlstands zu erzeugen – insbesondere in der autofreien Buchanan Street, die mit jungen Bäumen, geschliffenen Steinbänken und Flutlichtbeleuchtung rund um die neue Einkaufspassage Buchanan Galleries aufgewertet wurde. John Calcutt, seit 2006 Leiter des MFA-Programms an der Glasgow School of Art, merkte dazu an: „Ich finde, Glasgow ist mit der Neugestaltung der Buchanan Street sehr spektakulär gestaltet worden – es gibt eine andere Art von Geschäften, von Bars, von Restaurants. Die Stadt hat sich selbst als „stylish" inszeniert ... besonders, was die Bars angeht. Manchmal nennst du einem Taxifahrer den Namen einer Bar, und der kennt sie nicht, also sagst du, sie hieß soundso, und wenn er sie dann immer noch nicht kennt, sagst du, *davor* hieß sie so ... Dieses ständige Bauen und Erneuern, das ist für mich mit dem Aufstieg Douglas Gordons und Christine Borlands nicht zu trennen. Und die Stadt ist *damit* wiederum untrennbar verbunden."[13]

Die vielen Veränderungen der letzten Jahre rühren zum Teil daher, dass viel Geld in den Imagewandel Glasgows hin zu einem Einkaufs- und Tourismuszentrum gesteckt wurde, doch der Löwenanteil des erzielten Fortschritts geht zurück auf die ineinandergreifenden Initiativen in Kunst, Musik und Politik durch Personen, die mit ihrer anderen „Währung", mit Zeit und Idealismus, in die Glasgower Szene investiert haben; sie teilen ihre Ressourcen, geben sich Ratschläge, erledigen Dinge für andere, helfen einander aus und sind bei Eröffnungen und Ausstellungen präsent.

Viele der bedeutendsten Künstler, die Glasgow im vergangenen Jahrzehnt hervorgebracht hat, arbeiten in weniger leicht konsumierbaren Kunstformen. Ihre Werke sind häufig ortsspezifisch, prozessbezogen und performativ [Abb. 5]. In den letzten zehn Jahren hat dieser Ansatz weltweit zunehmend Anerkennung gefunden. Seit 1996 waren nicht weniger als 14 mit Glasgow verbundene Künstler für den Turner-Preis nominiert: Douglas Gordon (1996), Christine Borland (1997), Martin Creed (2001), Jim Lambie und Simon Starling (beide 2005), Nathan Coley (2007), Cathy Wilkes (2008), Lucy Skaer und Richard Wright (beide 2009), Susan Philipsz (2010), Karla Black und Martin Boyce (2011), Luke Fowler (2012) und David Shrigley (2013). Sechs von ihnen haben den Preis auch gewonnen: Gordon, Creed, Starling, Wright, Philipsz und Boyce. Unterdessen hat sich das Glasgow International Festival of Visual Art von

The many changes in Glasgow in recent years had partly sprung from investment in rebranding the city as a retail and tourist centre, but many more of those advances had been generated through the intertwined art, music and politics of people who had invested in the Glasgow scene with an alternative currency of time and love: by sharing resources and advice, doing favours, helping out and turning up at shows and openings.

Many of the most significant artists to emerge from Glasgow in the last decade work with less readily consumable forms of art, producing work that is often site-specific, process-based and performative [fig. 5], and this approach has begun to win plaudits across the world. Since 1996, no fewer than 14 artists associated with Glasgow have been nominated for the Turner Prize, including Douglas Gordon (1996), Christine Borland (1997), Martin Creed (2001), Jim Lambie and Simon Starling (both 2005), Nathan Coley (2007), Cathy Wilkes (2008), Lucy Skaer and Richard Wright (both 2009), Susan Philipsz (2010), Karla Black and Martin Boyce (both 2011), Luke Fowler (2012) and David Shrigley (2013). Of these, six won: Gordon, Creed, Starling, Wright, Philipsz and Boyce. Meanwhile, Glasgow International Festival of Visual Art (GI) has grown from a small event sustained by the goodwill of the local art community when it launched in 2005, to an ambitious and highly anticipated biennial festival, described in 2009 by *The Guardian* as "the UK's best annual visual arts festival."[14] With Glasgow routinely cited as the biggest centre for art in the UK after London, it made perfect sense when in January 2013 it was announced that the 2015 Turner Prize would be hosted in Glasgow, at Tramway.

However, despite the significant recent changes in Glasgow's international profile, the city still lacks the established infrastructure and opportunities of a major centre like New York or London (although it is certainly easier to negotiate and cheaper to live in than either of those cities). The establishment of The Modern Institute by Will Bradley, Charles Esche and Toby Webster in 1998 has been followed more recently by the young galleries Mary Mary, Kendall Koppe, The Duchy, David Dale Gallery and artist-led projects such as Market, SWG3 and the Glue Factory, but Glasgow remains a city in which many artists make work that they do not expect to sell. However, the relative absence of a commercial scene has also allowed the development of an art scene built with an economy of means and materials, and this 'make do and mend' approach has stood the city's artists in good stead. Francis McKee, director of Glasgow's

einer bescheidenen Veranstaltung, die bei ihrer Einführung 2005 vom guten Willen der örtlichen Künstlergemeinde getragen wurde, zu einer ehrgeizigen und immer wieder sehnlichst erwarteten Biennale entwickelt, die der *Guardian* 2010 als „Großbritanniens bestes jährliches Festival für bildende Kunst" bezeichnete.[14] Nachdem Glasgow regelmäßig als größtes britisches Kunstzentrum nach London erwähnt wurde, erscheint die Ankündigung vom Januar 2013, dass der Turner-Preis 2015 im Glasgower Kulturzentrum Tramway verliehen werden soll, nur folgerichtig.

Doch trotz der bedeutenden jüngeren Veränderungen in Glasgows internationalem Profil fehlt der Stadt bis heute eine gängige Infrastruktur mit den Möglichkeiten, wie sie große Städte wie New York oder London haben (auch wenn es hier sicherlich einfacher ist zu agieren und es sich günstiger leben lässt als in jeder dieser Metropolen). Der 1998 von Will Bradley, Charles Esche und Toby Webster gegründeten Galerie The Modern Institute folgten in jüngerer Zeit neben den Galerien Mary Mary, Kendall Koppe, The Duchy und der David Dale Gallery auch künstlergeführte Projekte wie Market, SWG3 und die Glue Factory. Dennoch bleibt Glasgow eine Stadt, in der viele Künstler Werke schaffen, von denen sie nicht erwarten, dass diese auch verkauft werden können. Dabei hat gerade die Abwesenheit einer Galerienszene diese Entwicklung einer mit sparsamen Mitteln und Materialien operierenden Kunstszene erst ermöglicht, und dieser Ansatz des Improvisierens und Zurechtkommens ist den Künstlern der Stadt zugutegekommen. Francis McKee, Direktor des Centre for Contemporary Arts in Glasgow (und Direktor der ersten drei Biennalen des Glasgow International Festival of Visual Art in den Jahren 2005, 2006 und 2008) bemerkte in einer Fußnote zu seinem aufschlussreichen Essay „The Eight Moves of the Submerged Dragon" von 1997: „Letztlich ist Glasgows Wiedererwachen eine Sache des Glaubens. Unser Glaube an die Umsetzung von Ideen ist dem Vertrauen sehr ähnlich, das wir in das Ansehen von Banken haben."[15] Dennoch hat das Weiterbestehen der Glasgower Kunstszene nach dem Zusammenbruch des Kunstmarkts 2008 bewiesen, dass die Mischung aus gesellschaftlicher Beteiligung und dem Interesse an prozessbezogenen Arbeitsweisen, die für die Kunstszene der Stadt charakteristisch ist, bis zu einem gewissen Grad den Launen des Marktes überlegen ist.

Die Kuratorin Katrina Brown gehörte Anfang der 1990er Jahre dem Transmission-Gremium an, leitete 2010 und 2012 das Glasgow International Festival of Visual Art und ist heute Direktorin des Kunstvereins The Common Guild

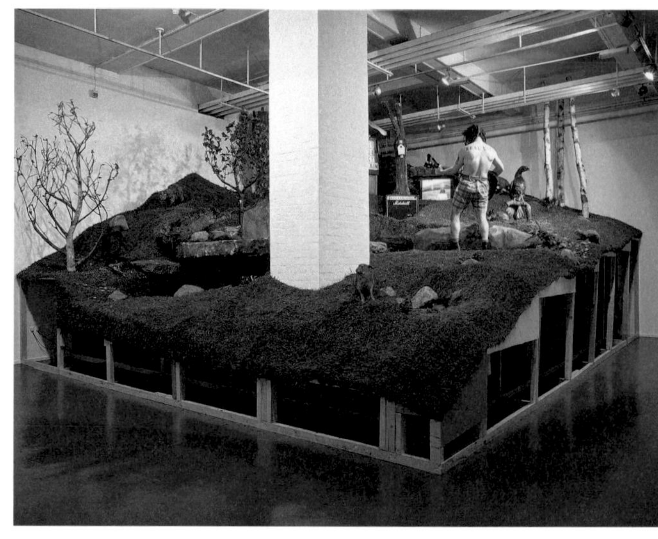

5 Ross Sinclair, *Real Life Rocky Mountain*, Centre for Contemporary Arts (CCA), Glasgow 1996

Centre for Contemporary Arts (and director of the first three editions of Glasgow International in 2005, 2006 and 2008) observed in a footnote to his insightful 1997 essay "The Eight Moves of the Submerged Dragon": "Ultimately, Glasgow's renaissance is the product of faith. Likewise our belief in the translation of ideas is very like the trust we place in the credit of banks."[15] However, the survival of the Glasgow art scene following the collapse of the art market in 2008 proved that the combination of social cooperation and interest in the process-based practices that characterise the city's art scene is one that, to a certain extent, transcends the vagaries of the marketplace.

Curator Katrina Brown, who served on the Transmission committee in the early 1990s, is now director of the Glasgow-based arts organisation The Common Guild and also directed the 2010 and 2012 editions of Glasgow International. Brown's second outing as GI director in 2012 showcased 130 artists across almost 50 venues, attracted 205,067 visitors and generated £1.7m for Glasgow's economy, as well as a further £436,878 for the rest of the country. The arts sector in the city now employs more people than shipbuilding did. She says: "There's far *more* activity in Glasgow now: more people coming to study, live, work here from elsewhere than back then. If you look at the committees at Transmission from the early 1990s we were almost all born or at least educated in Glasgow. And of course the single biggest difference is that there are now commercial galleries in the city taking artists from Glasgow to fairs – and therefore collectors and collections – all over the world. It's entirely possible now to be based here, have a successful, international career and a market for your work. What's exciting about now is that the next step seems possible – with so

mit Sitz in Glasgow. In ihrer zweiten Amtszeit als Festivaldirektorin im Jahr 2012 präsentierte sie 130 Künstler an fast 50 Schauplätzen, die 205.067 Besucher anzogen und 1,7 Millionen Pfund für die Glasgower Wirtschaft sowie weitere 436.878 Pfund für den Rest des Landes generierten. Der Kunstsektor der Stadt beschäftigt heute mehr Menschen als früher der Schiffbau. Brown sagt: „In Glasgow ist heute *viel mehr* los: Mehr Menschen als damals kommen von außerhalb, um hier zu studieren, zu leben und zu arbeiten. Wenn man sich die Gremien bei Transmission aus den frühen 1990er Jahren ansieht, waren wir fast alle in Glasgow geboren oder zumindest ausgebildet worden. Und natürlich ist der mit Abstand größte Unterschied der, dass es heute kommerzielle Galerien in der Stadt gibt, die Künstler aus Glasgow auf Messen – und damit bei Sammlern und Sammlungen – rund um den Erdball vertreten. Es ist heute durchaus möglich, hier zu leben, international erfolgreich Karriere zu machen und einen Markt für seine Werke zu haben. Das Aufregende am Hier und Jetzt ist, dass der nächste Schritt möglich scheint – bei so vielen Menschen mit so erstaunlicher gesammelter Erfahrung in der Stadt."[16]

Der von Brown beschriebene Wandel spiegelt sich auch bei den sechs Glasgower Künstlern wider, deren Werk das Neue Museum in Nürnberg in der Ausstellung *Funktion/Dysfunktion* präsentiert. Drei von ihnen wurden in Glasgow und Umgebung geboren: Martin Boyce (geb. 1967 in Hamilton, 19 km südöstlich von Glasgow), Claire Barclay (geb. 1968 in Paisley, 11 km westlich von Glasgow) und Mary Redmond (geb. 1973 in Glasgow). Die anderen drei gehören einer etwas jüngeren Generation an, die in den 1990er und 2000er Jahren zum Studieren nach Glasgow kam: Nick Evans (geb. 1976 in Mufulira, Sambia), Ciara Phillips (geb. 1976 in Ottawa, Kanada) und Nicolas Party (geb. 1980 in Lausanne). Alle sechs in der Ausstellung vertretenen Künstler haben entweder am Fachbereich Sculpture and Environmental Art der Glasgow School of Art studiert oder das MFA-Programm der Schule absolviert. Während die Kunsthochschule bis in die 1980er Jahre hinein überwiegend Studierende aus der Region anzog, ist die geografische Herkunft der Studierenden heute wesentlich breiter gefächert: 20 Prozent aller Studierenden kommen aus dem Ausland und weitere 20 Prozent aus anderen Teilen Großbritanniens.

Interessanterweise hat sich in den letzten zehn Jahren auch das offizielle Branding der Stadt Glasgow verändert, weg von den mit „Einkaufen" assoziierten Werten hin zum „Schaufensterbummel"-Erleben einer Kunstszene. 2004 wurde eine neue Imagekampagne unter dem Motto „Glas-

many people with such amazing collected experience in the city."[16]

The shift described by Brown is reflected in the six Glasgow-based artists whose work will be showcased in *Function / Dysfunction* at the Neues Museum in Nuremberg. Three were born in Glasgow or its vicinity: Martin Boyce (b. 1967, Hamilton, 12 miles from Glasgow), Claire Barclay (b. 1968, Paisley, 7 miles from Glasgow) and Mary Redmond (b. 1973, Glasgow). The remaining three artists are of a slightly younger generation, who moved to Glasgow to study in the 1990s and 2000s: Nick Evans (b. 1976, Mufulira, Zambia), Ciara Phillips (b. 1976, Ottawa, Canada) and Nicolas Party (b. 1980, Lausanne, Switzerland). All of the artists in the exhibition studied either in the Sculpture and Environmental Art Department at Glasgow School of Art, or on the school's MFA programme. The School of Art, which attracted a largely local student body up until the 1980s, now has a much more geographically diverse demographic: 20% of the total cohort are international students and a further 20% are from the rest of the UK.

Interestingly, Glasgow's official branding has also shifted in the last decade, moving away from the values associated with 'shopping' and closer to the 'window-shopping' values of the art community. In 2004, a rebranding of the city under the slogan "Glasgow: Scotland with Style" was launched. This campaign focused upon the city's shopping and fashion credentials through the promotion of the "Style Mile" of city centre retail outlets, and a further £80m was spent to support the expansion of the city centre shopping mall Buchanan Galleries. However, recent retail figures show that while Glasgow has retained its position as the biggest shopping destination in the UK outside of London, overall retail takings have decreased, from £2.4bn in 2011 to £1.94bn in 2012. In January 2013, with a view towards Glasgow's role as host of the 2014 Commonwealth Games, the latest iteration of Glasgow's official branding was revealed. The new slogan, "People Make Glasgow", marks a partial return to the popular "Glasgow's Miles Better"[18] slogan of the early 1980s, which successfully fostered an image of Glasgow as both friendly and welcoming.

Since 1954, when Alexander Trocchi wrote *Young Adam*, Glasgow has moved on in all kinds of ways. The

gow: Scotland with Style" (Schottland mit Stil) ins Leben gerufen, die sich auf die Shopping- und Modeattraktionen der Stadt konzentrierte und für die innenstädtischen Einzelhandelsgeschäfte auf der Glasgower „Style Mile" warb. Weitere 80 Millionen Pfund flossen in die Erweiterung der Buchanan Galleries im Zentrum. Jüngste Verkaufszahlen zeigen jedoch, dass Glasgow zwar seine Stellung als zweitgrößtes britisches Einkaufsziel nach London behaupten konnte, die Einzelhandelseinnahmen insgesamt aber gesunken sind: von 2,4 Milliarden Pfund im Jahr 2011 auf 1,94 Milliarden Pfund im Jahr 2012. Im Januar 2013 wurde im Hinblick auf Glasgows Rolle als Gastgeber der Commonwealth Games 2014 der nächste Schritt einer Glasgower Imagestrategie vorgestellt: Der neue Slogan „People Make Glasgow" (Menschen machen Glasgow aus) markiert teilweise eine Rückkehr zu dem populären Werbespruch „Glasgow's Miles Better" aus den frühen 1980er Jahren, mit dem das Image von Glasgow als freundliche und einladende Stadt erfolgreich gepflegt und gefördert wurde.

Seit 1954, als Alexander Trocchi seinen Roman *Wasserläufe* schrieb, hat sich Glasgow in alle möglichen Richtungen vorwärtsbewegt und dabei neu erfunden – als erfolgreiche und wirtschaftlich so lebensfähige Stadt wie in der Blütezeit des Schiffbaus. Die Straßenbahn, in der Trocchi einst fuhr, ist aus dem Stadtbild verschwunden, aber das Depot, in dem sie untergebracht war, ist als international angesehene „Insel aus Fenstern" neu geboren worden. Das Werk der in Glasgow tätigen Künstler wird heute sowohl gehandelt als auch im „Schaufenster" von Museen und Galerien auf der ganzen Welt betrachtet. Und dennoch ist die Glasgower Szene im Kern dieselbe geblieben. Sie definiert sich über den gesellschaftlichen Impuls, der in den Touristenslogans „Glasgow's Miles Better" und „People Make Glasgow" artikuliert wird. Trocchi beschrieb ihn auf poetischere Weise als Impuls, der vom einzelnen verlangt, hinter das eigene Spiegelbild zu blicken, und der „den Mut" erfordert, „mich bekannt zu machen."[17]

city has reinvented itself as successful and commercially viable, as in its shipbuilding heyday. The tram that Trocchi rode is no longer on the road, but the depot that once housed it is reborn as an internationally renowned "island of windows". The work of the artists based in Glasgow is now both traded and 'window-shopped' in museums and galleries all over the world. But still, the essence of the Glasgow scene remains the same. It is defined by the social impulse, articulated in the promotional slogans "Glasgow's Miles Better" and "People Make Glasgow". It is an impulse Trocchi described more poetically, as being one that requires the individual to look beyond their own reflection: one that demands "the courage […] to introduce myself."[17]

1   Alexander Trocchi, *Wasserläufe* (1954), Berlin 1997, S. 150–151 (teilweise neu übersetzt).

2   Kirsty Milne, „Inside the Glasgow Glass Envelope", *New Statesman*, 21.11.1986.

3   Cathy Wilkes, im Gespräch mit der Autorin, August 2001, zit. n. Sarah Lowndes, *Social Sculpture. The Rise of the Glasgow Art Scene*, Edinburgh 2010, S. 231.

4   Eine Parallele lässt sich zwischen dem Glasgower Fachbereich Environmental Art und dem Fachbereich Fine Art am Londoner Goldsmiths College ziehen, wo Jon Thompson und Michael Craig-Martin zwischen 1974 und 1988 einer Studentenkohorte, der auch die Young British Artists (YBAs) Damien Hirst, Sarah Lucas, Simon Patterson und Gary Hume angehörten, eine multimediale, ideenbasierte Kunst nahebrachten.

5   David Harding, *Decadent. Public Art: Contentious Term and Contested Practice*, Glasgow 1997, S. 17. Harding bezieht sich auf Michel de Certeau, *Kunst des Handelns*, Berlin 1988.

6   Sam Ainsley, im Gespräch mit der Autorin, Mai 2001, zit. n. Lowndes 2010, S. 88.

7   Milne 1986.

8   Douglas Gordon, im Gespräch mit Graham Fagen, zit. n. *Transcript*, Bd. 3, Nr. 3, Dundee 2001.

9   Nicola White, „Perpetual Motion" (1995), unveröffentlichter Essay über Transmission, zit. n. Lowndes 2010, S. 118–119.

10 Richard Wright, im Gespräch mit der Autorin, September 2001, zit. n. Lowndes 2010, S. 203.

11 Nicola White, im Gespräch mit der Autorin, November 2002, zit. n. Lowndes 2010, S. 128.

12 Claire Barclay, Katalogbeitrag für *Studio 58. Women Artists in Glasgow Since World War II*, hrsg. von Sarah Lowndes, Ausst.-Kat. Glasgow School of Art 2012, S. 36.

13 John Calcutt, im Gespräch mit der Autorin, April 2001, zit. n. Lowndes 2010, S. 329.

14 „What to See in 2010", *The Guardian*, 31. Dezember 2009, http://www.guardian.co.uk/culture/2009/dec/31/what-to-see-in-2010 (zuletzt abgerufen 25.7.2013).

15 Francis McKee, „The Eight Moves of the Submerged Dragon", in: *Made in Glasgow*, Brüssel 1997, unpaginiert.

16 Katrina Brown, in Erwiderung auf schriftlich gestellte Fragen der Autorin, April 2010, zit. n. Lowndes 2010, S. 414.

17 Trocchi 1997, S. 151 (teilweise neu übersetzt).

1   Alexander Trocchi, *Young Adam* [1954] (New York: Grove Press, 2003), p. 132.

2   Kirsty Milne, 'Inside the Glasgow Glass envelope', *New Statesman*, 21 November 1986.

3   Cathy Wilkes in conversation with the author, August 2001, quoted in Sarah Lowndes, *Social Sculpture: The Rise of the Glasgow Art Scene* (Edinburgh: Luath Press, 2010), p. 231.

4   A parallel can be drawn between the Environmental Art Department and the Fine Art Department at Goldsmiths' College, London, where from 1974 to 1988 Jon Thompson and Michael Craig-Martin promoted multimedia, ideas-based art to a student cohort that included the Young British Artists (YBAs) Damien Hirst, Sarah Lucas, Simon Patterson and Gary Hume.

5   David Harding, *Decadent: Public Art, Contentious Term and Contested Practice* (Glasgow: Foulis Press, 1997), p. 17, referencing Michel de Certeau, *The Practice of Everyday Life,* trans. Steven Rendall (Berkeley: University of California Press, 1984).

6   Sam Ainsley, in conversation with the author, May 2001, quoted in Lowndes, *Social Sculpture*, p. 88.

7   Milne, 'Inside the Glasgow Glass envelope'.

8   Douglas Gordon, in conversation with Graham Fagen, *Transcript*, Volume 03, Issue 03, Dundee, 2001.

9   Nicola White, "Perpetual Motion", 1995, unpublished essay on Transmission, quoted in Lowndes, *Social Sculpture*, pp. 118–119.

10 Richard Wright, in conversation with the author, September 2001, quoted ibid., p. 203.

11 Nicola White, in conversation with the author, November 2002, quoted ibid., p. 128.

12 Claire Barclay, catalogue text for Sarah Lowndes (ed.) *Studio 58: Women Artists in Glasgow Since World War II*, exh. cat. (Glasgow: Glasgow School of Art, 2012), p. 36.

13 John Calcutt, in conversation with the author, April 2001, quoted in Lowndes, *Social Sculpture*, p. 329.

14 'What to See in 2010', *The Guardian*, 31 December 2009.

15 Francis McKee, 'The Eight Moves of the Submerged Dragon', in *Made in Glasgow,* exh. cat. (Brussels: De Markten Arts Centre, 1997), unpaginated.

16 Katrina Brown, in response to questions sent by the author, April 2010, quoted in Lowndes, *Social Sculpture*, p. 414.

17 Trocchi, *Young Adam*, p. 132.

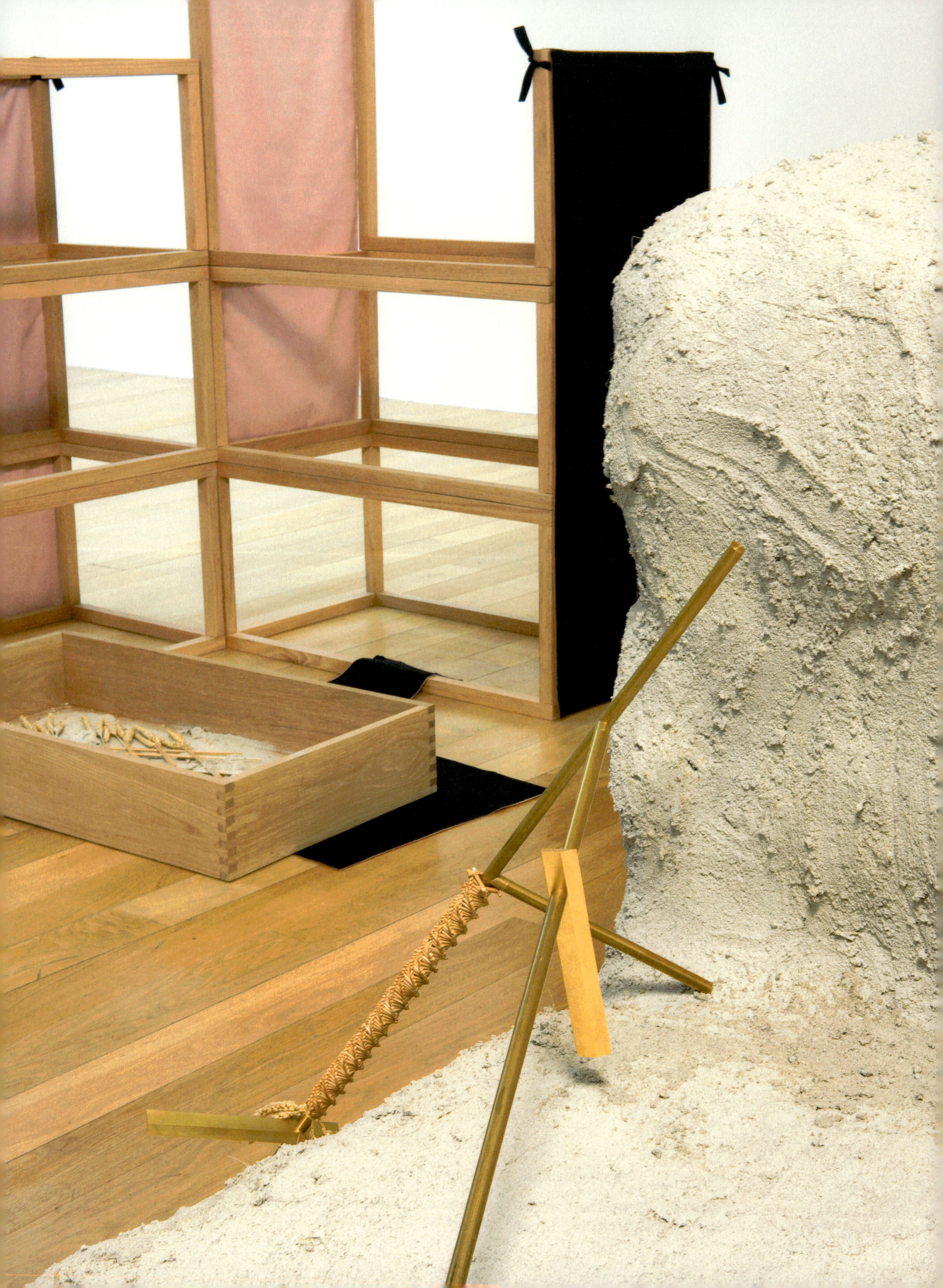

Caught In Corners, 2009, Installationsansicht /
Installation view, The Fruitmarket Gallery,
Edinburgh 2009

Biografie / Biography

Claire Barclay lebt und arbeitet / lives and works
in Glasgow, Schottland / Scotland
1968   geboren / born in Paisley, Schottland / Scotland

Studium / Education
1986–1990   Bachelor of Fine Art (Environmental Art),
    Glasgow School of Art, Glasgow
1991–1993   Master of Fine Art, Glasgow School of Art, Glasgow

Stipendien und Preise / Scholarships and Awards
1997   Artist in Residence, 200 Gertrude Street, Melbourne
2000   Three Year AHRB Fellowship, Glasgow School of Art
2007   Paul Hamlyn Foundation, Visual Artist Award
2008   The Hospital Club Creative Award for Art
2011   Residency, Statens Vaerksteder for Kunst,
    Kopenhagen / Copenhagen
2013   Residency, The Banff Centre, Banff

Ausgewählte Ausstellungen / Selected Exhibitions
„Nettverk Glasgow", Museet for Samtidskunst, Oslo (1998)
„Zenomap", 50. Biennale Venedig / Venice (2003)
„Art Now: Claire Barclay. Half-Light", Tate Britain, London (2004)
„Claire Barclay. Silver Gilt", Stephen Friedman Gallery,
London (2005)
„Claire Barclay. Shifting Ground", Camden Arts Centre,
London (2008)
„Claire Barclay. Openwide", The Fruitmarket Gallery,
Edinburgh (2009)
„Claire Barclay. Pale Heights", MUDAM, Luxemburg /
Luxembourg (2009)
„Claire Barclay. Shadow Spans", Whitechapel Gallery,
London (2010)
„Abstract Possible", Museo Tamayo, Mexiko-Stadt /
Mexico City (2011)

Ausgewählte Publikationen / Selected Publications
„Claire Barclay. Ideal Pursuits", Ausst.-Kat. / exh. cat. Dundee
Contemporary Arts, Dundee 2003
„Claire Barclay. Fault On The Right Side", Ausst.-Kat. / exh. cat.
Kunstverein Braunschweig 2007
„Claire Barclay. Openwide", Ausst.-Kat. / exh. cat. The Fruitmarket
Gallery, Edinburgh 2009

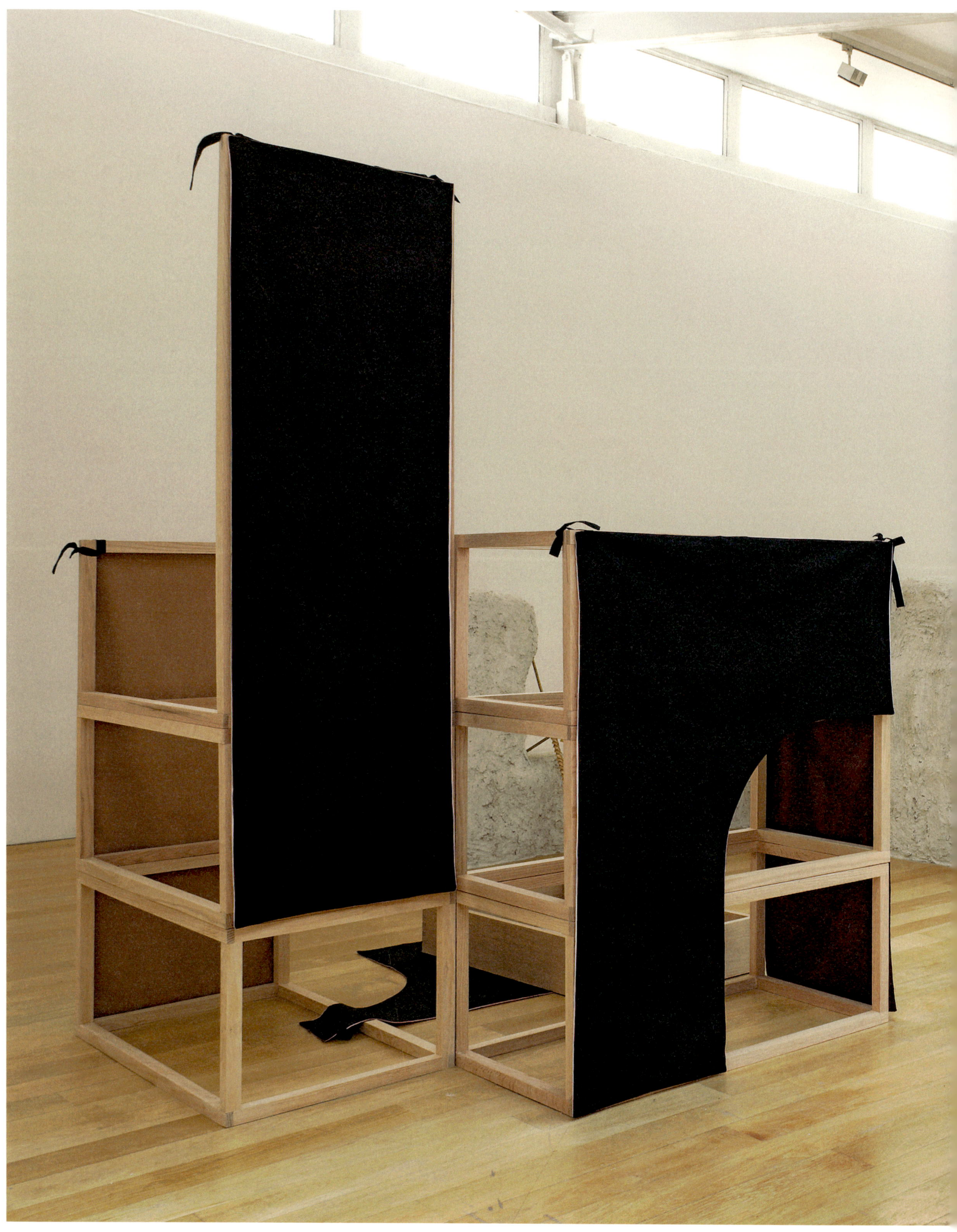

   Caught In Corners, 2009, Installationsansicht / Installation view, The Fruitmarket Gallery, Edinburgh 2009

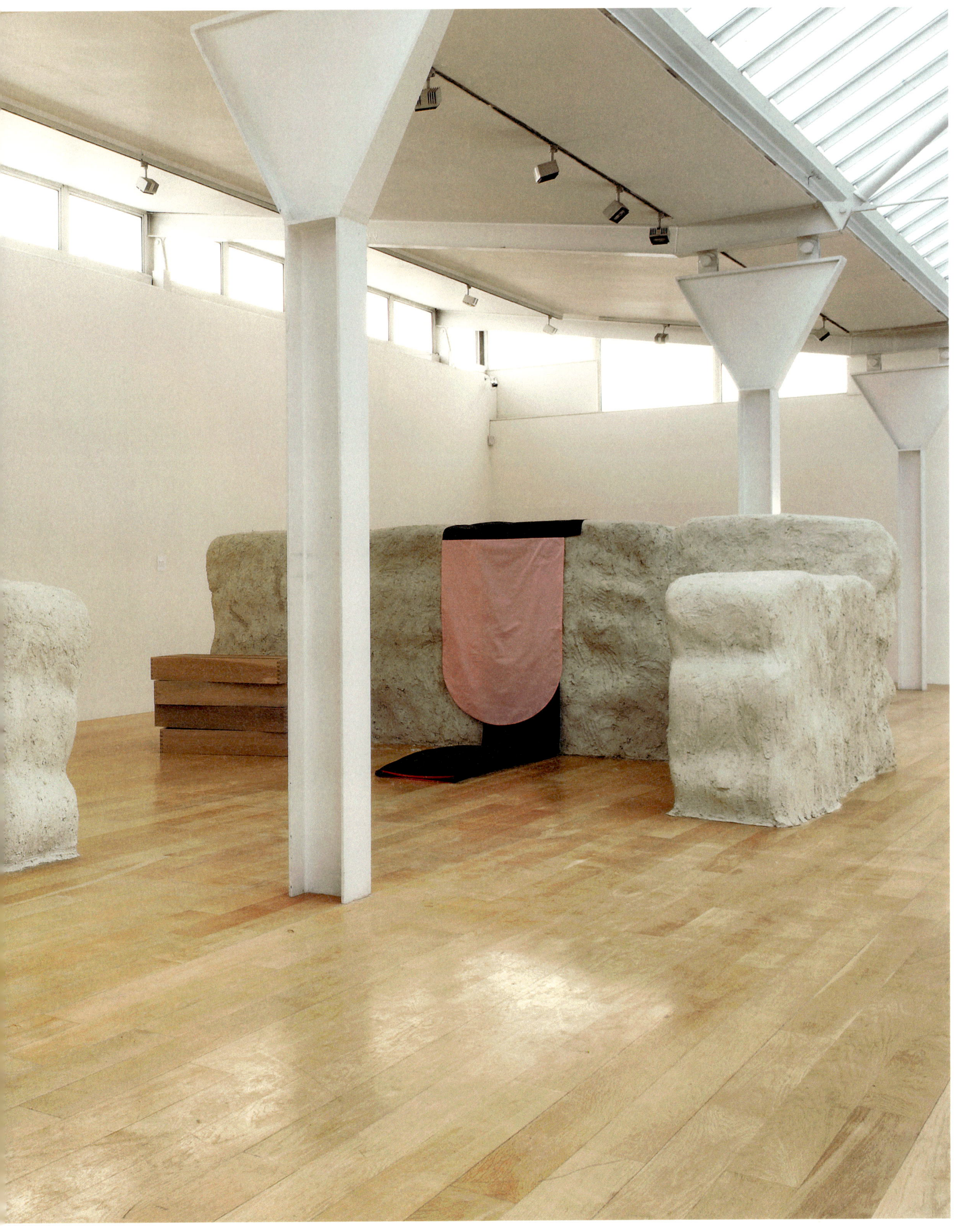

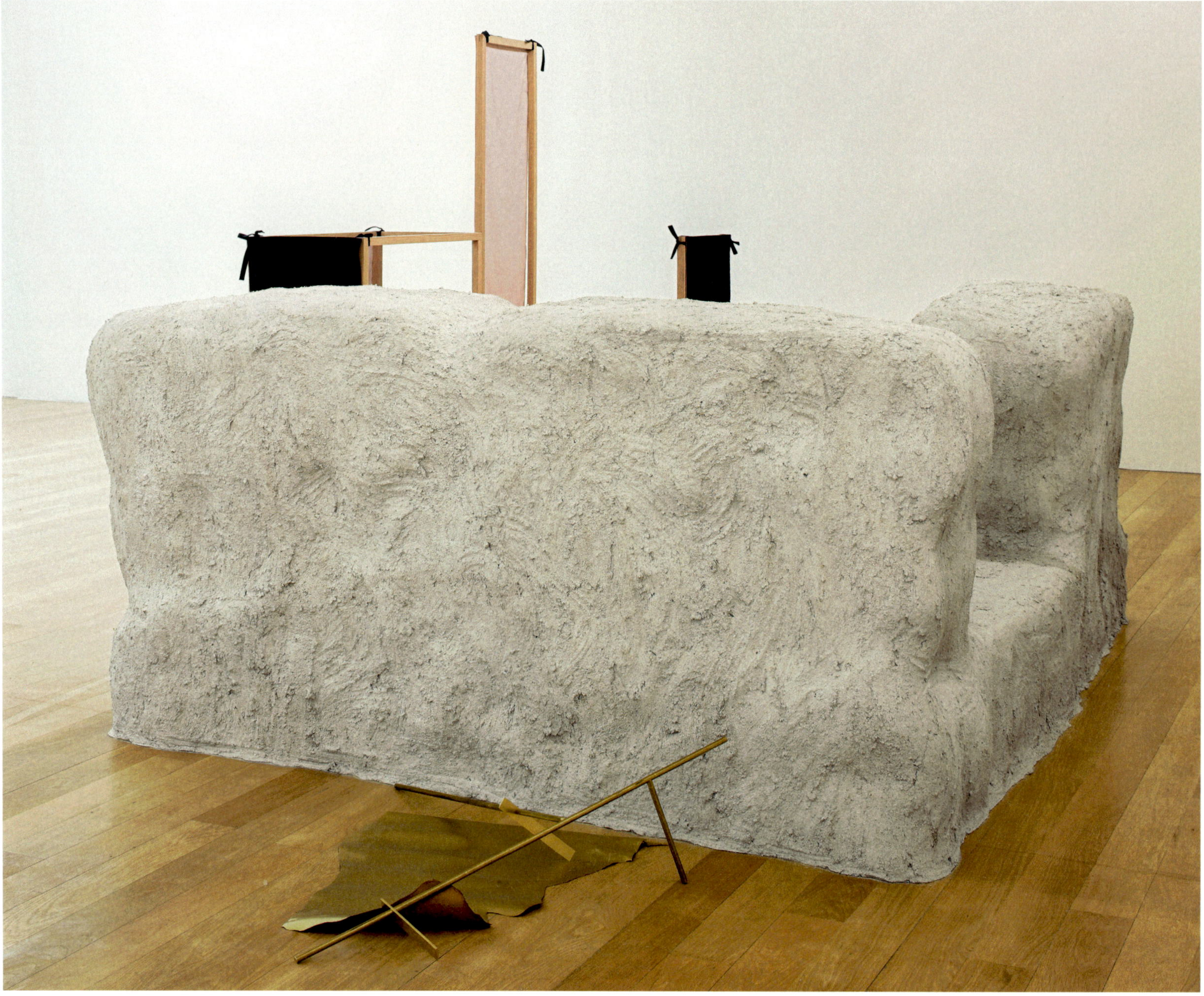

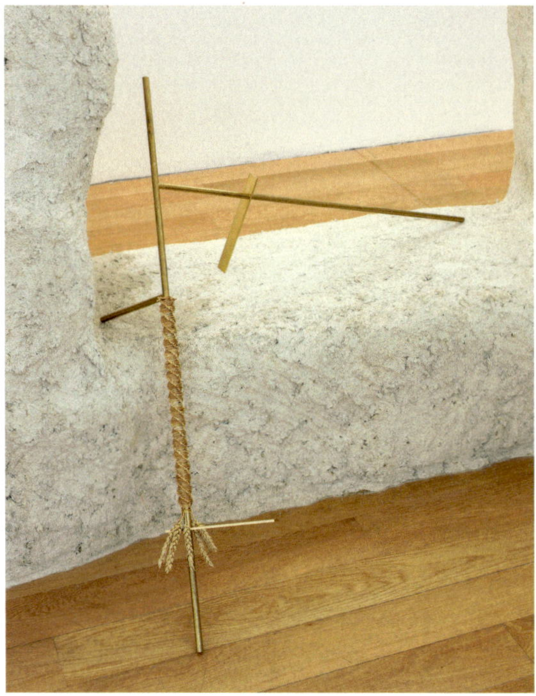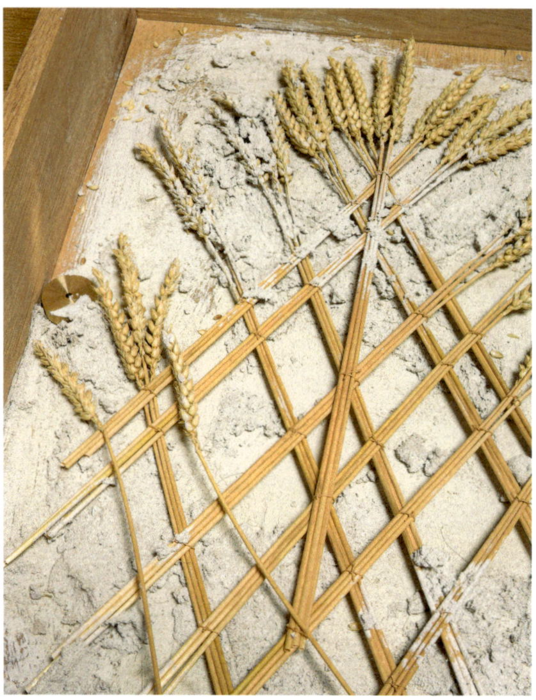

  Caught In Corners, 2009, Installationsansicht / Installation view, The Fruitmarket Gallery, Edinburgh 2009

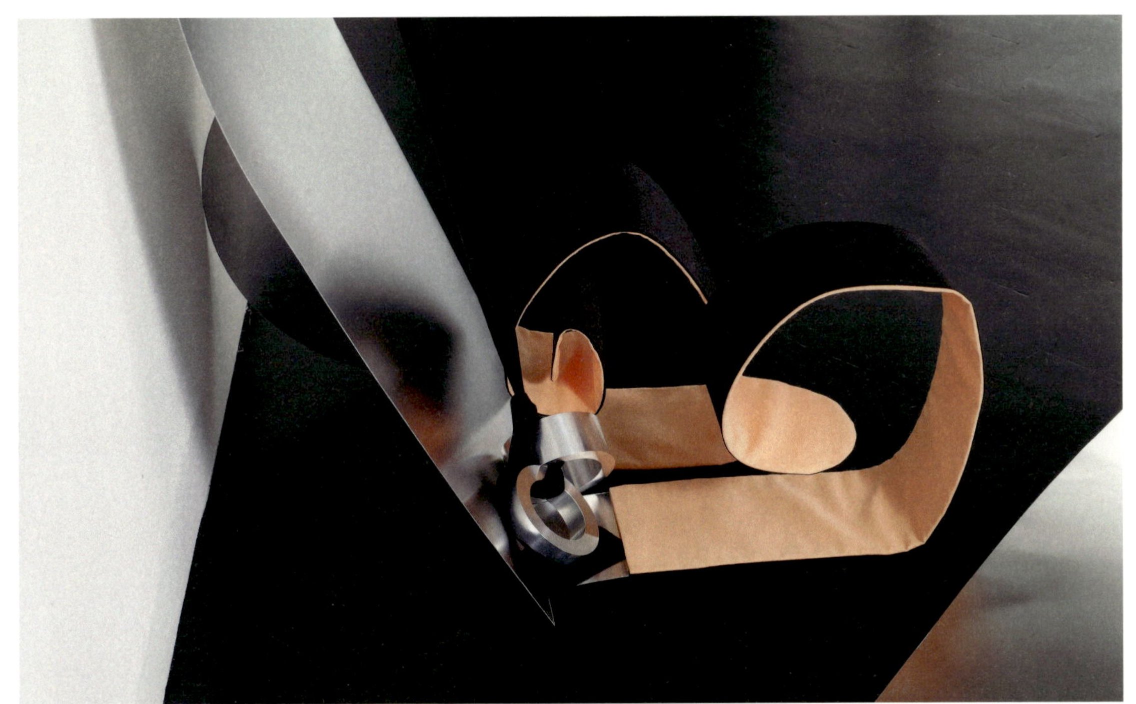

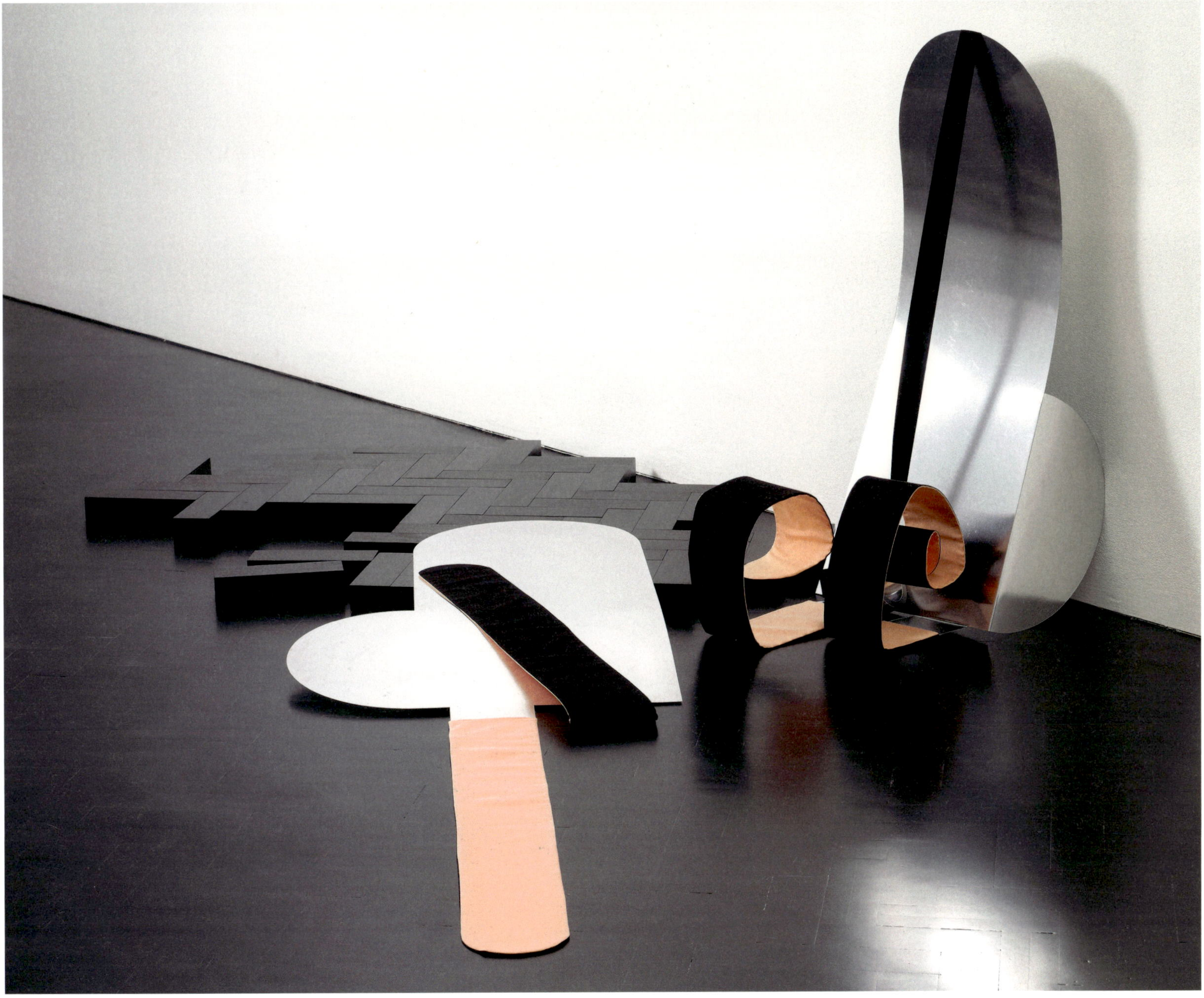

Claire Barclay 51

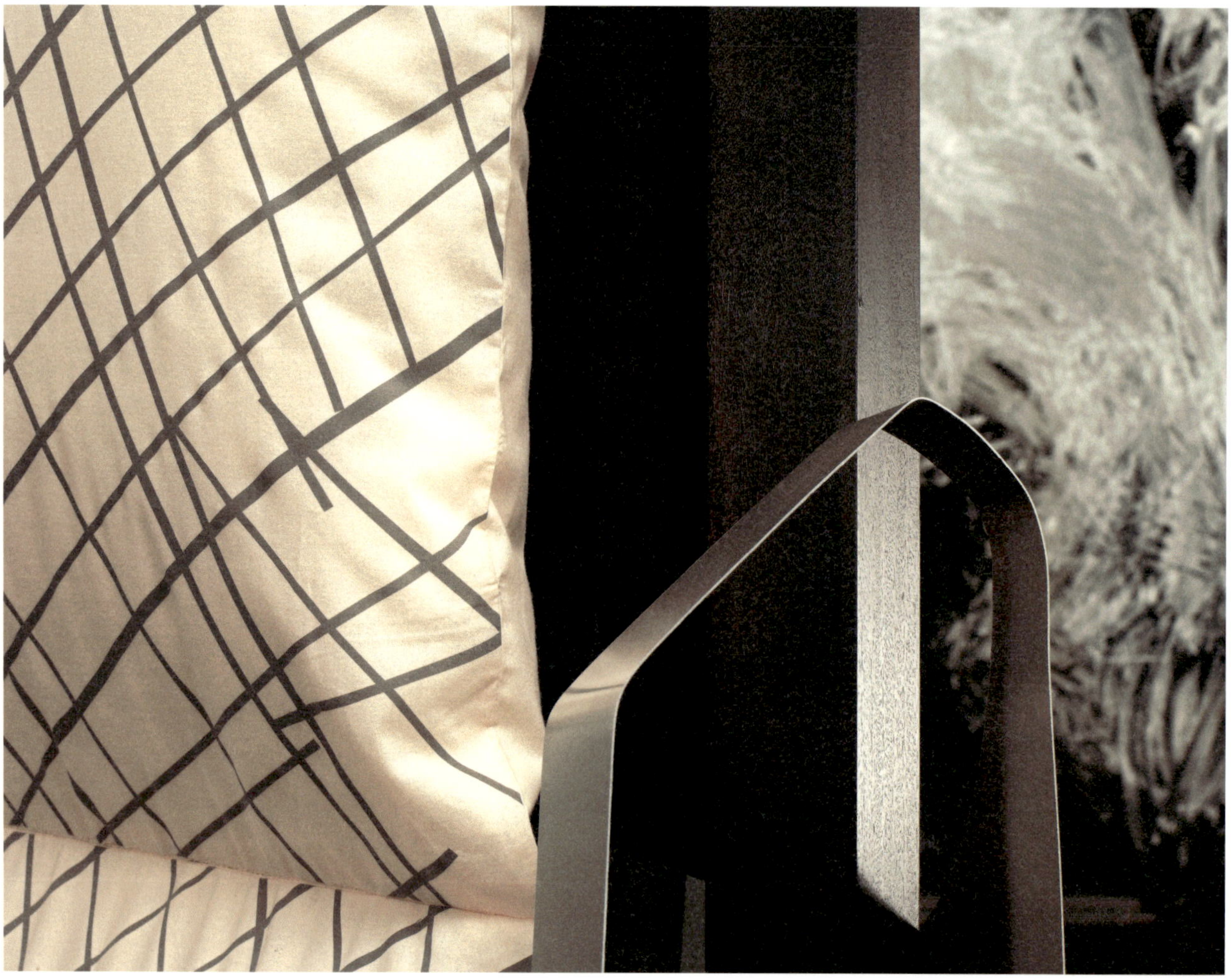

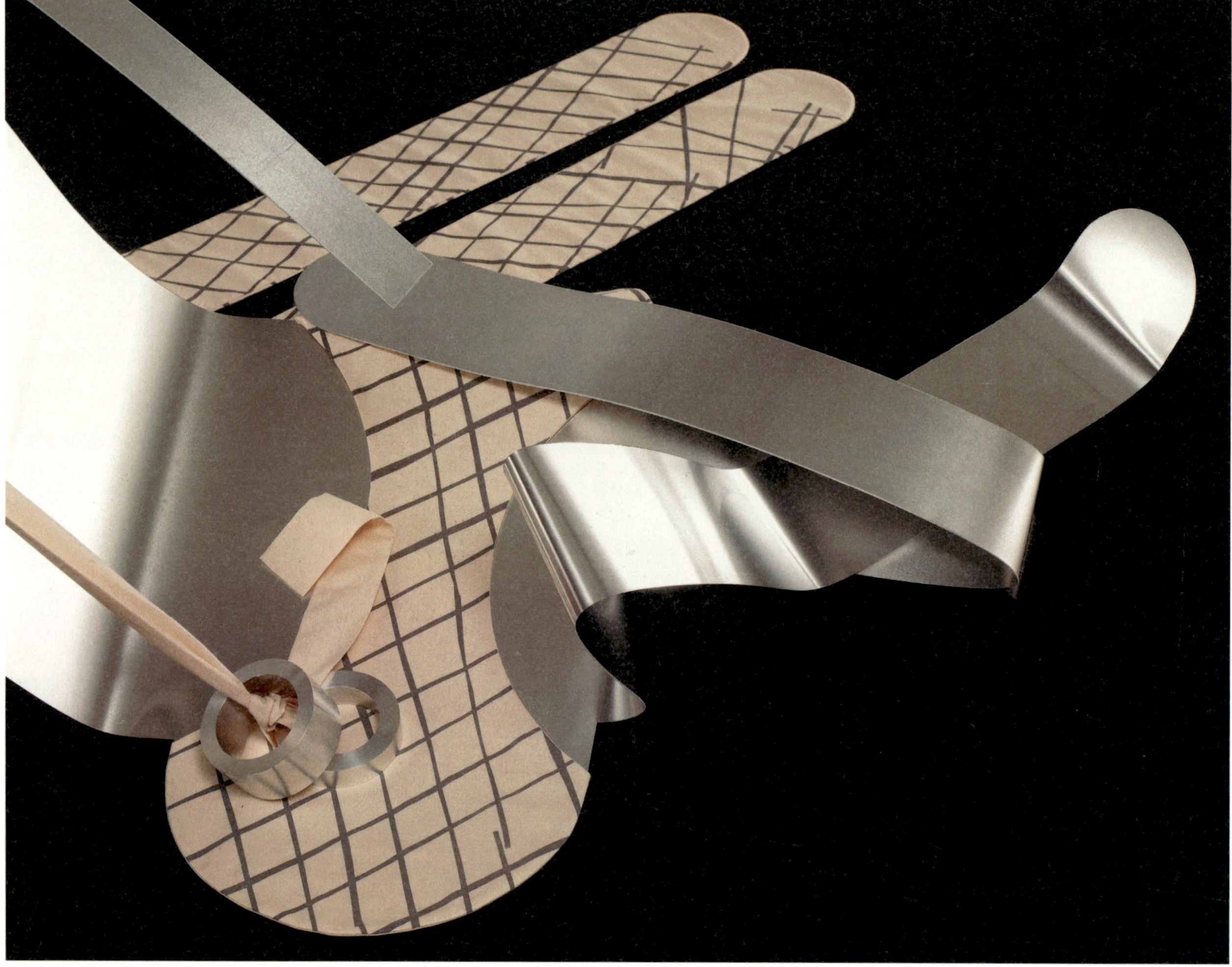

  Flat Peach, 2010, Installationsansicht / Installation view *Flat Peach*, Stephen Friedman Gallery, London 2010

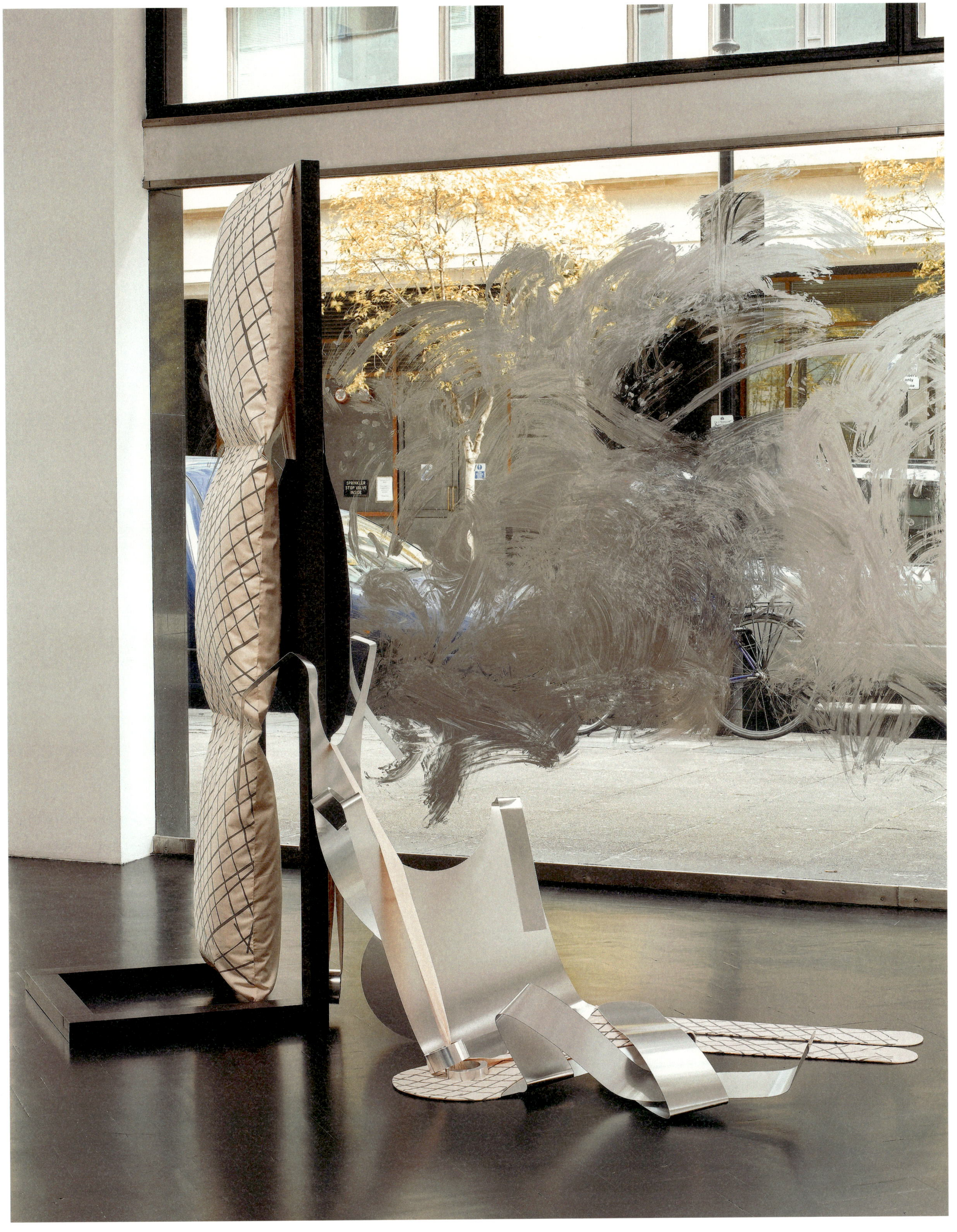

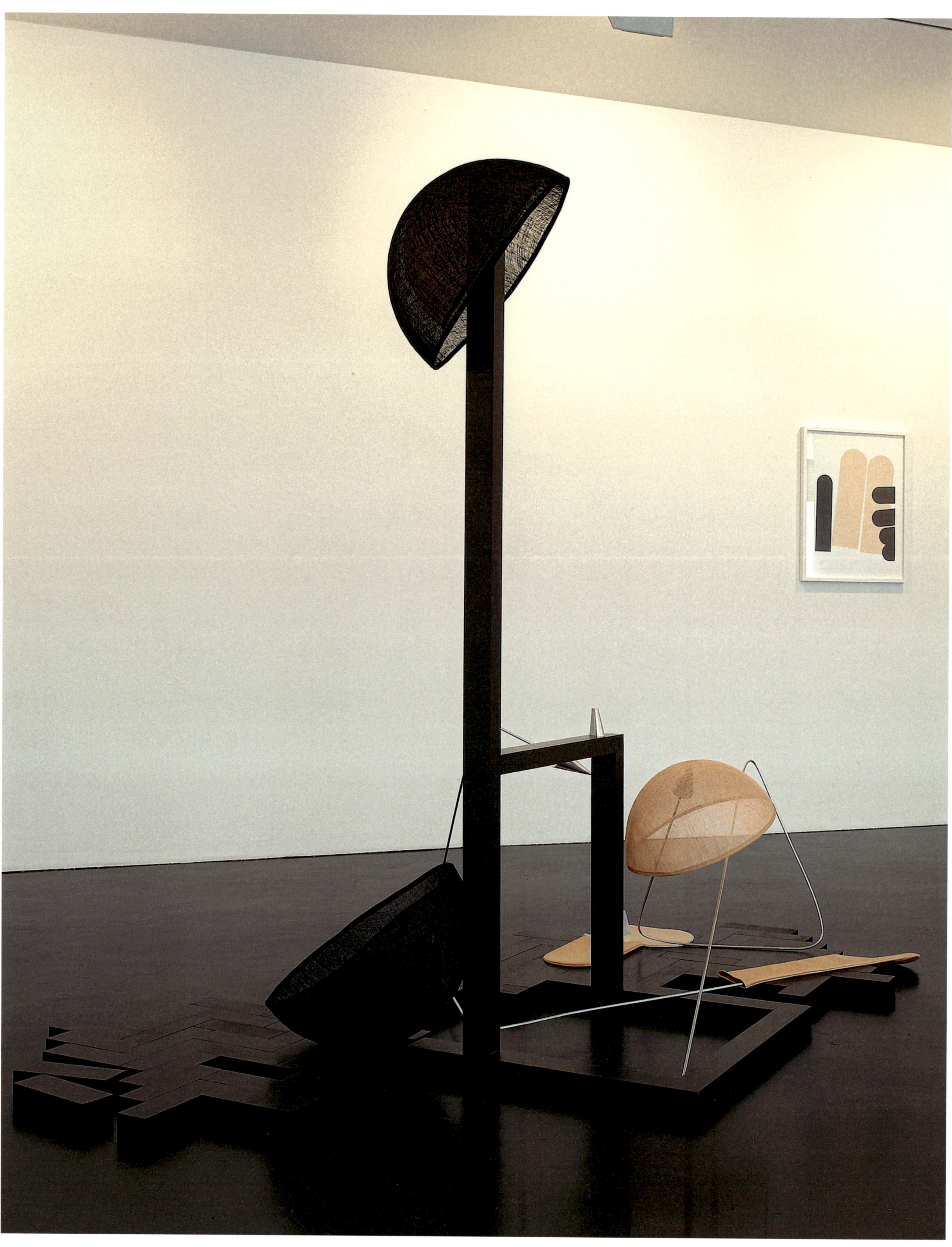

54   *Flat Peach*, 2010, Installationsansicht / Installation view *Flat Peach*, Stephen Friedman Gallery, London 2010

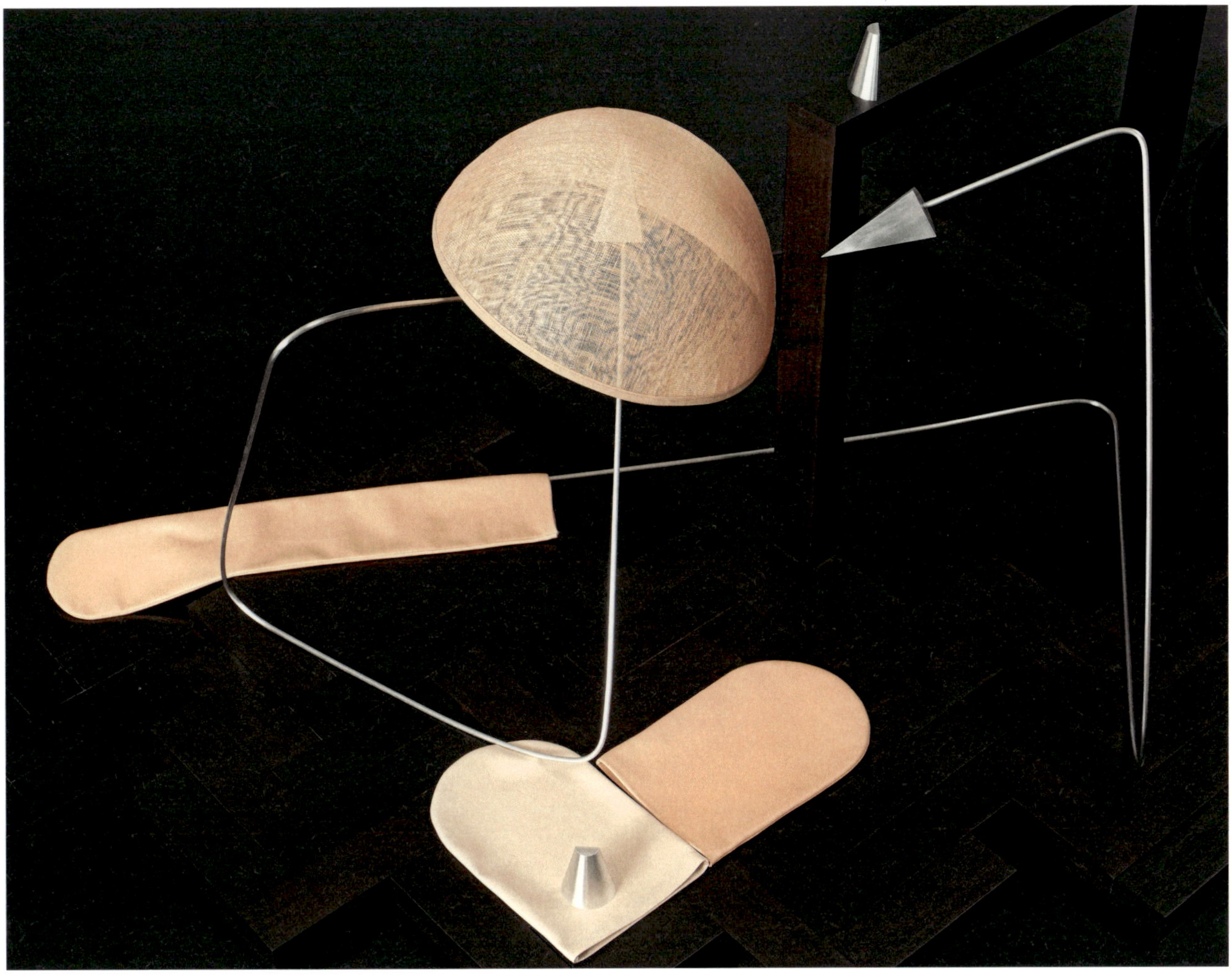

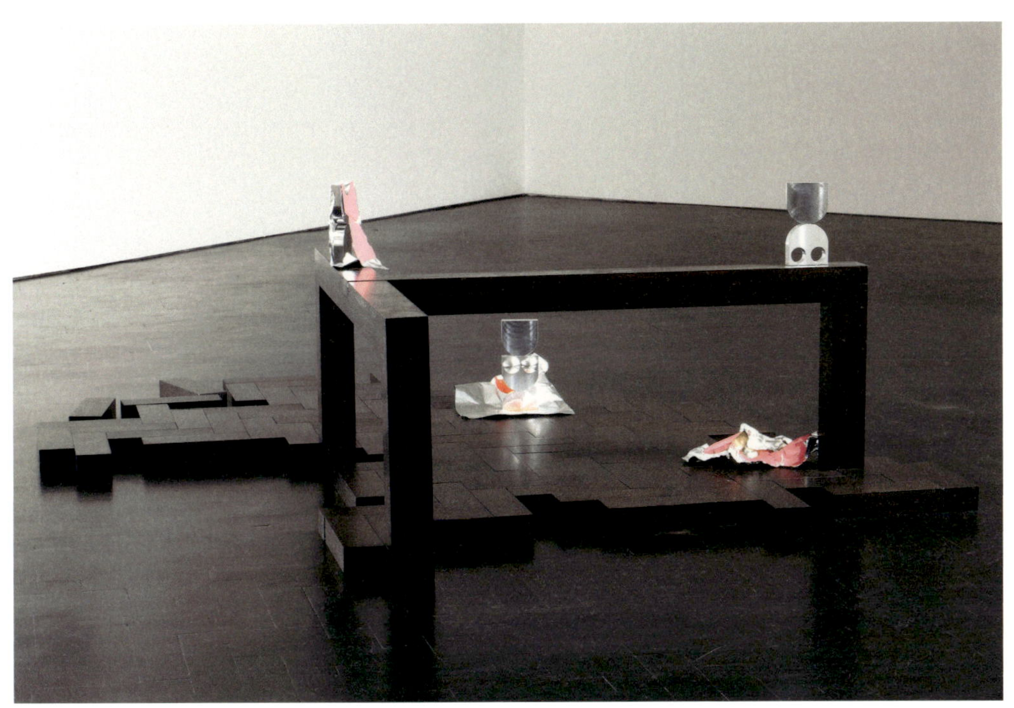

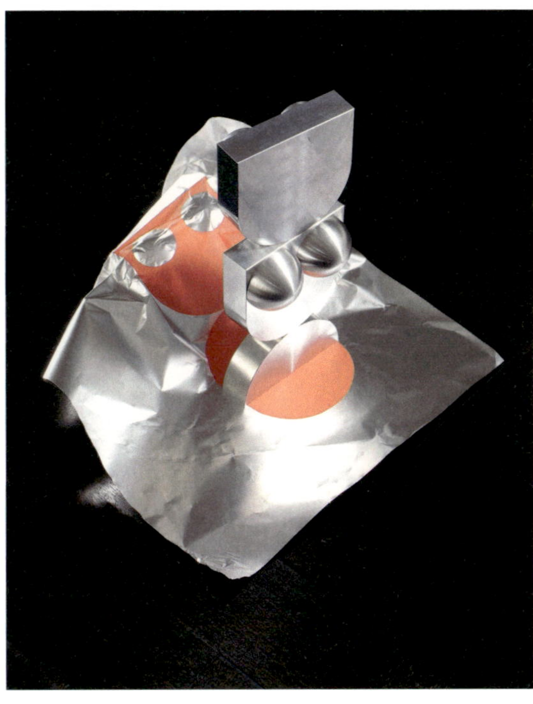

Flat Peach (oben / top), *Soft Group* (unten / bottom), 2010
Installationsansicht / Installation view *Flat Peach*, Stephen Friedman Gallery, London 2010

Claire Barclay 55

Claire Barclay

Claire Barclay ist als Künstlerin bekannt, deren Installationen speziell in bestimmten Räumen und für bestimmte Orte entstehen. Ihre vielfältigen Fragestellungen untersucht sie in verschiedenen aufeinanderfolgenden Zusammenhängen; jede Einladung, auszustellen, ist eine Einladung zum Nachdenken – zum Nachdenken über einen neuen Ort und zum Reflektieren über ihre Arbeit und wie sie diese dort fortsetzen könnte. Obwohl Barclay in großem Maßstab und mit interventionistischer Zielsetzung arbeitet, funktioniert jede ihrer Installationen wie ein Gedicht: eine in hohem Maße durchkomponierte Ansammlung von einzelnen Objekten, die eine Vielfalt an psychologischen und emotionalen Reaktionen auslösen kann. Und wie in der Dichtkunst sind es häufig die kleinsten Elemente, die die größten Ideen freisetzen.

Während ich dies schreibe, muss Barclays Beitrag zu dieser Ausstellung erst noch eine Form annehmen. Sie hat allerdings schon eine Vorstellung, woraus dieser Beitrag bestehen wird: aus einer Kombination ihrer eigenen Ideen und Materialien, die zugleich spezifisch für den Ausstellungsraum und den Zeitpunkt der Ausstellung sind. Während sie über die Ausstellung nachdachte, hat Barclay andere Projekte fertiggestellt. Für ein Krankenhaus in Edinburgh beschäftigte sie sich mit Geisteskrankheit und der Geschichte der Irrenhäuser und für eine Arbeit in einer englischen Küstenstadt mit der nicht weniger eindrucksvollen Geschichte des Kaspertheaters. Sie hat über Wahnsinn gelesen und sich von der Allegorie des „Narrenschiffs" fesseln lassen, aber auch von der Tatsache der Verbannung und der Gefangenschaft als Methoden im Umgang mit Geisteskranken in der Vergangenheit. Sie hat darüber nachgedacht, wie Geisteskrankheit und Puppenspiel Autorität infrage stellen, und über Kunst als „notwendigen Unsinn" – der Künstler als Narr, der die Wahrheit sagt. Mit diesen Gedanken im Kopf in Nürnberg angekommen, will sie ein losgelöstes, ungebundenes Werk schaffen, ein Werk, das einige dieser Gedanken zum Ausdruck bringt, wie subtil auch immer.

Es erscheint als Herausforderung, eine Installation zu schaffen, die dazu imstande ist. Doch genau darin besteht der Kern von Barclays Methode: Die Frage, wie man mit Material Bedeutung schaffen kann. Die Arbeit mit Materialien ist für sie genauso wichtig wie das Lesen von Büchern, die theoretische Auseinandersetzung mit diversen Themen. In das aktuelle Projekt fließt so nicht nur ihre Lektüre rund um Geisteskrankheit und Puppenspiel und ihre anhaltende Faszination für bedruckte und genähte Textilien und bearbeitetes Metall ein, sondern auch ihr derzeitiges Interesse an der fleischigen Transparenz von Latex, an den knochenartigen, kreidigen Feuersteinbrocken von der Küste und am Holz eines Schiffsmastes und dem Tuch seiner Segel.

Typischerweise nimmt Barclays Werk die Form einer Struktur an, in die und um die herum Gegenstände platziert werden. Diese Gegenstände sind die „Bomben", welche die Bedeutung des Werks sprengen. Von Barclay selbst oder jemandem gefertigt, der in der Bearbeitung des Materials geübter ist, sind sie mehrdeutig – oft erscheinen sie wie etwas anderes, doch diese Irreführung ist nur oberflächlich. Bei genauerem Hinsehen entpuppen sie sich stets als Dinge, die nur in der Welt des Werks existieren können. Wie etwa bei *Subject to Habit*, einer Installation für The Fruitmarket Gallery in Edinburgh aus dem Jahr 2009. Ein Stahlrahmen mit bankähnlichen Elementen aus Holz, eine Vinylmatte, die daneben ausgerollt ist, und strategisch positionierte, maschinell bearbeitete Metallscheiben erinnern an ein Fitnessstudio, an männliche Anstrengung und Betätigung. Doch die Matte ist keine Gymnastikmatte, die Bänke sind nicht funktionstüchtig und die Me-

Claire Barclay is known as an artist who makes installations in and for particular spaces. Her work collapses her own concerns into successive contexts, each invitation to show an invitation to think – to think about a new place, and to think again about what she makes and how she might continue to make it there. Though Barclay's work is large in scale and interventionist in ambition, each installation functions like a poem: a highly crafted assemblage of individual elements capable of triggering a range of psychological and emotional responses. And, as in poetry, it is often the smallest elements that set free the biggest ideas.

As I write, the work Barclay will contribute to this exhibition has yet to take shape. But she has already in her mind what it will be shaped out of: a combination of ideas and materials at once her own and particular to the space and time of the exhibition. While thinking about the exhibition, she has been completing other projects, working with mental illness and the history of the mental asylum for a hospital in Edinburgh, and with the equally potent history of the Punch and Judy puppet show for a project in an English seaside town. She has been reading about madness, and has become captivated with the allegory of the 'ship of fools', and with the twin conditions of banishment and confinement in historical methods of dealing with the insane. She has been thinking about how both mental illness and puppetry challenge authority, and about art as a 'necessary nonsense' – the artist as the fool who speaks the truth. Arriving in Nuremberg with these thoughts in her head, she wanted to make something unmoored, untethered – something that might speak, however obliquely, of some of this.

It seems a tall order, making something that can do that. Yet this is at the heart of Barclay's practice: how to make material make meaning. Working with materials is as important to her research as reading books, and as well as her reading around madness and puppetry, she brings to this present project her current interest in the fleshy transparency of latex, the bone-like, chalky flint nodules found at the seaside, the wood and canvas of a ship's mast and sails, and her ongoing fascination with printed and stitched fabric, and with machined metal.

Typically, Barclay's work takes the form of a structure into and onto which objects are placed. These objects are the bombs which detonate the work's meaning. Made either by Barclay herself or by someone more skilled in handling the material, the objects are ambiguous – they often look a bit like something else, but this is only a surface seduction. On close inspection they always turn out to be things which can only exist in the world of the work. So, for example, *Subject to Habit*, a work made for The Fruitmarket Gallery in Edinburgh in 2009. A steel frame with wooden bench-like elements, a vinyl mat extending away from it and strategically placed machined metal discs, it speaks of the gym, of masculine endeavour and exertion. Yet the mat is not a gym mat, the benches not functional, the metal discs neither dumb-bells nor barbells. And three 'hats' disrupt the work, their potential meanings unravelling along chains of reference encompassing dunces' caps, the hoods of the Ku Klux Klan, children's party hats or the tools of some psychological team-building or ice-breaking game.

Of her process, Barclay has commented: "I often choose to work with materials which are familiar and omnipresent. Leather, clay, cloth, wood, metal and so on. They've been used to make the objects that shape our lives for a very long time. I like these materials in particular because they transcend time and place and even culture. I try to form them into objects which defy specific categorisation, being at once recognisable and foreign, domestic and

tallscheiben weder Kurz- noch Langhanteln. Drei „Hütchen" schließlich stören das Werk. Ihre potenziellen Bedeutungen entspinnen sich entlang von Bezugsketten, die Narrenkappen, Ku-Klux-Klan-Kapuzen, Partyhüte von Kindergeburtstagen und auch das Zubehör eines psychologischen Teambuilding- oder Kennenlernspiels einschließen.

Barclay selbst sagt über ihre Arbeitsweise: „Ich arbeite häufig mit vertrauten, allgegenwärtigen Materialien: Leder, Ton, Stoff, Holz, Wolle, Metall und so weiter, aus denen die Dinge bestehen, die unser Leben schon sehr lange prägen. Mir gefallen diese Materialien besonders, weil sie Zeit, Ort und selbst Kultur transzendieren. Ich versuche, aus ihnen Objekte herzustellen, die sich einer klaren Kategorisierung widersetzen, da sie zur gleichen Zeit erkennbar und fremd, häuslich und industriell, zeitgenössisch und antik sind. Ich versuche immer, Arbeiten zu schaffen, die auf diese Weise mehrdeutig sind."[1] Aus diesem Grund, glaube ich, lässt mich Barclays Werk an Poesie denken. Es ist – wie ein Gedicht – aus Dingen komponiert, die von ihr oder für sie geschaffen wurden und die genauso, oder zumindest ähnlich, wie Dinge der realen Welt erscheinen, die jedoch vollständig unter Barclays Kontrolle funktionieren, auch wenn sie damit vielleicht gerade die Vorstellung von Kontrolle untergraben. Barclays Werk lässt das Material sprechen, lässt es sein eigenes Netz von Anspielungen aufbauen, indem es uns von Gegenständen erzählt, die wir vielleicht besser kennen und die aus dem gleichen Material bestehen. Gleichzeitig manifestiert sich auch der Prozess, durch den das Material zur Kunst geformt wird – das Metall wurde maschinell bearbeitet, der Stoff bedruckt und genäht, das Holz gedrechselt. Die Künstlerin spricht nicht von einer „fertigen" Installation, sondern vom Erreichen einer zufriedenstellenden Zäsur im Prozess, einem Moment vielleicht, in dem das sich stetig weiterentwickelnde Gedicht ihres Werks anderen gezeigt, von ihnen gelesen werden und seinen geheimnisvollen, anspielungsreichen Zauber ausüben kann.

industrial, contemporary and antique. I always try to make work which is ambiguous in this way."[1] This is why, I think, her work makes me think of poetry. It is composed, like a poem, of things made by or for her that seem the same as, or at least similar to, things that exist out in the world, but which are operating entirely under her control, even as they may be doing so precisely to undermine the very idea of control. Her work lets the material speak, lets it set up its own network of allusions, talking to us of objects we may know better that are made of the same thing. At the same time, the process through which the material is fashioned into art also speaks – the metal has been machined, the cloth printed and stitched, the wood turned. The artist talks not of an installation being 'finished', but of reaching a satisfactory pause in the process, a moment perhaps at which the ever-developing poem of her work may be shown to others, be read by them, and work its particularly elusive, allusive magic.

1   „Ein Gespräch zwischen Claire Barclay und Janneke de Vries", in: *Claire Barclay. Fault on the Right Side*, Ausst.-Kat. Kunstverein Braunschweig, Köln 2007, S. 67.

1   'A Conversation between Claire Barclay and Janneke de Vries', in *Claire Barclay: Fault on the Right Side*, exh. cat. Kunstverein Braunschweig (Cologne: Walther König, 2007), p. 73.

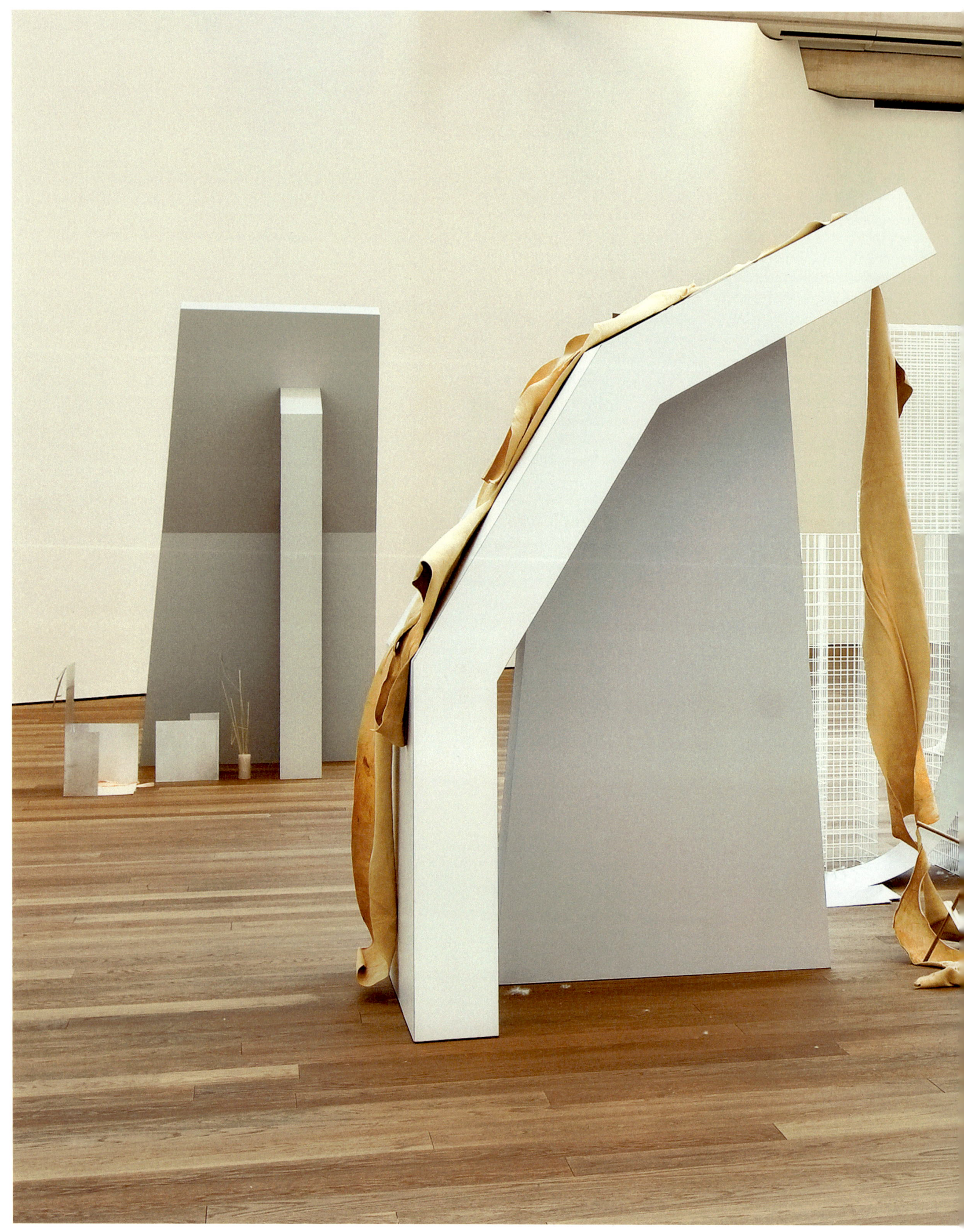

 Pale Heights, 2009, Installationsansicht / Installation view, MUDAM Luxembourg, Musée d'Art Moderne Grand-Duc Jean, Luxemburg / Luxembourg 2009

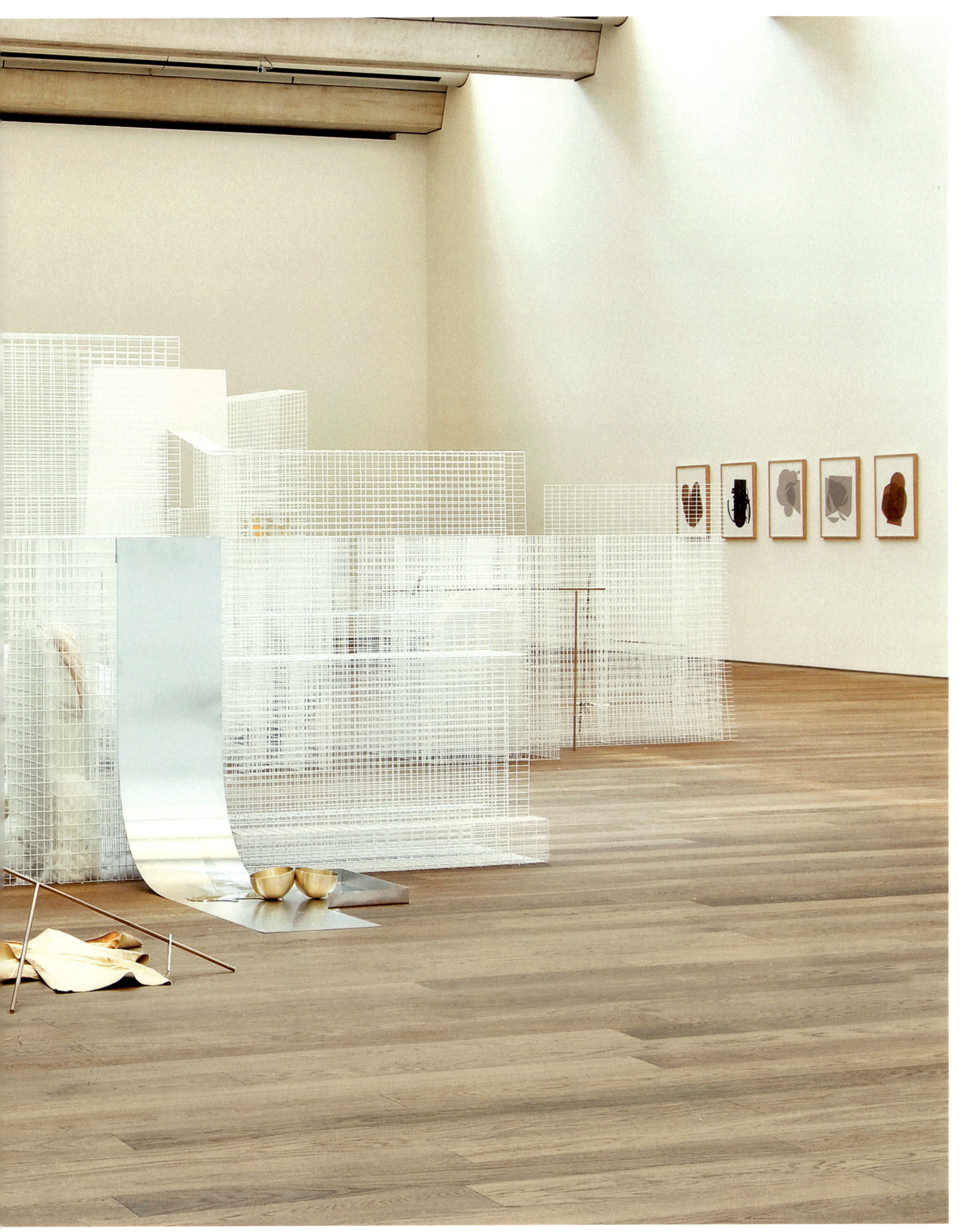

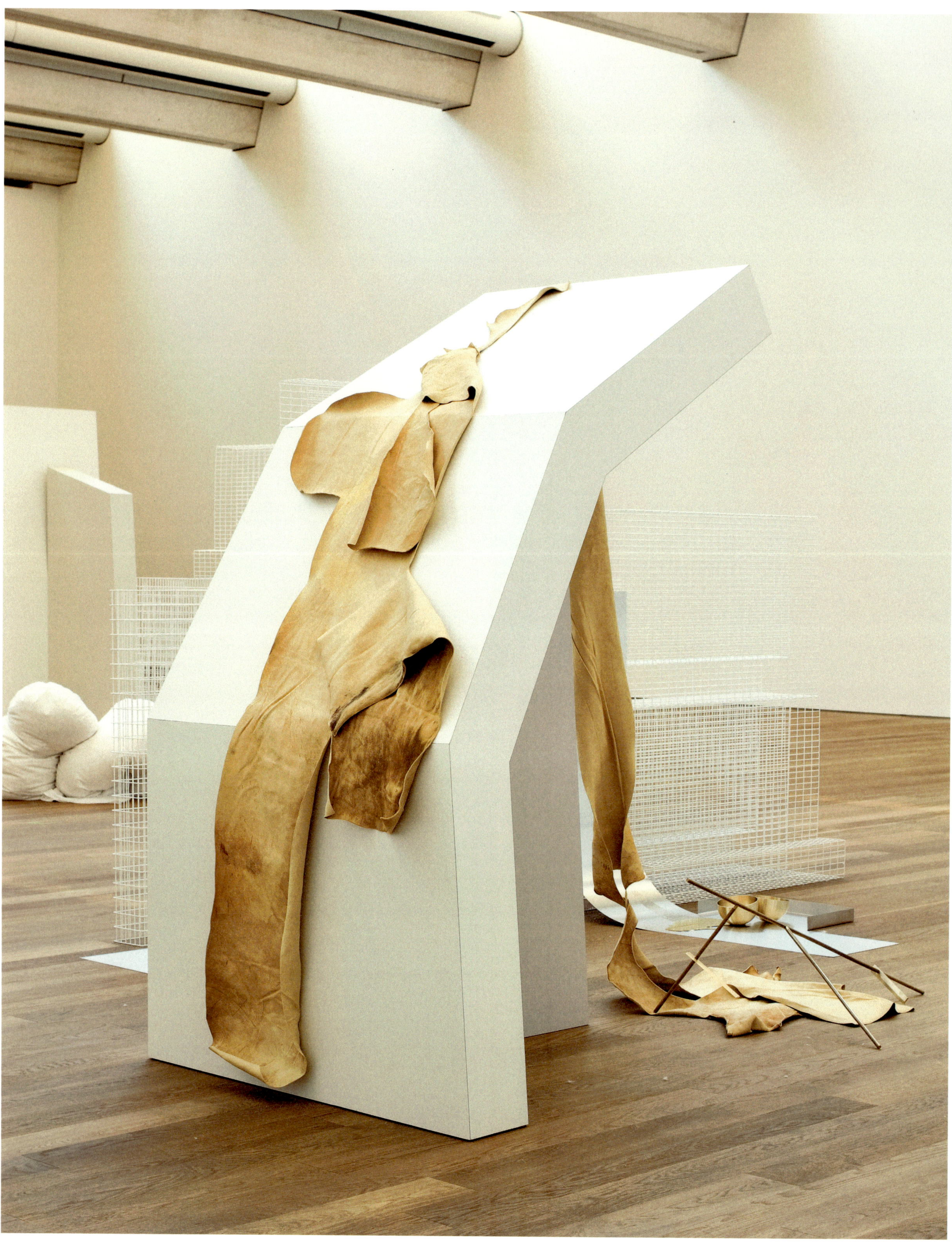

   Pale Heights, 2009, MUDAM Luxembourg, Musée d'Art Moderne Grand-Duc Jean, Luxemburg / Luxembourg 2009

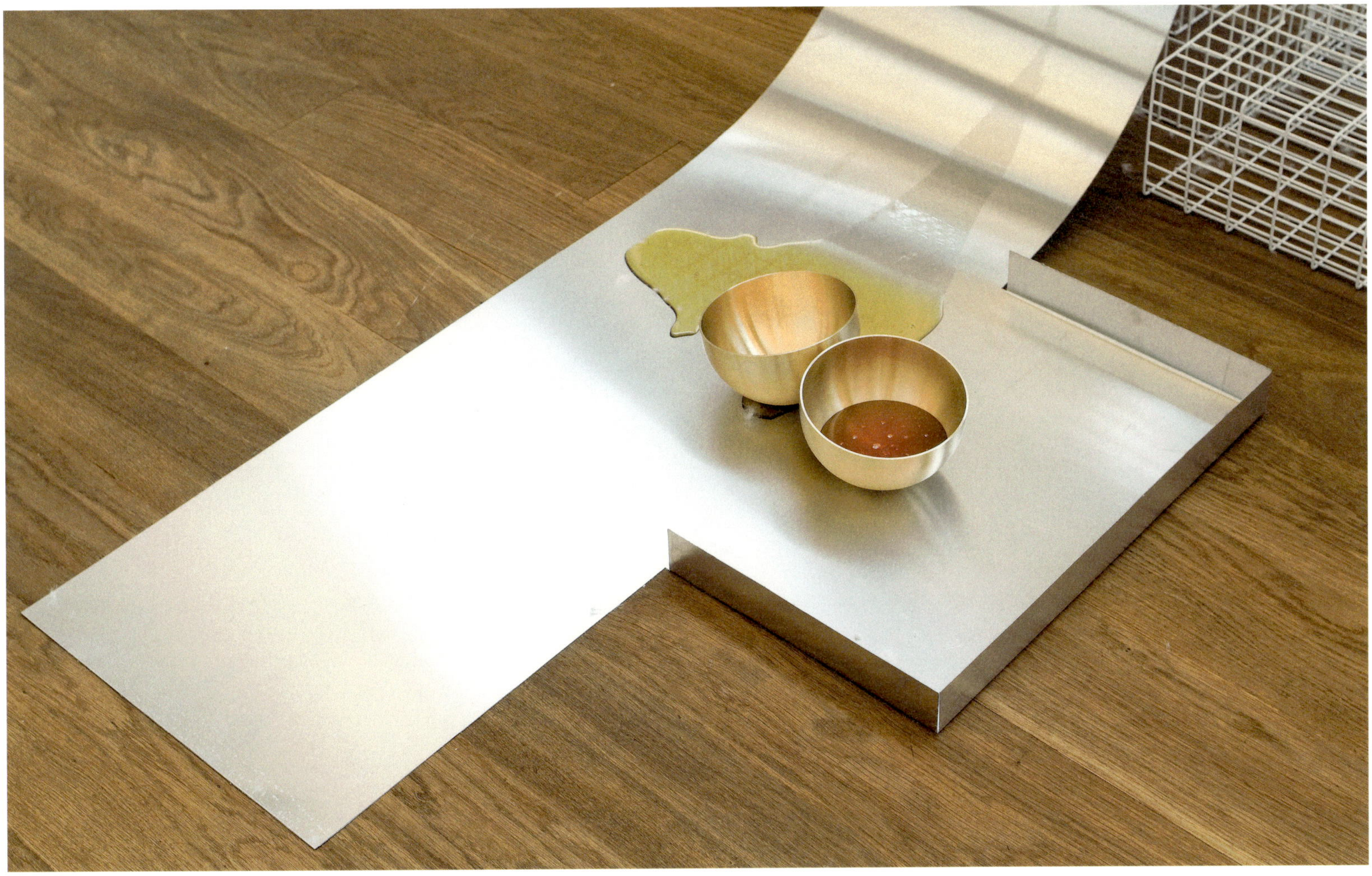

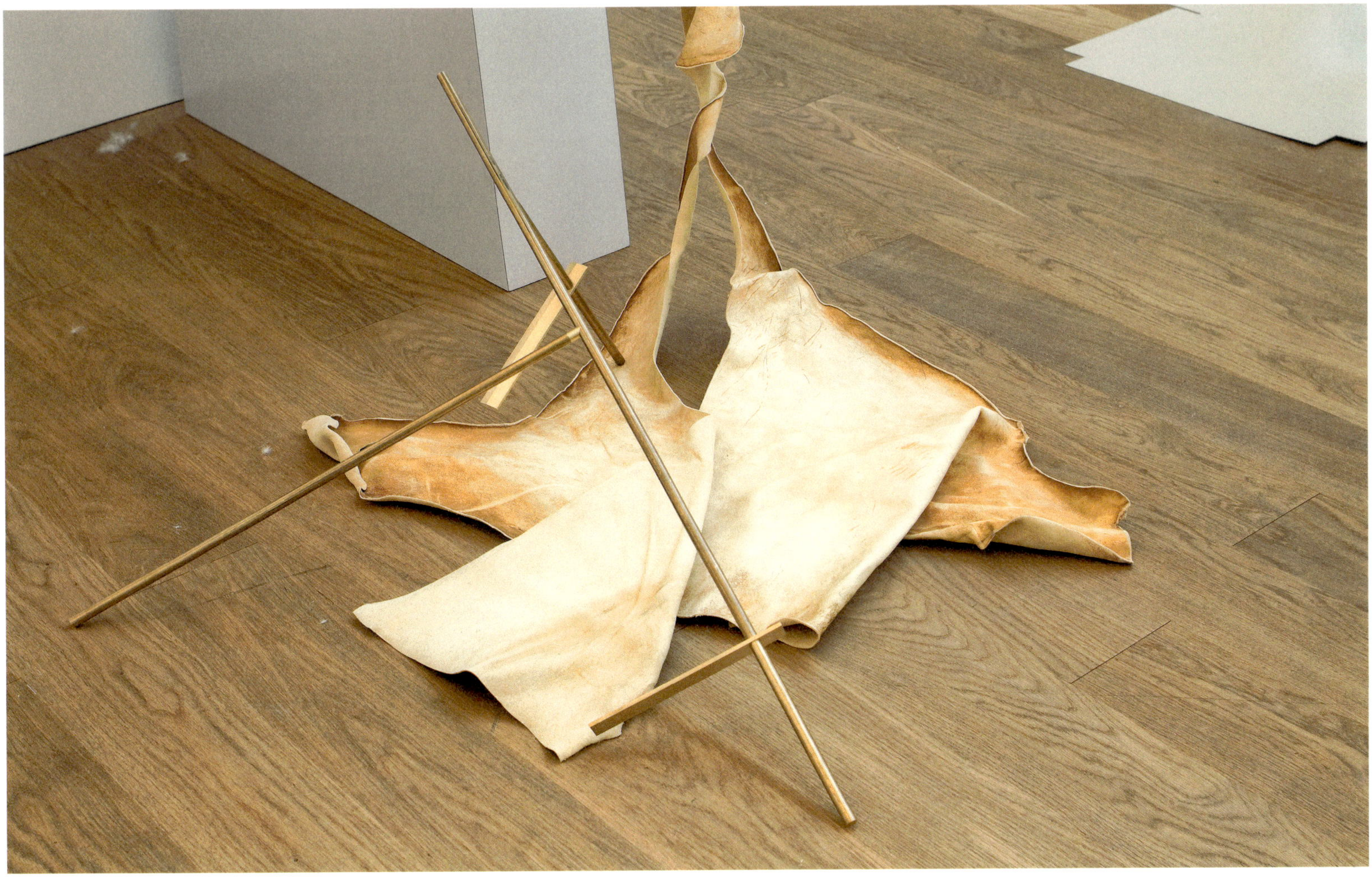

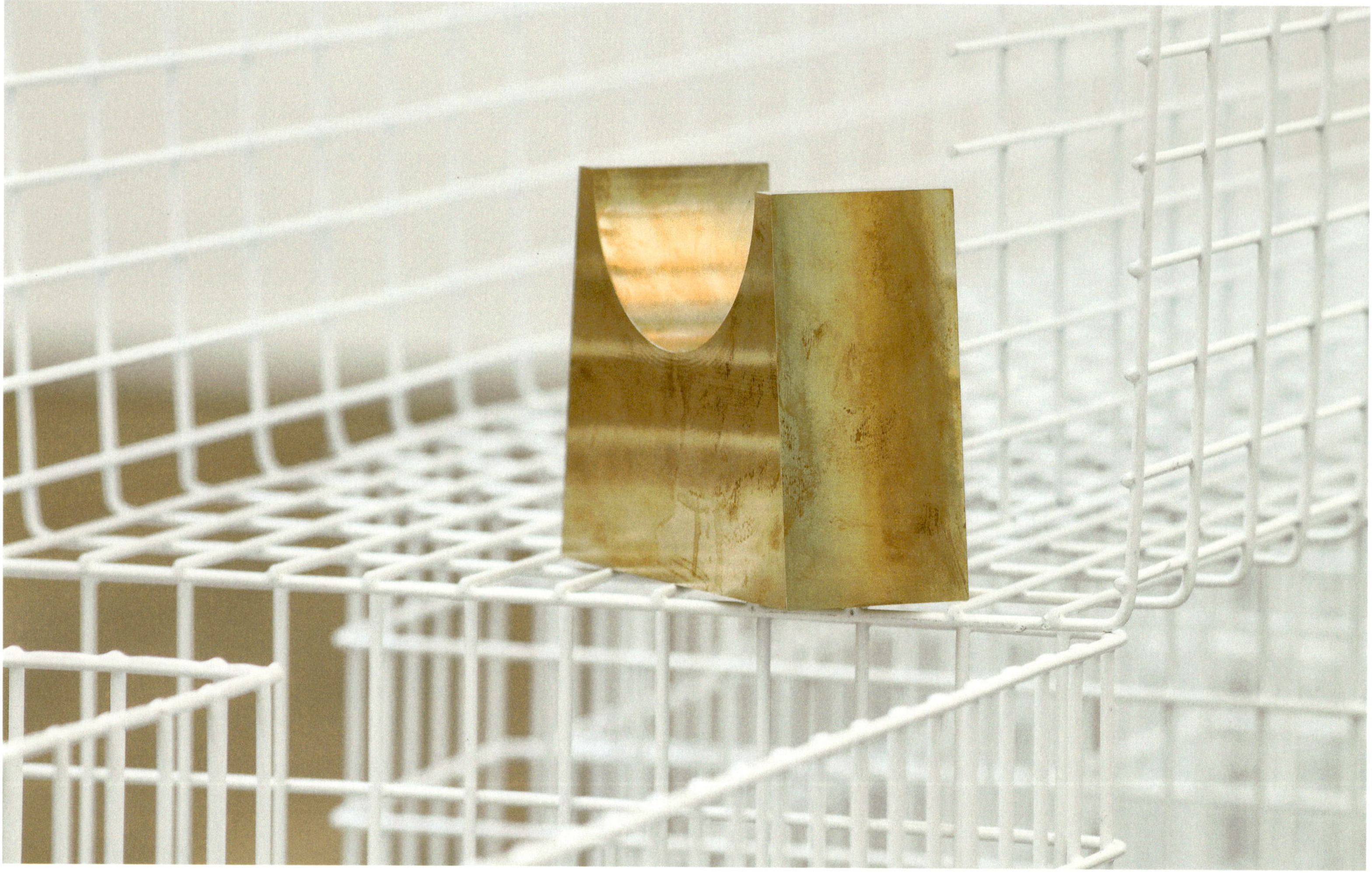

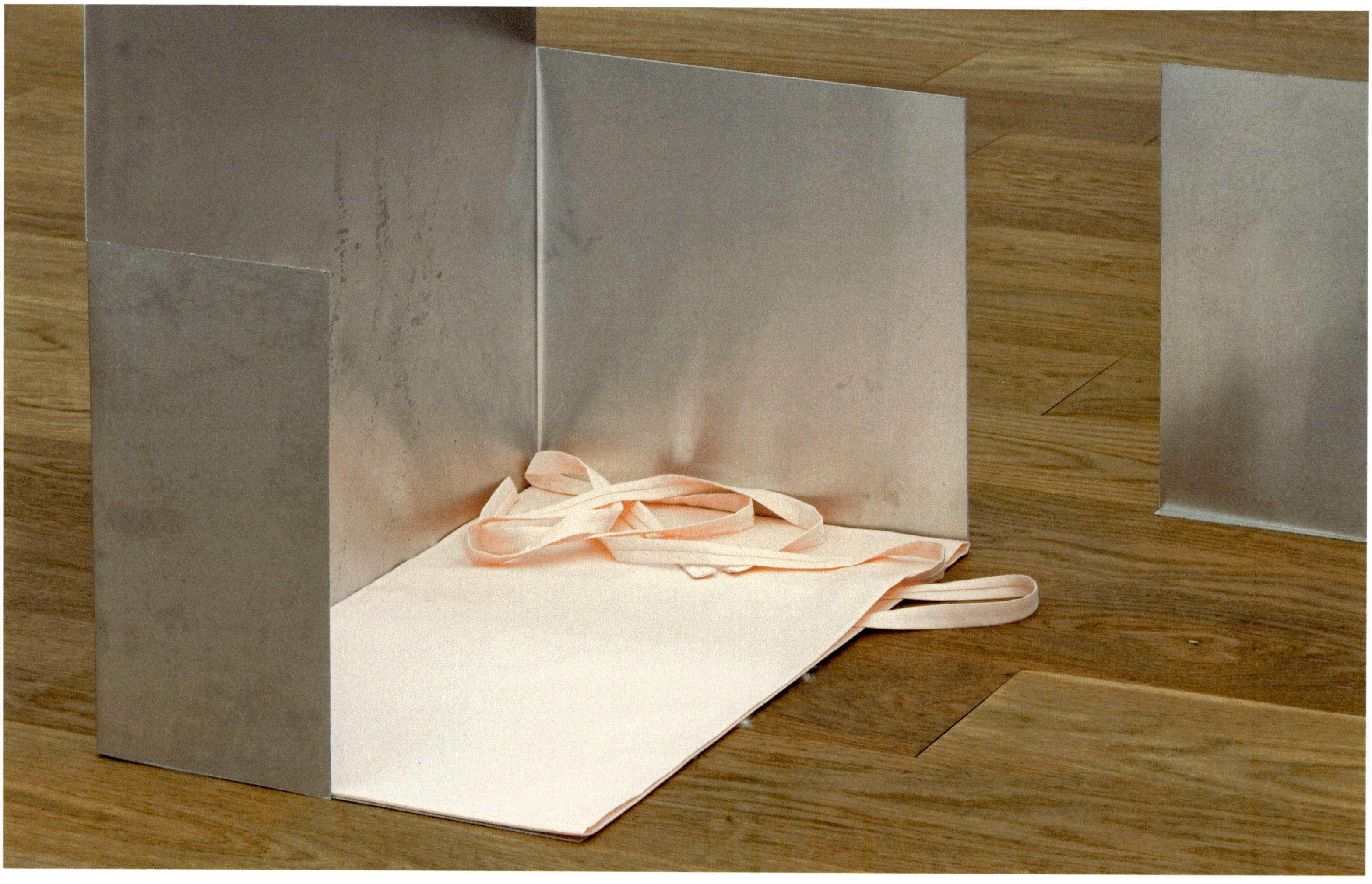

Pale Heights, 2009, MUDAM Luxembourg, Musée d'Art Moderne Grand-Duc Jean, Luxemburg / Luxembourg 2009

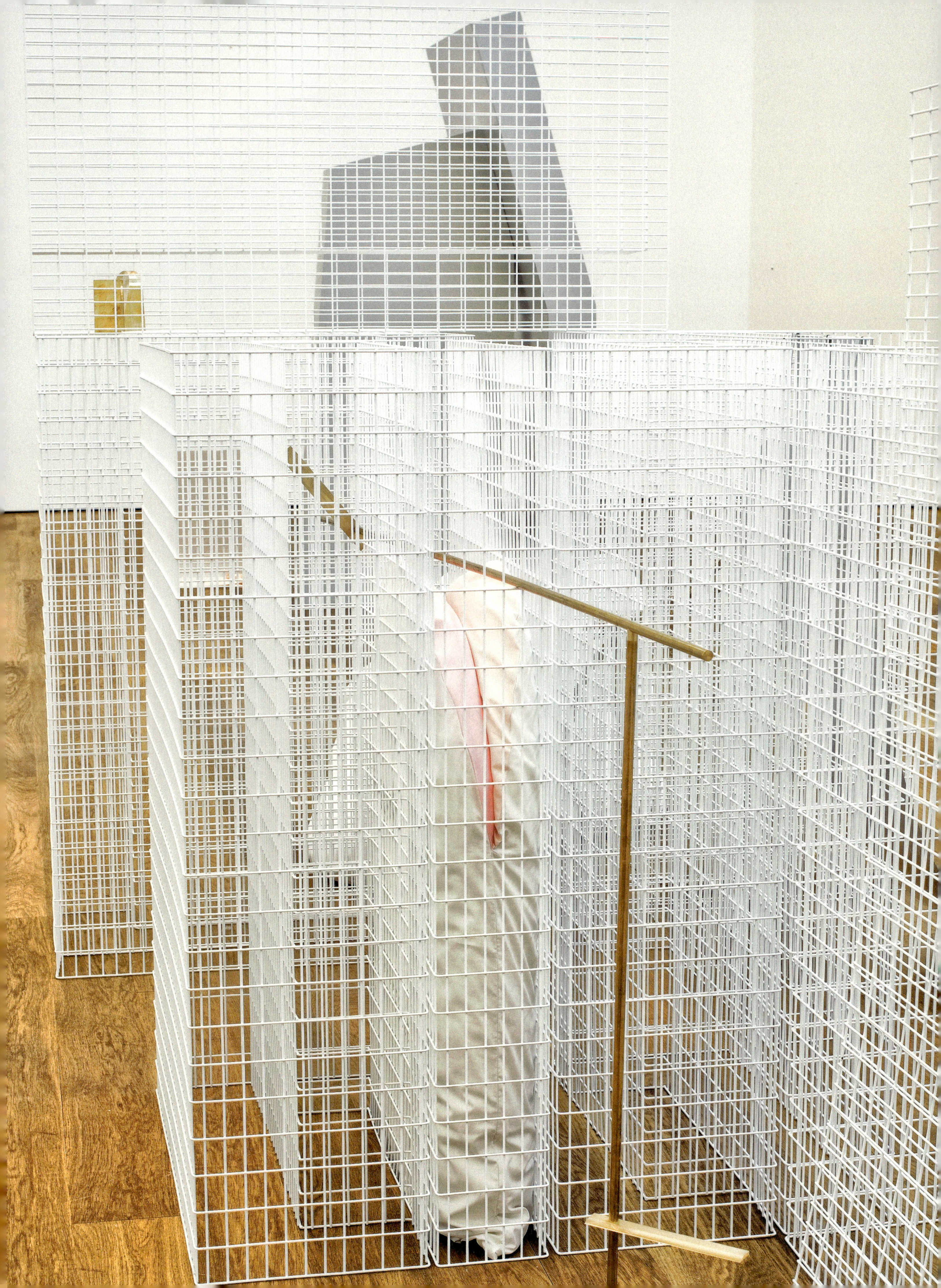

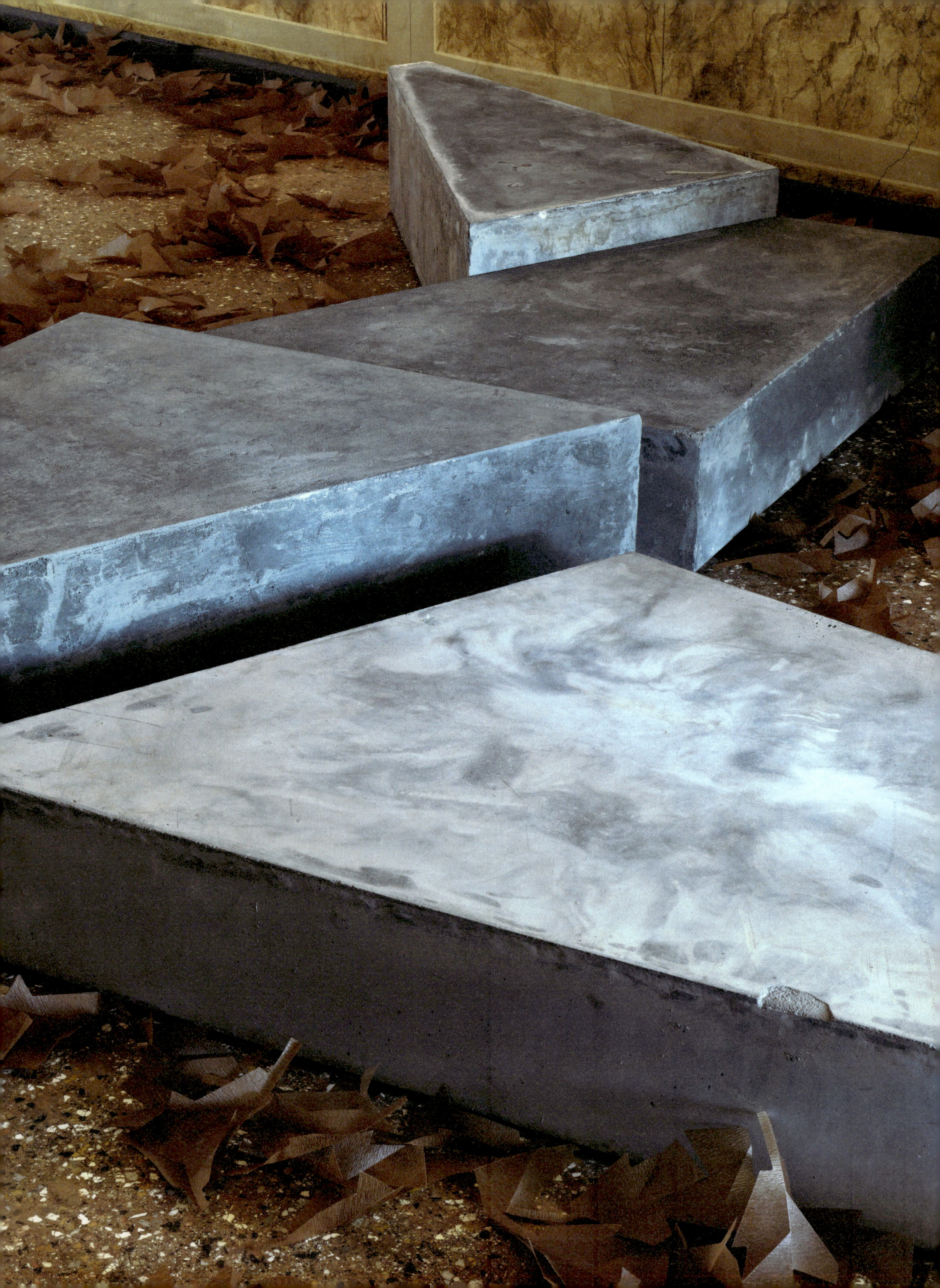

Martin Boyce

A River in the Trees, 2009, und / and *Evaporated Pools*, 2009, Installationsansicht / Installation view *No Reflections*, Scotland + Venice, Palazzo Pisani, Biennale Venedig / Venice Biennale, Venedig / Venice 2009

Biografie / Biography

Martin Boyce lebt und arbeitet / lives and works in Glasgow, Schottland / Scotland
1967   geboren / born in Hamilton, Schottland / Scotland

Studium / Education

1986–1990   Bachelor of Fine Art (Environmental Art), Glasgow School of Art, Glasgow
1995–1997   Master of Fine Art, Glasgow School of Art, Glasgow
1996   California Institute for the Arts, Los Angeles

Stipendien und Preise / Scholarships and Awards

2004   Paul Hamlyn Foundation, Visual Artist Award
2004   Kunstpreis der Adolf-Luther-Stiftung, Krefeld
2005   Stipendium / scholarship, Europäisches Kolleg der Künste, Universität der Künste, Berlin
2011   Turner Prize

Ausgewählte Ausstellungen / Selected Exhibitions

„Here + Now: Scottish Art 1990–2001", Dundee Contemporary Arts; Aberdeen Art Gallery (2001)
„Our Love is Like the Flowers, the Rain, the Sea and the Hours", Tramway, Glasgow (2002)
„Martin Boyce. For 1959 Capital Avenue", Museum für Moderne Kunst, Frankfurt am Main (2002)
„Martin Boyce. Brushing Against Strange Weeds", The Modern Institute, Glasgow (2004)
„Martin Boyce. A Lost Cat and Alleyways, Back Gardens, Pools and Parkways", Centre d'Art Contemporain, Genf / Geneva (2007)
„Skulptur Projekte Münster", Münster (2007)
„Martin Boyce. This Place is Close and Unfolded", Westfälischer Kunstverein, Münster (2008)
„Martin Boyce. No Reflections", Scotland and Venice, 53. Biennale Venedig / Venice (2009)
„Modern British Sculpture", Royal Academy of Arts, London (2011)
„Martin Boyce. In Praise of Shadows", Johnen Galerie, Berlin (2012)
„Martin Boyce. It's Over / and Over", Tanya Bonakdar Gallery, New York (2013)

Ausgewählte Publikationen / Selected Publications

„Martin Boyce", Ausst.-Kat. / exh. cat. The Fruitmarket Gallery, Edinburgh 1999
„Martin Boyce. Undead Dreams", Ausst.-Kat. / exh. cat. RomaRomaRoma, Rom / Rome 2003
„Martin Boyce", Ausst.-Kat. / exh. cat. Frac des Pays de la Loire, Carquefou; Westfälischer Kunstverein, Münster; Ikon Gallery, Birmingham; Zürich / Zurich 2009
„Martin Boyce. No Reflections", Ausst.-Kat. / exh. cat. Dundee Contemporary Arts, Dundee 2009
„Martin Boyce", Renate Wiehager, Christian Ganzenberg (Hg./eds.), Köln / Cologne 2012
Martin Boyce, „A Partial Eclipse", London 2013

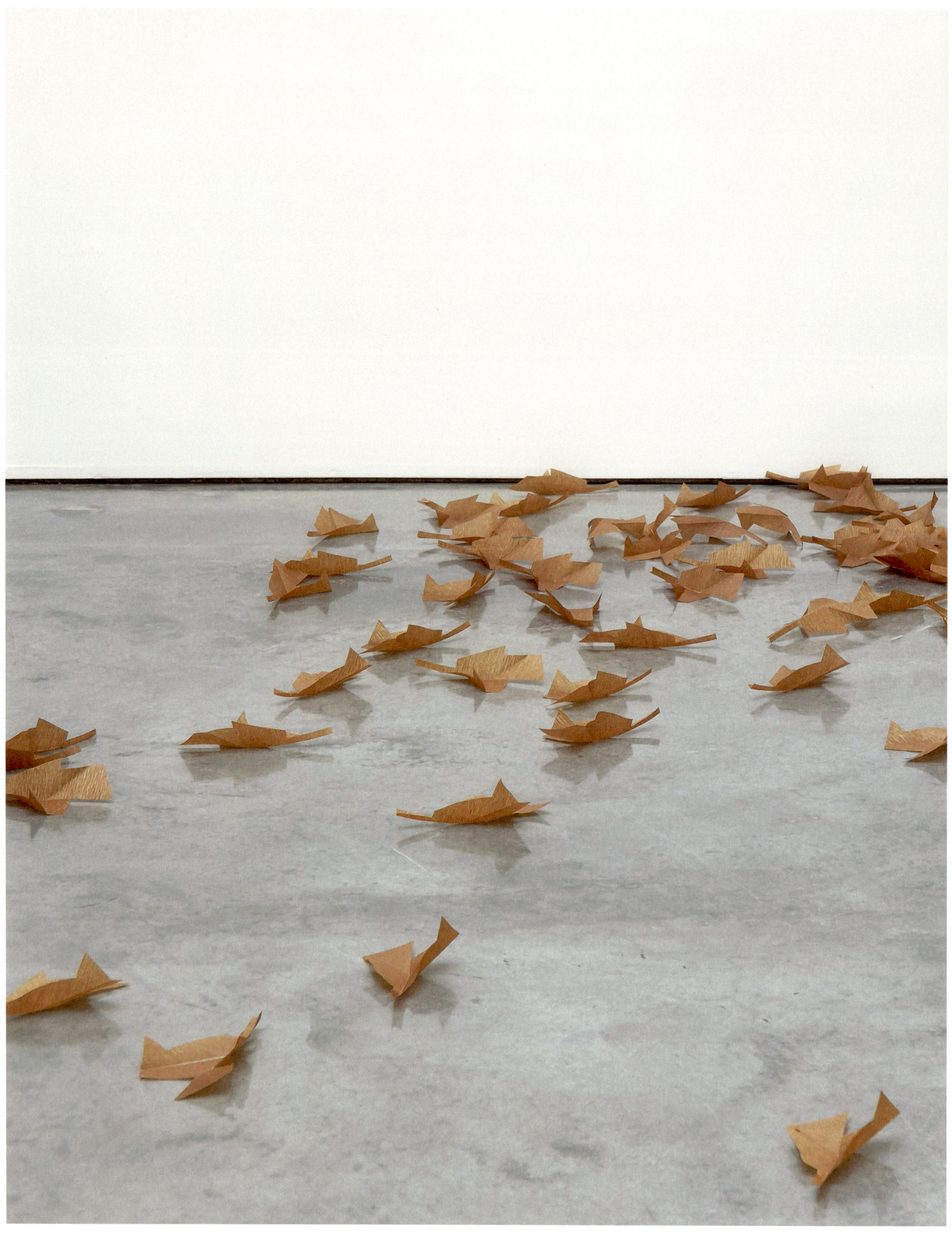

66 *Evaporated Pools*, 2009, Installationsansicht / Installation view *the spirit level*, Barbara Gladstone Gallery, New York 2012

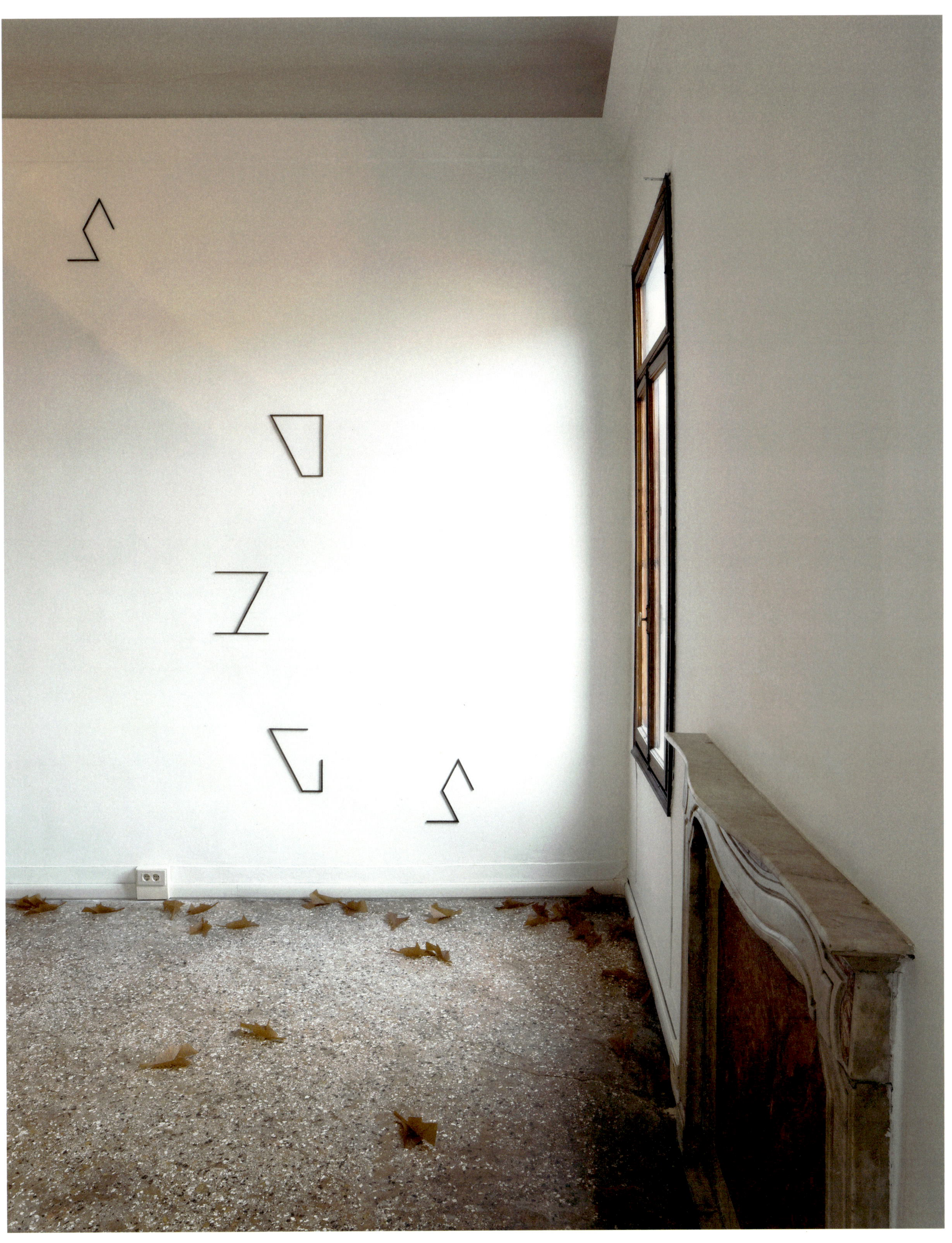

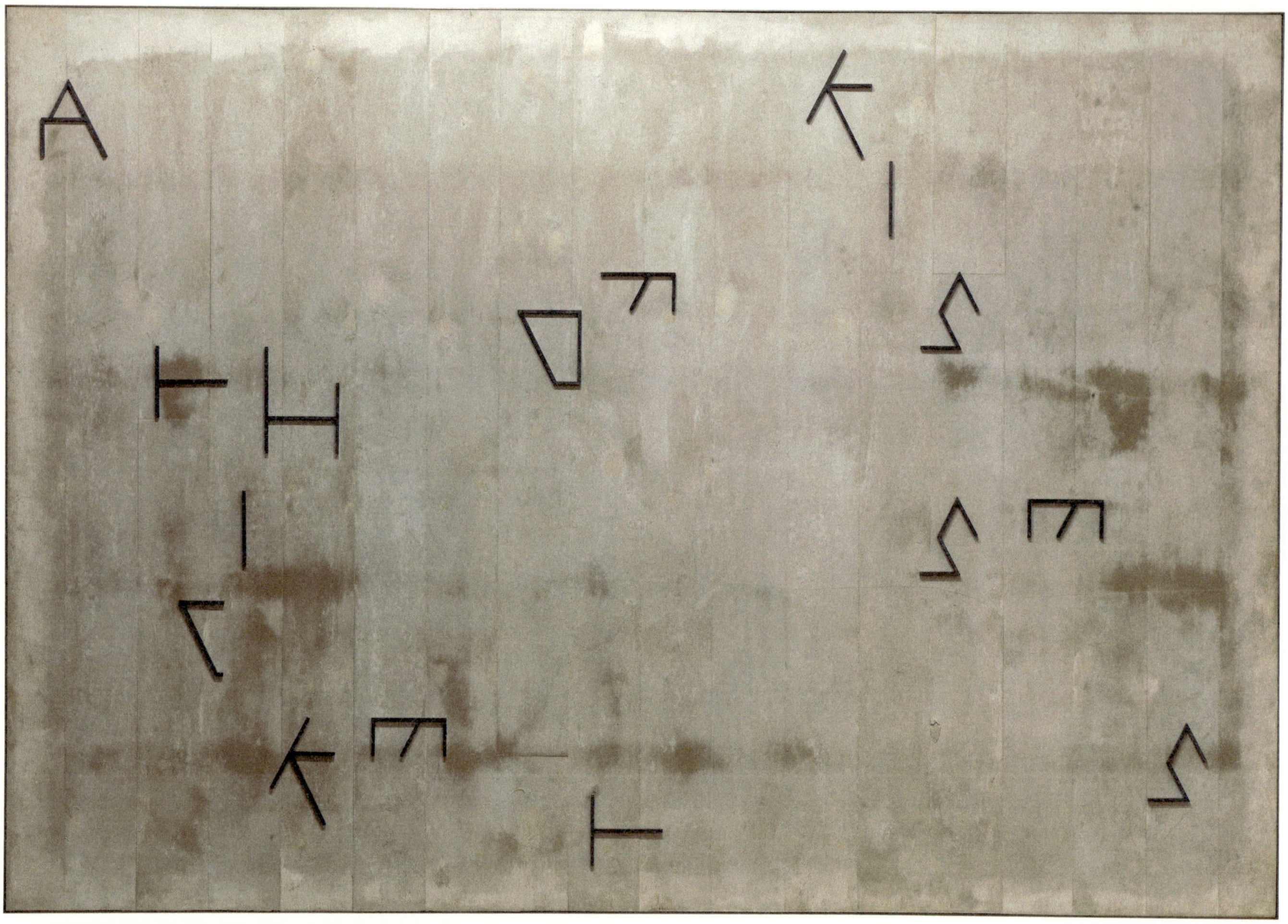

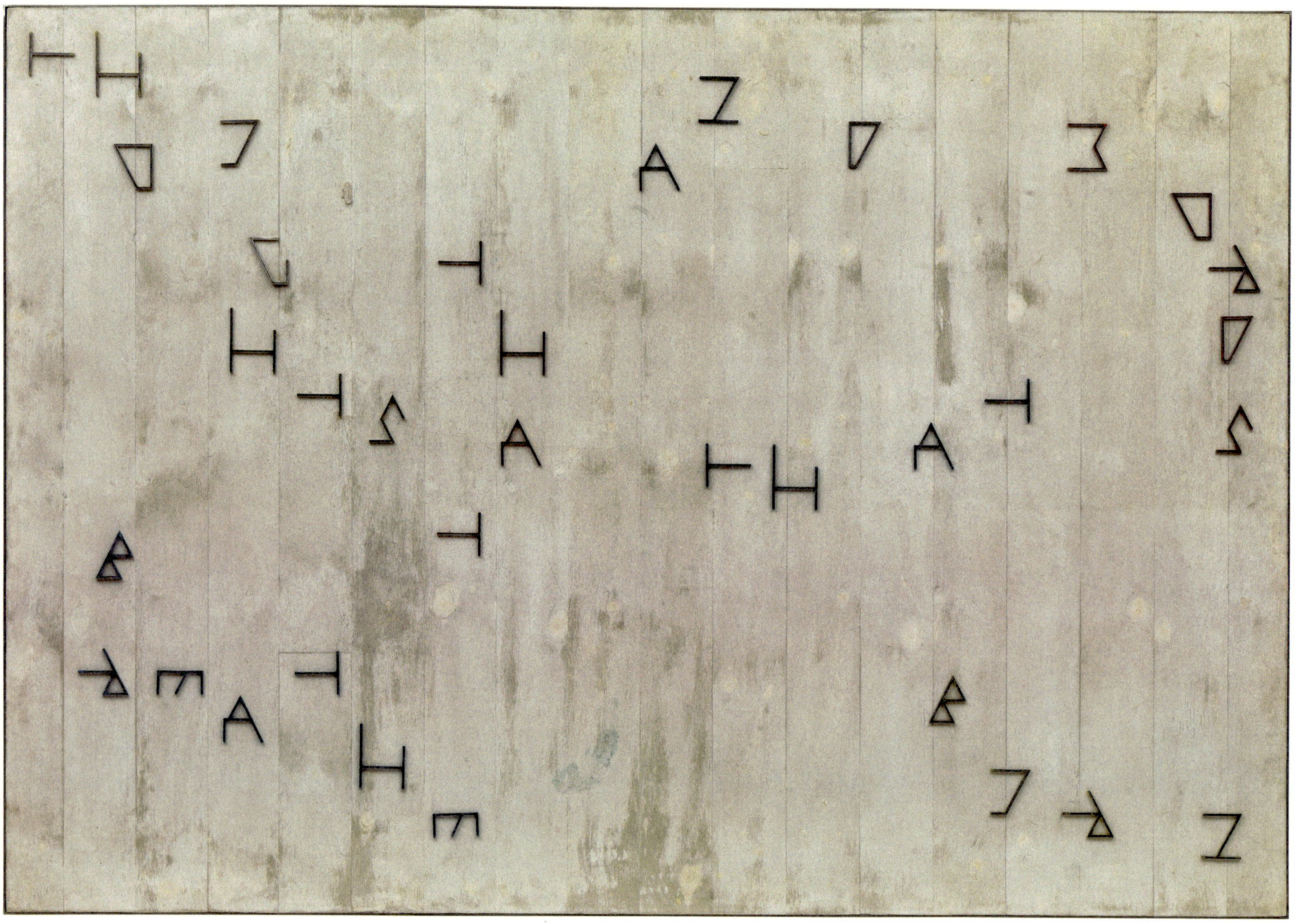

Of Kisses, 2009, Naomi Milgrom Collection, Australien / Australia (oben / top)
Thoughts That Breathe, 2010, Private Collection (unten / bottom)

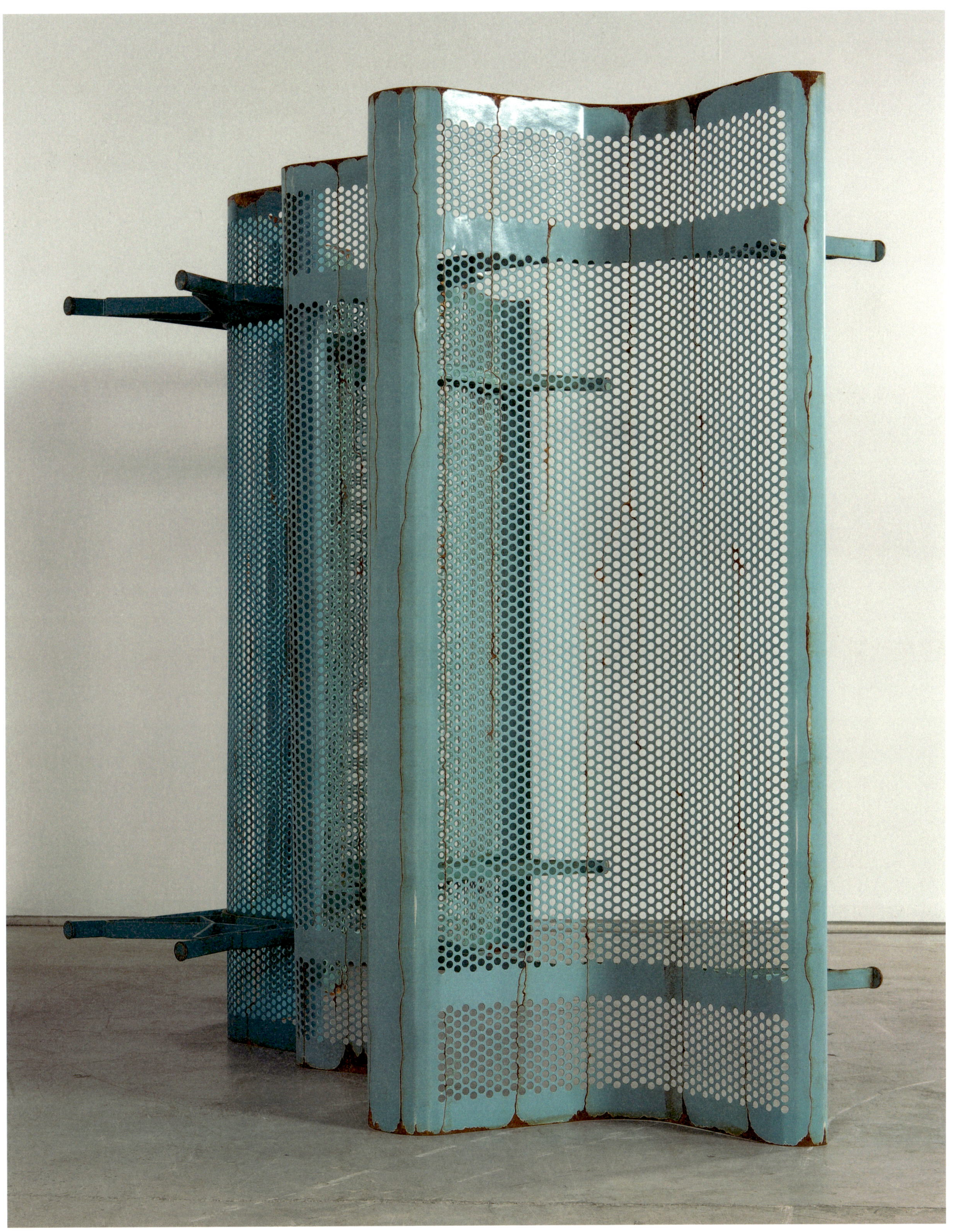

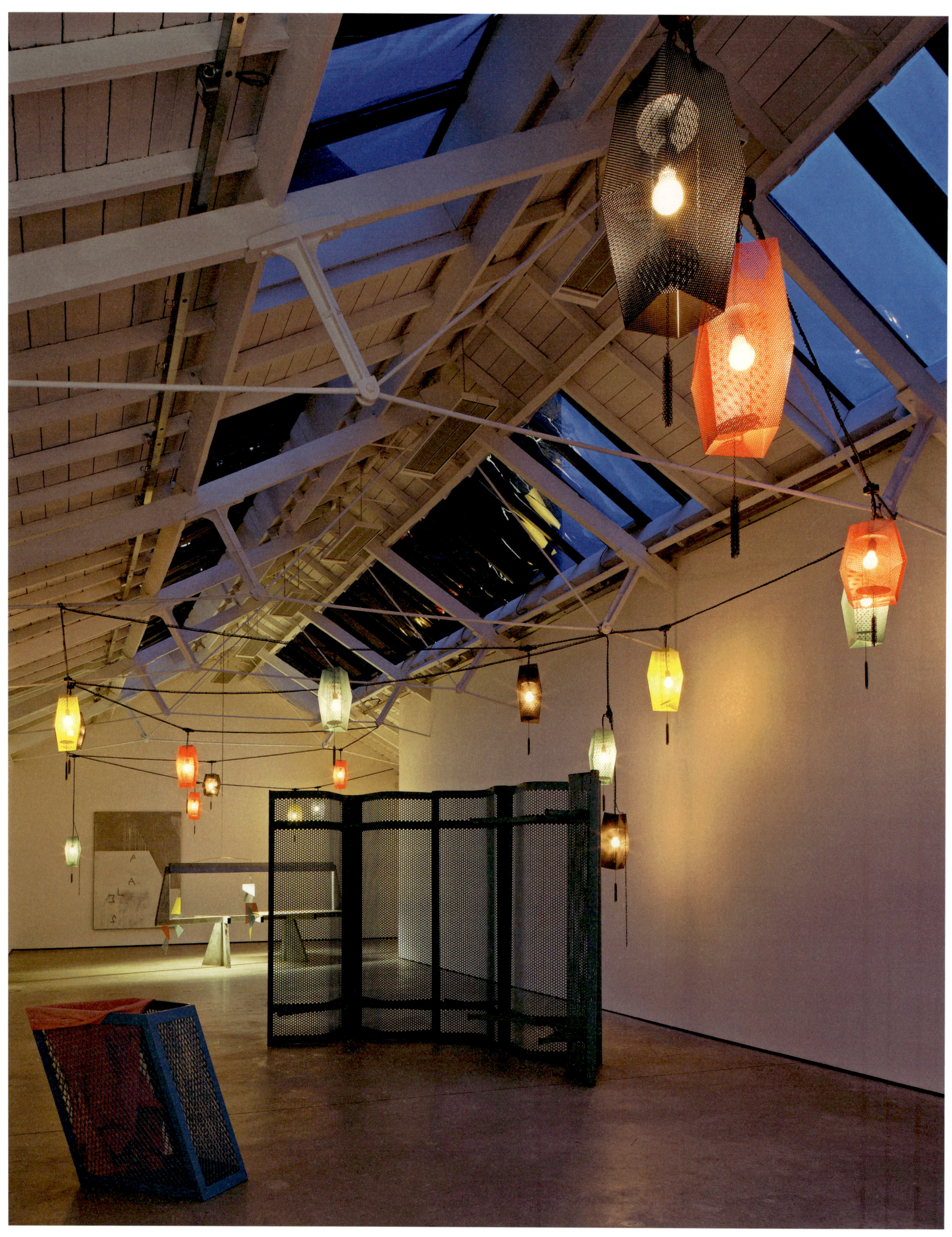

Installationsansicht / Installation view *night terrace – lantern chains – forgotten seas – sky*,
The Modern Institute/Toby Webster Ltd, Glasgow 2011

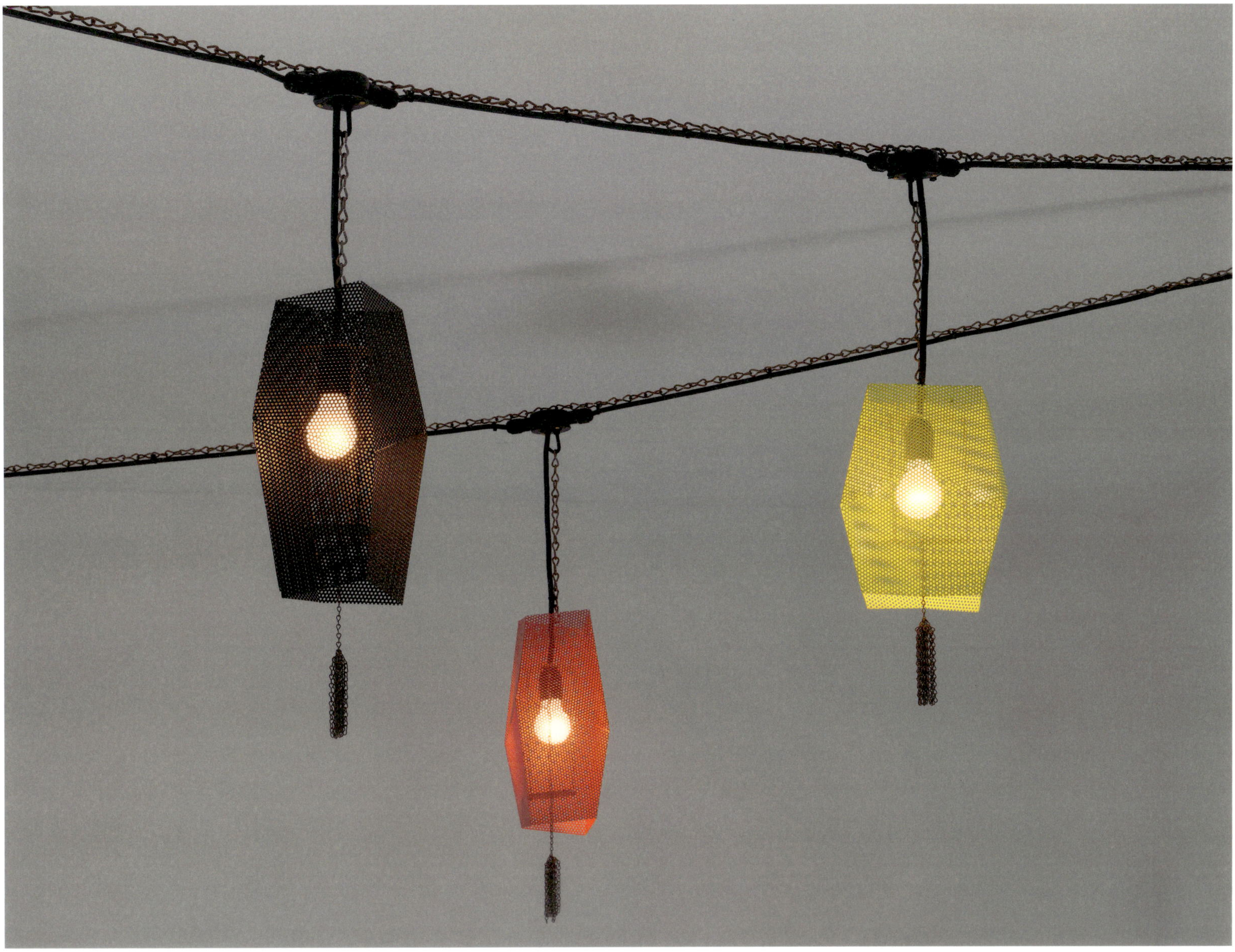

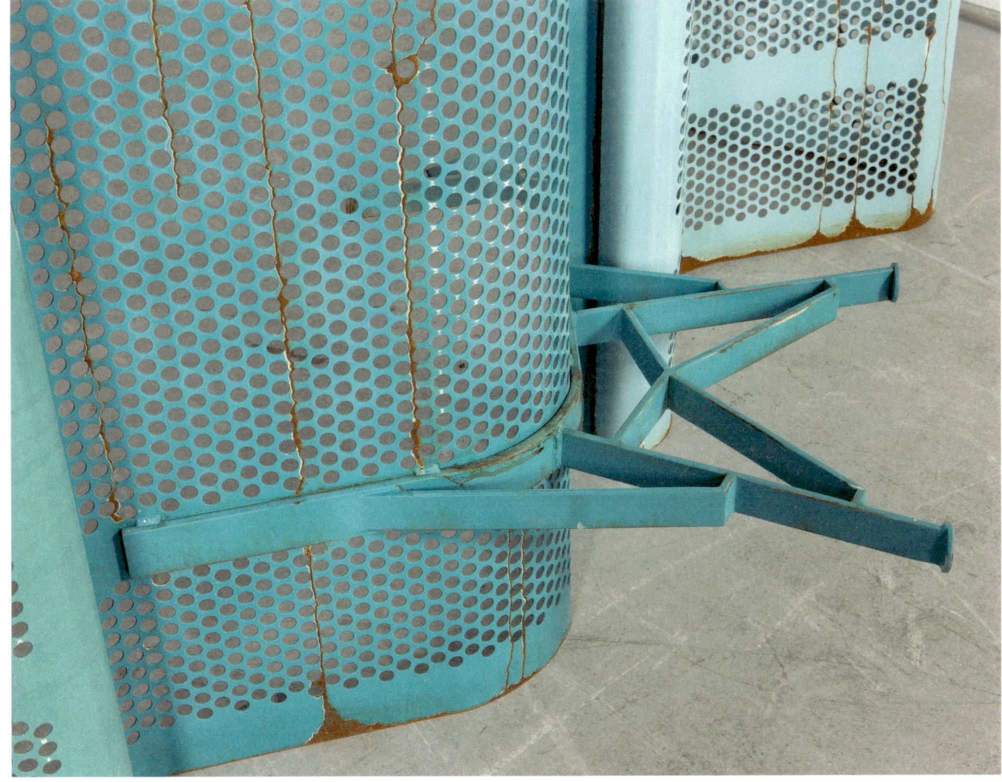

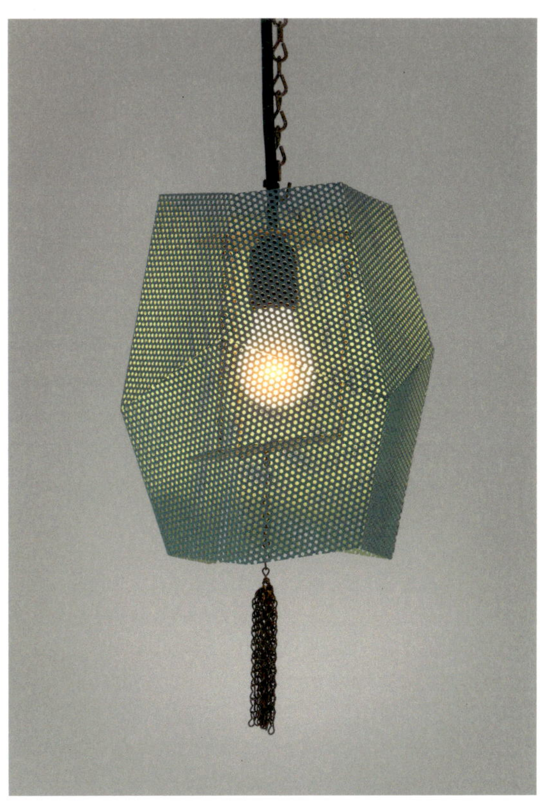

Years and Stars and Storms, 2012 (oben und unten rechts / top and bottom right)
The Waves, 2011 (unten links / bottom left)

Martin Boyce

Martin Boyce ist vor allem für seine atmosphärisch dichten skulpturalen Installationen bekannt, die Bezüge zur Designgeschichte des 20. Jahrhunderts und zum urbanen Raum verknüpfen und oft auch sparsame poetische Textelemente enthalten. Eine subtile, aber wesentliche Konzentration auf das Detail kennzeichnet seine Installationen, wobei viele seiner Skulpturen unverkennbar vom Mobiliar der Stadtlandschaft abgeleitet sind, etwa von Straßenlaternen, Telefonzellen, Zäunen oder Abfalleimern.

Obwohl seine Werke deutlich an die Kunst und das Design der Moderne angelehnt sind, so zum Beispiel an die heute hoch geschätzten und viel kopierten Designikonen von Charles und Ray Eames oder Jean Prouvé, erscheinen sie oft beschädigt, verblasst oder zerfallen, sind ihres neuen, futuristischen Glanzes und ihres Versprechens einer besseren Welt beraubt. Denn Boyce interessieren gerade die unbeachteten, verlassenen „Nicht-Orte", die dem Verfall, der Verwahrlosung überlassen werden.

Bezüge zum Herbst als Metapher allmählichen Niedergangs und vergangener Pracht durchziehen Boyce' Werk, eines Verblassens oder Schwindens, das seinem Interesse an aufgegebenen Orten entspricht. Das äußert sich in verschiedenen Formen: von Werktiteln über sonnenverbrannte Farben und Materialien bis hin zur Verwendung oder Andeutung von herabgefallenem Laub – und insbesondere in Boyce' Konstruktionen von kargen, baumähnlichen Strukturen. Sie tauchten erstmals in einer zentralen Installation aus dem Jahr 2002 auf, die den Titel *Our Love is Like the Flowers, the Rain, the Sea and the Hours* trug. Darin schuf Boyce zwar keinen ganzen Wald, vielmehr einen Park, bestückt mit stark stilisierten „Bäumen" aus Neonröhren und deren Stahlgehäusen, die an einfachen Ketten von der Decke herabhingen und knapp über dem Boden schwebten. Diese (beleuchteten) Bäume waren innerhalb der gesamten Installation verteilt, zusammen mit einer Reihe von skulpturalen Formen, die Ähnlichkeiten mit Funktionsgegenständen wie Abfalleimern, Bänken, Liegen und Maschendrahtzaun aufwiesen. Wo die Maschendrahtgebilde wie Kürzel für rudimentäre städtische Umzäunungen wirken, evozieren die Bänke eine Art zielloses Nichtstun, während die Licht-Bäume das Ganze in ein künstliches, kaltes Zwielicht tauchen.

Vergleichbare Licht-Bäume und andere baumähnliche Formen kommen bei Boyce seither regelmäßig vor. Sie geben seinen Installationen einen Maßstab und deuten einen Außenraum an, wenn auch nur den begrenzten und kontrollierten Außenraum des städtischen Parks oder Gartens und nicht die raue Wildnis, sagt Boyce doch selbst: „dass ein Garten nicht zur Natur, sondern zur Architektur gehört".[1]

Die Fotografie eines modernistischen Gartens, die Boyce 2005 entdeckte, wurde in den letzten Jahren zu einer wichtigen Quelle für zahlreiche seiner Werke. Die Aufnahme zeigt eine Gartenkulisse mit vier stark stilisierten Bäumen aus Beton, die Jan und Joël Martel 1925 für einen Garten auf der *Exposition Internationale des Arts Décoratifs et Industriels Modernes* in Paris entwarfen. Sie sind eher geometrisch als organisch und bestehen vollständig aus glatten Flächen und geraden Linien: Zwei hohe, schmale Streifen durchkreuzen sich im rechten Winkel zum „Stamm", an dessen Spitze eine Ansammlung von unterschiedlich geneigten Flächen das Laub bildet. Boyce sah darin „eine perfekte Einheit von Architektur und Natur". Heute finden die Bäume der Martels ihr Echo in vielen daraufhin entstandenen Boyce-Skulpturen, darunter auch solchen, die andere, ausdrücklich funktionale Objekte wie die Dächer von Telefonzellen und Deckenleuchten imitieren. Neben diesen dreidimensionalen Arbeiten hat Boyce das ur-

Martin Boyce is best known for his atmospheric sculptural installations that combine references to both twentieth-century design history and the urban environment, often incorporating sparse, poetic text. His installations are marked by a subtle but significant attention to detail, while many of his sculptures are recognisably derived from the furniture of many a cityscape, such as street lights, phone booths, fencing and litter bins.

Although his work draws substantially on modernism, both in art and design, including the now iconic, highly valued and muchcopied designs of, for example, Charles and Ray Eames or Jean Prouvé, it often appears damaged, faded or degraded, stripped of its shiny, future-focussed newness and promise of a better world. For Boyce is equally if not more concerned with places and spaces of decay, disregard, dereliction and abandonment.

References to autumn permeate Boyce's work, a metaphor of gradual decline, past glory, a fading or diminishing that parallels his interest in abandoned places. It occurs in many forms: from the titles of works, through sun-scorched colours and materials, to the appearance of or allusion to fallen leaves, and notably in Boyce's rendering of sparse, tree-like structures. The first of these appeared in a major installation in 2002, entitled *Our Love is Like the Flowers, the Rain, the Sea and the Hours*. In this Boyce created, if not quite a forest, then at least a park, furnished with highly stylised 'trees' made of fluorescent tube lights and their steel casings, suspended from the ceiling by rudimentary chains, not quite touching the ground. These (illuminated) trees were dispersed throughout the installation, alongside an array of sculptural forms that reference functional objects, such as litter bins, benches, daybeds and chain-link fencing. If the chain-link structures act as a shorthand for rudimentary urban enclosures, the benches evoke a kind of purposeless idling, while the tree/lights infuse the whole with a kind of artificial, cold twilight.

Similar tree/lights and other tree-like forms have appeared repeatedly since, lending both scale and a suggestion of outdoor space to Boyce's installations, albeit the contained and managed outdoors of the urban park or garden, rather than rugged wilderness. As Boyce has said, "the garden does not belong to nature but to architecture".[1]

It was the discovery of a photograph of a modernist garden in 2005 that has come to influence the development of many works in recent years. The photograph showed four highly stylised, concrete trees in a garden setting. The trees were designed by Jan and Joël Martel in 1925 for a garden at the *Exposition Internationale des Arts Décoratifs et Industriels Modernes* in Paris. They are geometric rather than organic, comprised entirely of flat planes and straight lines: two tall, narrow strips intersect to create the 'trunk', atop which sits a cluster of differently angled planes, in what Boyce has described as "a perfect collapse of architecture and nature". The Martels' trees now find an echo in many of Boyce's subsequent sculptures, including those that mimic other, explicitly functional objects, such as phone-booth canopies and ceiling lights. In addition to these three-dimensional works, Boyce has also extended the original design through drawing and re-drawing the trees, rendering them entirely linear and flat, which, through a process of juxtaposition and repetition, generated a regular pattern. It is this two-dimensional pattern – its shapes, angles and distinctive lines – that now appears in an extensive body of work, providing the format for sculptures that suggest gates, screens, window grilles, ventilation grilles and other partitions.

sprüngliche Design auch durch Zeichnungen und Neukonzeptionen der Bäume erweitert, sie gänzlich linear und flach abgebildet und so in einem Prozess von Gegenüberstellung und Wiederholung ein regelmäßiges Muster erzeugt. Diese zweidimensionale Struktur – seine Formen, Winkel und charakteristischen Linien – manifestiert sich heute in einem umfangreichen Schaffenswerk: Sie bildet die Vorlage für Skulpturen, die an Tore, Wandschirme, Fenstergitter, Lüftungsgitter oder andere Trennelemente erinnern.

Aus dieser Struktur hat Boyce inzwischen ein Alphabet entworfen, seine *Concrete Tree Typography* – buchstabenartige Formen, die er herausgelöst hat. Den Ausgangspunkt dazu bildete sein anhaltendes Interesse an Text und Typografie. Sprache spielt schon seit Langem eine Rolle in seinem Werk, ist jedoch, ob als Zitat[2] oder als Neuformulierung, zunehmend in den Mittelpunkt gerückt. Wie andernorts bemerkt wurde, kommt Text sowohl in Boyce' Titeln als auch in den Werken selbst in einer Art zum Einsatz, dass „sich kaum zwischen entwendeten Originalen und eigens angefertigten Kopien unterscheiden"[3] lässt.

Die von ihm begründete Typografie verwendet Boyce heute zur Erstellung kurzer Texte in vielfältiger Form: in Drucken, auf Gemäldeoberflächen und für Messingbeschriftungen, die direkt auf die Wand montiert werden. Boyce' Arbeit für die *Skulptur Projekte Münster* im Jahr 2007 beispielsweise bestand aus Steinplatten, die als Einzelelemente musterartig zusammengesetzt ein großes Betonplateau bildeten. Ausgewählte Fugen zwischen den Platten wurden mit Messingeinlagen versehen, die zusammen den Satz *We Are Still and Reflective* ergaben. Auch Boyce' Werk für den schottischen Beitrag zur Biennale von Venedig 2009 enthielt Text. In seiner Ausstellung mit dem Titel *No Reflections* zog sich in einem Raum der Messingschriftzug „Petrified Songs" (Versteinerte Lieder) über zwei Wände, während an anderer Stelle ein großformatiger Siebdruck die Worte „No Brilliantly Coloured Birds" (Keine bunt schillernden Vögel) trug. In diesen und vielen anderen Werken verläuft die Schrift aber vertikal anstatt horizontal, also von oben nach unten – eine Verschiebung, die das Fallen von Blättern anzudeuten vermag und an die Bäume erinnert, von denen die Formen ursprünglich abstammen. Die Buchstaben liegen meist auf der Seite, ihre Reihenfolge erschließt sich nicht unmittelbar, was das Entziffern der Worte selbst erschwert. Sie sind Texten jedoch ähnlich genug und gerade so weit als Sprache zu erkennen, dass der Drang, zu lesen anstatt nur zu betrachten, nicht zu unterdrücken ist. Die Sprache selbst und ihre Fähigkeit, Bedeutung zu generieren, scheinen sich aufzulösen.

Zu der Ausstellung in Venedig gehörte auch ein Raum mit großen, flachen Betonformen, die ebenfalls von Boyce' Strukturelementen abgeleitet worden waren und, an Trittsteine erinnernd, eine Art Garten im Innenraum bildeten. Diese „Steine" wurden von einer weiteren Arbeit begleitet, die sich durch alle Räume zog: Es waren verstreute Blätter – Formen aus braunem, mit Paraffin beschichtetem Krepppapier, ausgeschnitten, stilisiert und kantig wie die Betonbäume in jenem Pariser Garten, die bis heute unvermindert in Boyce' Arbeiten nachhallen.

From within this pattern, Boyce has since created an alphabet: letterforms picked out in the pattern he had created, his *Concrete Tree Typography*. That he should do so is an extension of an enduring interest in both text and typography. Language has long played its part in Boyce's work, though it has increasingly moved to the centre, whether in quotation[2] or newly composed phrases. As one writer has noted, text is used both in his titles and in the works themselves "in a manner not dissimilar to the oscillation between the use of purloined originals and fabricated copies in the sculptures".[3]

The typography he established is now used to create short texts in multiple forms: in prints, on the surface of paintings and in brass lettering that is attached directly to the wall. Boyce's work for the 2007 *Skulptur Projekte Münster*, for example, created a large concrete plateau comprised of slabs formed to the pattern, with a text picked out in the spaces between the slabs by means of occasional brass inlays (the text reads *We Are Still and Reflective*). Text also featured in Boyce's 2009 exhibition for the Scottish project at the Venice Biennale. In an exhibition entitled *No Reflections*, one room was adorned with brass lettering that read "Petrified Songs", the lettering running over two walls, while elsewhere a large screenprint bore the words "No Brilliantly Coloured Birds". In these and many other works, the words run vertically rather than horizontally, and from top to bottom, a shift that tends to suggest falling leaves, and recall the trees from which the forms originate. The letters lie mostly on their sides, the sequence not immediately apparent, making the words themselves difficult to discern. They are, however, sufficiently text-like, just recognisable as language, which means the urge to read, rather than simply look, is undeniable. Language and its capacity for generating meaning seems itself to be disintegrating.

The exhibition in Venice included a room of large, low concrete forms, like stepping stones, their forms again derived from Boyce's pattern, creating a kind of indoor garden. These 'stones' were accompanied by another work, one that disperses throughout the spaces in which it is shown. It takes the form of a scattering of leaves: shapes cut from brown, paraffin-coated crêpe paper, stylised and angular just like those concrete trees in the garden in Paris, which continue to resonate.

1   Ein Gespräch zwischen Martin Boyce und Christian Ganzenberg, in: Renate Wiehager und Christian Ganzenberg (Hrsg.), *Martin Boyce*, Köln 2012, S. 66.
2   Boyce' Werktitel *Our Love is Like the Flowers, the Rain, the Sea and the Hours* zum Beispiel ist ein Zitat aus einem Lied der englischen New-Wave-Band New Order (*The Village*, 1983).
3   Caoimhín Mac Giolla Léith, „Permanente Dämmerung: Das Nachleben der Formen", in: *Martin Boyce*, Zürich 2009, S. 121.

1   Martin Boyce, in an interview with Christian Ganzenberg, in Renate Wiehager and Christian Ganzenberg/Daimler Art Collection (eds.), *Martin Boyce* (Cologne: Snoeck, 2012), p. 56.
2   *Our Love is Like the Flowers, the Rain, the Sea and the Hours* is, for example, a lyric in a song by New Order (*The Village*, 1983)
3   Caoimhín Mac Giolla Léith, 'Permanent Dusk: The Afterlife of Forms', in *Martin Boyce* (Zurich: JRP|Ringier, 2009), p. 121.

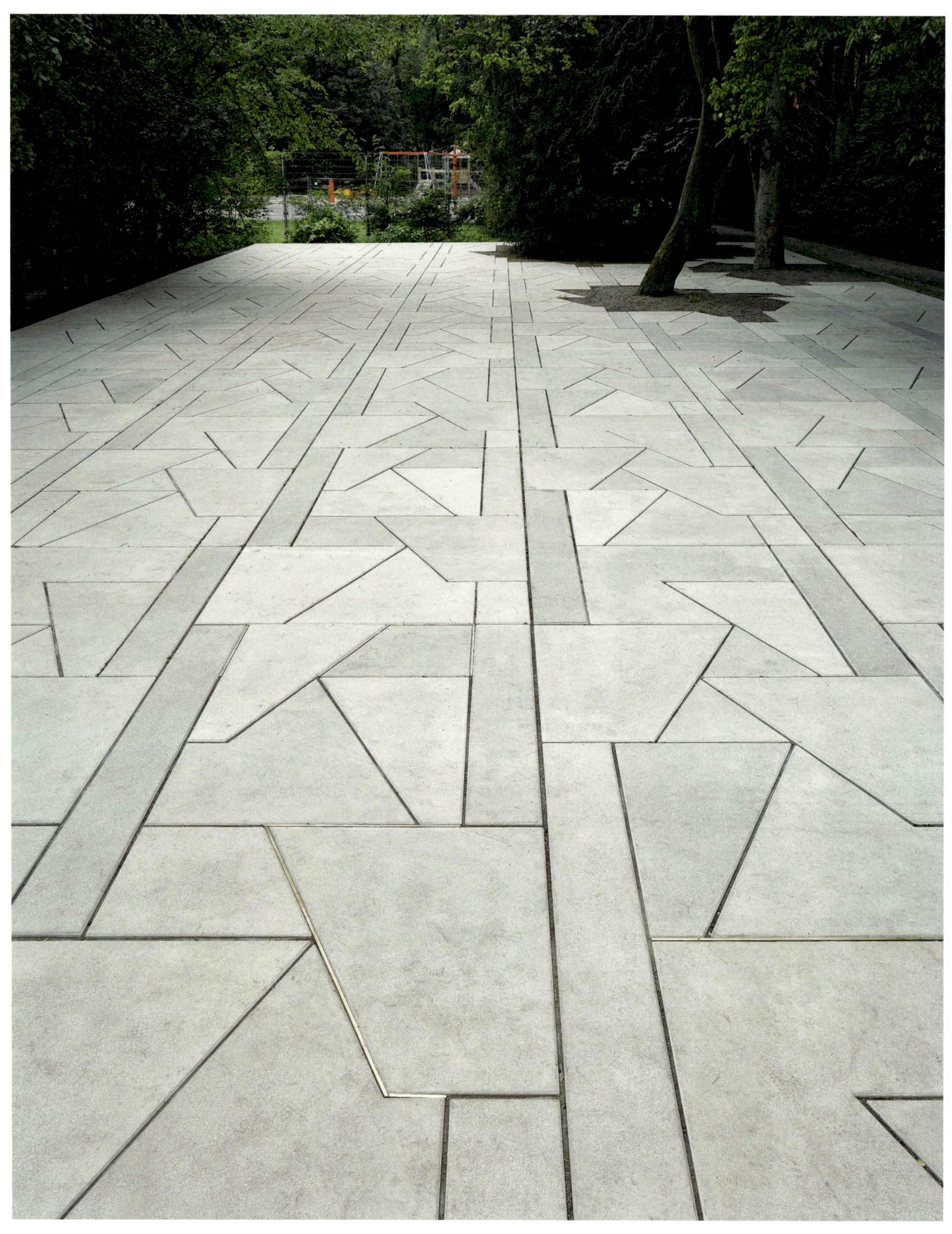

We Are Still and Reflective, 2007, Ausstellung / Exhibition *Skulptur Projekte Münster*, Westfälisches Landesmuseum, Münster 2007,
Sammlung / Collection LWL-Museum für Kunst und Kultur. Westfälisches Landesmuseum, Münster

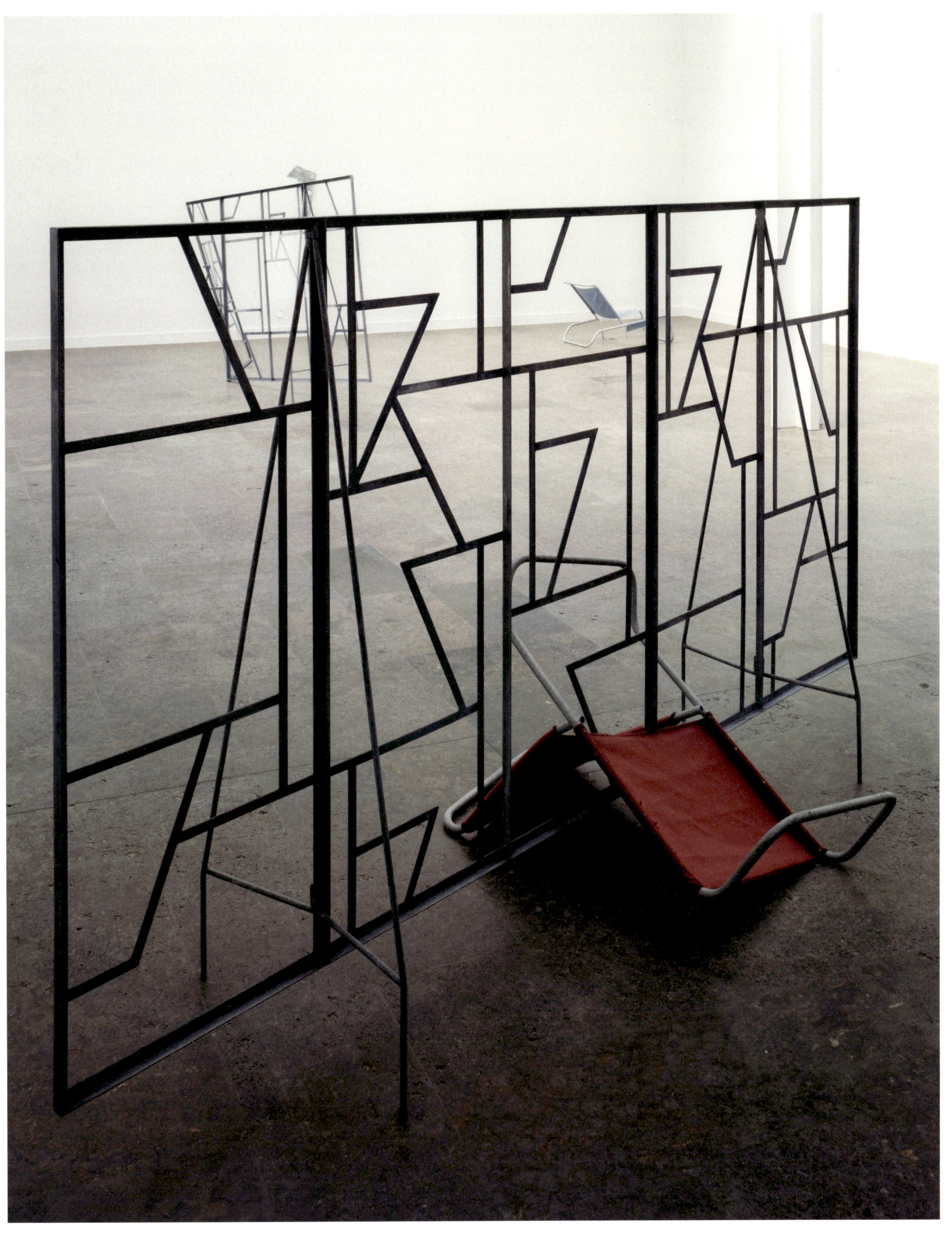

The After and The Before, 2008, Installationsansicht / Installation view *This Place is Close and Unfolded*,
Westfälischer Kunstverein, Münster 2008

Martin Boyce 75

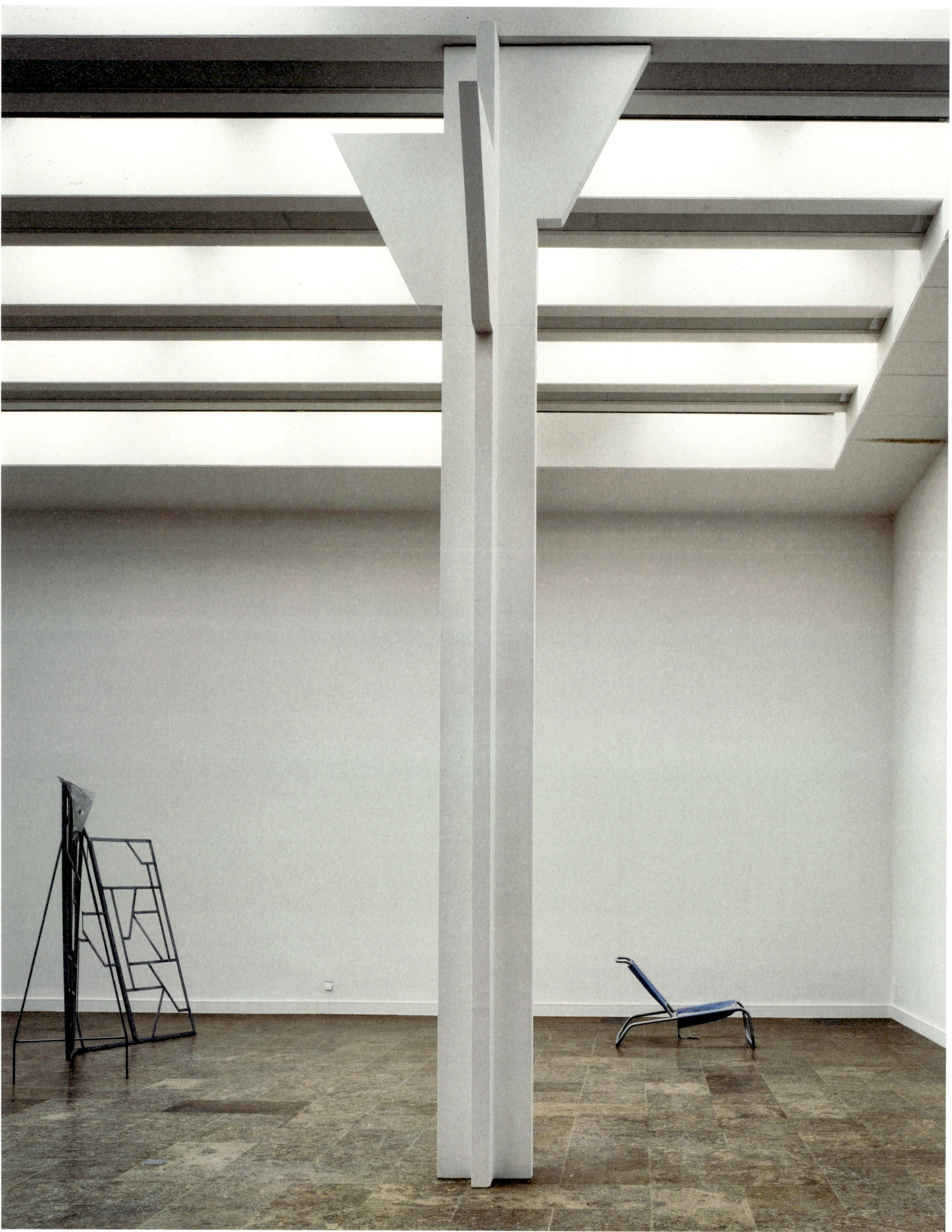

 Installationsansicht / Installation view *This Place is Close and Unfolded*, Westfälischer Kunstverein, Münster 2008

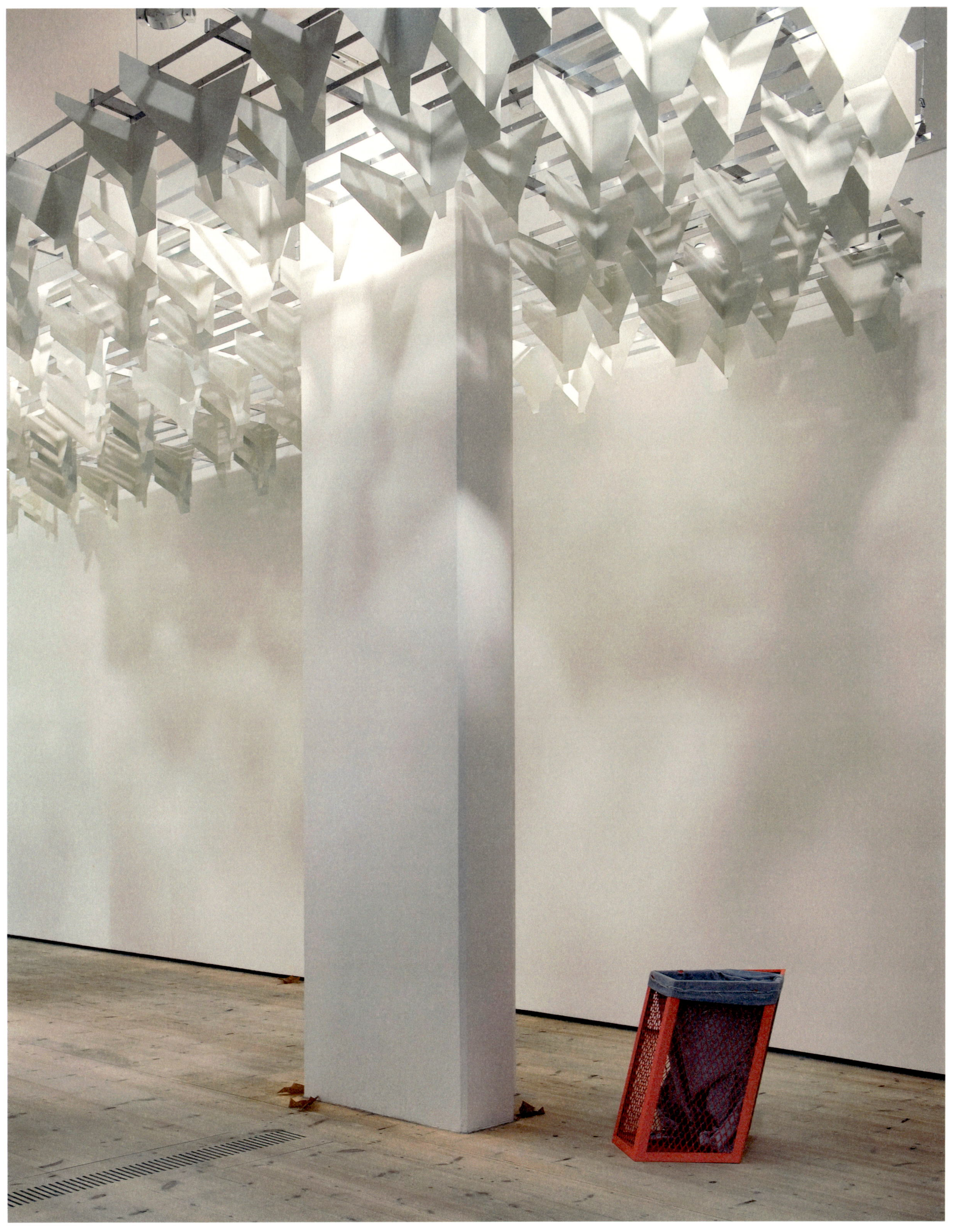

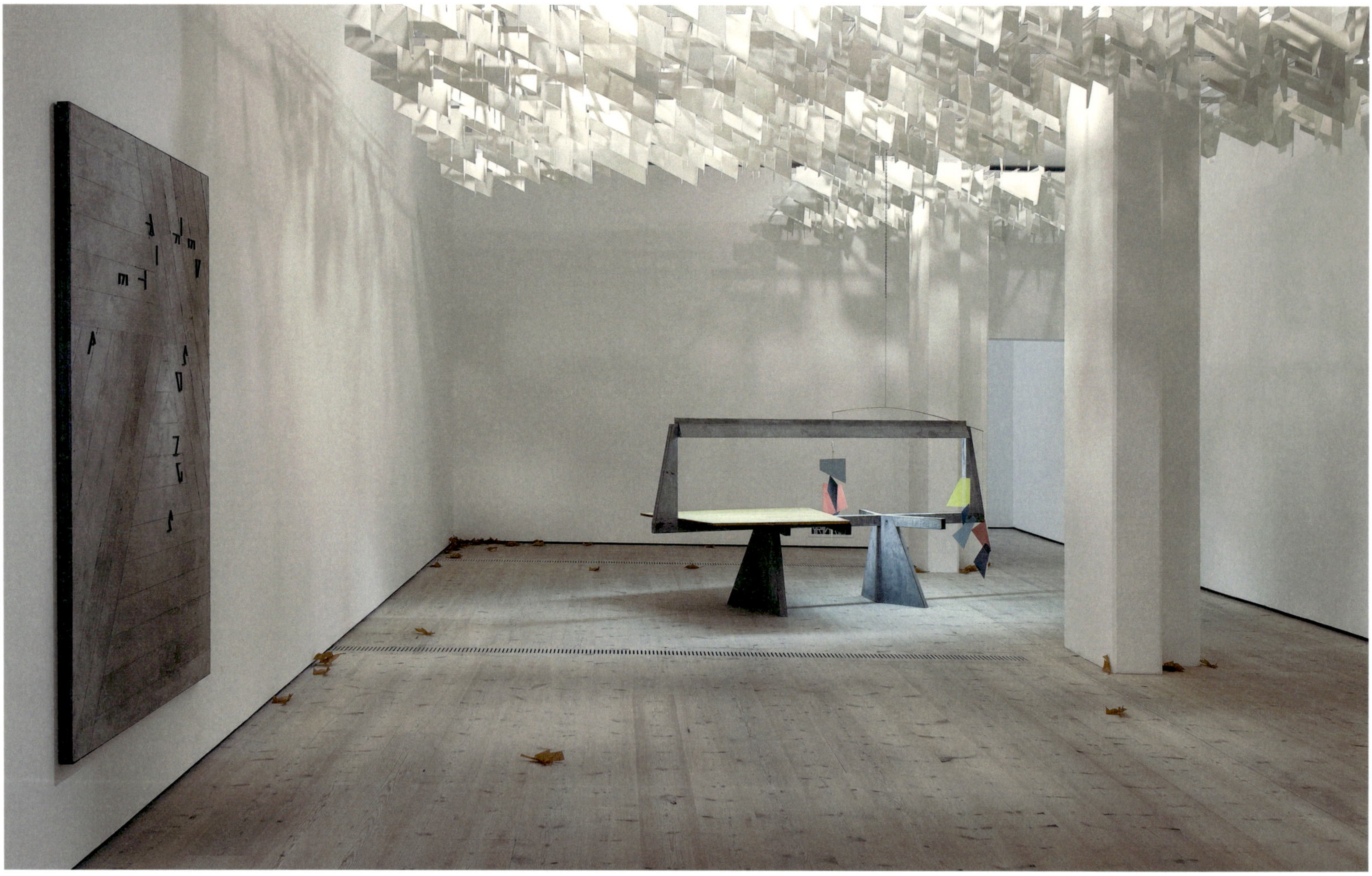

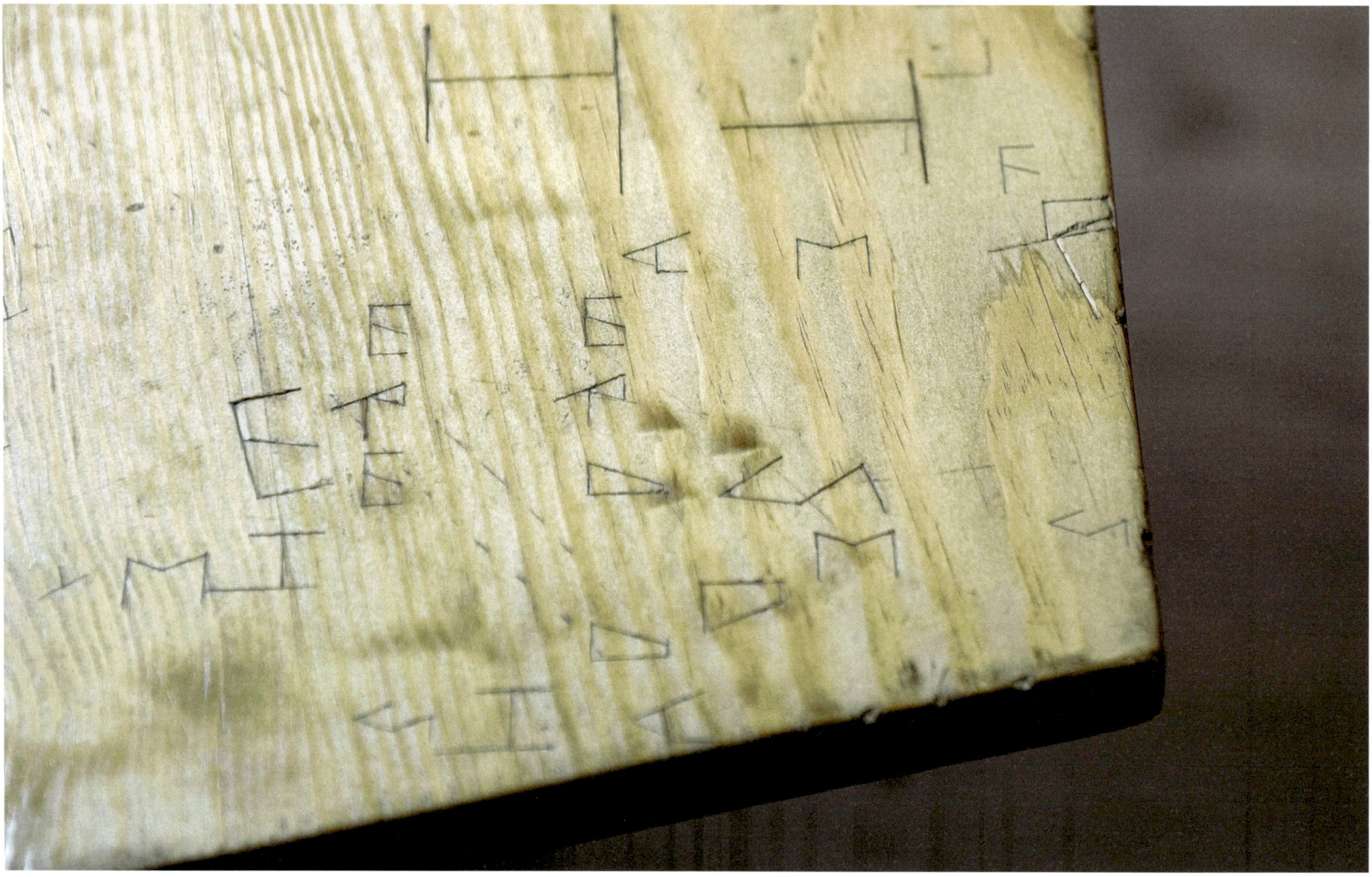

Installationsansicht / Installation view *Turner Prize 2011*, Baltic Centre for Contemporary Art, Gateshead 2011 (oben / top)
Do Words Have Voices, 2011 (Ausschnitt / detail, unten / bottom)

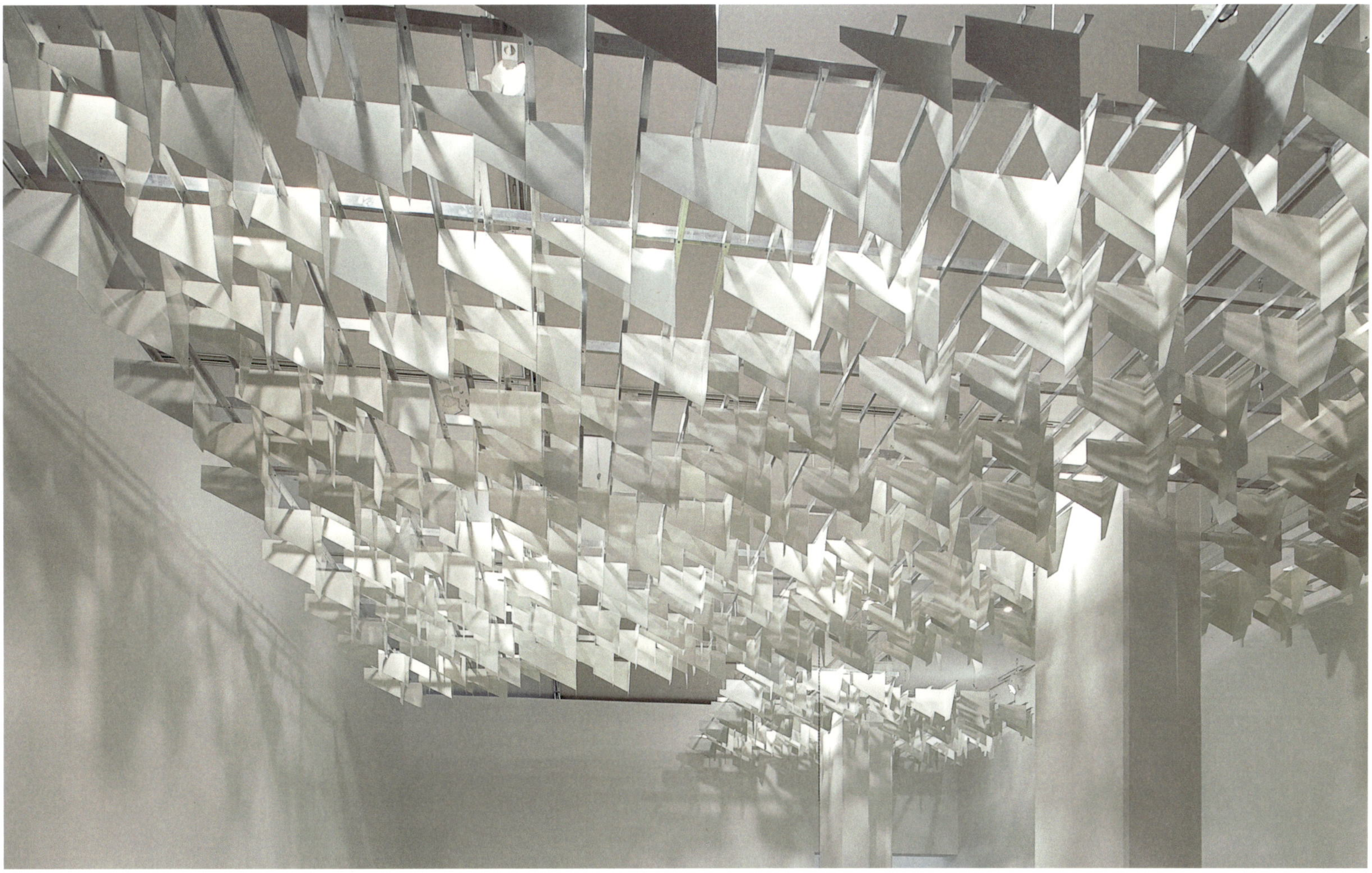

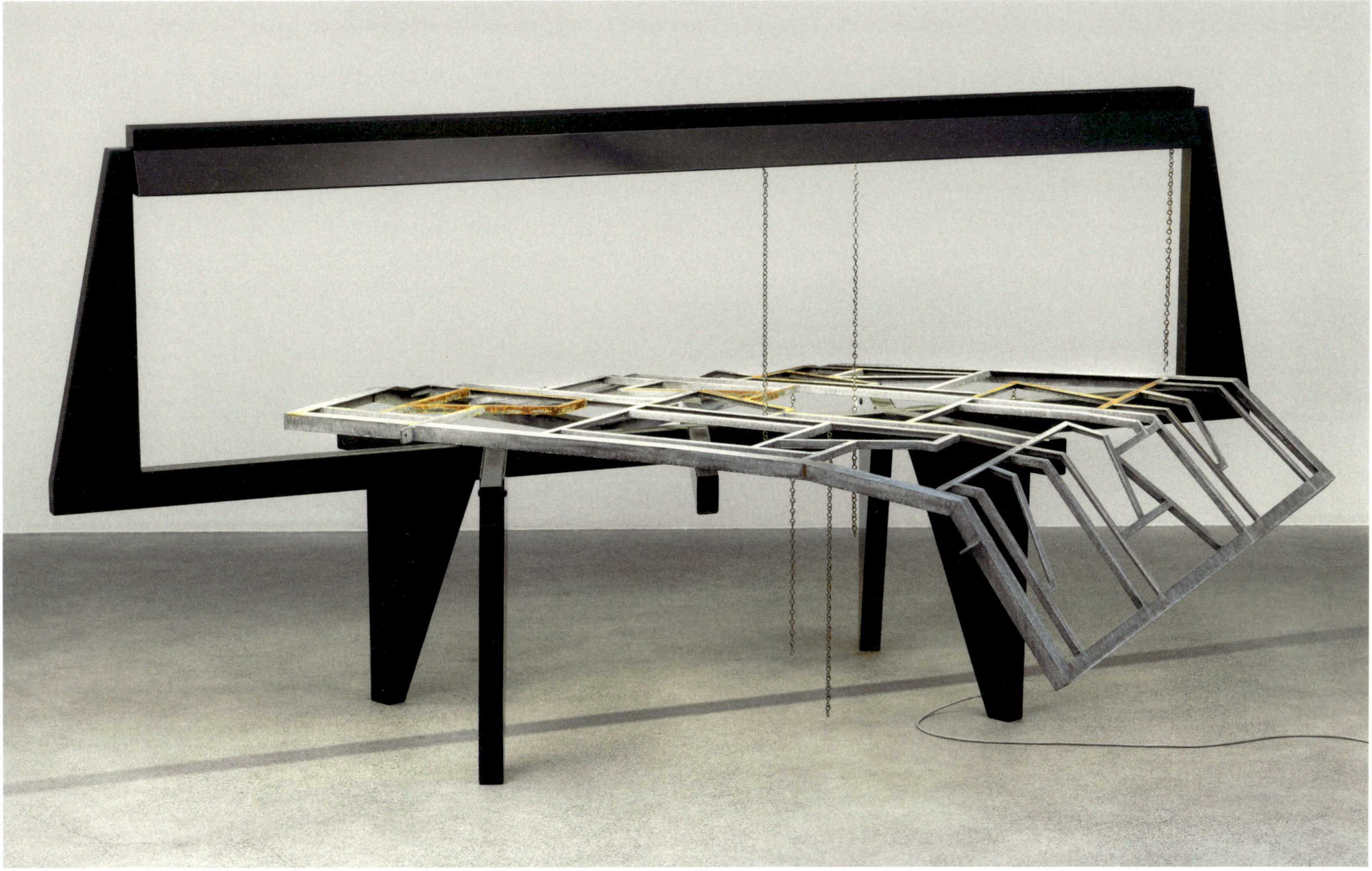

Beyond the Repetition of High Windows, Intersecting Flight Paths and Opinions (A Silent Storm is Painted on the Air), 2011, Installationsansicht /
Installation view *Turner Prize 2011*, Baltic Centre for Contemporary Art, Gateshead 2011 (oben / top) · *Open (The End)*, 2010, Installationsansicht /
Installation view *A Library of Leaves*, Galerie Eva Presenhuber, Zürich / Zurich 2010, Fondazione Sandretto Re Rebaudengo, Turin (unten / bottom)   **Martin Boyce**   79

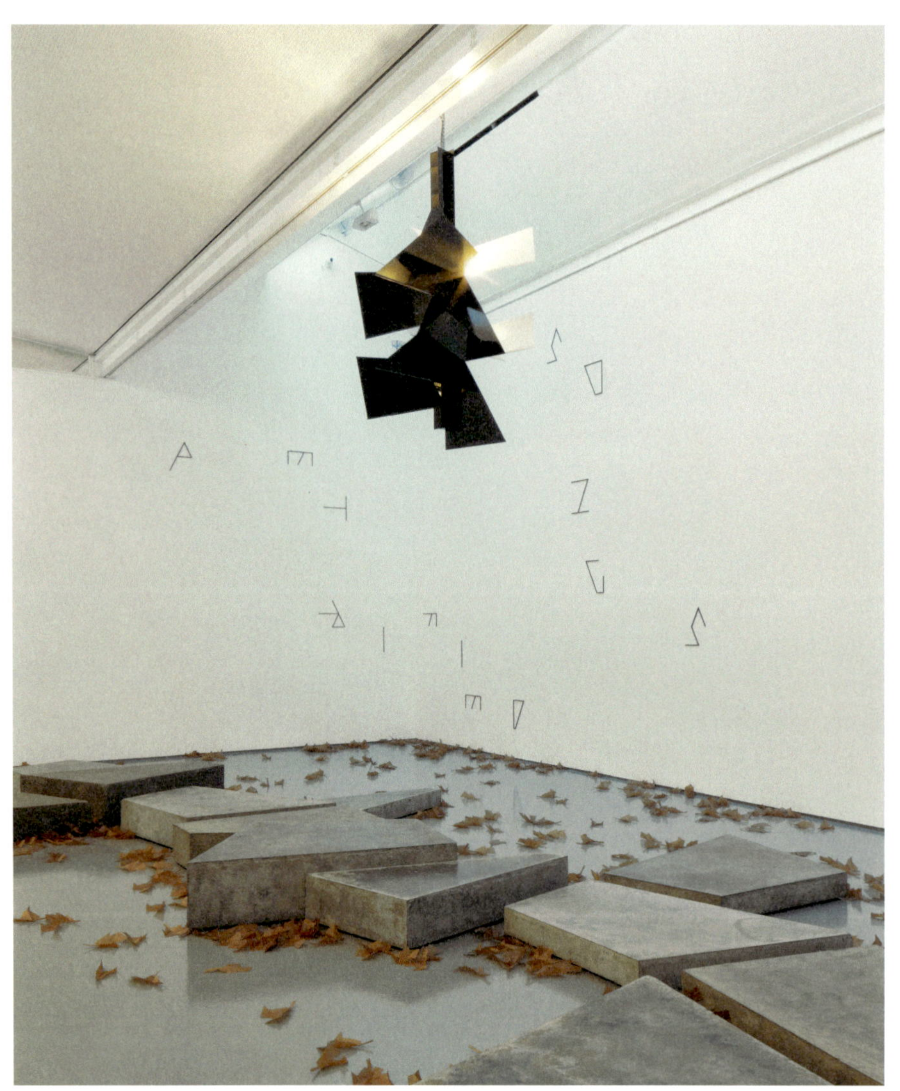
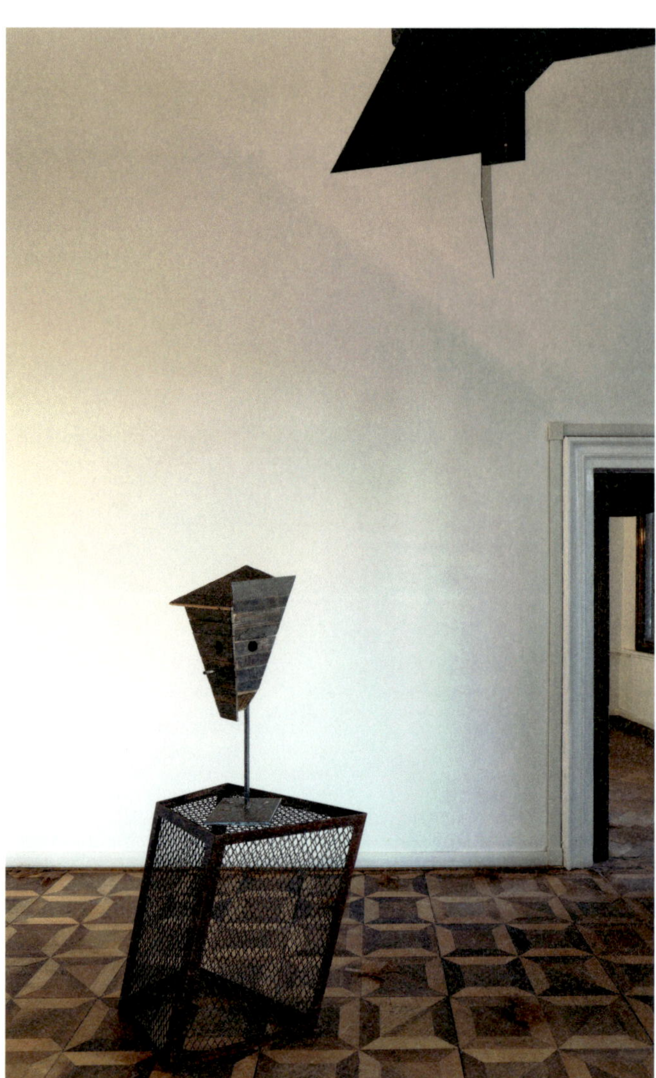

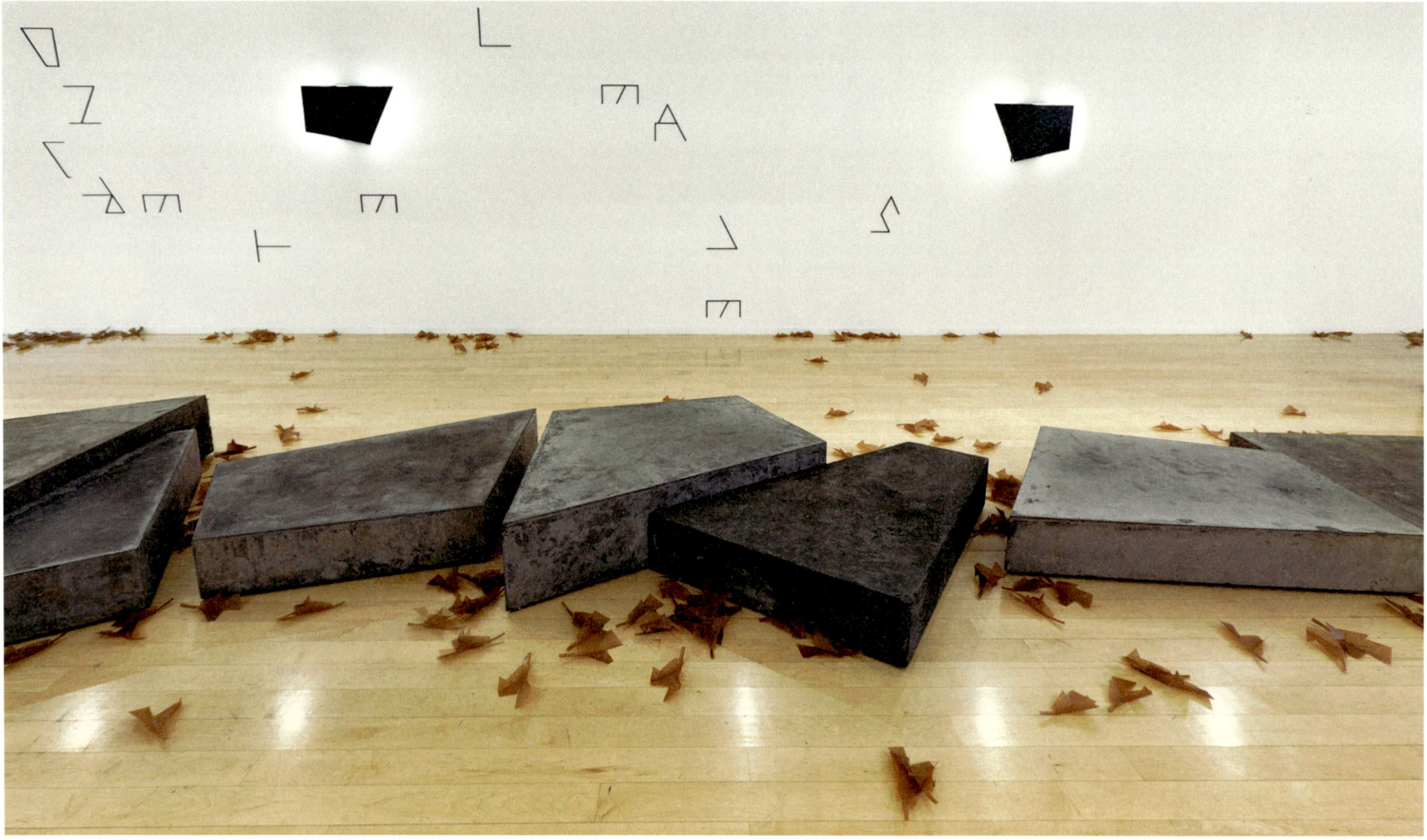

Installationsansicht / Installation view *No Reflections*, 2009, Scotland + Venice, Dundee Contemporary Arts, Dundee 2009 (oben links / top left) · *There are Places*, 2009, Installationsansicht / Installation view *No Reflections*, Scotland + Venice, Palazzo Pisani, Biennale Venedig / Venice Biennale, Venedig / Venice 2009, Collection Köser, Köln / Cologne (oben rechts / top right) · Installationsansicht / Installation view *Conceptual Tendencies*, Daimler Contemporary, Berlin 2011 (unten / bottom)

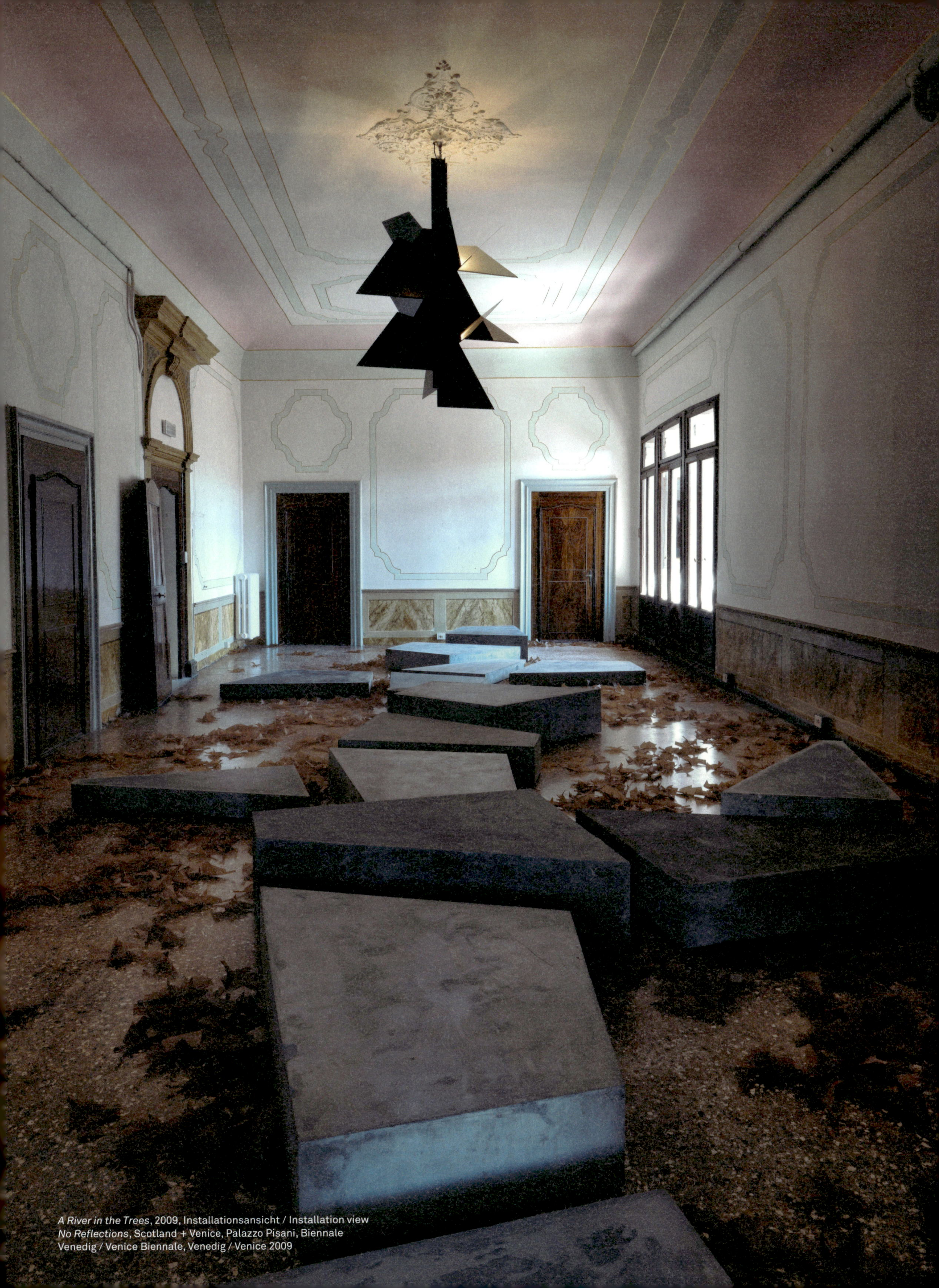

A River in the Trees, 2009, Installationsansicht / Installation view
No Reflections, Scotland + Venice, Palazzo Pisani, Biennale
Venedig / Venice Biennale, Venedig / Venice 2009

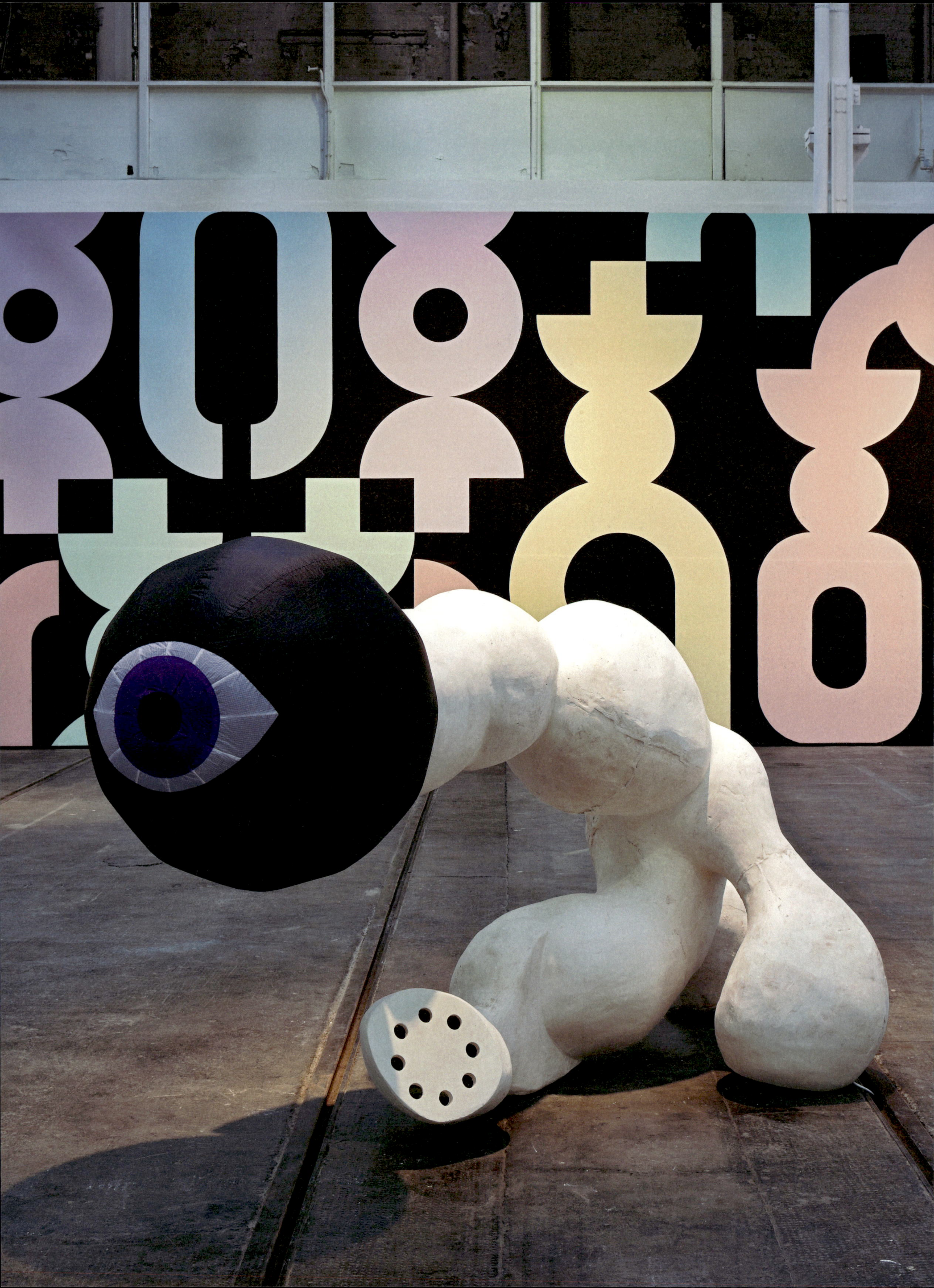

Black Eye, 2013, Installationsansicht /
Installation view *Solar Eyes*, Tramway,
Glasgow 2013

Biografie / Biography

Nick Evans lebt und arbeitet / lives and works
in Glasgow, Schottland / Scotland
1976   geboren / born in Mufulira, Sambia / Zambia

Studium / Education
1997   Foundation Studies in Art and Design, Yeovil College,
    Somerset
1999   Royal College of Fine Arts, Stockholm
2000   Bachelor of Fine Art (Fine Art, Sculpture, Environmental
    Art), Glasgow School of Art, Glasgow

Stipendien und Preise / Scholarships and Awards
2008   Residency, European Ceramic Work Centre,
    's-Hertogenbosch
2011   Artists' Fellowship Programme, Scottish National Gallery
    of Modern Art and Creative Scotland, Edinburgh

Ausgewählte Ausstellungen / Selected Exhibitions
„Nick Evans. Lumumba is Dead", Transmission Gallery,
Glasgow (2002)
„Nick Evans. Abstract Machines", Tate St Ives (2006)
„Nick Evans. Rational Slab", Mary Mary, Glasgow (2007)
„Nick Evans. Primary School", Inverleith House, Edinburgh (2008)
„Zwischenraum: Space Between", Kunstverein Hamburg (2010)
„You, Me, Something Else", Gallery of Modern Art, Glasgow (2011)
„Nick Evans. Flesh and Bones", Liste 16, Basel (2011)
„Nick Evans. Oceania", Scottish National Gallery of Modern Art,
Edinburgh (2012)
„Nick Evans. Solar Eyes", Tramway, Glasgow (2013)

Ausgewählte Publikationen / Selected Publications
„Nick Evans. Abstract Machines", Ausst.-Kat. / exh. cat.
Tate St Ives 2006

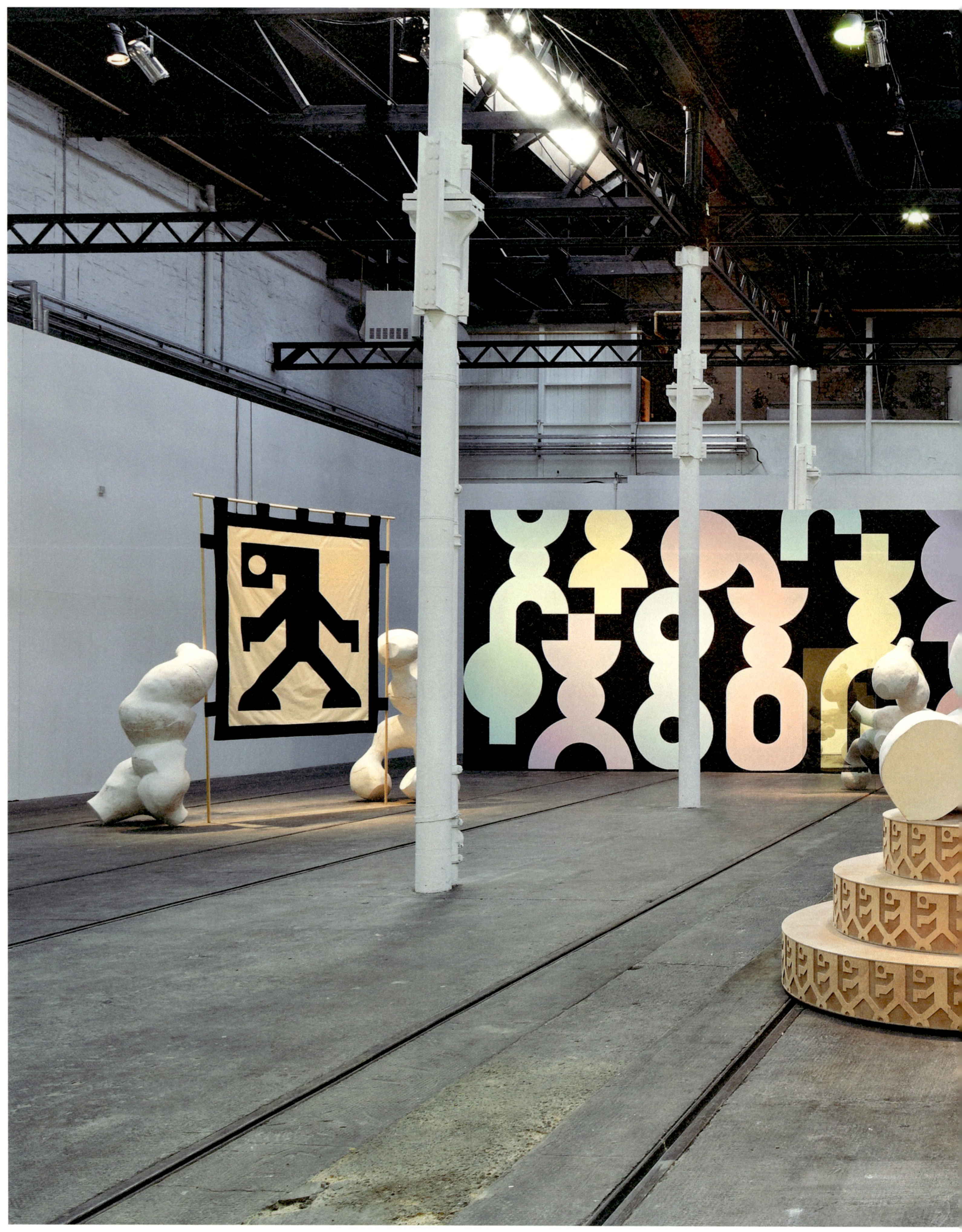

  Installationsansicht / Installation view *Solar Eyes*, Tramway, Glasgow 2013

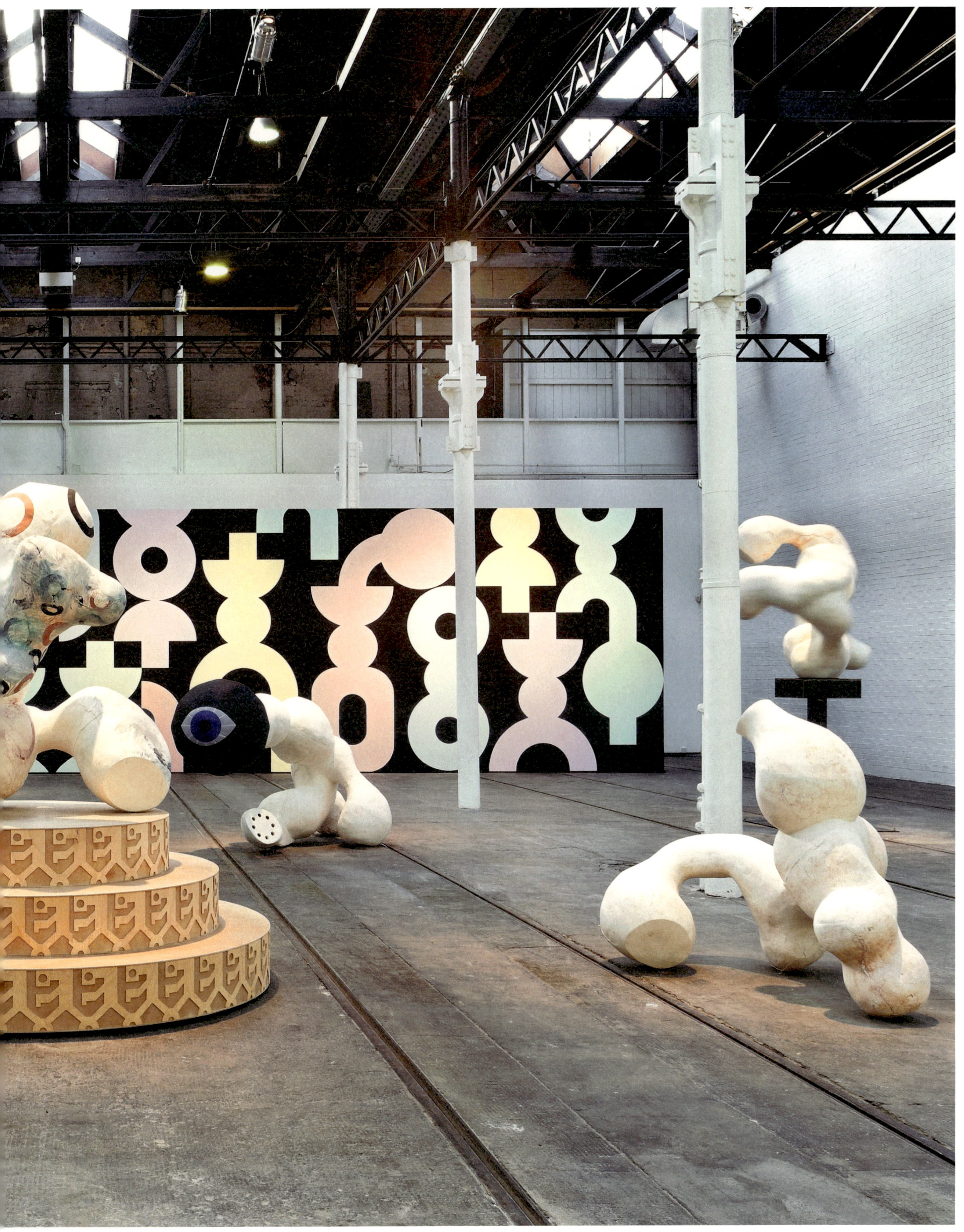

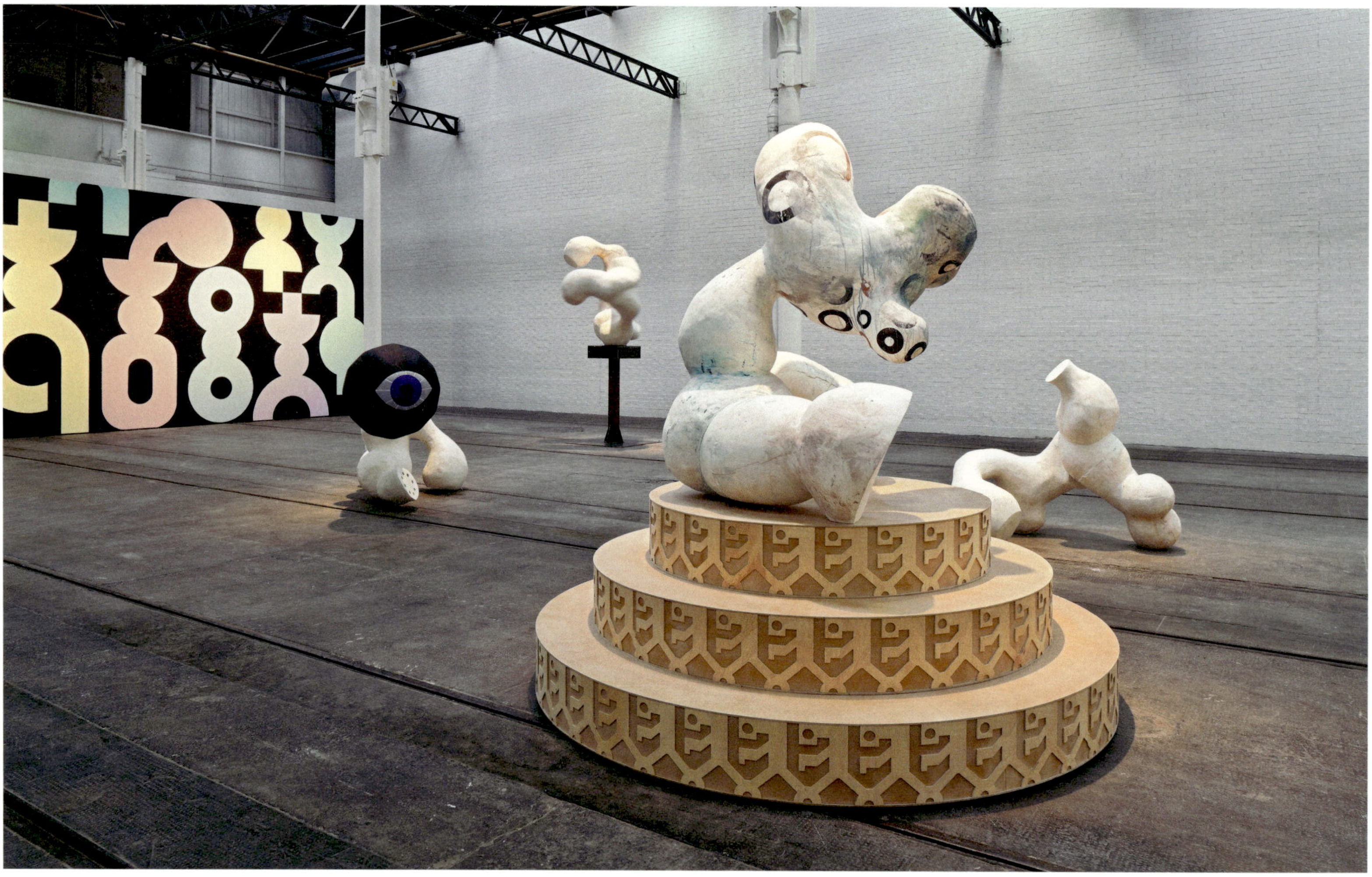

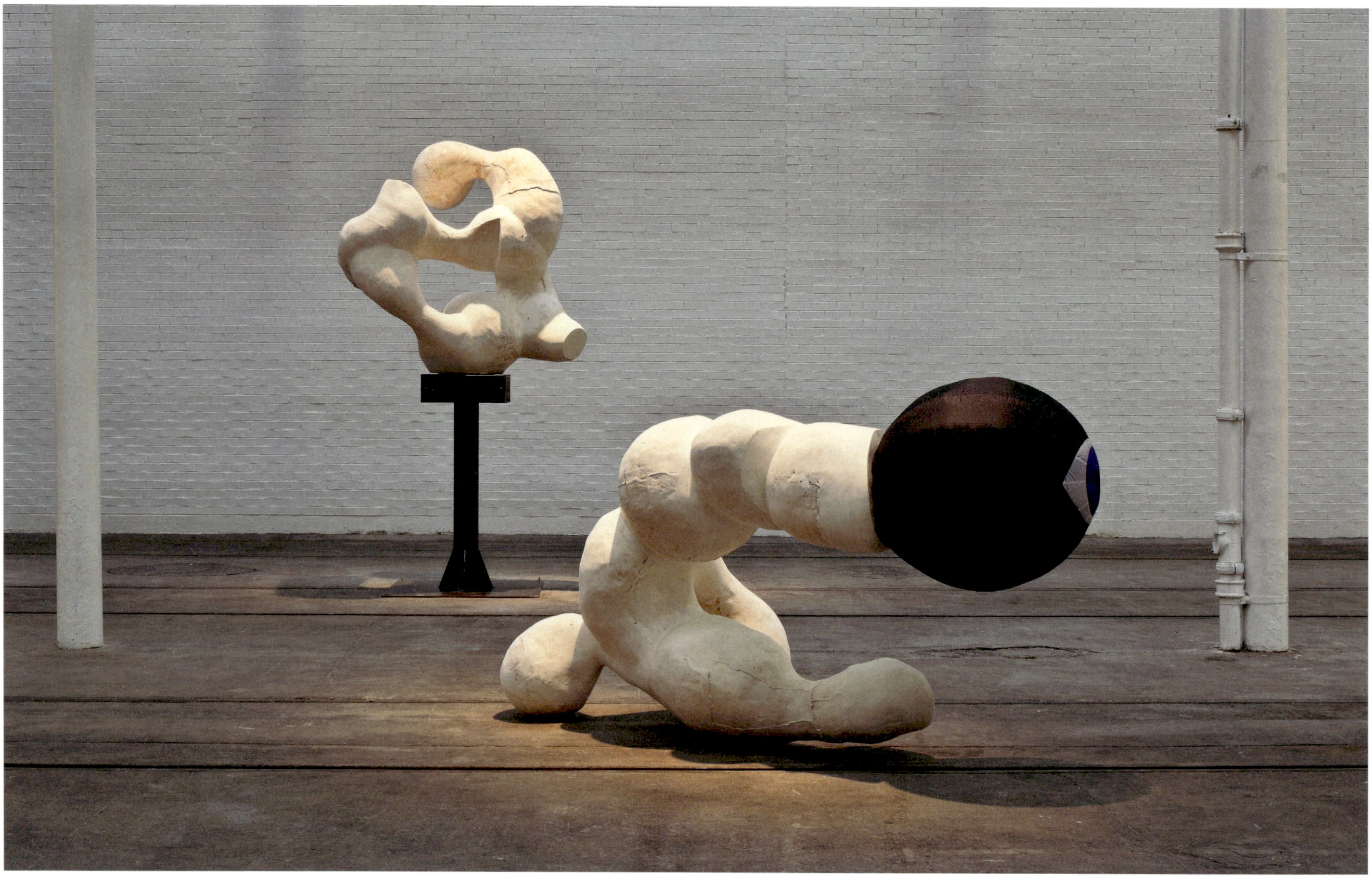

Black Eye, 2013, *Unseeing Eye*, 2013, *Mother*, 2013, *The Ox*, 2013, Installationsansicht / Installation view *Solar Eyes*, Tramway, Glasgow 2013 (oben / top)
Unseeing Eye, 2013, *Black Eye*, 2013, Installationsansicht / Installation view *Solar Eyes*, Tramway, Glasgow 2013 (unten / bottom)

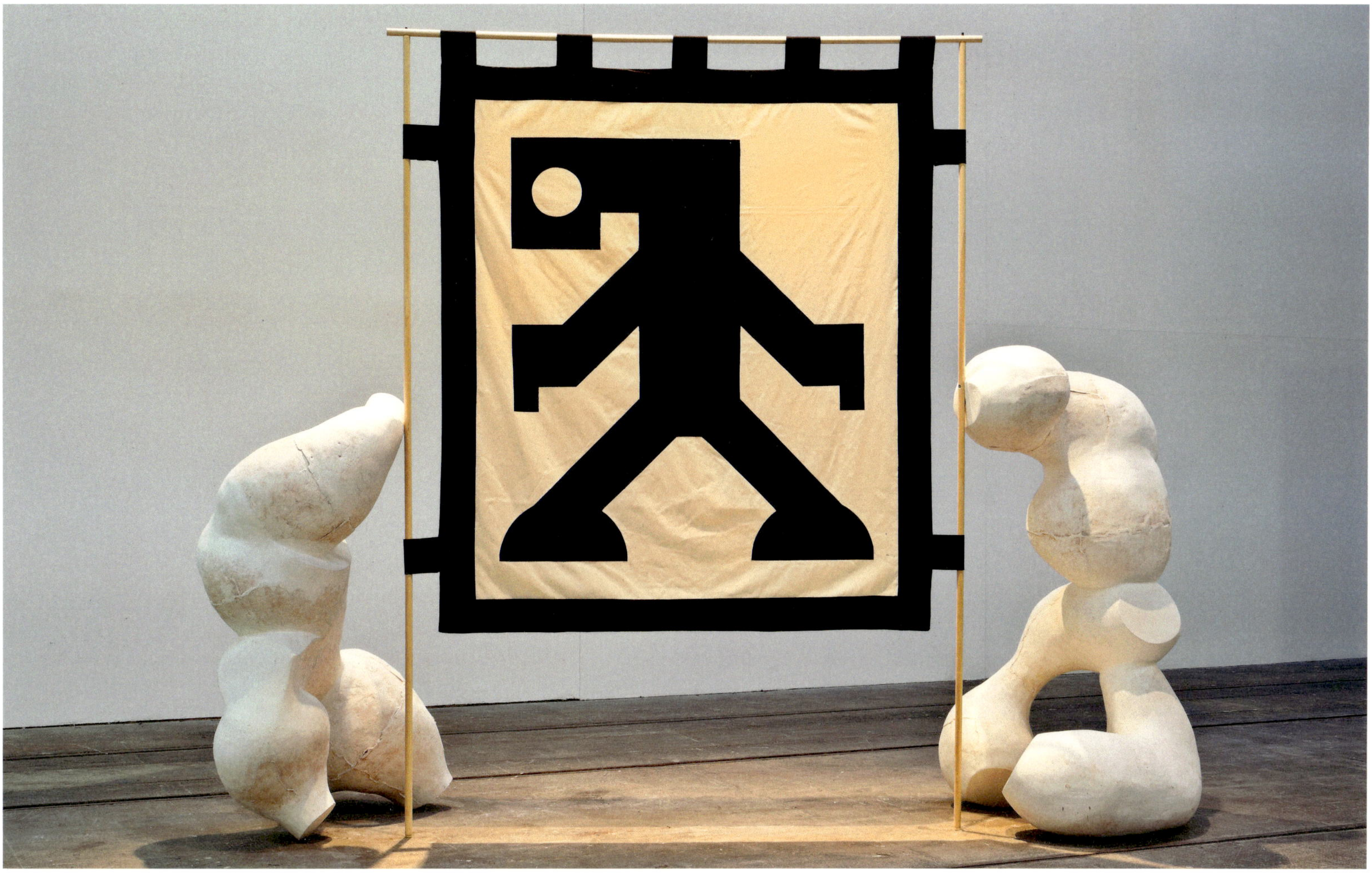

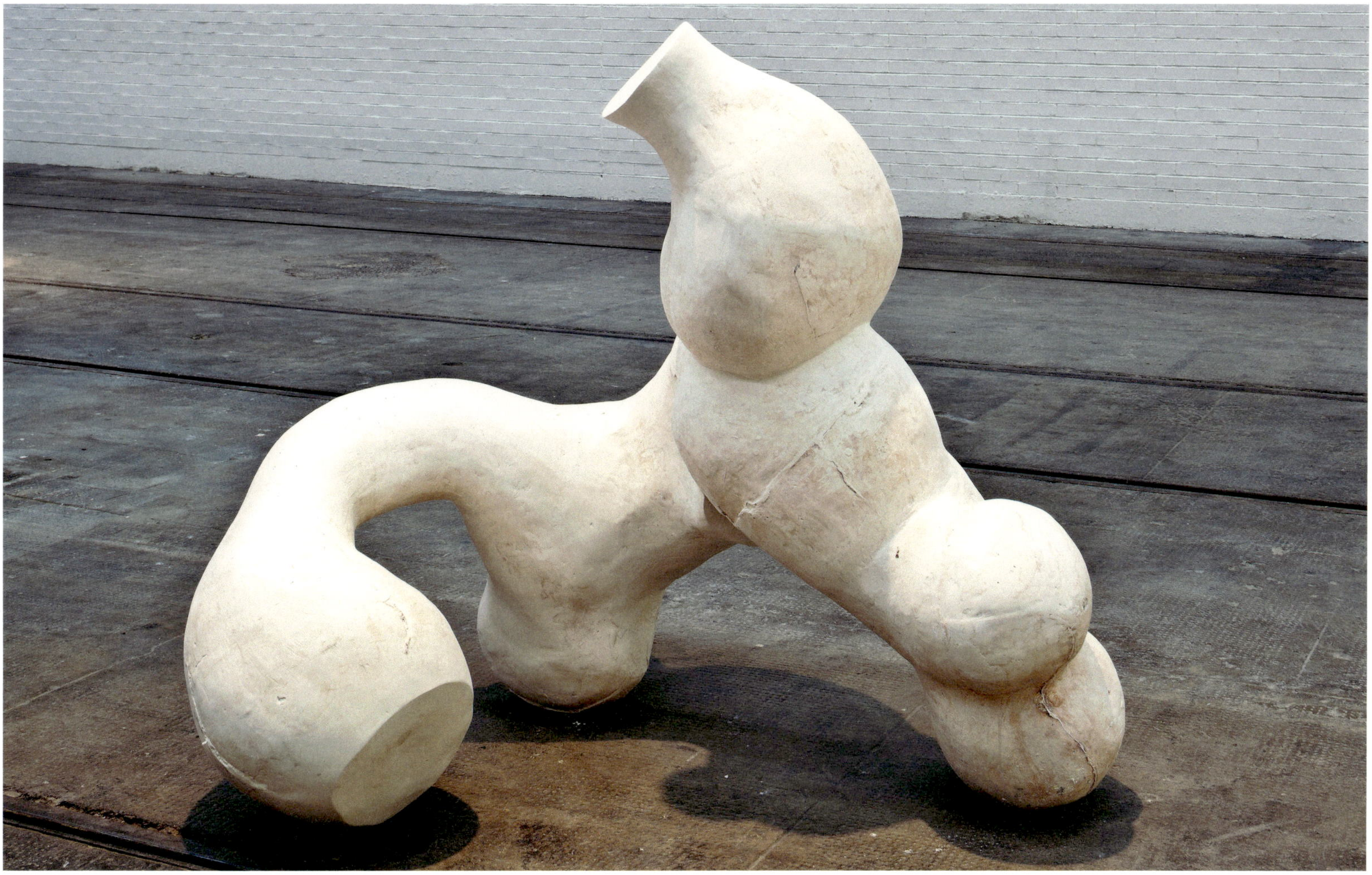

Nothing to do, Nowhere to go, Nothing to be, No-one to know, 2013, Installationsansicht / Installation view *Solar Eyes*, Tramway, Glasgow 2013 (oben / top) · *The Ox*, 2013, Installationsansicht / Installation view *Solar Eyes*, Tramway, Glasgow 2013 (unten / bottom)

Nick Evans 87

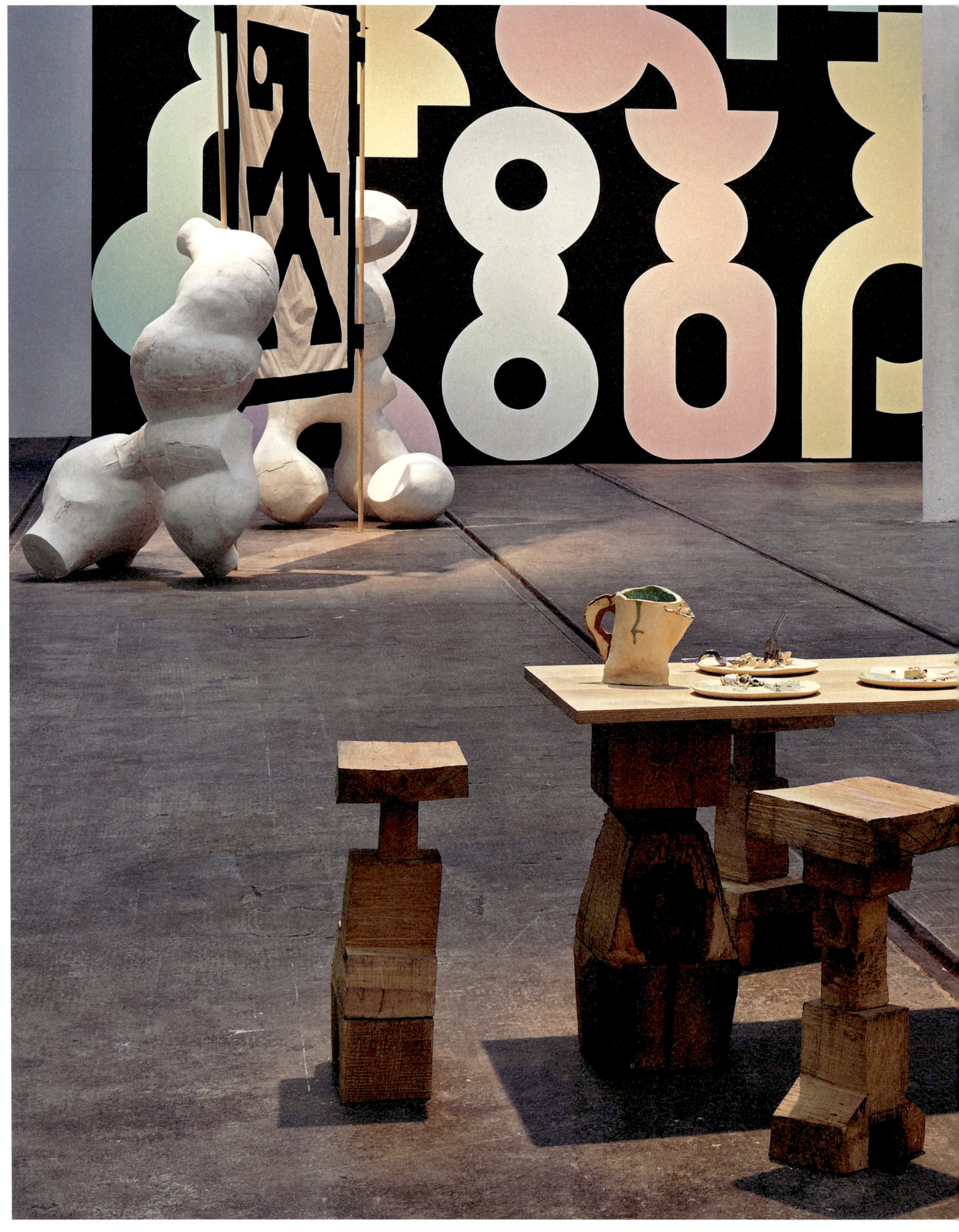

 The Eaten, 2013, Installationsansicht / Installation view *Solar Eyes*, Tramway, Glasgow 2013

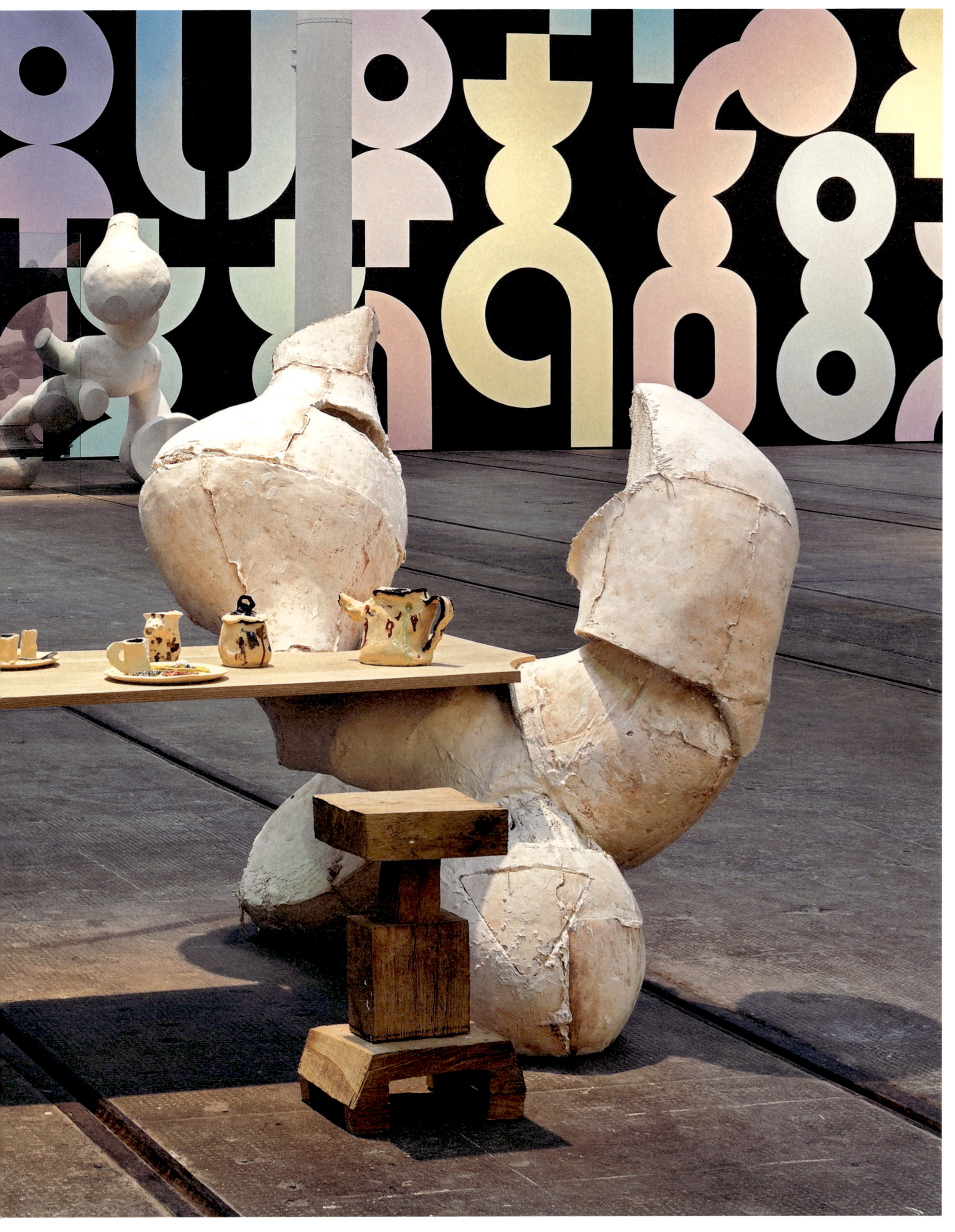

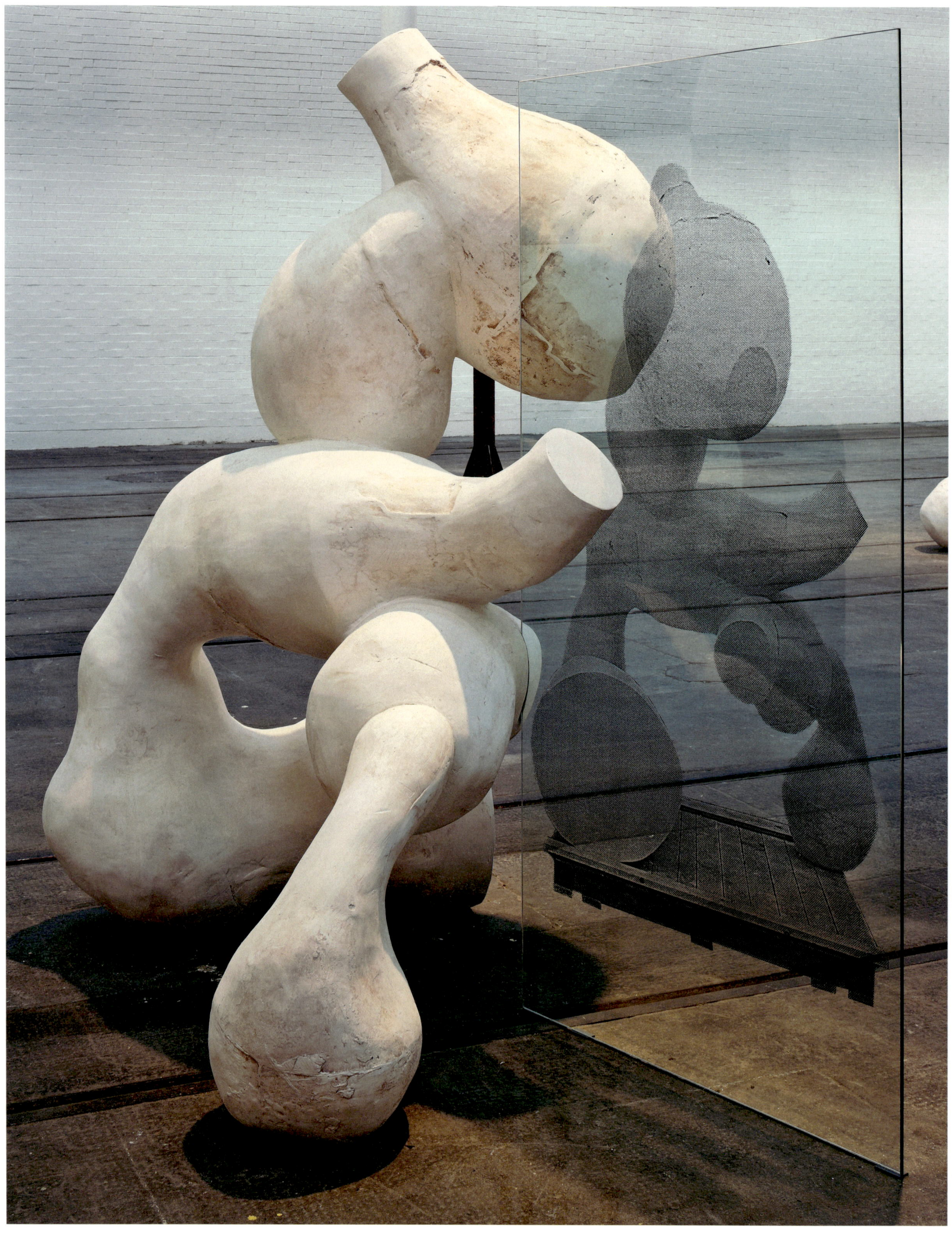

 Guardian with Image, 2013, Installationsansicht / Installation view *Solar Eyes*, Tramway, Glasgow 2013

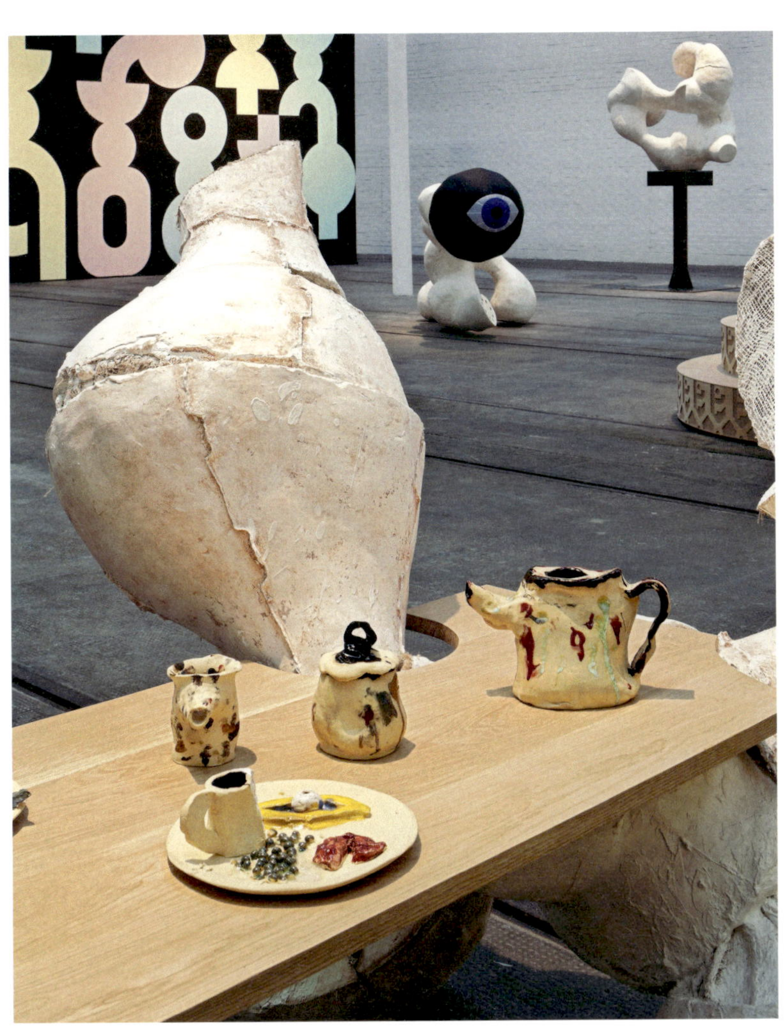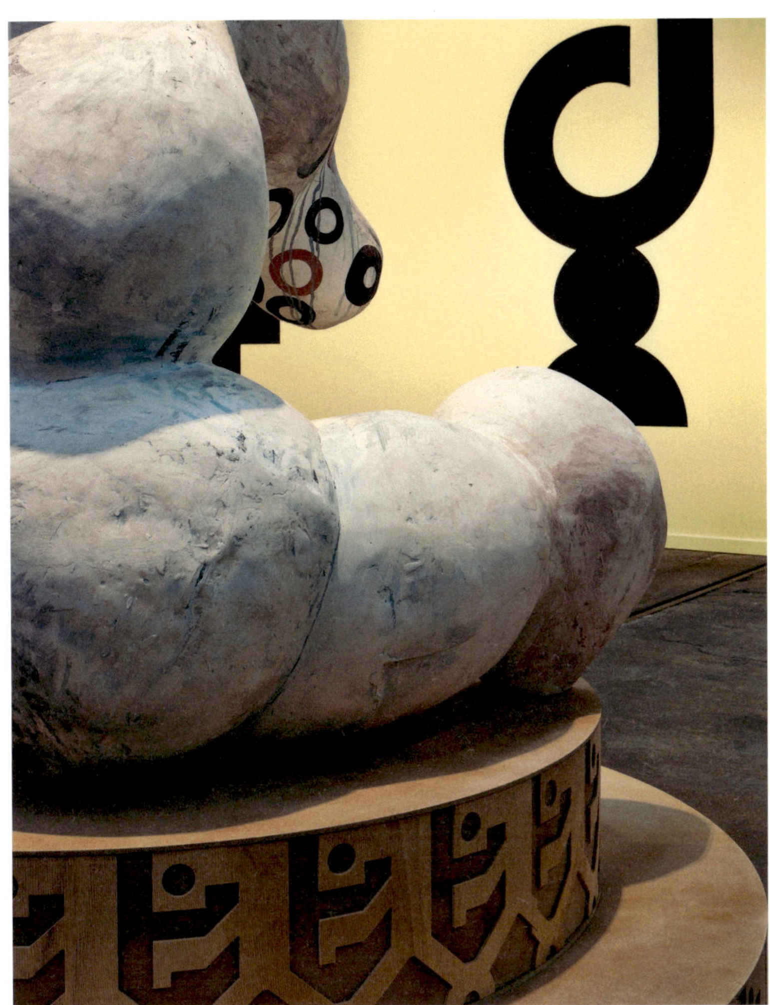

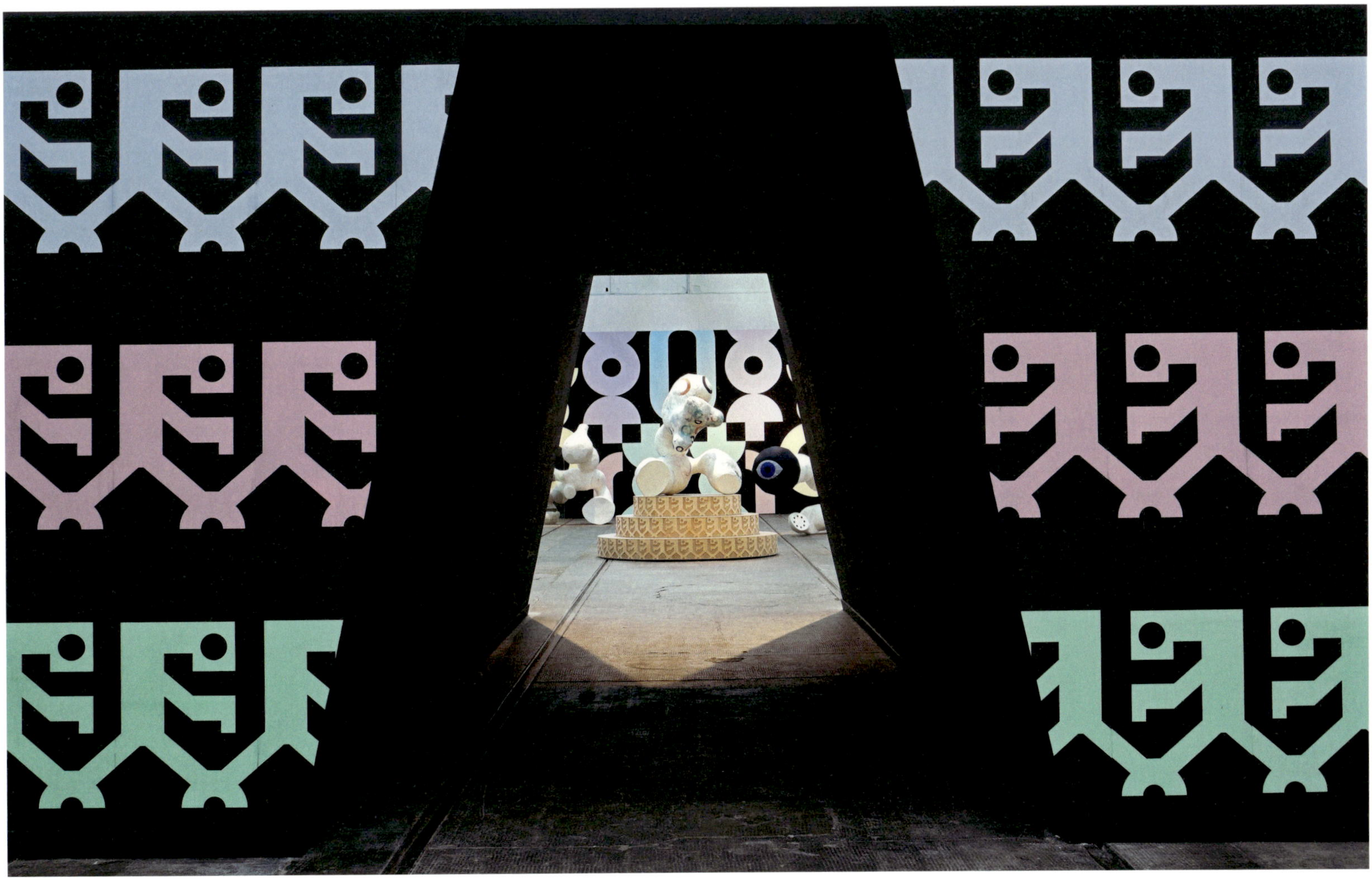

The Eaten, 2013 (oben links / top left), *Mother*, 2013 (oben rechts / top right)
Installationsansicht / Installation view *Solar Eyes*, Tramway, Glasgow 2013 (unten / bottom)

Nick Evans

Die heutige Medizin bewegt sich innerhalb des Horizonts von Zell- und Genforschung. Ihr gröberes Handwerk – die Orthopädie – ist ein Wissensbereich, der aus der Viktorianischen Zeit stammt. Selbst in diesem Kontext kann ich nicht mehr „von der Jahrhundertwende" sprechen und von Ihnen erwarten, dass Sie verstehen, dass ich die Wende vom 19. zum 20. Jahrhundert meine, aber ich tue es trotzdem. Ich möchte Ihren Blick auf die Technik und die Keramik lenken, die beim Eingipsen gebrochener Gliedmaßen zusammentreffen, ein Verfahren, das sich im Umfeld der gewaltigen eurasischen Landkriege entwickelte, wie sie in den Gemälden von Elisabeth, Lady Butler zu sehen sind.

Von ihrem Konzept her haben die modularen Formen, die Nick Evans in seinem Studio aus den Materialien für die ambulante Ruhigstellung von Gliedmaßen herstellt, mit Eimern voll Wasser und Säcken mit feuchtigkeitsbindendem Pulver zu tun. Zurechtgeklopfte Gipsklumpen werden mit Bandagen versehen, die entstehenden Gipsverbände herausgelöst und in Bogenlinien zusammengesetzt. Die charakteristischen länglichen Formen, die zuerst bei Barbara Hepworth und Henry Moore, Ben Nicholson und David Nash zu sehen waren, sind ein vage vertrauter Anblick aus der Zeit zwischen den Weltkriegen, als die gesprengte menschliche Gestalt sich archaisch, neolithisch wieder festigte und Trost in Vorstellungen von idyllischer Landwirtschaft, Kindheit und reiner Farbe suchte. Vergehen und Bestehen (der Gips ist verschwunden) beeinflussen das Bewusstsein auf die gleiche Weise, sie überschatten sich gegenseitig. Was bleibt, wenn Geschichte das Archiv ausschöpft? Rätsel, Neukombinationen und ein großer Spiel-Raum zwischen den Ohren.

Evans verbrachte 2006 einige Zeit als *Artist in Residence* an der Tate St. Ives. Für ihn war die Erfahrung, in dem zum Atelier umgebauten Tanz- und Kinosaal auf die dort gelagerten Arbeiten Hepworths zu stoßen, besonders bedeutsam. In dem Lager befindet sich das Werk im Limbus, in einem Zwischenzustand – einem Tanzen und Schweben, Sich-Biegen und Sich-Verbinden –, der ihn inspiriert. Seine eigenen Skulpturen sind im Atelier, das ebenso ein Raum zum Ausprobieren wie zum Produzieren ist, Geschwister. Wie bei Beckett sitzen sie dort, umgeben von den primitiven Materialien und Gerätschaften, mit denen sie erschaffen wurden, und spielen mit Utensilien herum, die eigentlich in einen Putzschrank gehören – Besenstielen, Wischmops und Ähnlichem. Indem sie in Richtung Unabhängigkeit, wenn nicht Autonomie schlingern, zwingen sie ihren Schöpfer immer mehr, am Rand zu wohnen und auf die Wünsche zu reagieren, die von Zeit zu Zeit aus ihrem vertraulichen Kreis hervordringen. Er bringt Werkzeuge zum Einsatz und bietet ihnen Talmi an. Sie putzen sich heraus. Sogar wenn sie aus Gips sind, wollen die polierten, akkurat und elegant geformten Oberflächen Hepworths Stein und Bronze sein, Materialien, für die Evans' Skulpturen keine Zeit haben (natürlich qualifiziert „sogar" Gips als Hilfsmaterial – als vorläufig und prothetisch).

Herbert Read, der in Yorkshire geborene Künstler, Kurator und Autor, der dem britischen Modernismus so sehr Gestalt gegeben hat, schrieb einmal für ein BBC-Magazin namens *The Listener* einen Artikel mit dem Titel „Distortion". „Verzerrung ist ein Wort, das beim Zuhörer unangenehme Assoziationen hervorruft, aber wie manche der Zuschriften zu diesen wöchentlichen Notizen zeigen, verweist es auf eine tatsächliche Schwierigkeit im Verständnis der visuellen Künste. Ich müsste eigentlich sagen, dass auf eine sehr allgemeine und vielleicht paradoxe Art und Weise jede Kunst verzerrt ist. Sogar

Today, medicine takes the cellular and the genetic as its horizon. Its big mechanics – orthopaedics – are a Victorian epistemology. Even in this context, I can no longer say "at the turn of the century" and expect you to understand that I mean the nineteenth to twentieth, but I do. I mean to direct you to engineering and ceramics, which collide in the practice of setting broken limbs in plaster, a tactic that developed in proximity to the huge Eurasian land wars we see depicted in paintings by Elizabeth, Lady Butler.

In their conception, the modular forms Nick Evans produces in his studio from the materials of ambulatory immobilisation involve buckets of water and sacks of hygroscopic dust. Lumps of claggy earth, paddled into shape, are repeatedly set in bandages, the resulting casts prised off and reassembled along limber lines. Oblong characteristics, acquired from Barbara Hepworth and Henry Moore, Ben Nicholson and David Nash, are suggestively familiar of that period – interwar – when the exploded human form consolidated archaically, neolithically, seeking solace in ideas of genial agriculture, childhood and pure colour. Disappearance and permanence (the clay has slipped away) affect consciousness in the same way, shadowing each other. When history exhausts the archive, what's left? Riddles, recombinants and that vast ludic space between your ears.

Evans spent time on residency at the Tate St Ives in 2006 and marks the experience of encountering Hepworth's work, stored in the converted dance hall/cinema that was her studio, as especially significant. Stored, the work is in limbo, and it is limbo – a dance and a suspension, bending and binding – that informs him. His own sculptures are siblings in the studio, as much a room for rehearsal as for making. Beckettesque, they sit surrounded by the rudimentary implements that brought them into being, jesting with props that properly belong in a cleaning cupboard – broom handles, mop heads and sorts. Gradually, tottering towards independence if not autonomy, they force their maker to reside on the periphery, responding to the demands that issue forth now and then from their private huddle. He implements tools and offers them geegaws. They dress up. Even in plaster, the polished, deliberate surfaces of Hepworth aspire to stone and bronze, graceful and pedantic, materials that Evans' sculptures don't have time for (of course 'even' qualifies plaster as an auxiliary material – propositional and prosthetic).

Herbert Read, the Yorkshire-born artist, curator and writer who gave so much body to British modernism, once wrote an article entitled *Distortion* for a BBC magazine called *The Listener*. "Distortion is a word with unpleasant associations for listeners, but as some of the letters evoked by these weekly notes bear witness, it indicates one of the real difficulties in appreciation of the visual arts. I should be prepared to say, in a very general and perhaps paradoxical way, that all art is distorted. Even classical Greek sculpture, which I dealt with last week, was distorted in the interests of the ideal. Was the line of the brow ever in reality so straight, the face so oval, the breasts so round ...?" Distortion is a process of appropriation and reproduction – there is no appropriation or re-presentation without distortion and re-orientation. With the action of a vortex, Evans' post-colonial process spins Hepworth and Moore together with the tribal artefacts that came to them as raw ideals; the splinters and weird bodies evident in Nash spin with the baby-boom psychedelics of Sergeant Pepper's Lonely Hearts Club Band.

Where Hepworth and Moore pegged their notions of home to the immemorial as represented by the English landscape and the

von / by FIONA JARDINE

die klassische griechische Skulptur, über die ich letzte Woche geschrieben habe, war in Richtung des Ideals verzerrt. War die Augenbraue tatsächlich so gerade, das Gesicht so oval, die Brust so rund …?" Verzerrung ist ein Prozess der Aneignung und Reproduktion – ohne Verzerrung und Neuausrichtung gibt es keine Aneignung oder Re-Präsentation. In einer Strudelbewegung verspinnt Evans' postkoloniales Verfahren Hepworth und Moore mit den prähistorischen Artefakten, die als primitive Ideale zu ihnen gelangten; Nashs Bruchstücke und sonderbare Körper verschmelzen mit den Babyboom-Psychedelikern von Sergeant Pepper's Lonely Hearts Club Band.

Wo Hepworth und Moore ihre Vorstellungen von Zuhause an das durch die englische Landschaft und die spirituelle Integrität von Figuren, Masken und Reliquien kolonialen Ursprungs repräsentierte Unvordenkliche koppelten, beschäftigt sich Evans' Arbeit mit Häuslichkeit als Folge eines äußerst informiert, aber isoliert im Haus verbrachten Lebens in einer Zeit, in der die Bildung schwindelerregender Äquivalenzen der Kern einer neuen Groteske ist. In Galerien und Ausstellungsräumen besetzen seine Skulpturen Sockel, die wie die Beine von provisorischen Tischen Brâncuşis Säulen ähneln, und verlangen nach eklektischen, gemusterten Hintergründen, die ihre Knochenstruktur hervorheben. In diesem Zwischenzustand können sie eine Variante dessen vor Augen führen, was Psychedelia vom viktorianischen Ornament übernahm, was die Memphis Group vom Kente-Stoff übernahm (und durch Elvis in Tennessee vom Alten Ägypten).

Zu Beginn dieses Textes habe ich auf ein Wissensgebiet der Viktorianischen Zeit verwiesen, das von der Orthopädie repräsentiert wird. Sie hatte mit menschlichen Körpern und harten Werkstoffen zu tun und erreichte eine kritische Masse, die melancholische Ärzte hervorbrachte, die Anatomie ernst nahmen, aber auch – wenn wir die Metapher weiterführen wollen – komische Hilfspfleger, die Patienten im Rollstuhl zum Röntgen schieben (ich denke an Marcel Duchamp). Die Bewegungseinschränkung durch Streckung und Eingipsen wurde rasch zum Hauptgegenstand von Komödien und zum erzählerischen Kunstgriff. Ich würde behaupten, dass Evans' „verkalkte Gespenster" von modernistischen Tropen genau solche MacGuffins sind wie L. B. Jefferies' komplett eingegipstes Bein in *Fenster zum Hof* und ihm – gut sichtbar versteckt – einen Vorwand bieten, Flüchtiges gründlich zu betrachten und darüber zu spekulieren, was seine früheren Nachbarn im Schilde führen.

spiritual integrity of colonially sourced figures, masks and relics, Evans' work deals with domesticity as a consequence of life spent indoors, massively informed yet disconnected in a time when staggering equivalences are the bedrock of a new grotesque. On show in gallery and exhibition spaces, his sculptures adopt pedestals that relate Brâncuşi's columns as the legs of occasional tables and desire eclectic, patterned backgrounds, the better to emphasise their bone structure. In limbo, they can present a version of what psychedelia took from Victorian ornament, what the Memphis Group took from Kente cloth (and, by way of Elvis in Tennessee, from Ancient Egypt).

I started this piece making reference to a Victorian epistemology represented by orthopaedics. Involving human bodies and hard materials, it had a critical mass that produced melancholic physicians who took anatomy seriously but also, if we want to extend the metaphor, droll hospital porters to wheel patients to radiology (I have in mind Marcel Duchamp). The limits imposed on movement by traction and plaster casting quickly became comedy staples and plot devices. I would suggest that, like LB Jefferies' full leg cast in *Rear Window* – hidden in plain sight – Evans' 'calcified ghosts' of modernist tropes are just such MacGuffins, giving him the excuse to scope across temporalities and speculate about what his erstwhile neighbours have been up to.

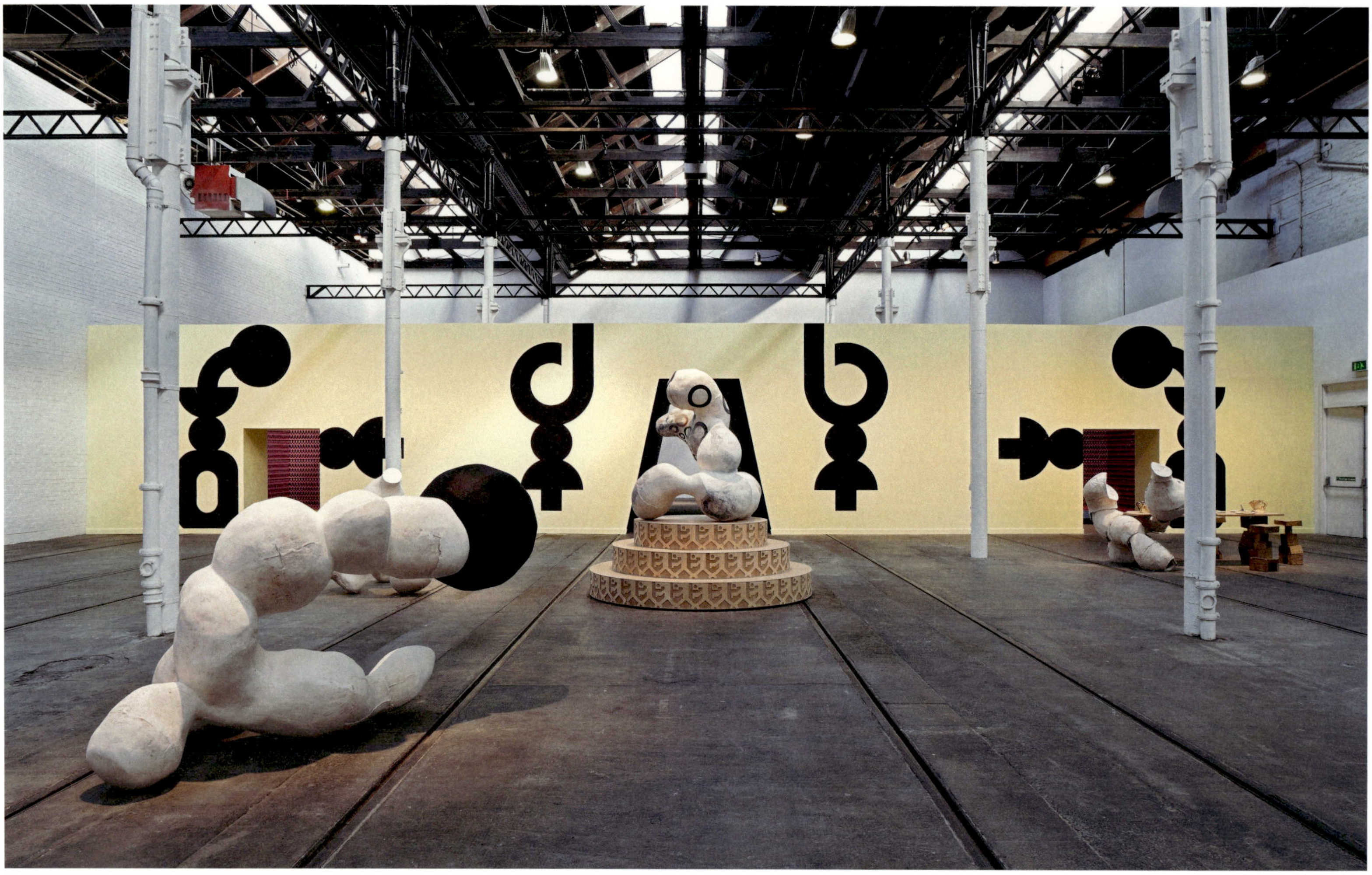

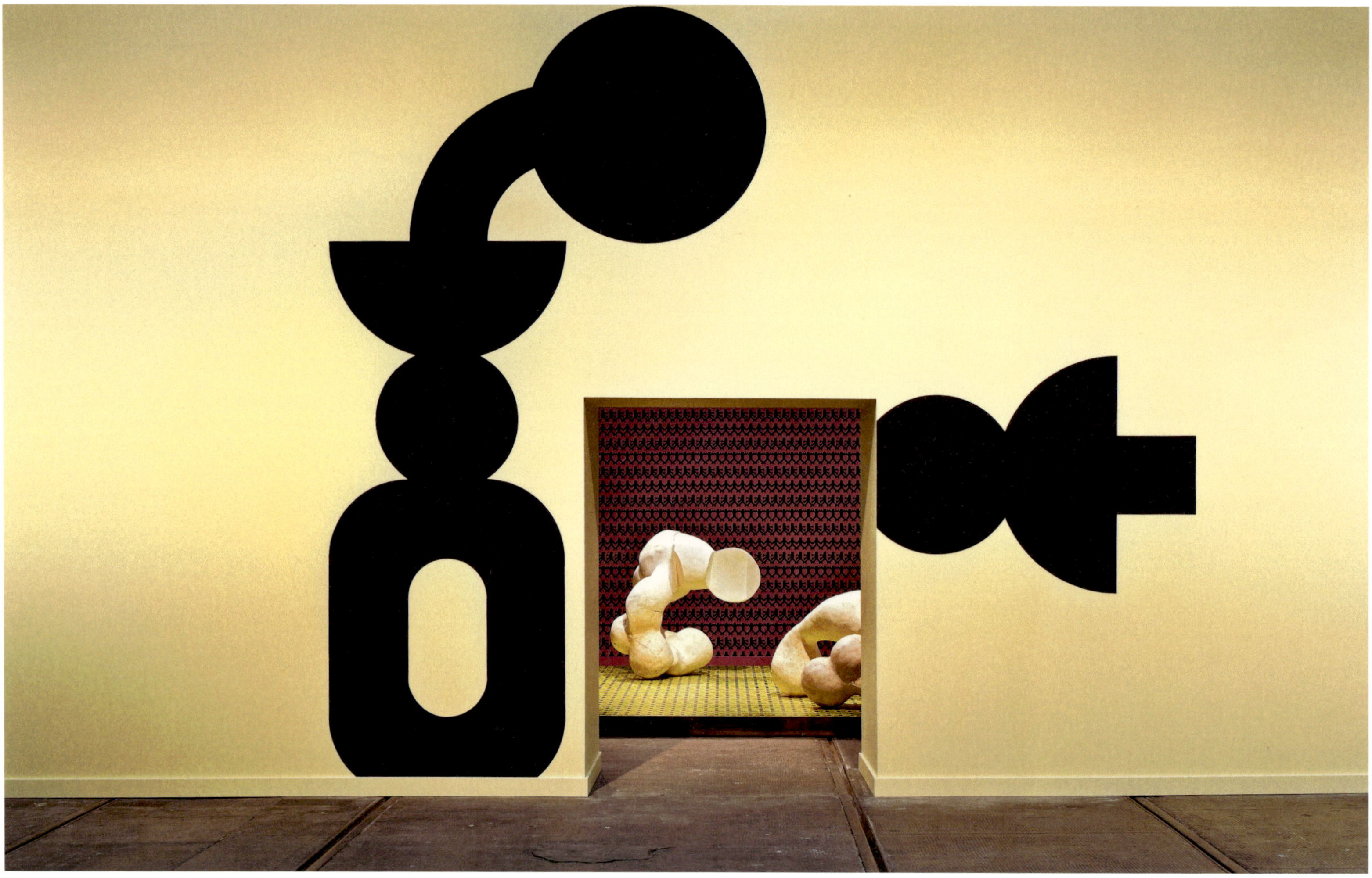

  Installationsansichten / Installation views *Solar Eyes*, Tramway, Glasgow 2013

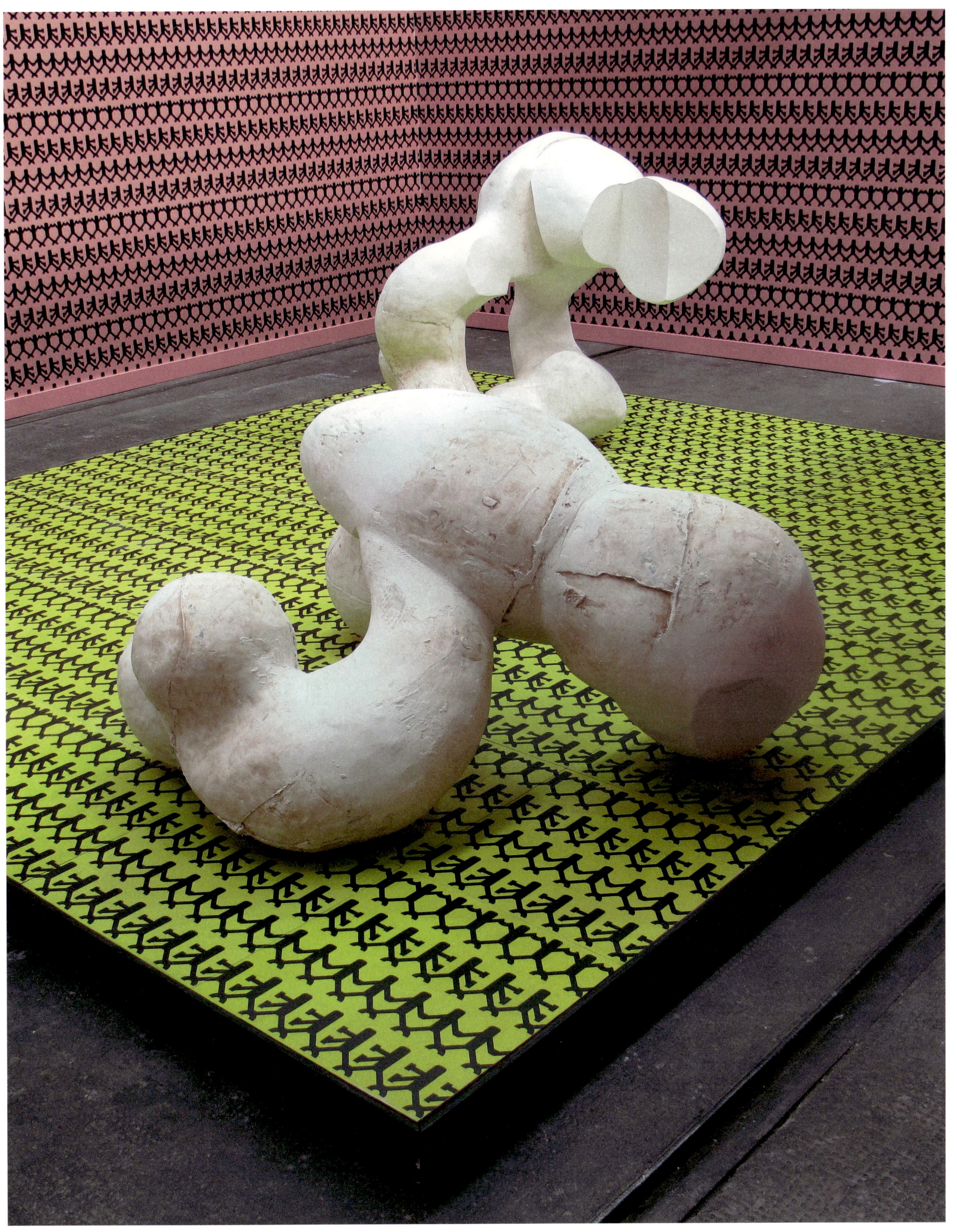

The Scandal, 2013, Installationsansicht / Installation view *Solar Eyes*, Tramway, Glasgow 2013

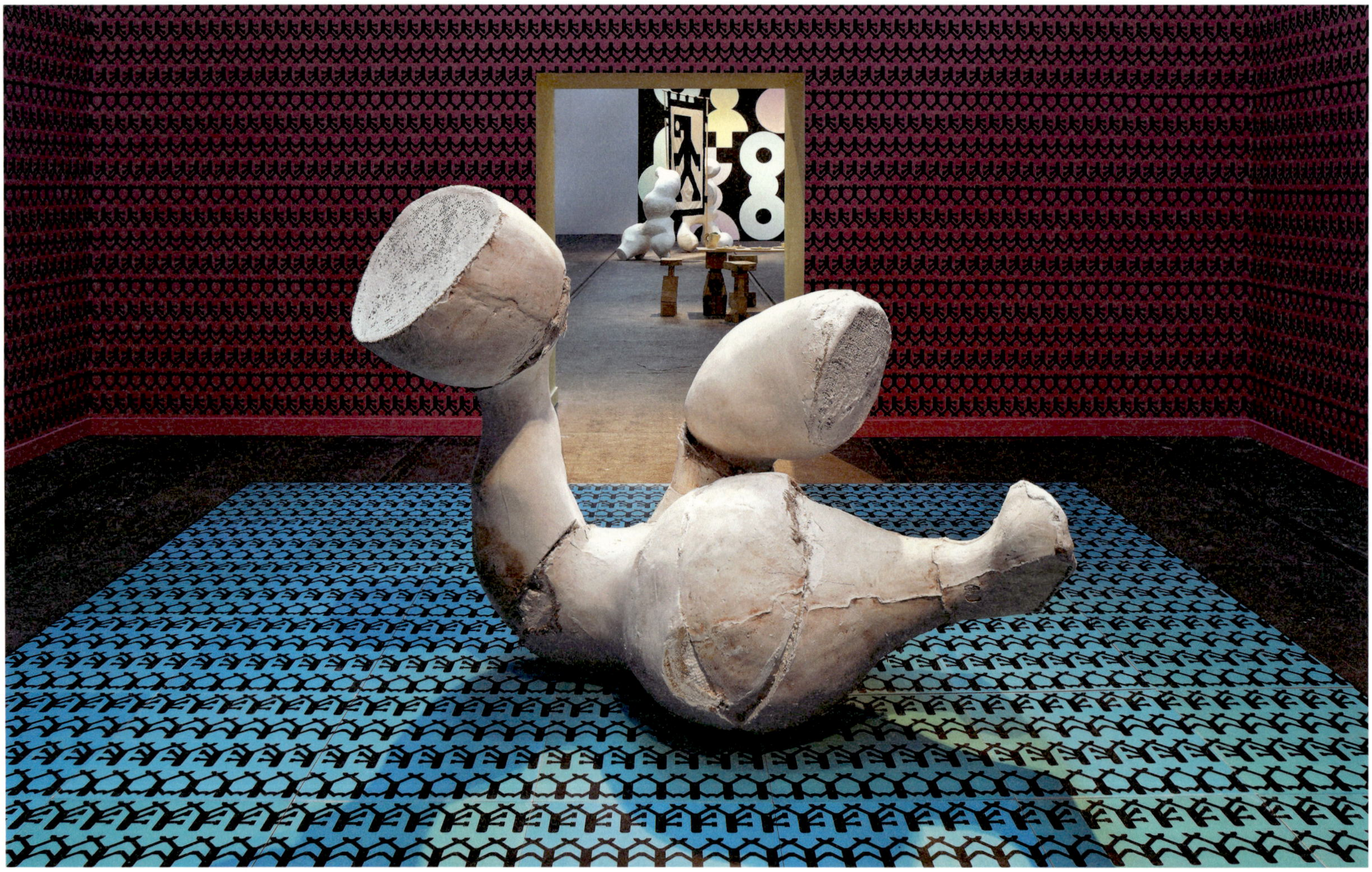

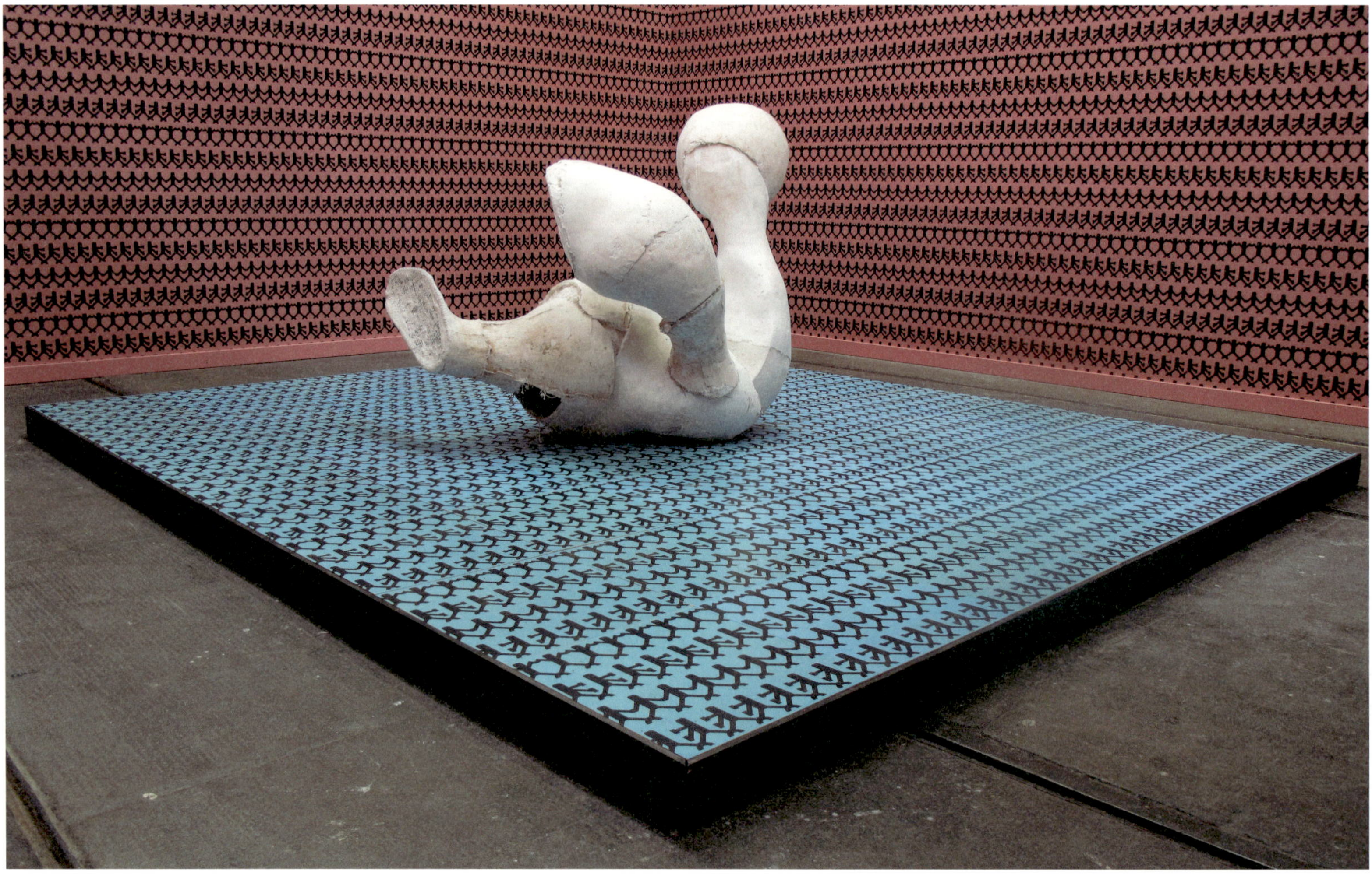

   The Scandal (1), 2013, Installationsansichten / Installation views *Solar Eyes*, Tramway, Glasgow 2013

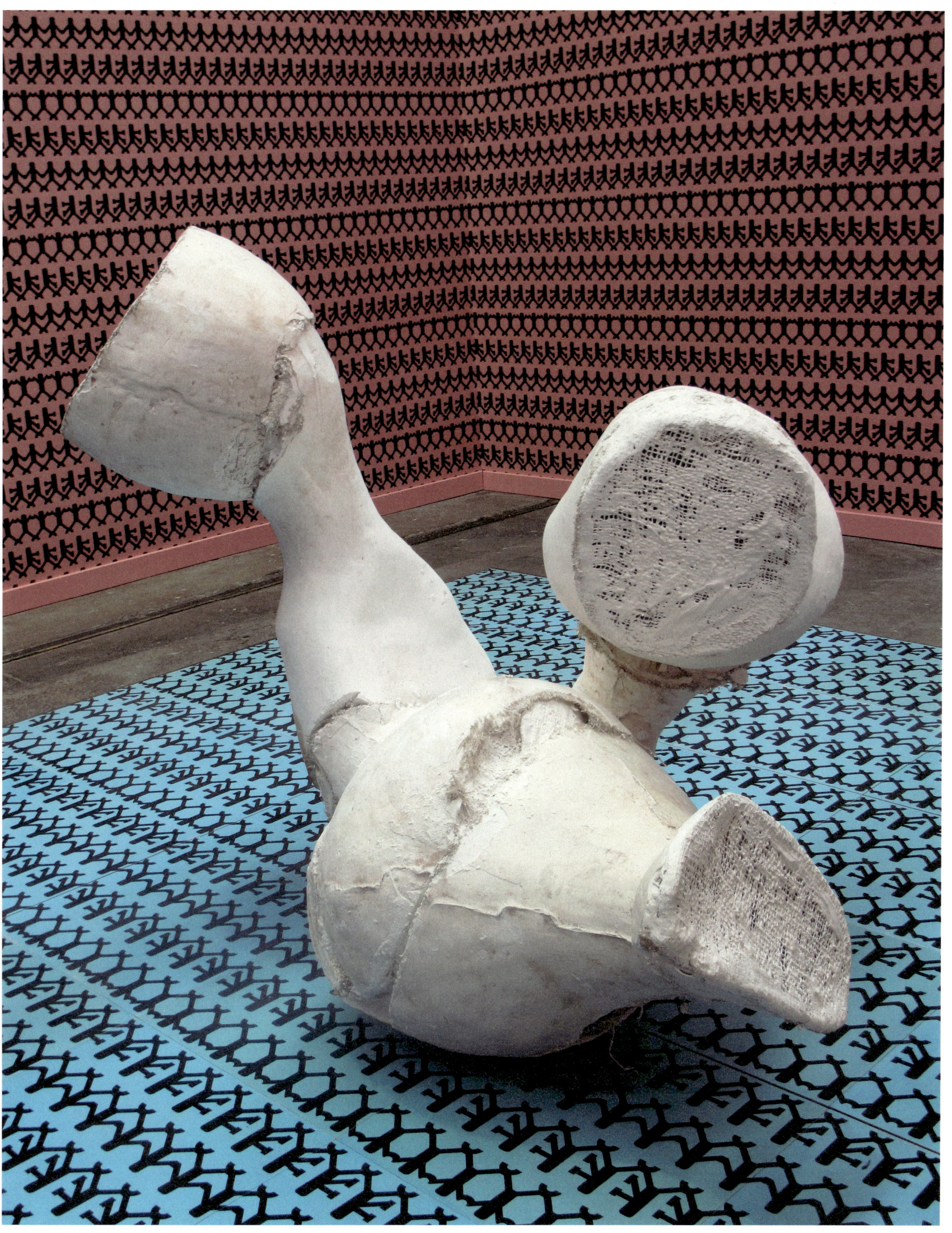

The Scandal (1), 2013, Installationsansicht / Installation view *Solar Eyes*, Tramway, Glasgow 2013

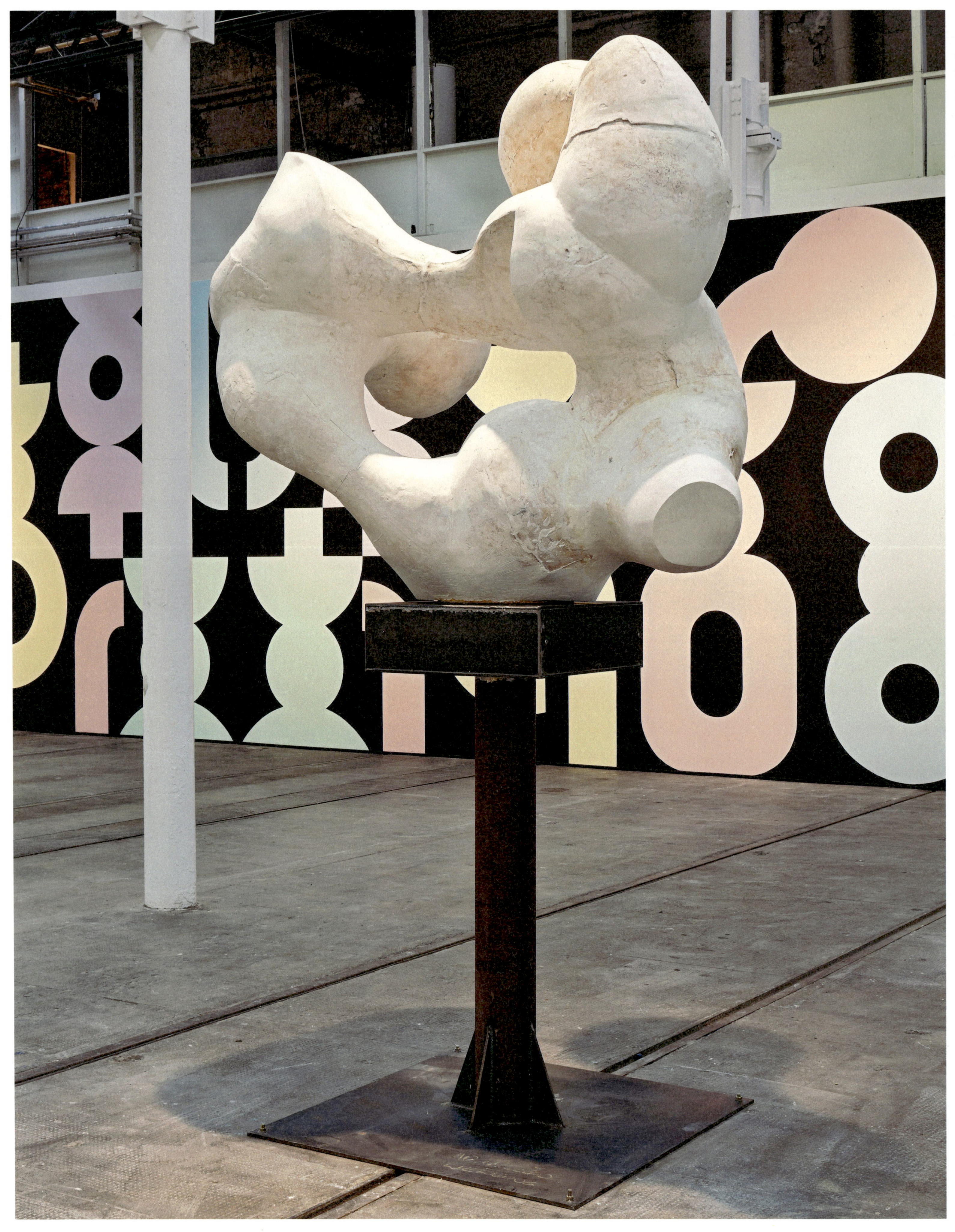

Unseeing Eye, 2013, Installationsansicht / Installation view *Solar Eyes*, Tramway, Glasgow 2013
Gatekeeper, 2013, Installationsansicht / Installation view *Solar Eyes*, Tramway, Glasgow 2013 (S./p. 99)

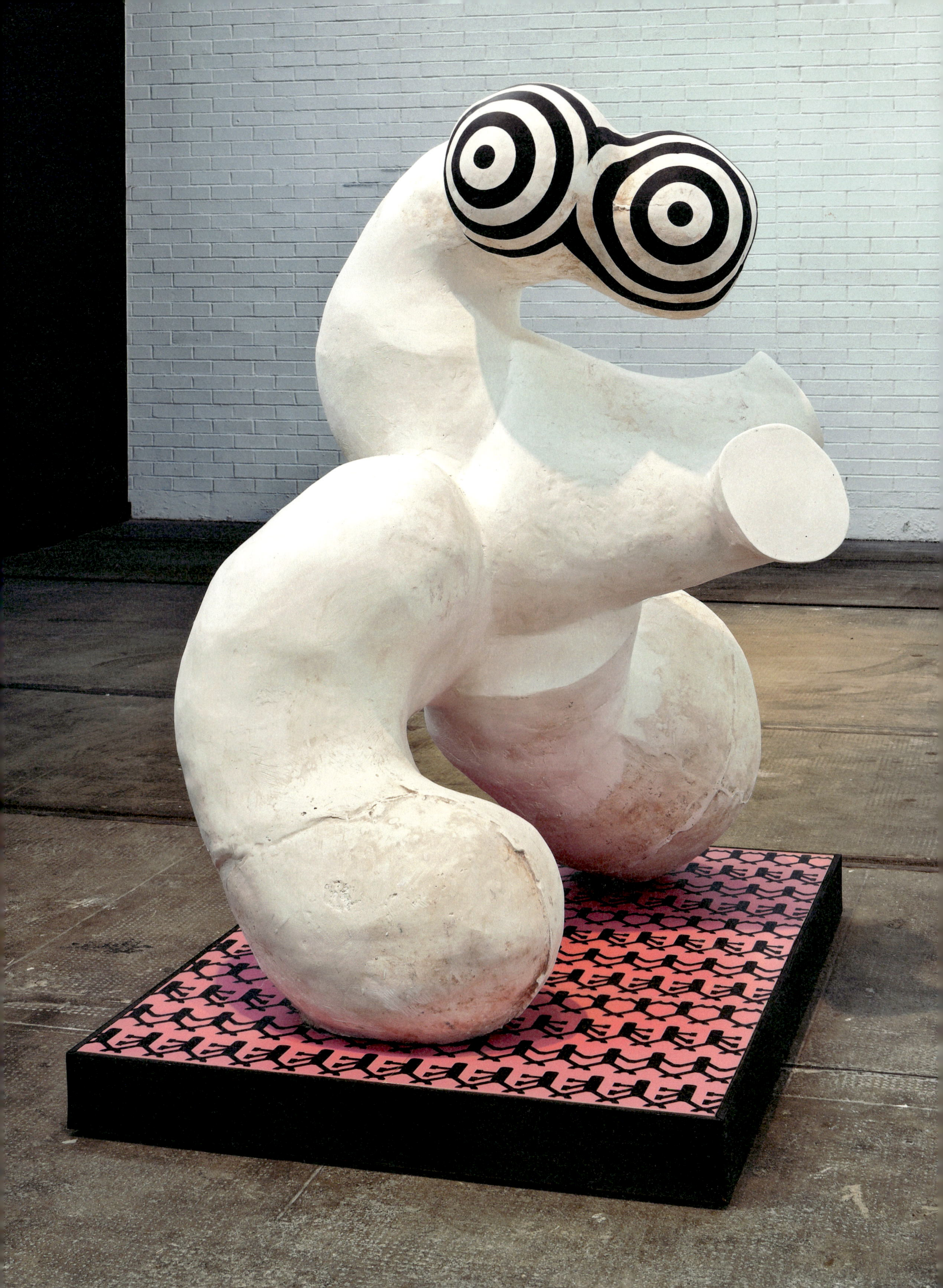

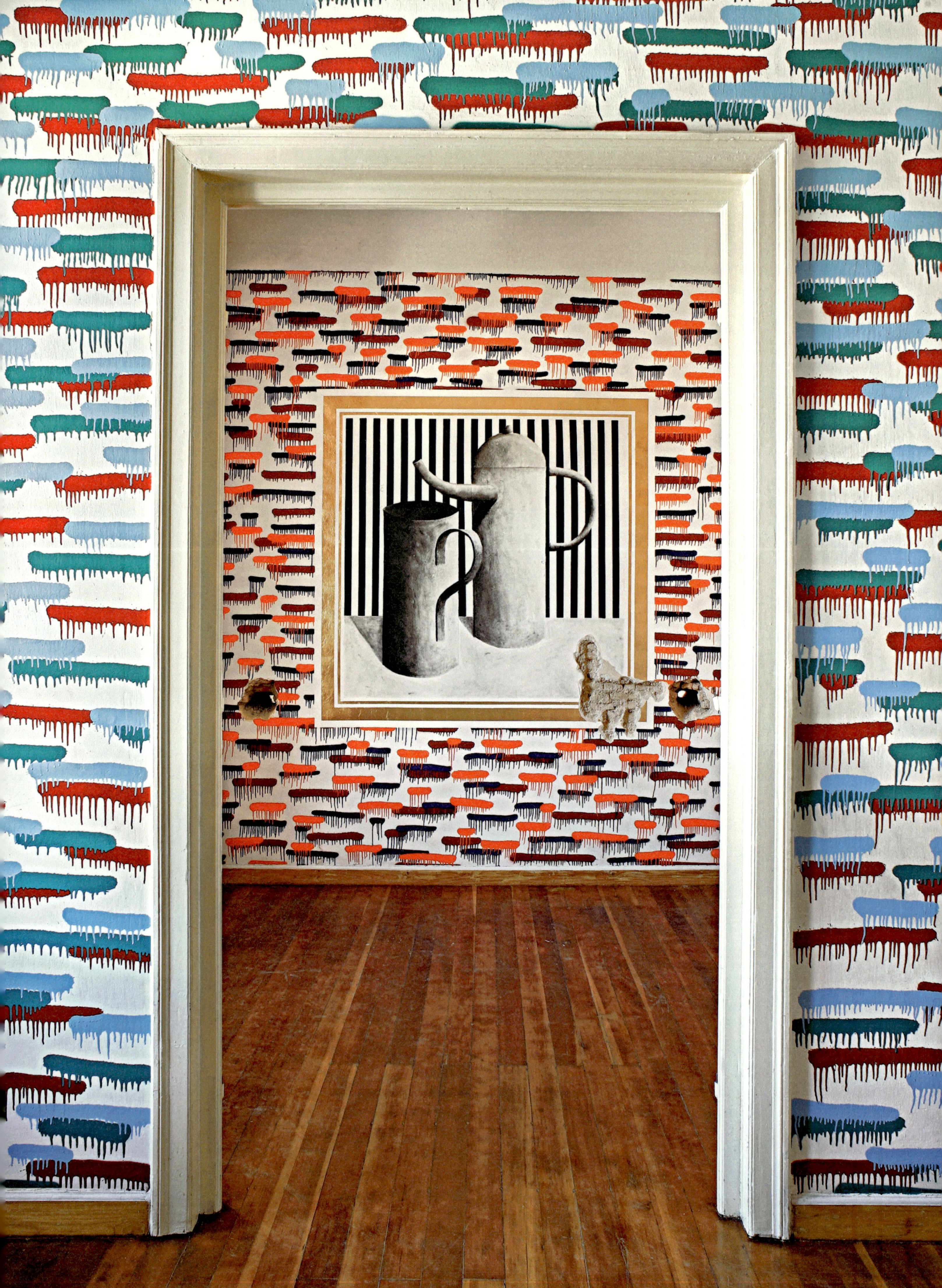

Installationsansicht / Installation view
Still Life, Gold and Peeling Paint, ReMap3,
Athen / Athens 2011

Biografie / Biography

Nicolas Party lebt und arbeitet / lives and works
in Glasgow, Schottland / Scotland
1980   geboren / born in Lausanne, Schweiz / Switzerland

Studium / Education
2001–2004   Bachelor of Fine Art, Lausanne School of Art,
Lausanne
2007–2009   Master of Fine Art, Glasgow School of Art,
Glasgow

Ausgewählte Ausstellungen / Selected Exhibitions
„Nicolas Party. New Work Scotland“, Collective Gallery,
Edinburgh (2010)
„Nicolas Party. Still Life, Gold and Peeling Paint“, ReMap3, Athen /
Athens (2011)
„Nicolas Party. Dinner for 24 Elephants“, The Modern Institute
Osborne Street, Glasgow (2011)
„Nicolas Party. Still Life, Stones, and Elephants“, Swiss Institute,
New York (2012)
„Nicolas Party. Still Life oil paintings and Landscape watercolours“,
The Modern Institute Osborne Street, Glasgow (2013)
„Just What Is Not Is Possible“, Museum Folkwang, Essen (2013)
„Ihre Geschichte(n)“, Bonner Kunstverein, Bonn (2013)

Ausgewählte Publikationen / Selected Publications
„Nicolas Party“, Ausst.-Kat. / exh. cat. The Modern Institute,
Glasgow 2011
John Calcutt, „Nicolas Party“, in: *Map*, Issue 25, 10/07/2011
Chris Sharratt, „Reviews“ (Ausstellungskritik / review: „Nicolas
Party. Still Life oil paintings and Landscape watercolours“, The
Modern Institute Osborne Street, Glasgow), in: *frieze*, Issue 156,
06/2013

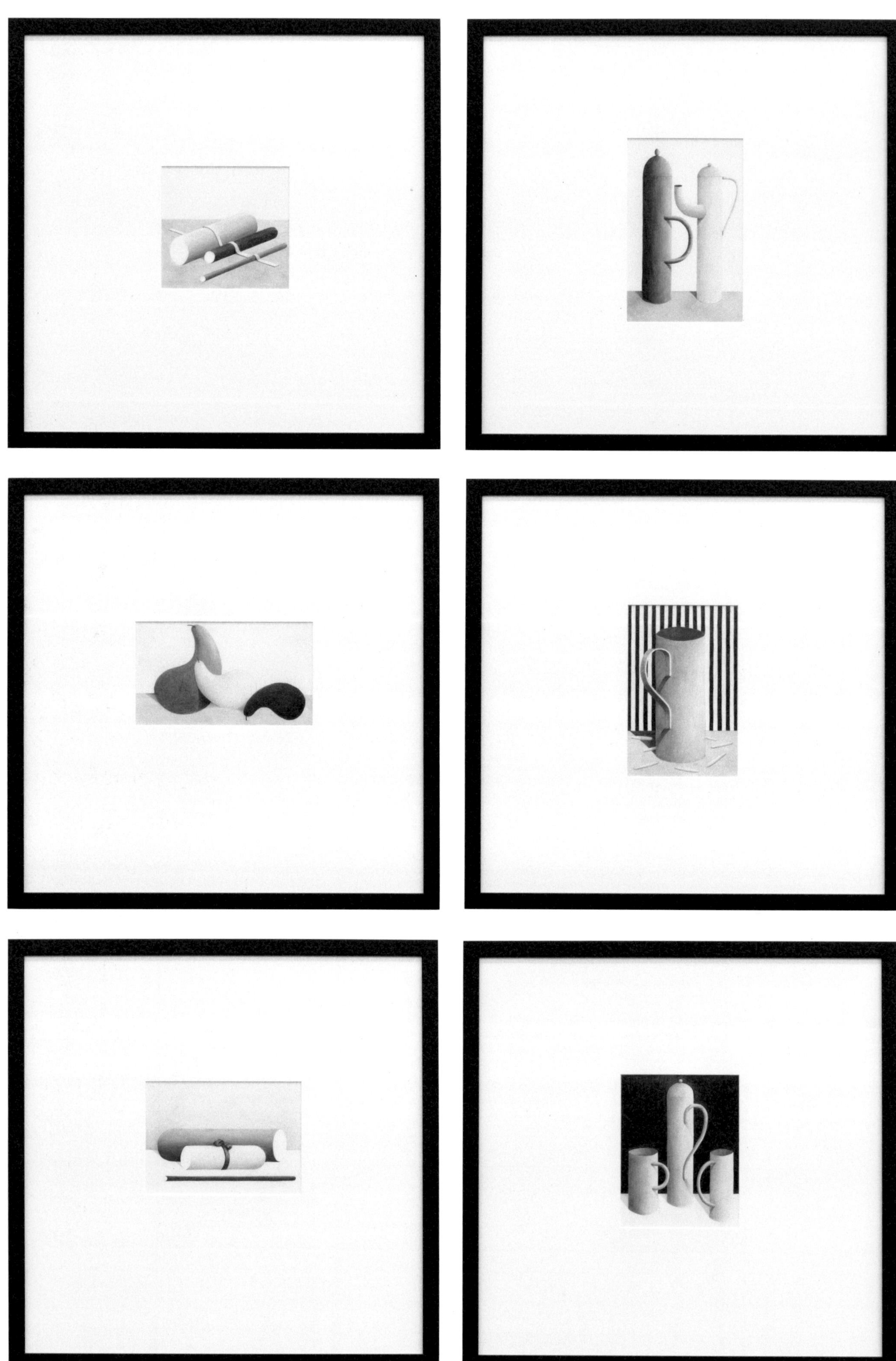

102 Alle Bilder je / all images each: *Still Life*, 2012, Private Collection, Switzerland (oben links, Mitte / top left, middle), Collection Eva Presenhuber, Zürich / Zurich (oben rechts, unten links / top right, bottom left)

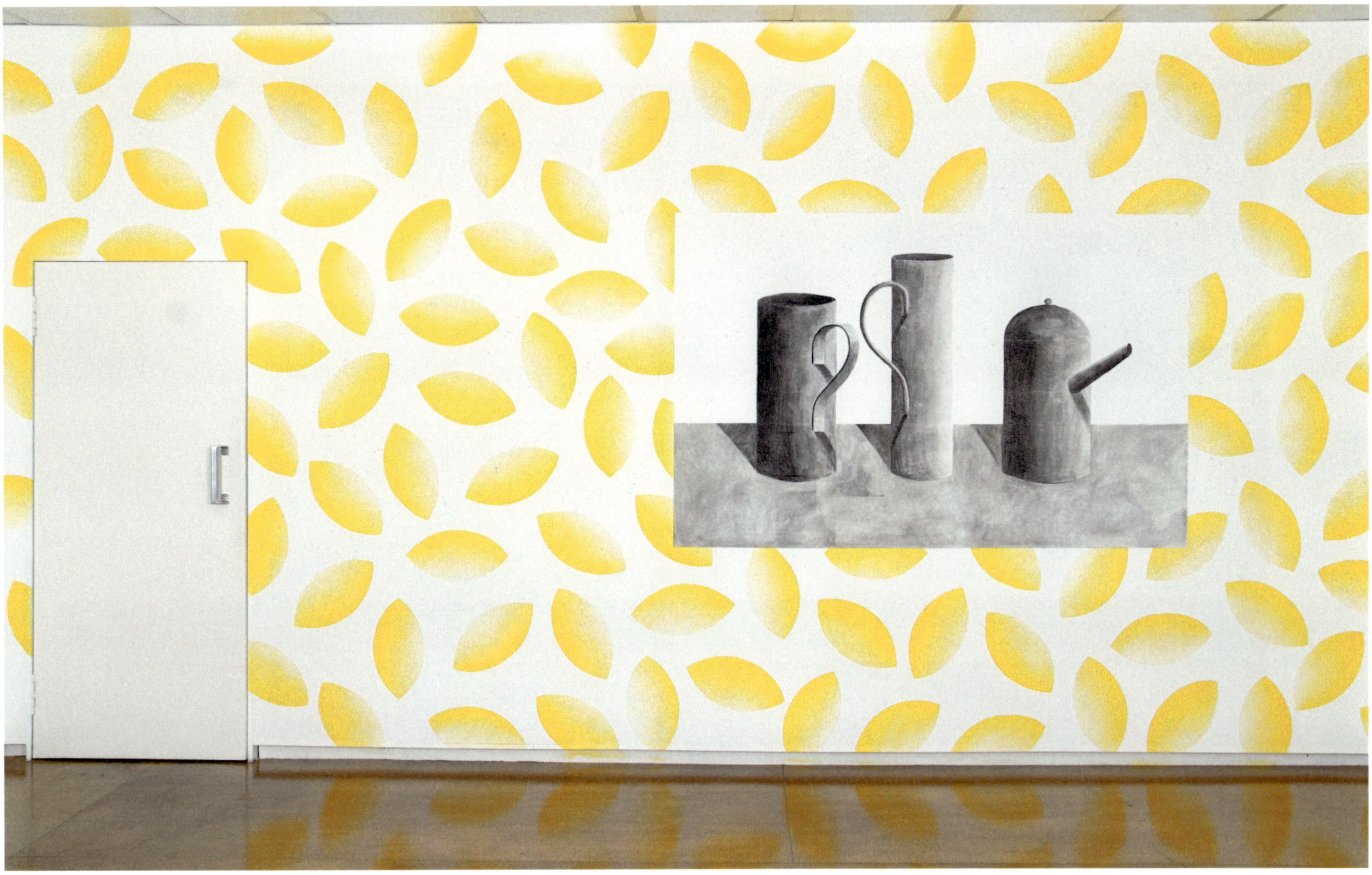

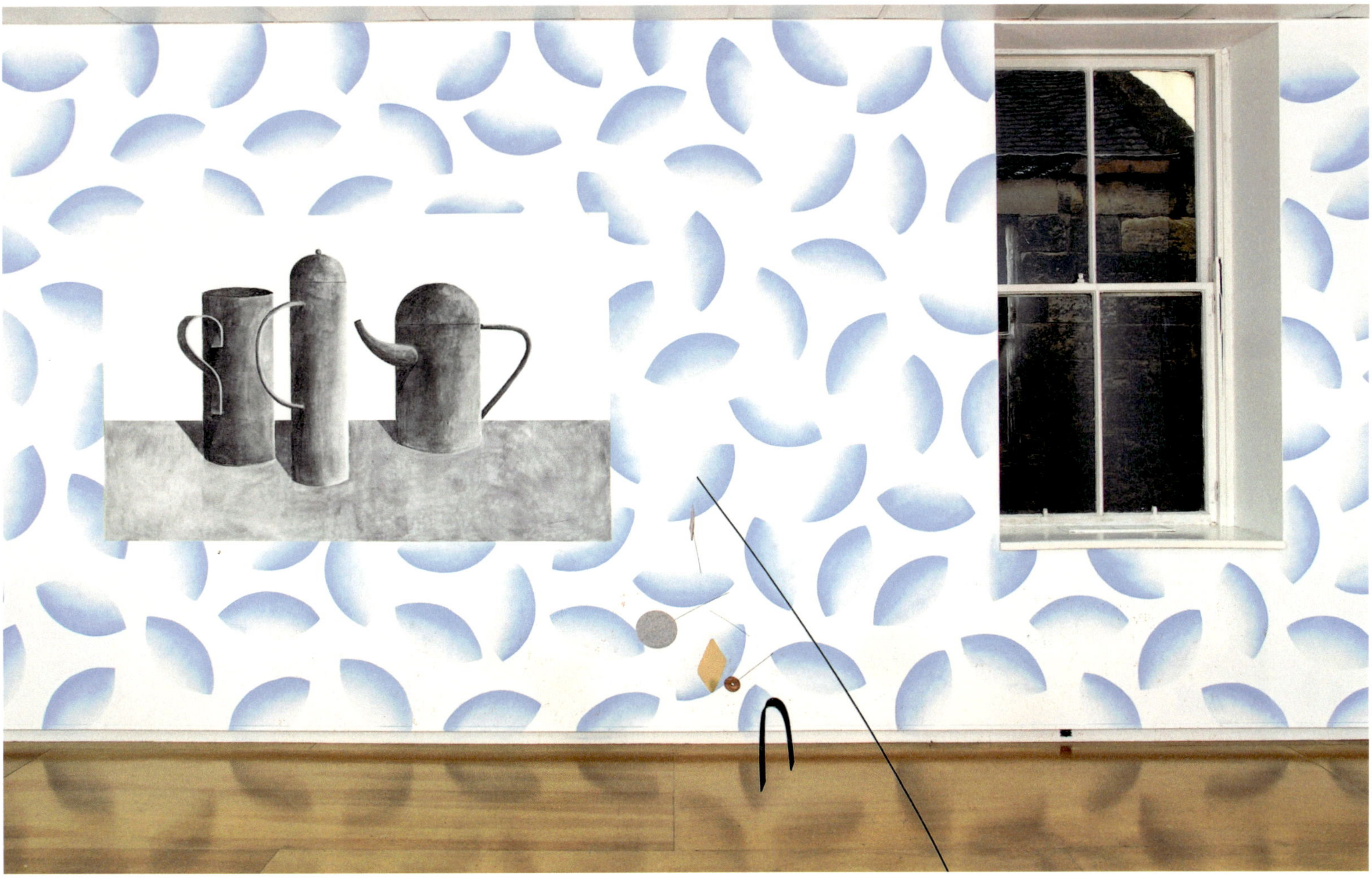

Decorative pattern Number 3 (+Still life), 2010, Installationsansichten / Installation views *Interference with twigs*,
Mary Mary, Glasgow 2010

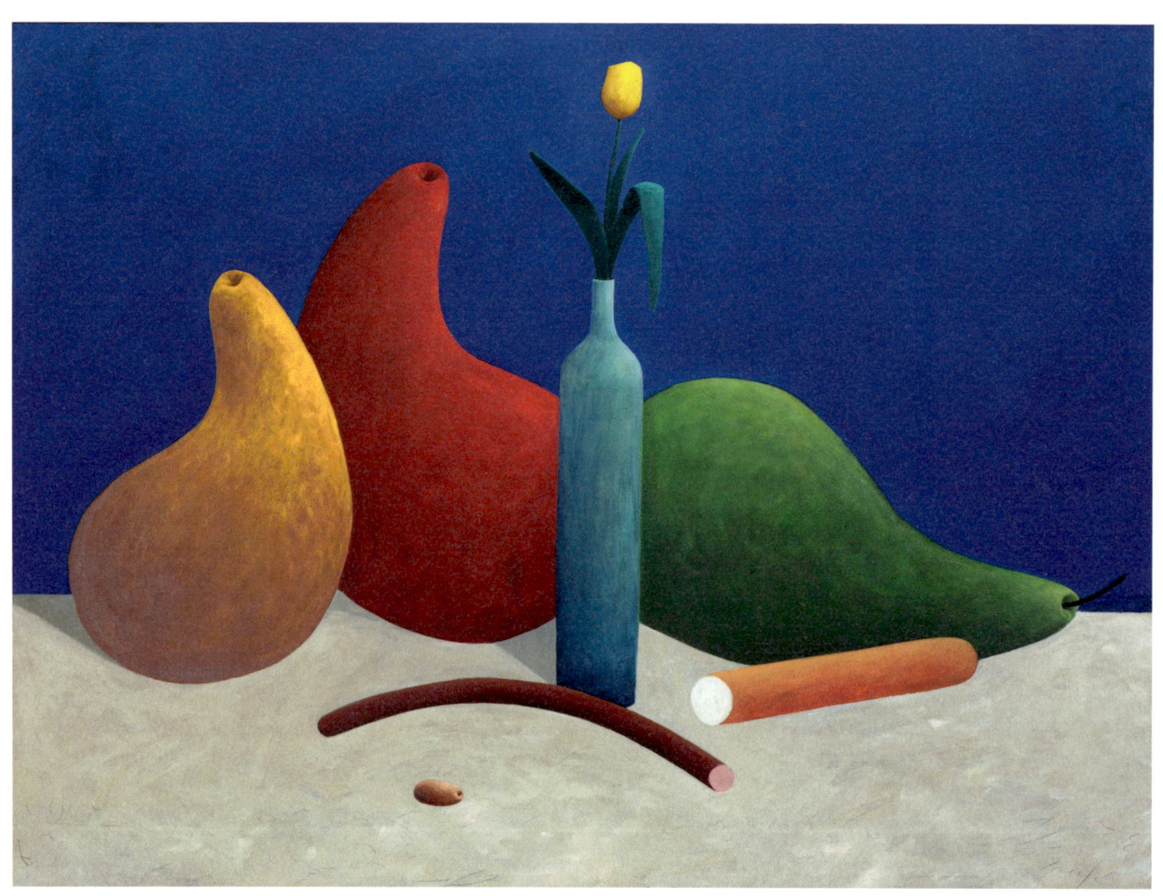

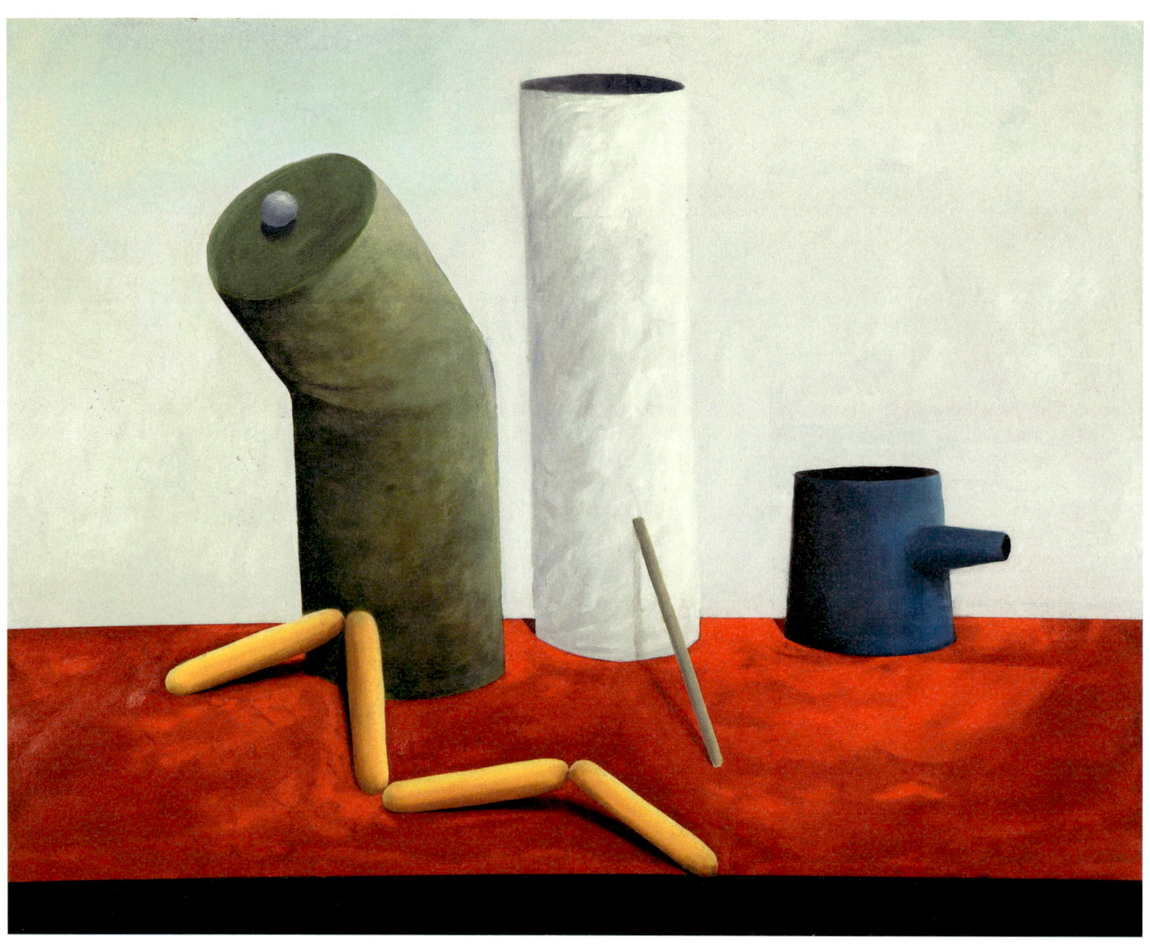

Still life with an olive, 2012–2013, Bert Kreuk Collection (oben / top)
Still life with a red table, 2010, Collection William and Anne Palmer (unten / bottom)

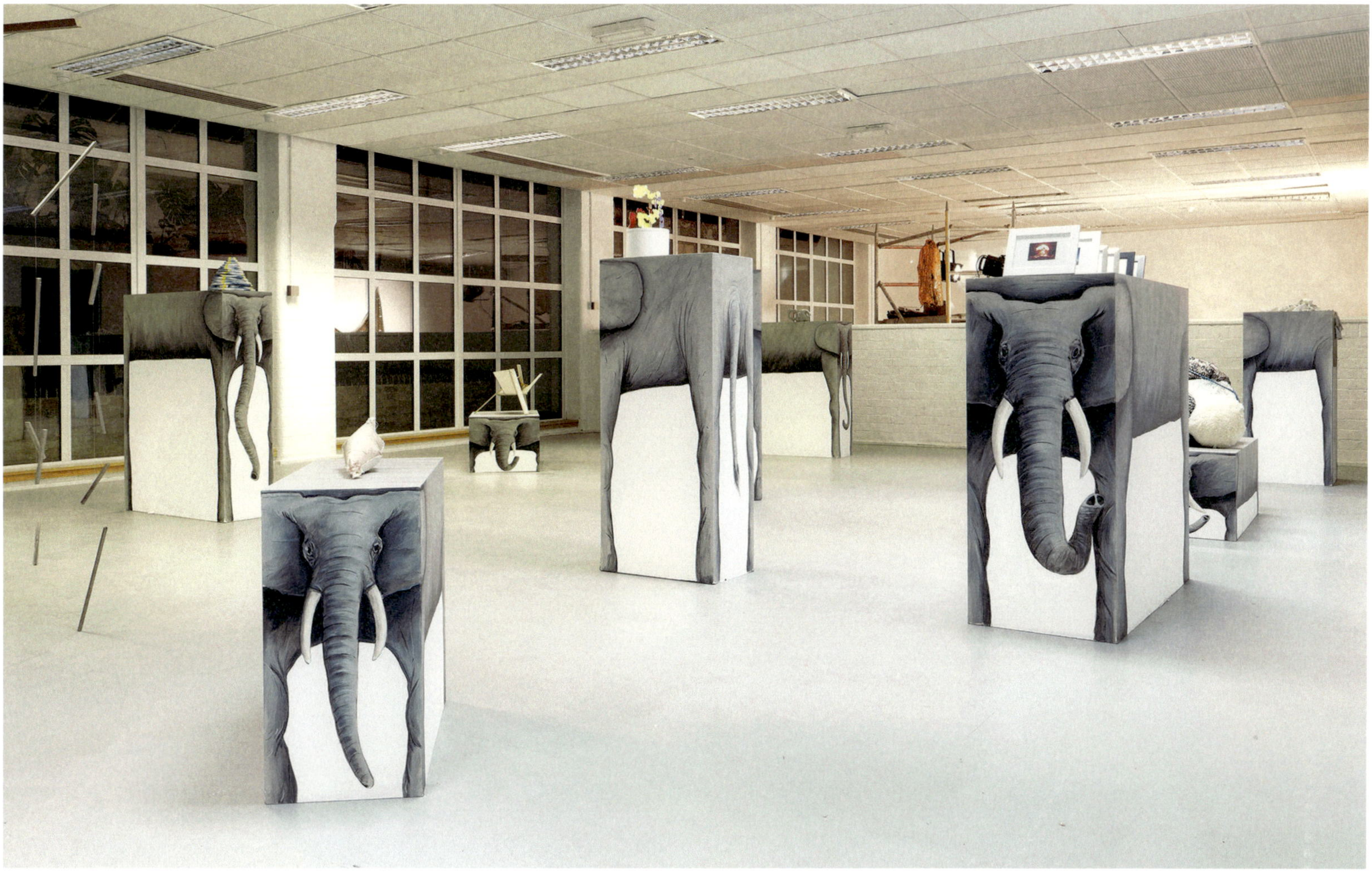

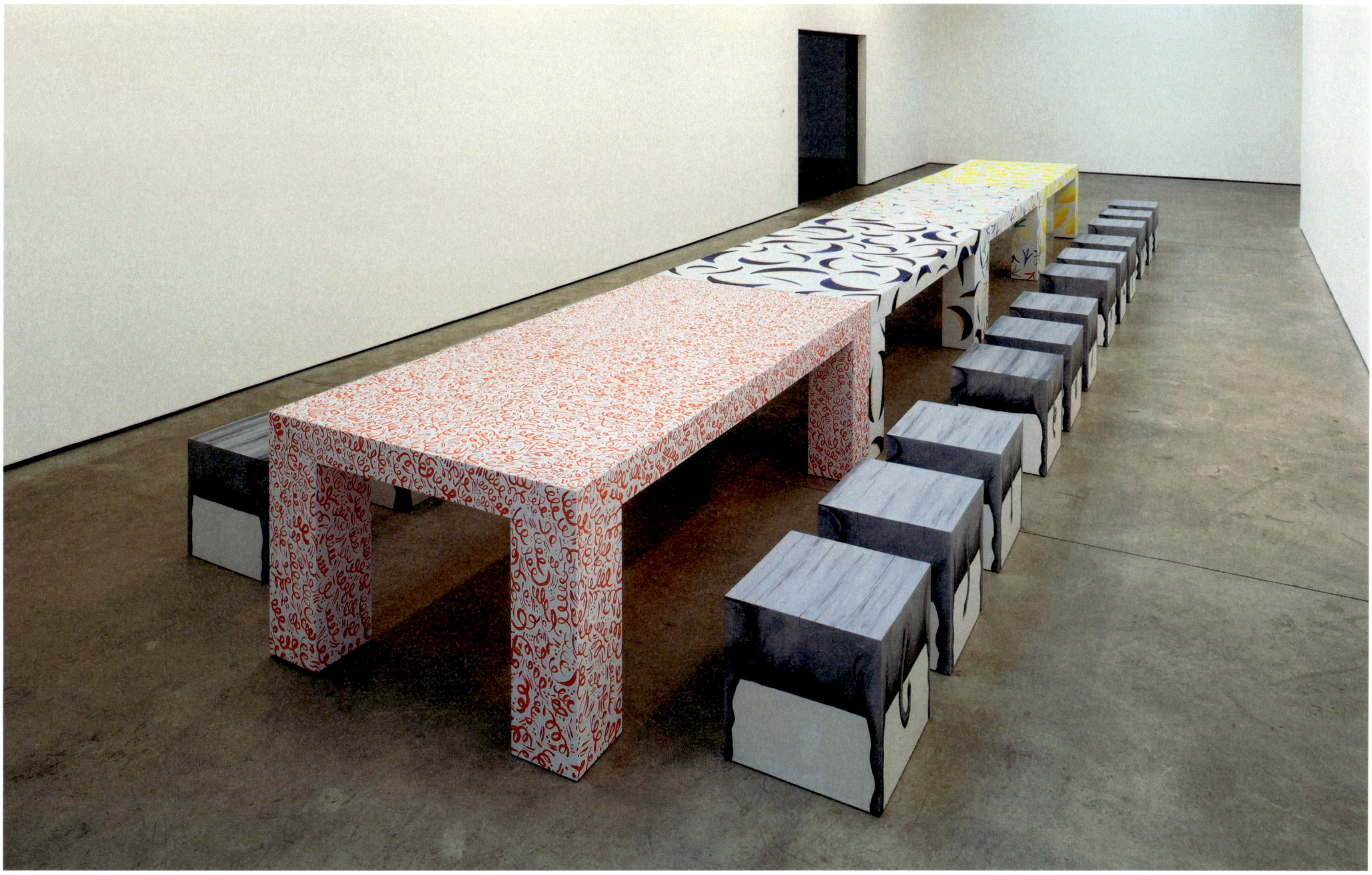

Installationsansicht / Installation view *Elephants at the Woodmill*, The Woodmill, London 2011 (oben / top)
Installationsansicht / Installation view *Dinner for 24 Elephants*, The Modern Institute/Toby Webster Ltd, Glasgow 2011 (unten / bottom)

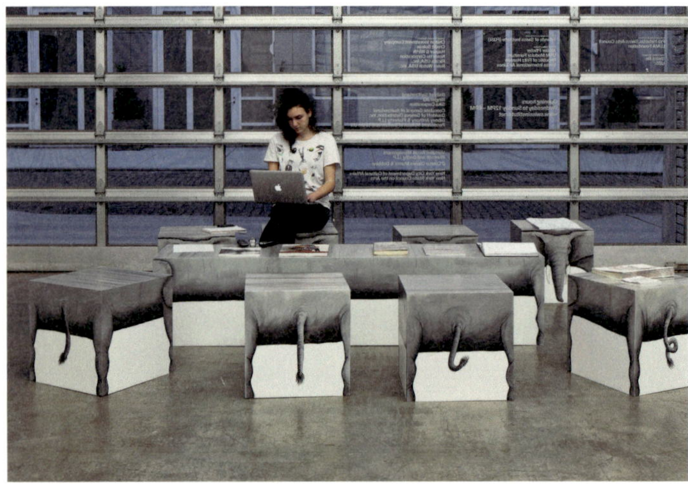
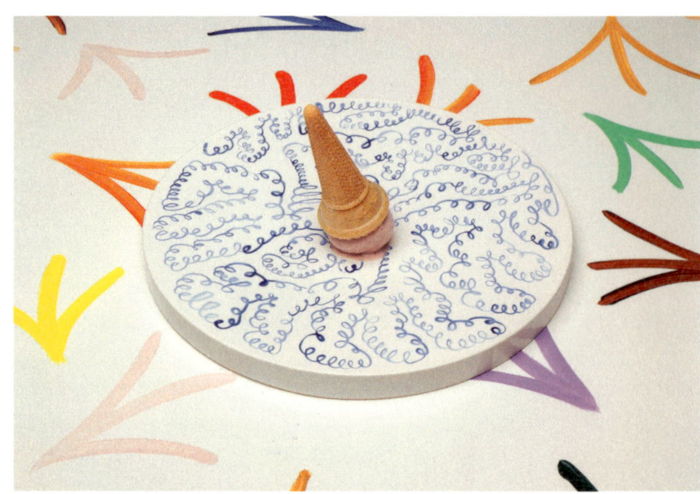
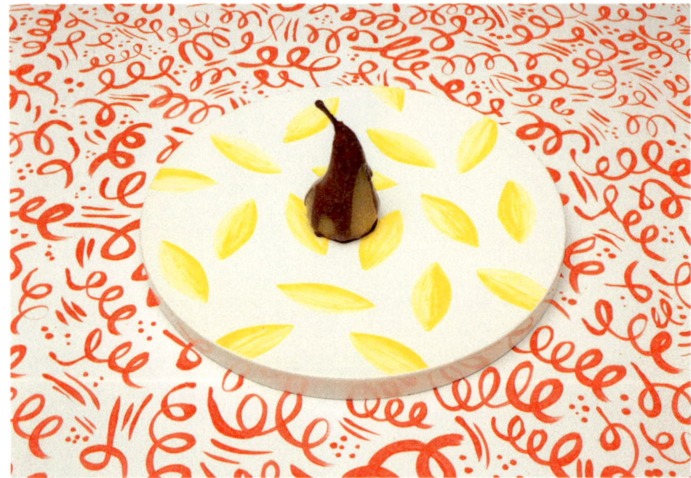
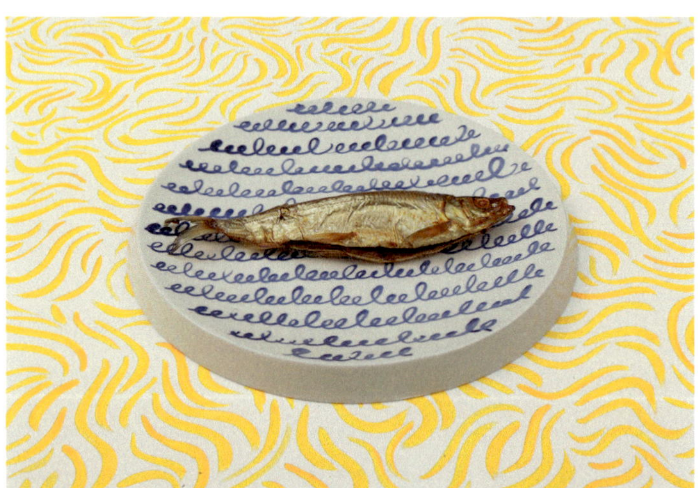
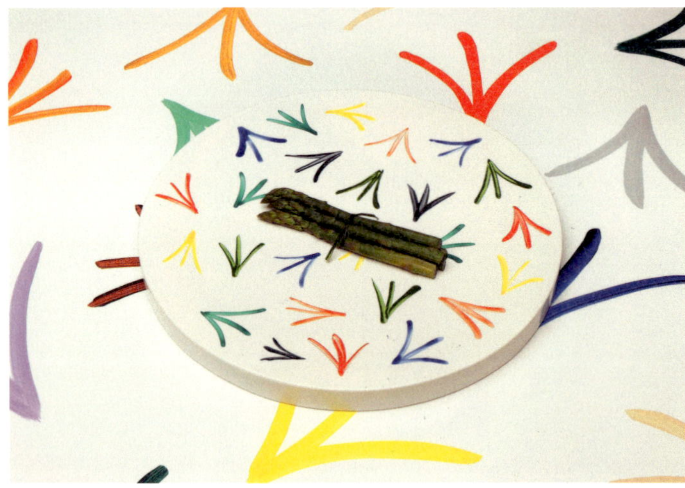
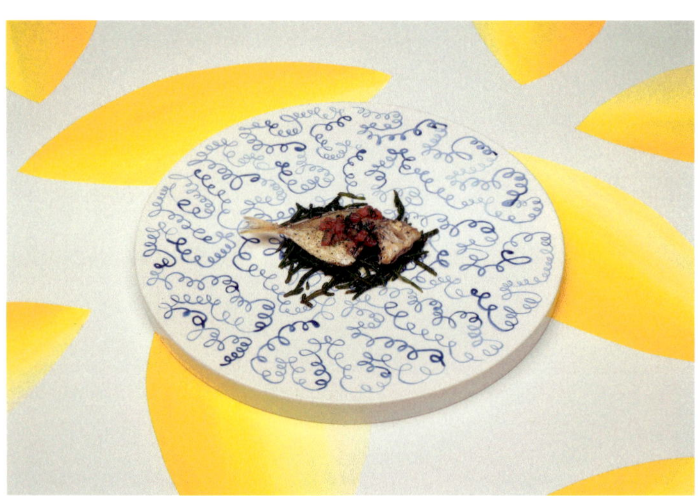
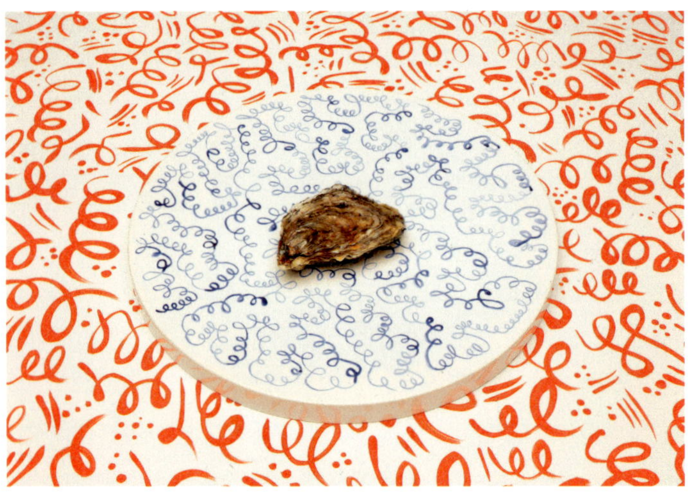
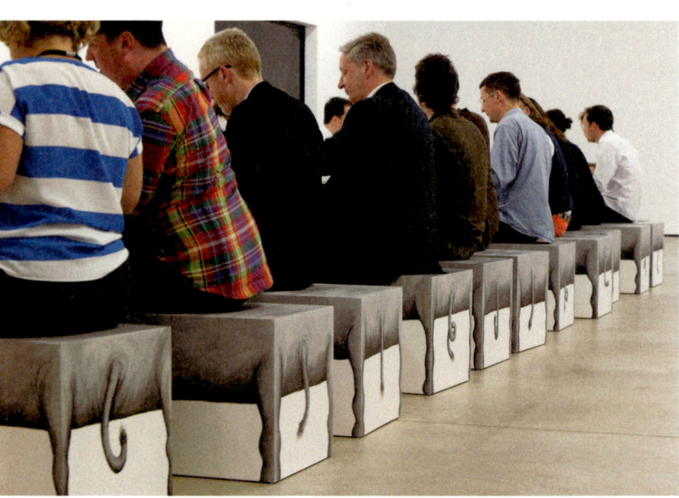

Installationsansicht / Installation view *Still Life, Stones and Elephants*, Swiss Institute, New York 2012 (oben links / top left)
Dinner for 24 Dogs, Salon 94 Freemans, New York, 2012 (zweite Reihe rechts / second row, right)
Dinner for 24 Elephants, The Modern Institute/Toby Webster Ltd, Glasgow, 2. September / 2 September 2011 (alle anderen / all the others)

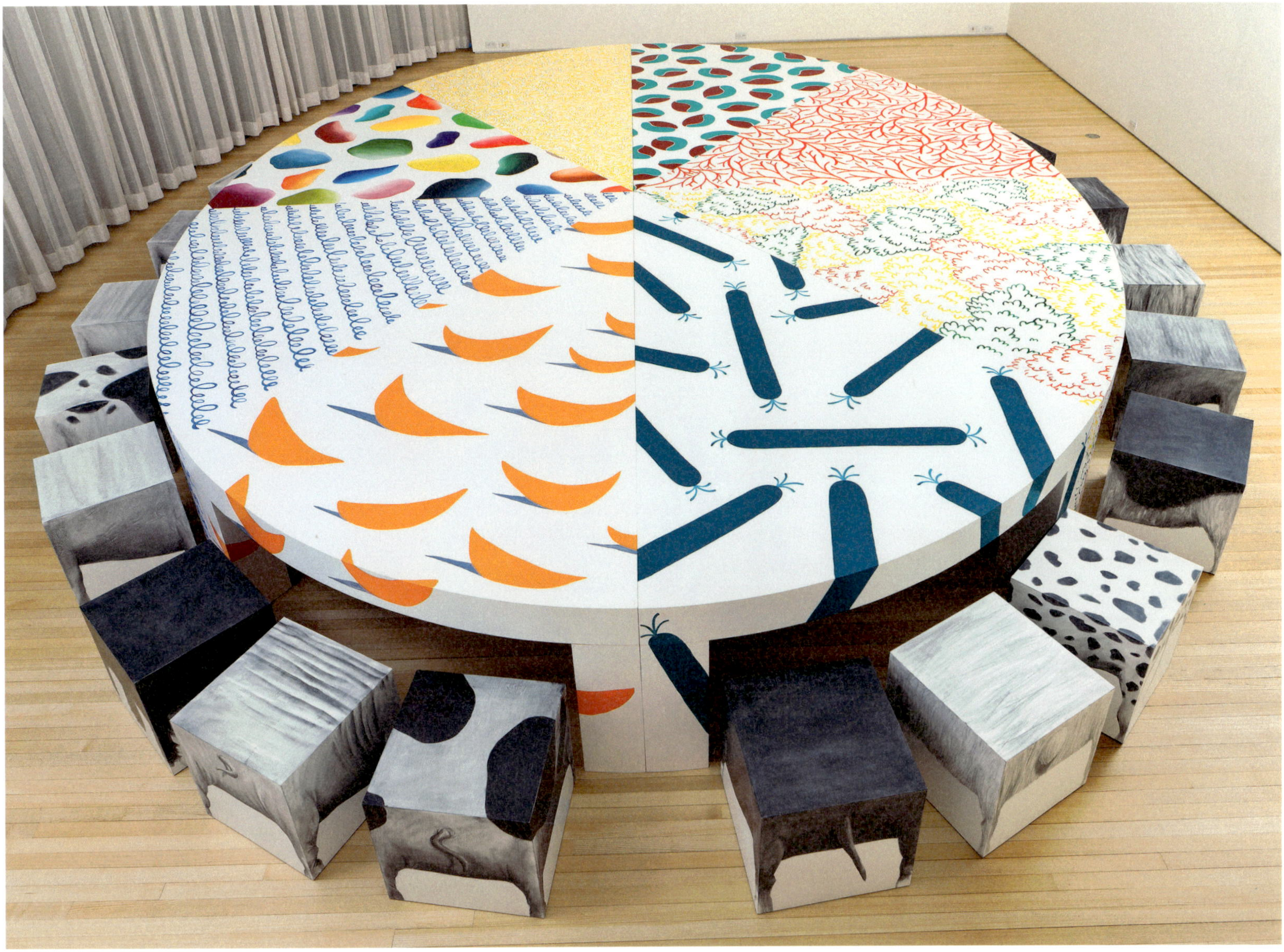

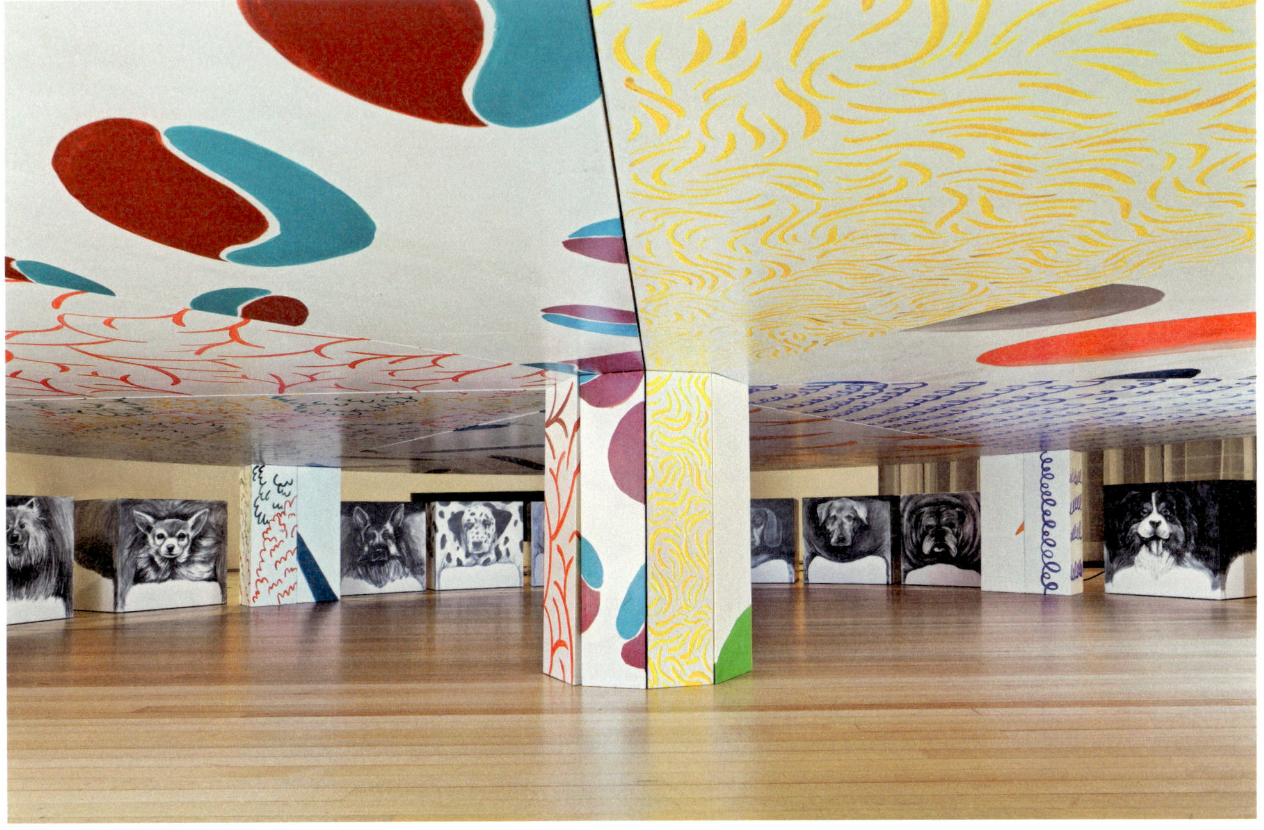

Dinner for 24 Dogs, 2012, Installationsansichten / Installation views *Dinner for 24 Dogs*, Salon 94 Freemans, New York 2012   **Nicolas Party**   107

Nicolas Party

Nicolas Party ist ein Maler, der in seinem Werk die eher konventionellen Gattungen des Stilllebens und der Landschaftsmalerei erforscht. Dennoch ist er kein konventioneller Maler und sein Werk nicht an die traditionellen Materialien oder Bildträger gebunden, die wir mit dem Medium assoziieren.

Partys „Leinwand" schließt vielmehr alles ein, von Galeriewänden bis zu Tischen, Stühlen, Geschirr, Steinen und sogar seinem eigenen Körper. Mit Materialien wie Ölfarbe, Aquarell, Kohle und Bleistift oder auch Sprühfarbe, Keramikglasur und Tattoofarben transformiert er Oberflächen, überzieht sie mit einer neuen Haut und überführt sie aus ihrer nüchternen Realität in seine heitere und oft surreale Welt. Felsbrocken und Steine werden angemalt, damit sie wie Früchte, Fleischstücke und überdimensioniertes Gemüse erscheinen; Stühle, Tische und Sockel verwandeln sich in eine Herde Elefanten; und aus Holzstämmen werden riesige Finger, die aus dem Boden herausragen, in dem sie stecken. Galeriewände werden mit leuchtenden Sprühfarben bearbeitet, die Zusammenhänge zwischen ungleichartigen Räumen herstellen und den traditionelleren Werken auf Leinwand oder Papier einen bewegten, lebendigen Hintergrund bieten. Mehr noch als ein Fenster in eine andere Welt zu öffnen, erschafft Party im Ausstellungsraum seine alternative Realität und stellt eine Bühne bereit, auf der das Werk (und das Publikum) ihr Spiel aufführen können.

Rund um Requisiten oder Möbelstücke, die er selbst entwirft und bemalt, hat Party eine Reihe von Veranstaltungen konzipiert: So präsentiert er auf Sockeln, an Wänden und auf Böden, die er mit seinen eigenen Entwürfen überzieht, die Werke anderer Künstler oder inszeniert Dinnerpartys, für die er Tische und Stühle minutiös bemalt, damit sie wie Tiere aussehen. Party schafft Situationen, die mit Humor und Genuss das Bewusstsein seines Publikums wecken und den Kontext offenlegen sollen, in dem sein Werk gezeigt wird. Durch die Umwandlung von Alltagsgegenständen wird das Publikum aufgefordert, die Welt ein wenig anders zu sehen, so das Potenzial einer ruhenden Situation freizusetzen und die Wirklichkeit mit der Fantasie verschmelzen zu lassen.

Zeit und Zeitlosigkeit liegen Partys künstlerischer Praxis und seinem Interesse an der Welt zugrunde. Weil er zeitgleich an aufwendigen Ölgemälden arbeitet, deren Fertigstellung mehrere Jahre in Anspruch nimmt, an Wandbildern, die einige Tage brauchen, und an Geschirrstücken, die eine Sache von Minuten sind, schwankt sein Verhältnis zur Zeit (und deren Verhältnis zum Wert) unaufhörlich. Die Zeit wird zu etwas Spielerischem, zu etwas, das sich nach Bedarf verlangsamen oder beschleunigen lässt. Party hat kein Interesse an der Trennung von Vergangenheit, Gegenwart und Zukunft, sondern an der Möglichkeit, dass ein Objekt – oder ein Kunstwerk – über den Moment hinaus existieren kann, in dem es geschaffen wird, jenseits unserer gegenwärtigen Vorstellung von Zeit und Wert. Partys Faszination für das Zeitlose wird durch sein Interesse an der sich niemals verändernden Landschaft und an den Grundformen der Stilllebenmalerei sichtbar gemacht; beides kehrt in seinen Ölgemälden und Aquarellen wieder. Indem er sich denselben essenziellen Bestandteilen der Landschaft (Bäume, Büsche, Gras und Blumen) und denen des Stilllebens (Kannen, Gefäße, Früchte und Gemüse) zuwendet, untersucht er die elementaren Grundeinheiten, die unsere Welt ausmachen und seit Jahrhunderten ausgemacht haben.

Partys künstlerische Praxis verweist fortwährend auf die Kunstgeschichte. Sein Werk reflektiert die Arbeiten etlicher Künstler vor ihm, die ähnliche Themen (und Malgründe) in Angriff genommen

Nicolas Party is a painter whose work explores the relatively conventional subjects of still life and landscape. He is not, however, a conventional painter, and his work is not bound by the traditional materials or surfaces that we might associate with the medium.

Instead, Party's 'canvas' includes everything from gallery walls to tables, chairs, crockery, rocks and even his own body. Working with anything from oil paint, watercolour, charcoal and pencil to spray paint, ceramic glaze and tattoo inks, Party transforms surfaces, covering them with a new skin and transporting them from their mundane reality into his humorous and often surreal world. Rocks and stones are painted to look like pieces of fruit, slabs of meat and overgrown vegetables; chairs, tables and plinths are transformed into a herd of elephants; and logs become giant fingers, reaching out of the ground in which they stand. Gallery walls are covered in brightly coloured spray paint, merging disparate spaces and providing an active, undulating backdrop to the more traditional works on canvas or paper. Rather than creating a window onto another world, Party creates his alternative reality in the exhibition space, providing a stage on which the work (and audience) can perform.

Party has produced a number of events staged around props or furniture designed and painted by him, ranging from exhibitions of other artists' work presented on plinths, walls and floors covered in his own designs, to dinner parties that take place on tables and chairs carefully painted to resemble animals. Party creates situations that use humour and pleasure to trigger awareness in his audience and to reveal the context in which the work is presented. By transforming everyday objects he invites the audience to see the world slightly differently, releasing the potential of a static situation and allowing reality to merge with imagination.

Time and timelessness underlie Party's practice and his interest in the world. Simultaneously working on laborious oil paintings that take several years to complete, murals that take a number of days, and pieces of crockery that take a matter of minutes, his relationship to time (and its relationship to value) fluctuates continuously. Time becomes something playful, something that can be slowed down or speeded up as necessary. He is not interested in the separation of past, present and future, but in the possibility that an object, or artwork, can exist beyond the moment in which it is made, outside our current notion of time and value. Party's fascination with timelessness is made visible through his interest in the unchanging rural landscape and the basic forms of still-life painting, which recur in his oil paintings and watercolours. By returning to the same essential ingredients of the landscape (trees, bushes, grass and flowers) and those of a still life (pots, vessels, fruits and vegetables), he examines the basic elements that make up our world, and have done for centuries.

Party's practice continually references art history, and his work echoes that of a number of artists who have tackled similar subjects (and surfaces) before him, from the cave paintings of France and Spain and the frescos of Greece and Rome, via the still-life painting of Jean-Siméon Chardin, Giorgio Morandi and Fernand Léger, to the multicoloured world of David Hockney and the signature stripes of Daniel Buren. Party positions himself and his work within an epic history that far exceeds his immediate context.

Within his work Party returns to a number of motifs, using his own practice (as much as anyone else's) to create a colourful language based on the history of his previous works. Using a lexicon of objects (such as the pots in his still-life paintings) and shapes (such

haben, von den Höhlenmalereien in Frankreich und Spanien und den antiken Fresken der Griechen und Römer über die Stillleben von Jean Siméon Chardin, Giorgio Morandi und Fernand Léger bis zur vielfarbigen Welt eines David Hockney und den charakteristischen vertikalen Streifen eines Daniel Buren. Party stellt sich und sein Werk in den Kontext einer langen und ehrwürdigen Geschichte, die weit größer ist als sein unmittelbares Umfeld.

Innerhalb seines Werks kehrt Party zu einer Reihe von Motiven zurück, wobei er sein eigenes Verfahren mit den Methoden der anderen kombiniert, um eine farbenfrohe Sprache zu erschaffen, die auf seinen früheren Arbeiten aufbaut. Mit einem Vokabular von Dingen (wie den Kannen in seinen Stillleben) und Formen (wie den „Zweigen", „Scheiben" und „Federn", die in seinen Wandbildern auftauchen) kennzeichnet er den Malgrund als seinen eigenen und generiert so einen wiedererkennbaren, charakteristischen Stil. Diese sich selbst fortsetzende Sprache eröffnet dem Künstler eine andere Möglichkeit, mit der Zeit zu spielen, sodass sich die Arbeiten auf sich selbst zurückbeziehen können.

Partys komplexes Verhältnis zur Zeit kommt vor allem in der Wahl seiner Themen zum Ausdruck, spiegelt sich aber auch in seinen unterschiedlichen Arbeitsweisen, vom zeitaufwendigen Malen im Atelier bis zur produktiven Tätigkeit als Teil einer Gruppe. Party arbeitet regelmäßig mit anderen Künstlern zusammen und hat in den letzten Jahren an zahlreichen Gemeinschaftsprojekten mitgewirkt oder sie angestoßen – von Publikationen und Ausstellungen bis hin zu gemeinschaftlich produzierten Arbeiten. Sein Interesse an diesen unterschiedlichen Arbeitsformen ist typisch für seine vielfältigen und interdisziplinären künstlerischen Aktivitäten und vielleicht auch für Glasgow. Noch nie hat sich Party festlegen lassen: Er ist Maler, Grafikdesigner, Graffitikünstler und Kurator, sein künstlerischer Ansatz schließt viele Rollen und Identitäten ein, sogar die der Menschen um ihn herum und der Stadt, in der er lebt.

as the 'sprigs', 'slices' and 'springs' that appear in his murals) he marks surfaces as his own, generating a recognisable, 'signature' style. This self-perpetuating language provides another way for Party to play with time, allowing the work to refer back to itself.

Although much of Party's complex relationship with time is articulated through his choice of subject, it is also reflected in the various ways in which he works, from his slow, solitary pursuits in the studio to his prolific practice as part of a collective. Party regularly works with other artists, and over recent years he has initiated and participated in numerous collaborative projects, from publications and exhibitions to collectively authored works. His interest in these varied modes of working is typical of his wide-ranging and cross-disciplinary practice, and perhaps also of Glasgow. Party has been (and still is) many things: a painter, a graphic designer, a graffiti artist and a curator, and his practice as an artist encompasses many roles and identities, including those of the people around him and the place where he lives.

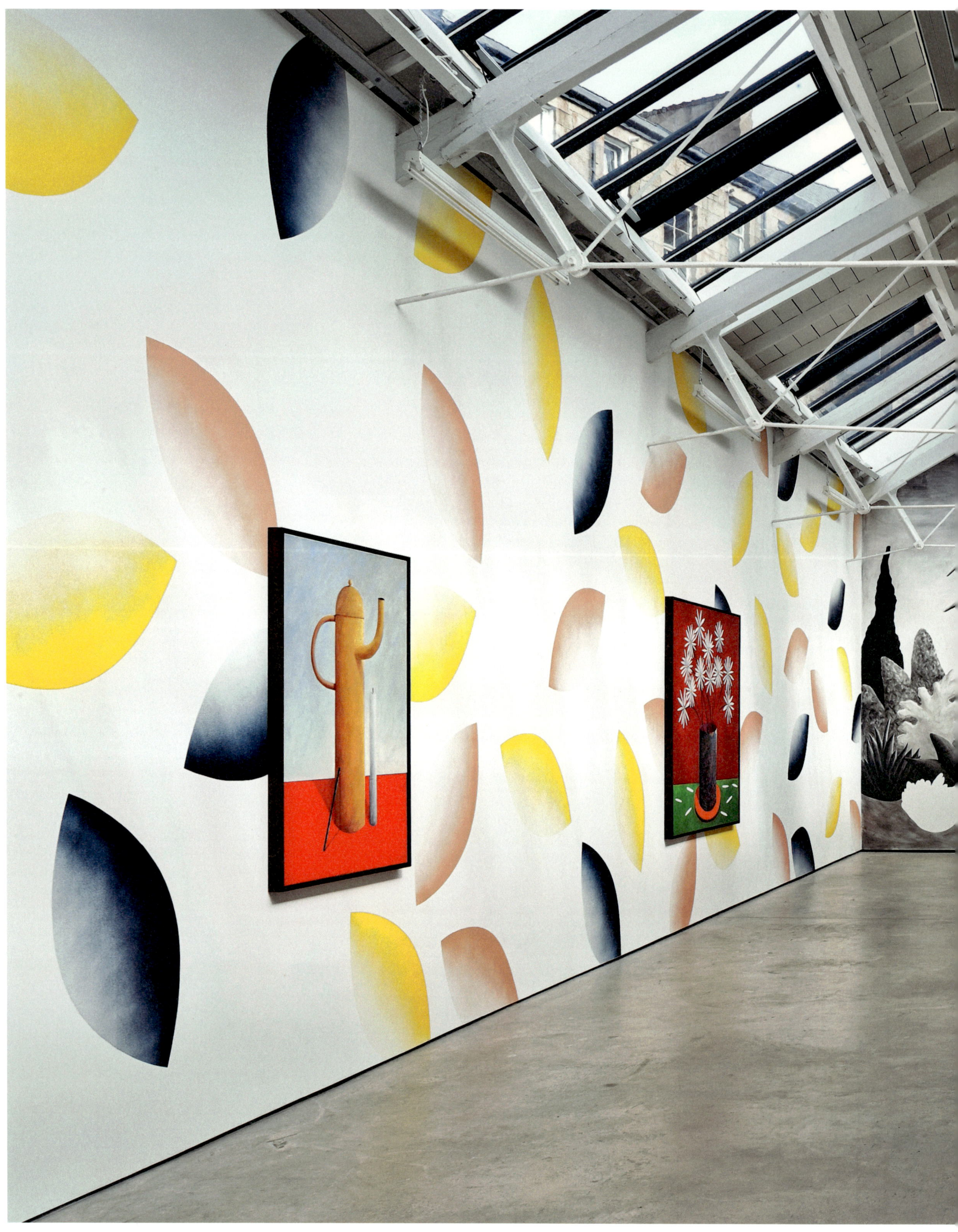

 Installationsansicht / Installation view *Still Life oil paintings and Landscape watercolours*, The Modern Institute/Toby Webster Ltd, Glasgow 2013

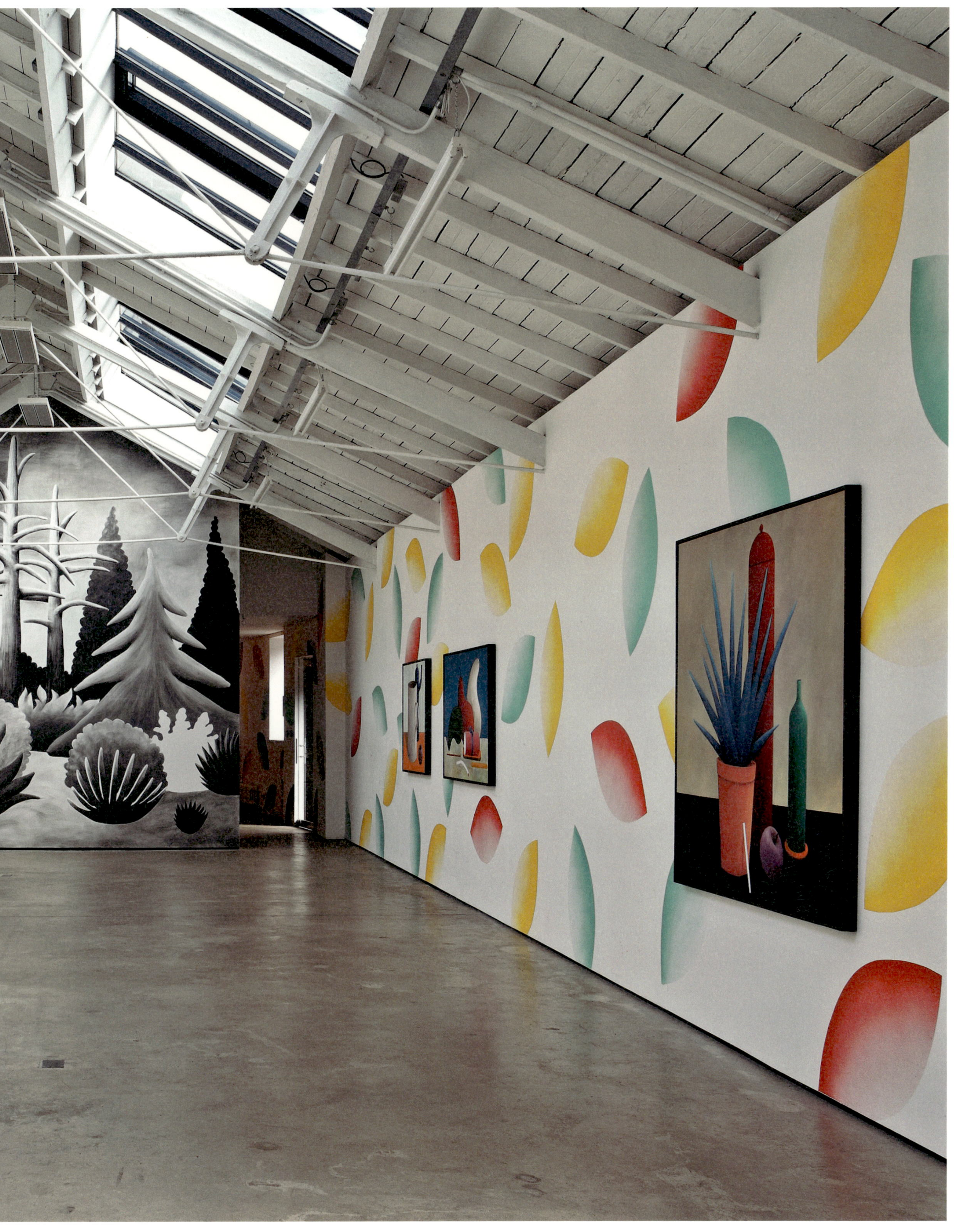

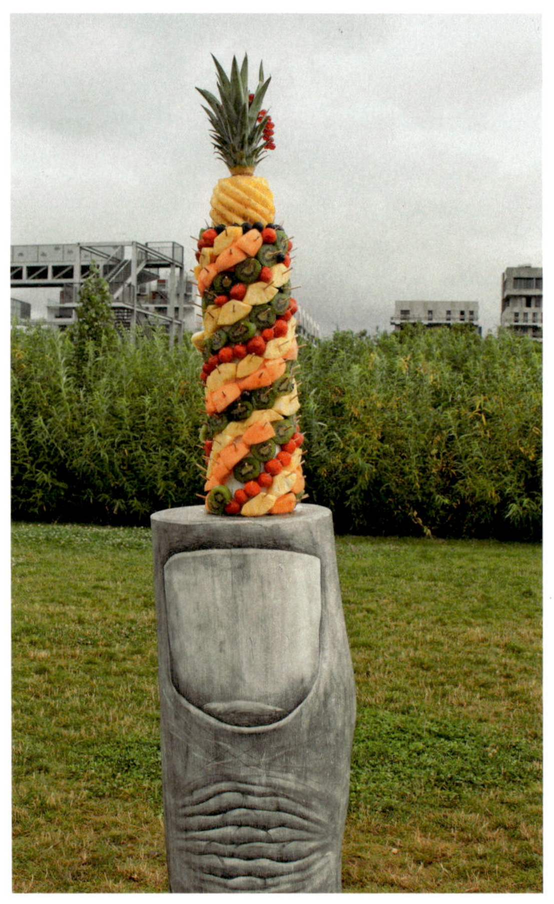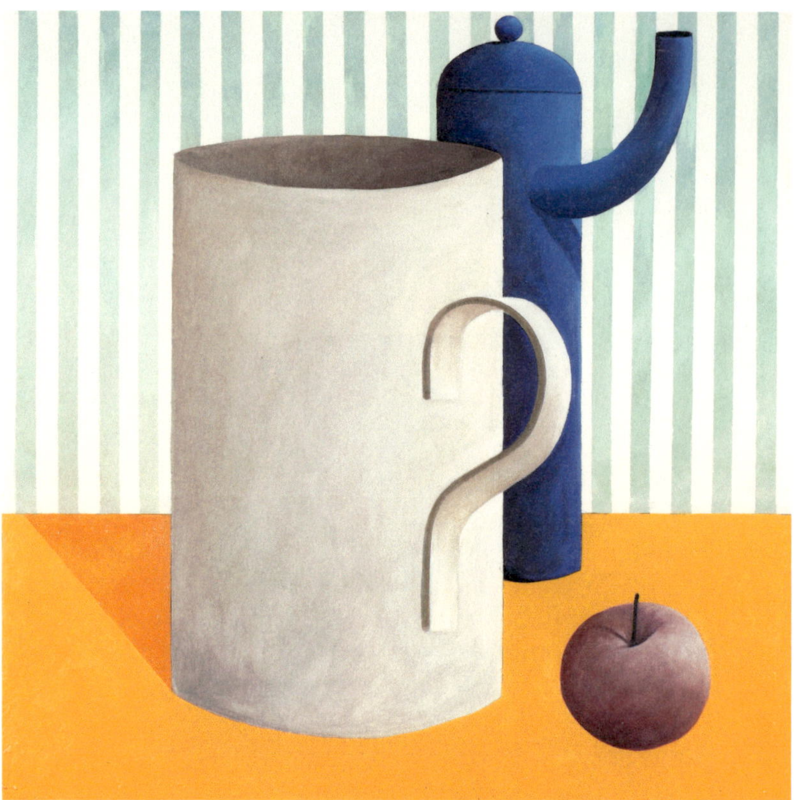

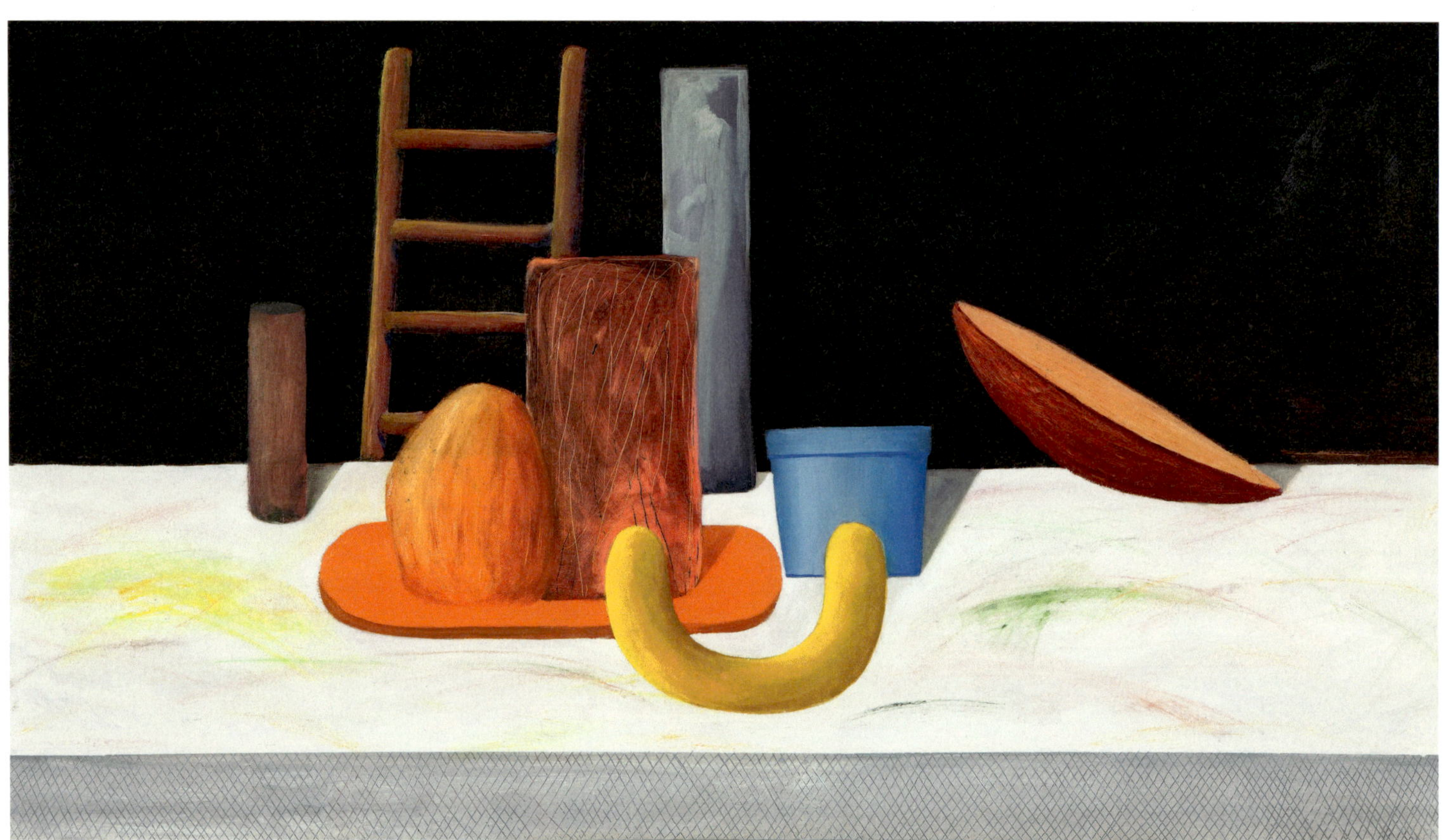

Fingers, 2012, Installationsansicht / Installation view *Allez-y*, R4, Ile Seguin, Paris 2012 (oben links / top left)
Still life with an orange table, 2012–2013, Collection of Kevin and Amy Gould, Singapore (oben rechts / top right)
Still life with a paint roller, 2009, Private Collection, Paris (unten / bottom)

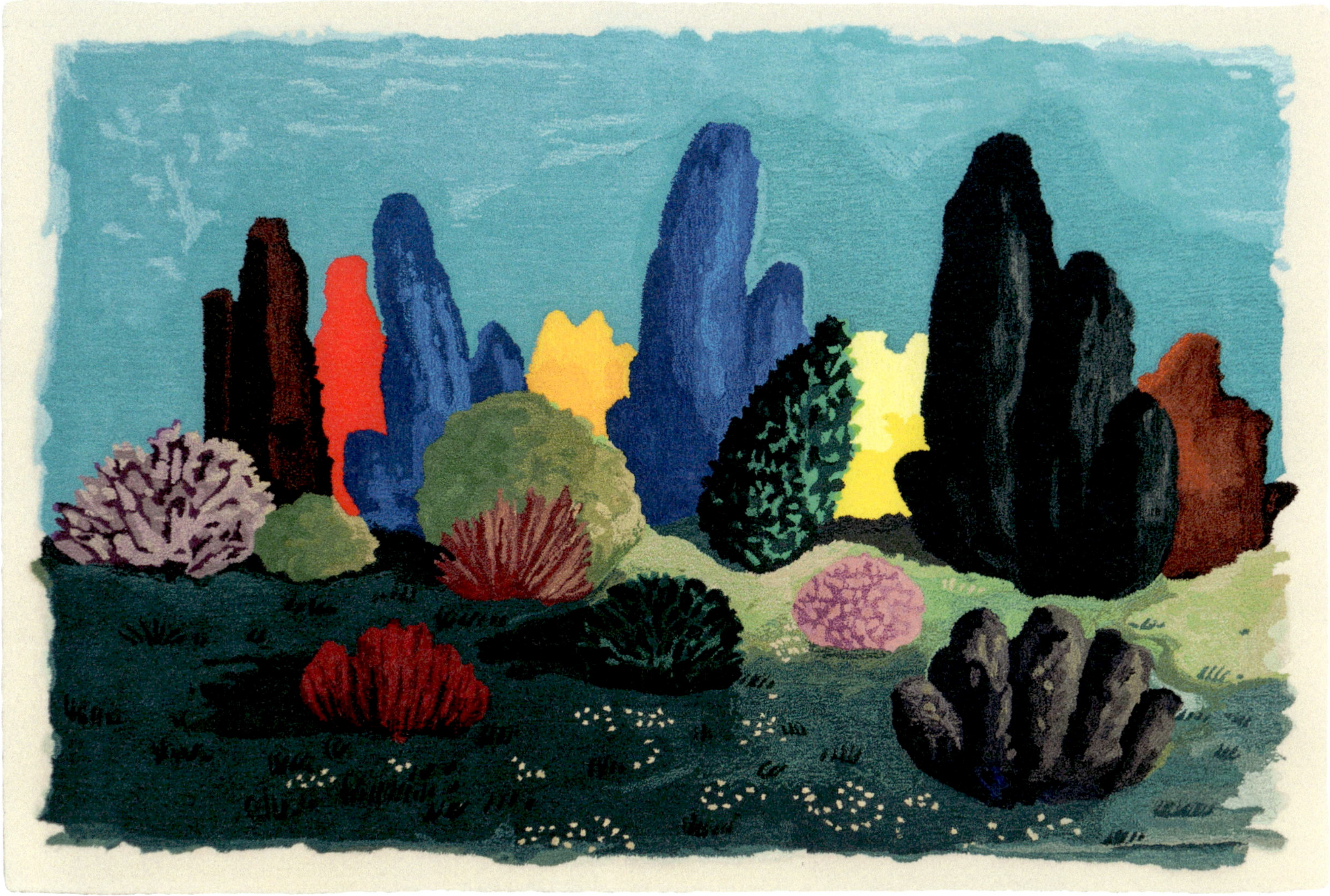

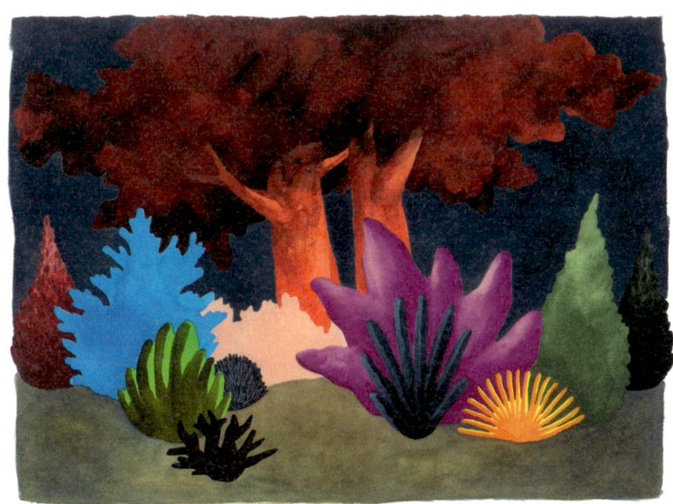

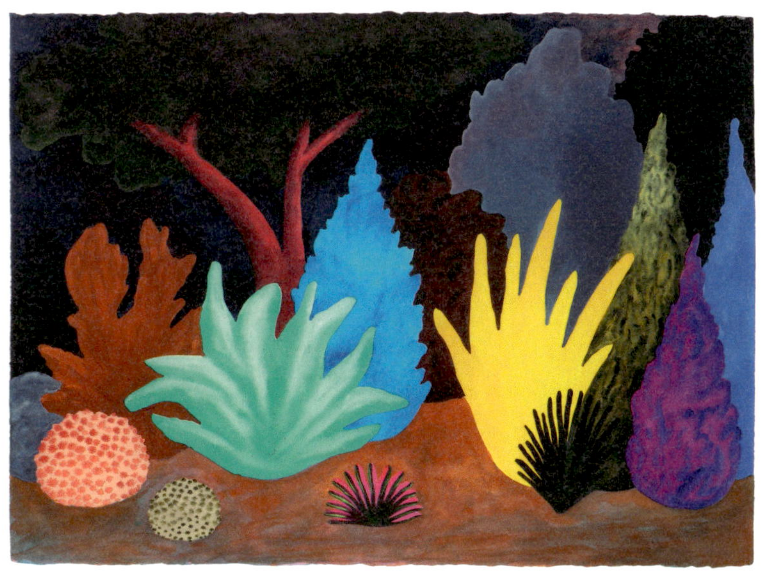

Landscape, 2012 (oben / top) · *Landscape*, 2013, Debbie and Mitchell Rechler Collection (Mitte / middle)
Landscape, 2013 (unten rechts / bottom right)

Nicolas Party   113

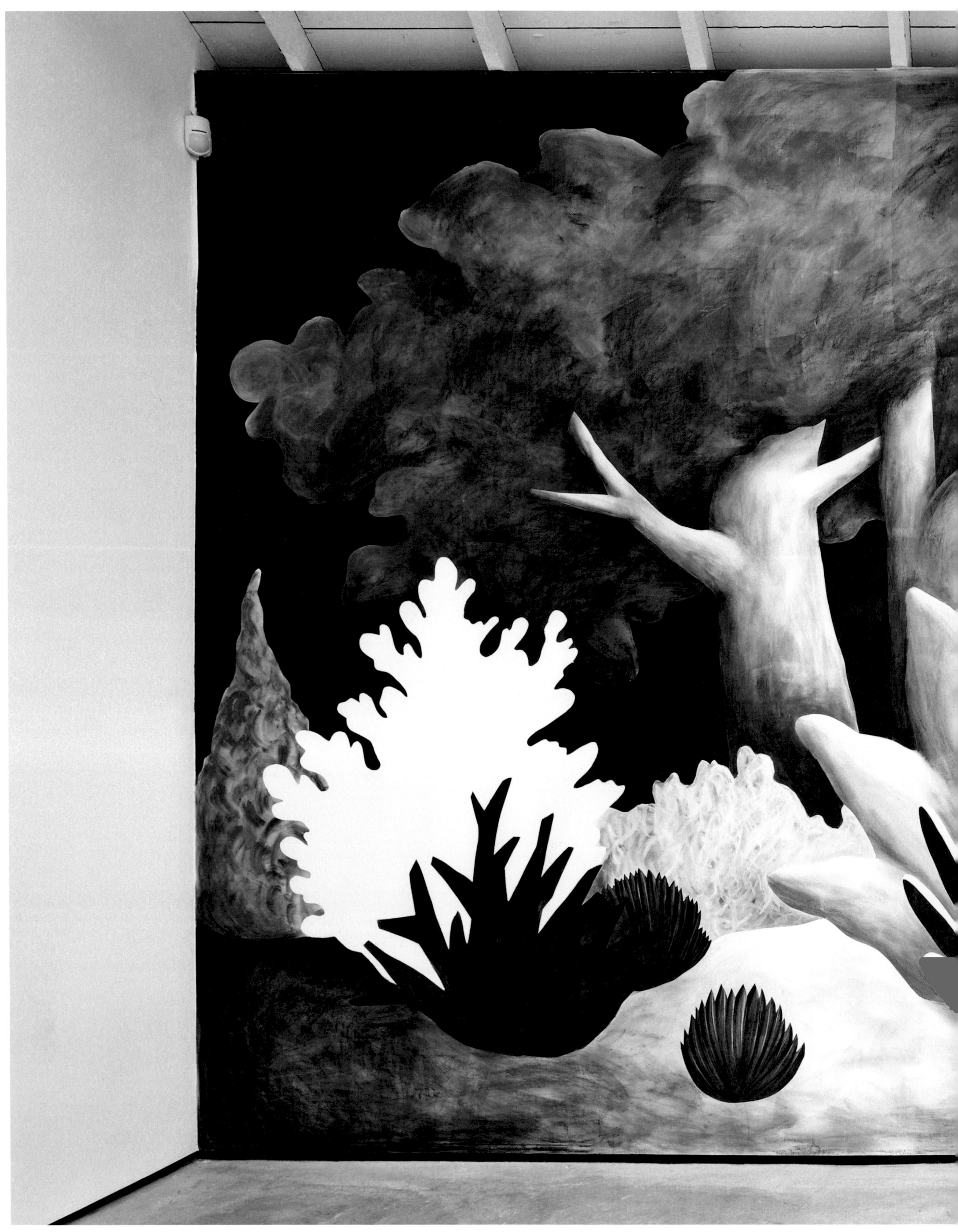

 Landscape, 2013, Installationsansicht / Installation view *Still Life oil paintings and Landscape watercolours*, The Modern Institute/Toby Webster Ltd, Glasgow 2013

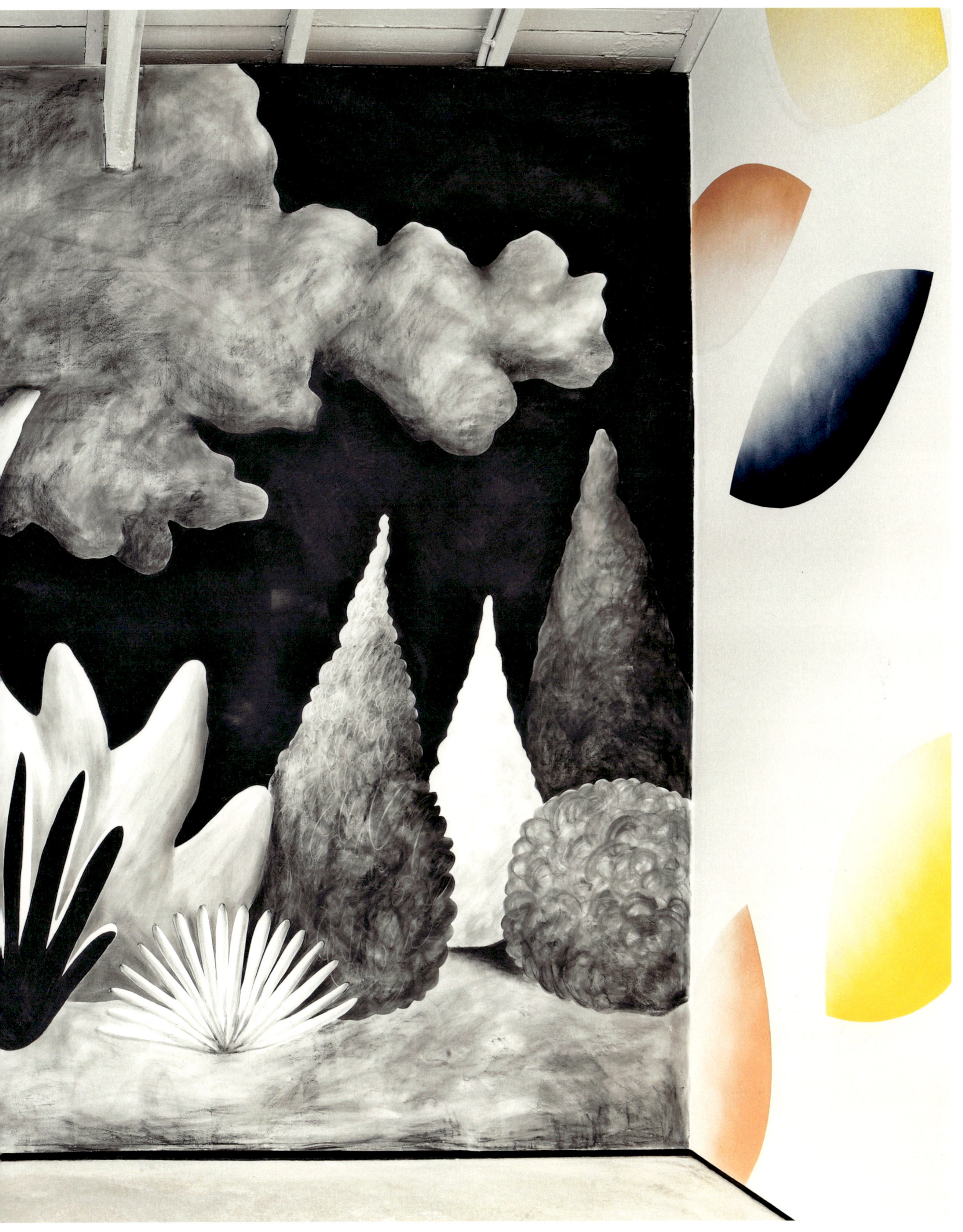

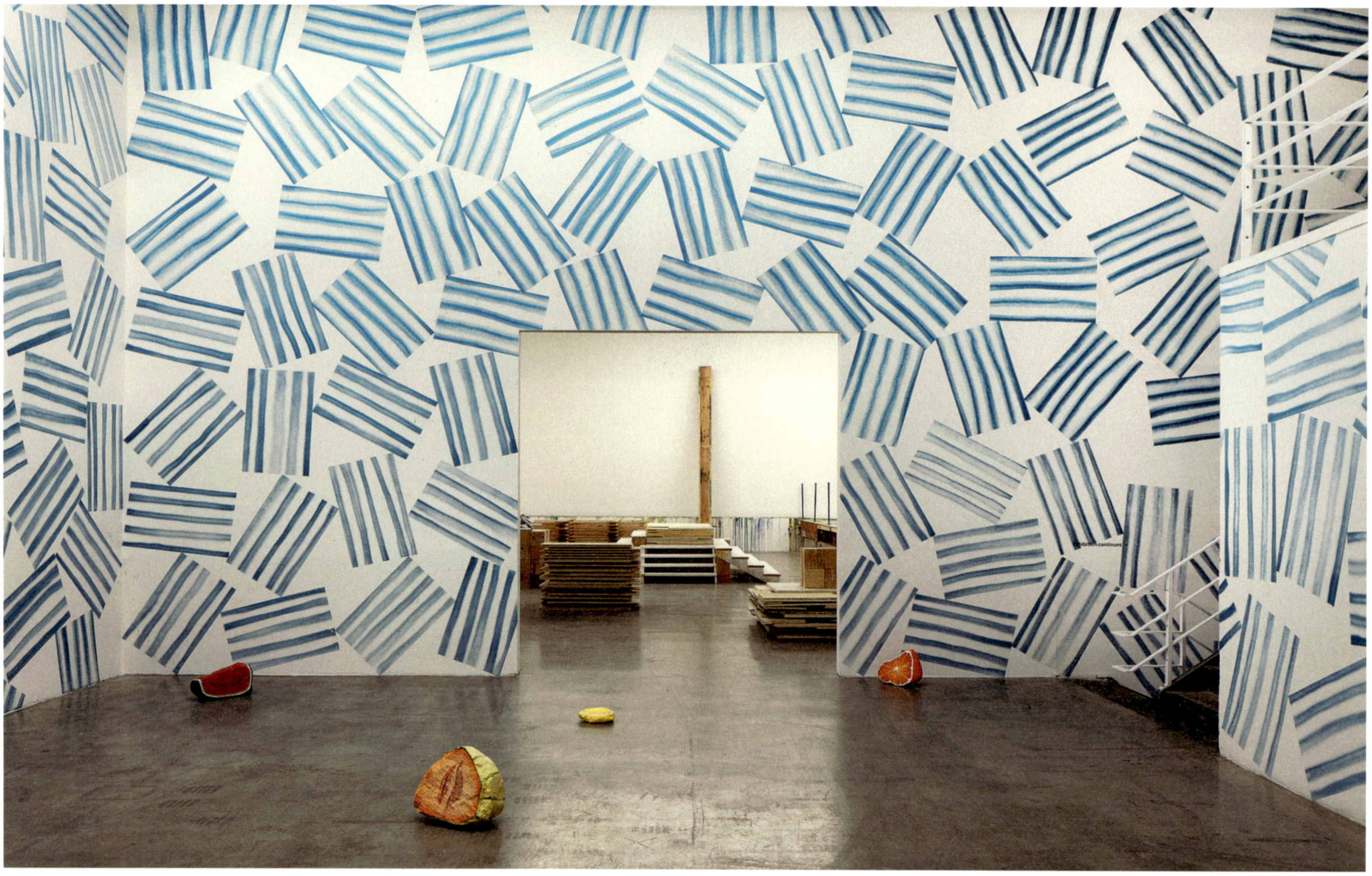

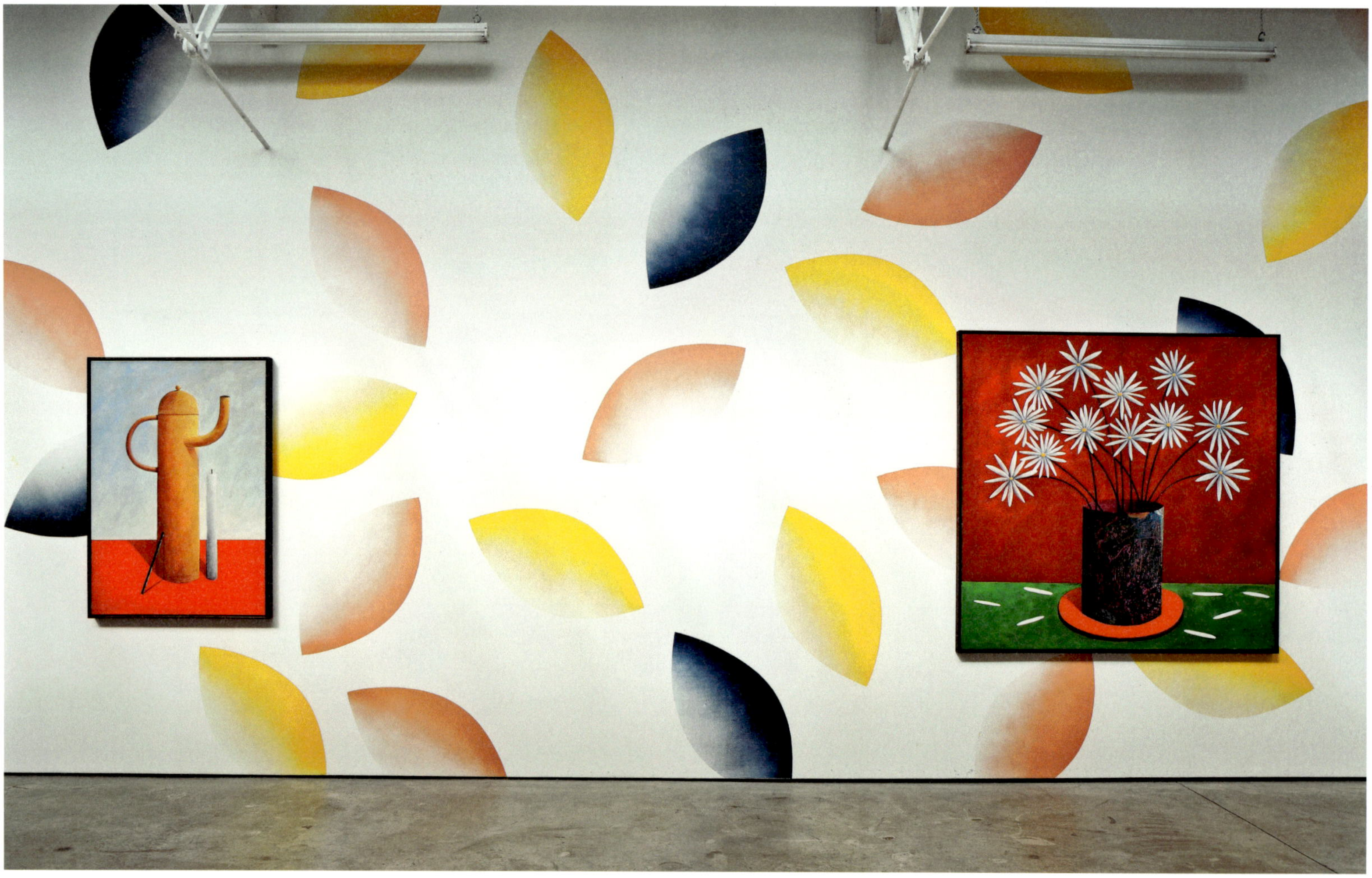

Installationsansicht / Installation view *Still Life, Stones and Elephants*, Swiss Institute, New York 2012 (oben / top)
Installationsansicht / Installation view *Still Life oil paintings and Landscape watercolours*, The Modern Institute/Toby Webster Ltd, Glasgow 2013 (unten / bottom)
Untitled, 2013, Installationsansicht / Installation view *Still Life oil paintings and Landscape watercolours*, The Modern Institute/Toby Webster Ltd, Glasgow 2013 (S. / p. 117)

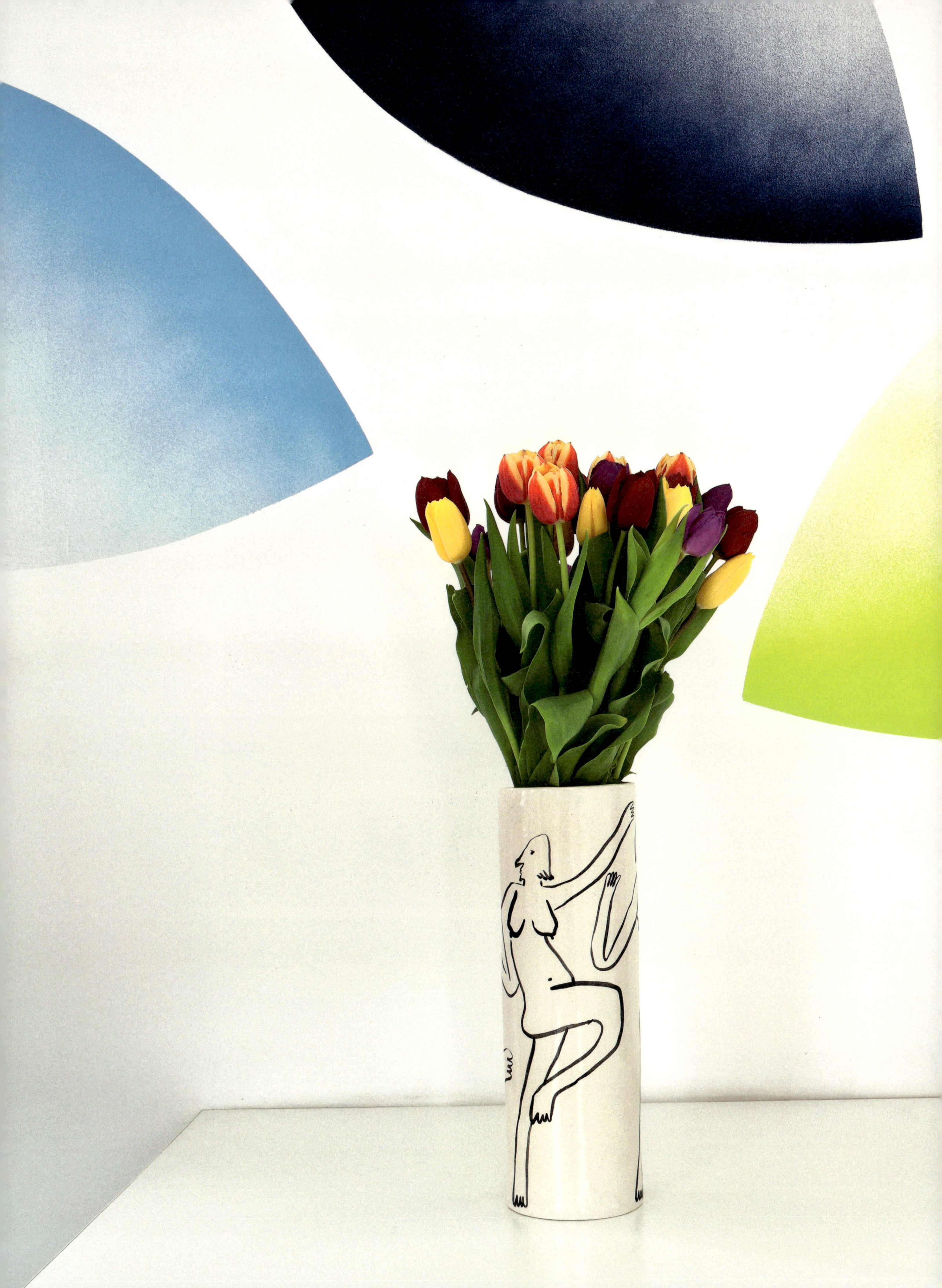

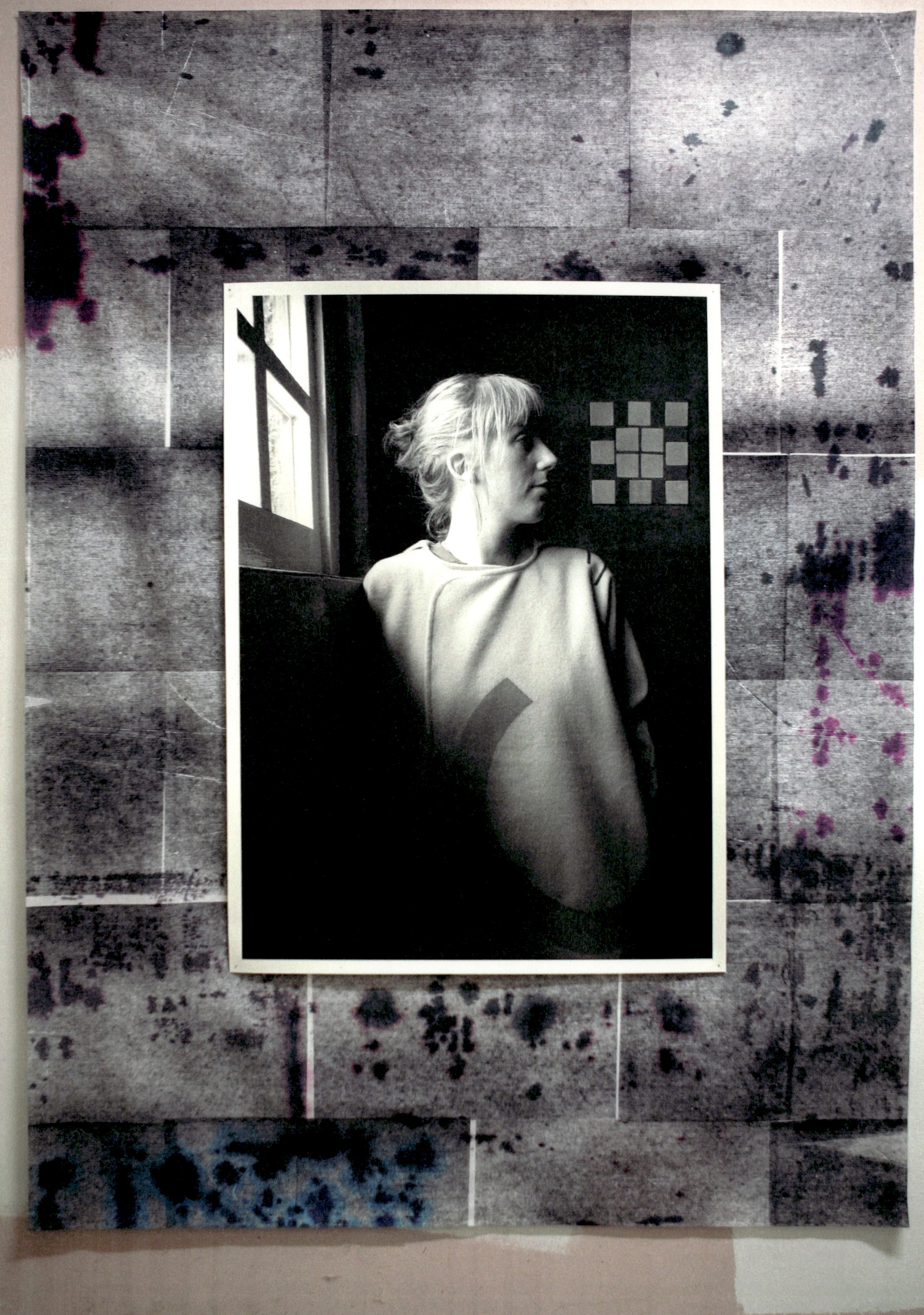

Printing Textiles, Laura, 2011

Biografie / Biography

Ciara Phillips lebt und arbeitet / lives and works
in Glasgow, Schottland / Scotland
1976   geboren / born in Ottawa, Kanada / Canada

Studium / Education

1996–2000   Bachelor of Fine Art, Queen's University, Kingston
2002–2004   Master of Fine Art, Glasgow School of Art, Glasgow

Stipendien und Preise / Scholarships and Awards

2009   Visual Arts Creative Development Residency, Cove Park
2010   Gastkünstlerin des Landes Nordrhein-Westfalen,
        Düsseldorf
2011   Visual Artist Grant, Creative Scotland
2013   Drawing Room Bursary Award, Drawing Room, London
2014   Artist in Residence, St John's College, Oxford

Ausgewählte Ausstellungen / Selected Exhibitions

„Aires de jeux", Le Quartier, Centre d'Art Contemporain,
Quimper (2010)
„Zwischenraum: Space Between", Kunstverein Hamburg (2010)
„Blueprint for a Bogey", Gallery of Modern Art, Glasgow (2011)
„Petrosphere", ReMap3, Athen / Athens (2011)
„Ciara Phillips. The only rule is work", Kendall Koppe,
Glasgow (2011)
„Ciara Phillips", Liste 17, Basel (2012)
„Ciara Phillips. Start with a practical idea", Gregor Staiger, Zürich /
Zurich (2012)
„Ciara Phillips. Slippery under pressure", OUTPOST,
Norwich (2012)
„The Souls, a Twice-Told Tale", Centre Européen d'Actions
Artistiques Contemporaines, Straßburg / Strasbourg (2013)
„Ciara Phillips. And more", Inverleith House, Edinburgh (2013)
„There Will Be New Rules Next Week", Dundee Contemporary
Arts, Dundee (2013)

Ausgewählte Publikationen / Selected Publications

Ruth Barker, Niall Macdonald, „Placed Upon the Horizon:
A Permanent Public Artwork", South Lanarkshire Council,
Hamilton 2006
Dawn Bothwell, „Corita Kent and Ciara Phillips: Pull Everything
Out", in: *This is Tomorrow*, Onlinemagazin / online magazine,
http://www.thisistomorrow.info/viewArticle.aspx?artId=1405
Gabriele Schaad, „Ciara Phillips – Start with a practical idea", in:
frieze d/e, Issue 6, 09/2012

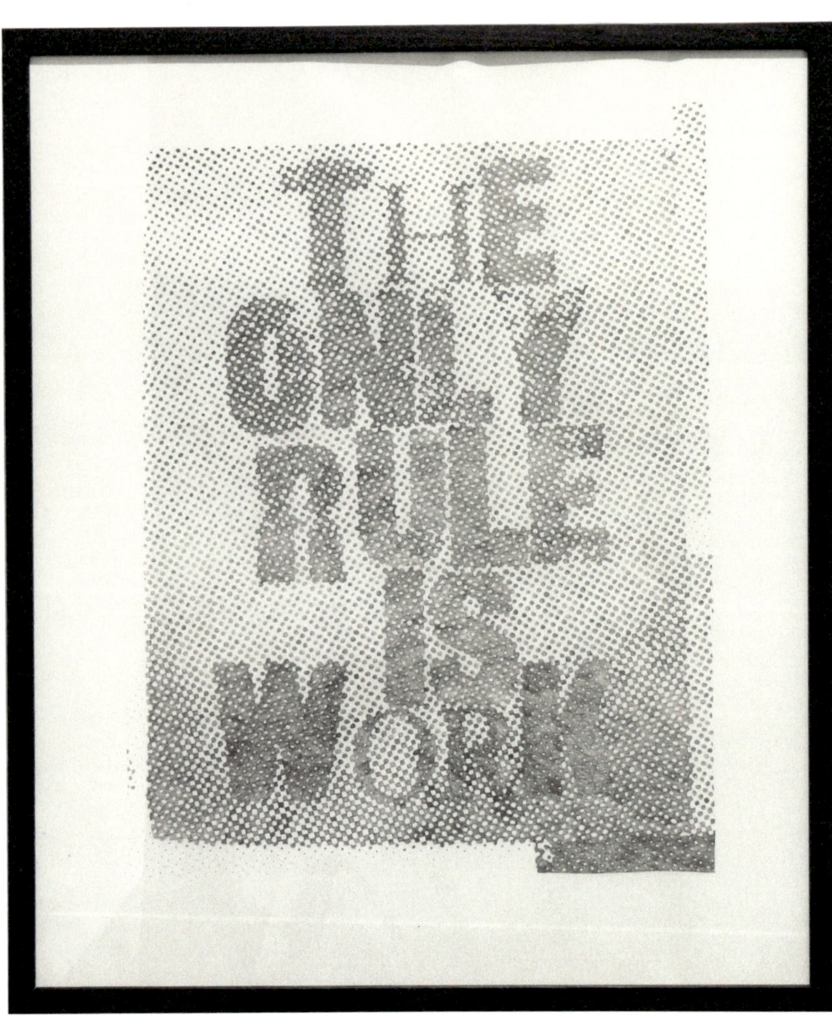

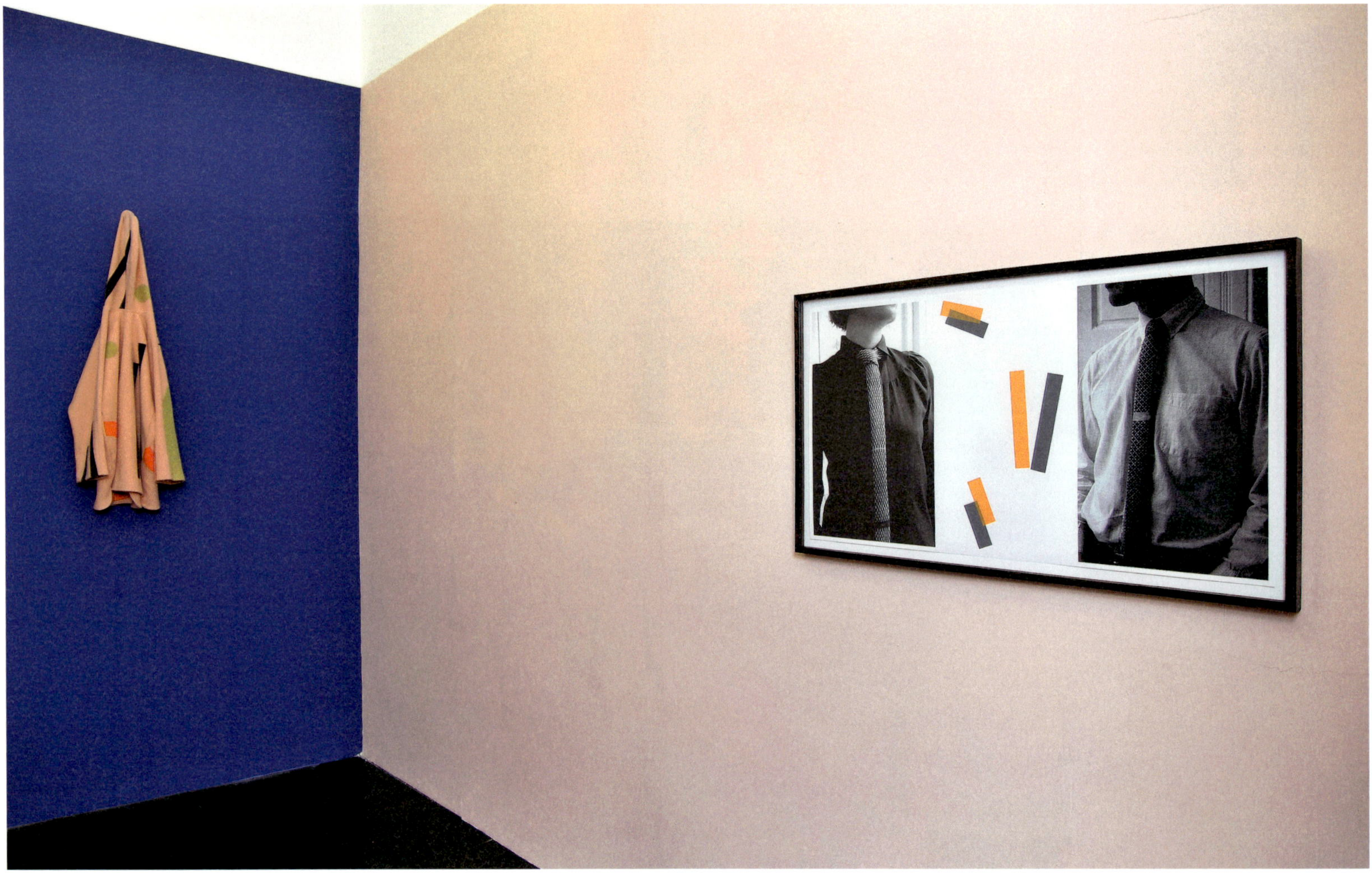

Rule 7, 2010 (oben / top)
Jacket, 2011, und / and *The only rule is work,* 2011, Installationsansicht / Installation view *The only rule is work*, Kendall Koppe, Glasgow 2011 (unten / bottom)

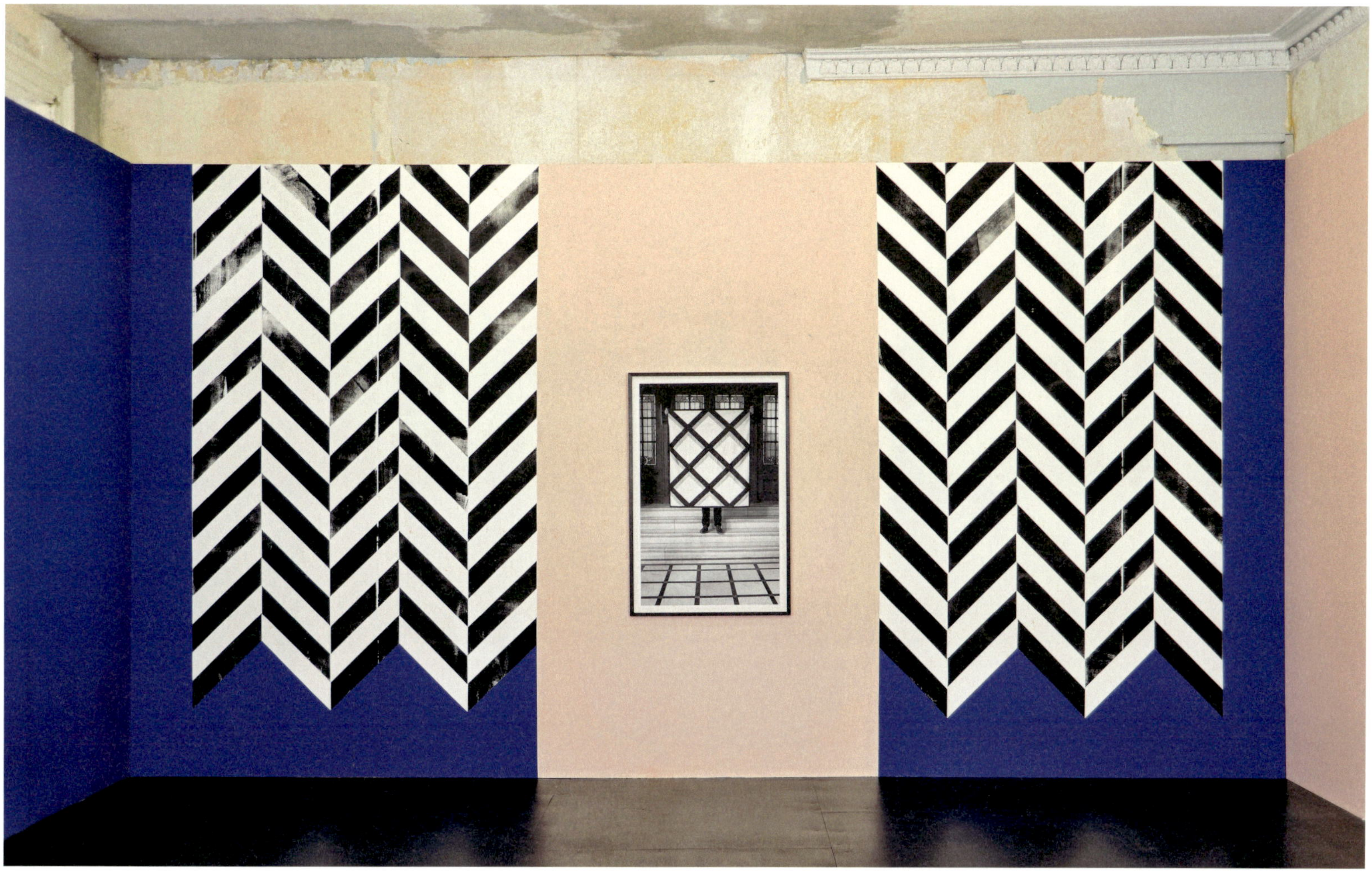

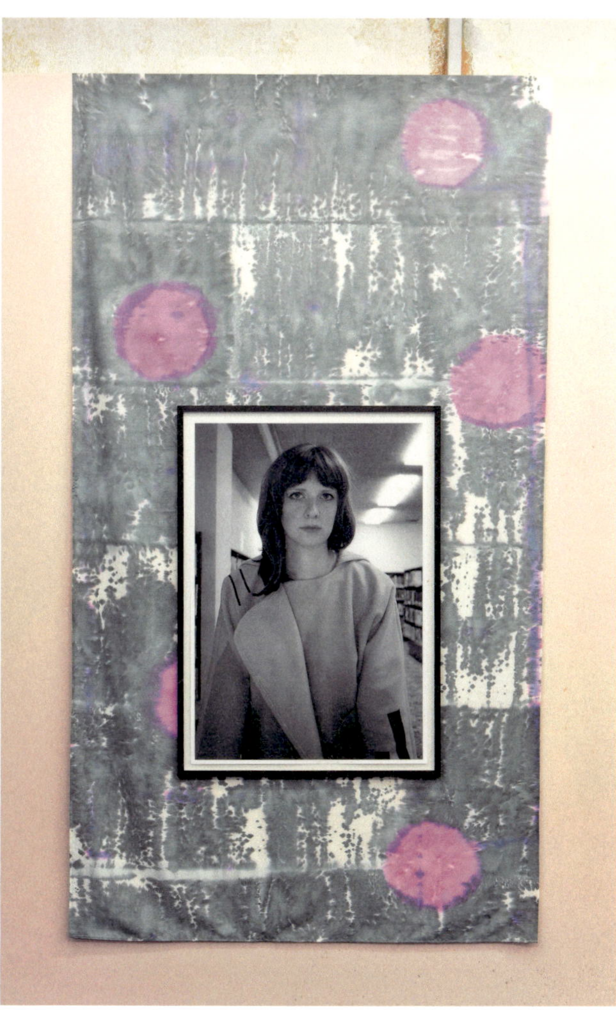

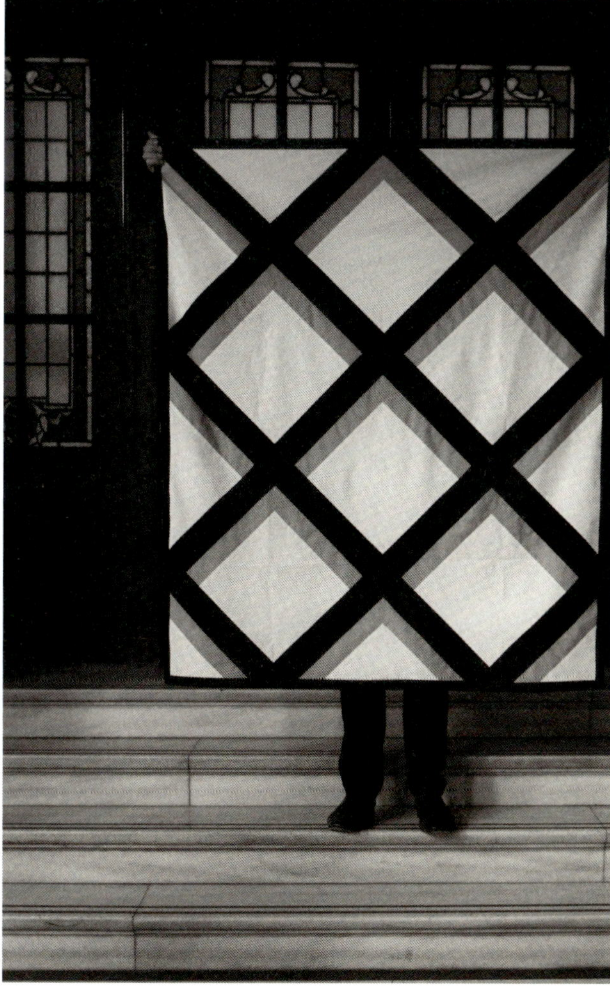

Shadow Work (conceal), 2011, Installationsansicht / Installation view *The only rule is work*, Kendall Koppe, Glasgow 2011 (oben / top) · *Catriona, Mitchell Library,* 2011, Installationsansicht / Installation view *The only rule is work*, Kendall Koppe, Glasgow 2011 (unten links / bottom left) · *Shadow work*, 2011 (unten rechts / bottom right)

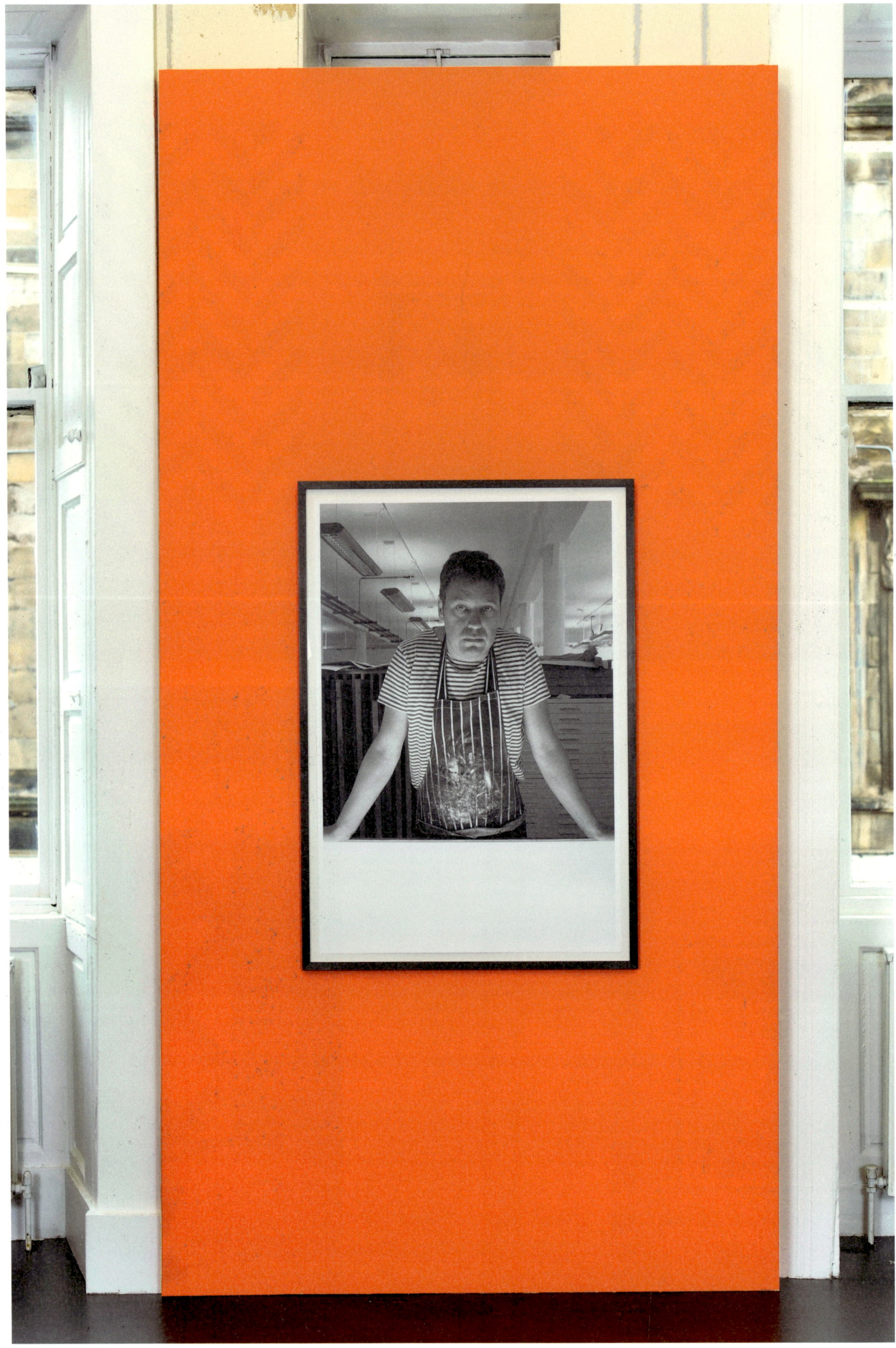

 Scott, Print Studio, 2011, Installationsansicht / Installation view *The only rule is work*, Kendall Koppe, Glasgow 2011

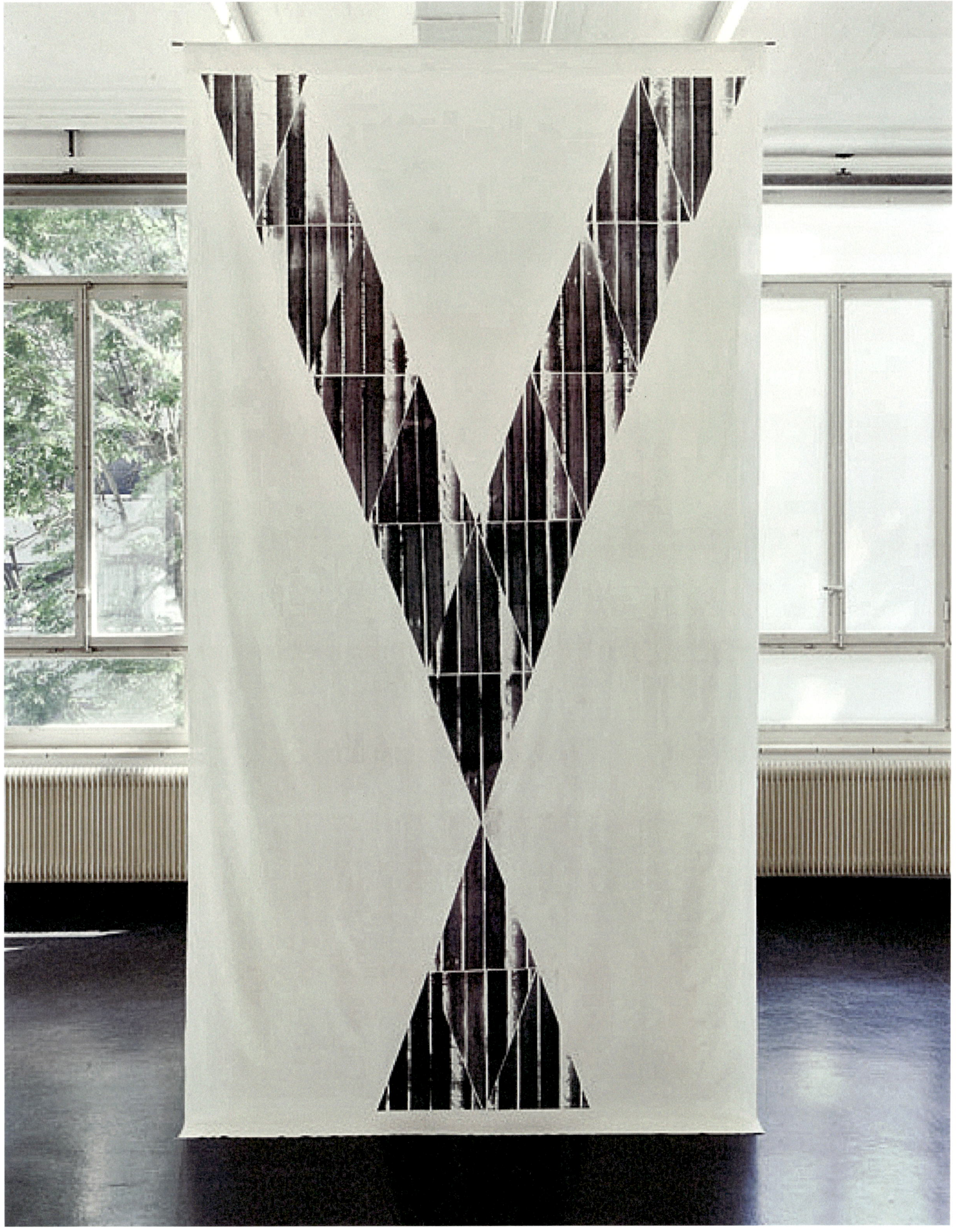

Very, 2012, Installationsansicht / Installation view *Start with a practical idea*, Gregor Staiger, Zürich / Zurich 2012   **Ciara Phillips** 123

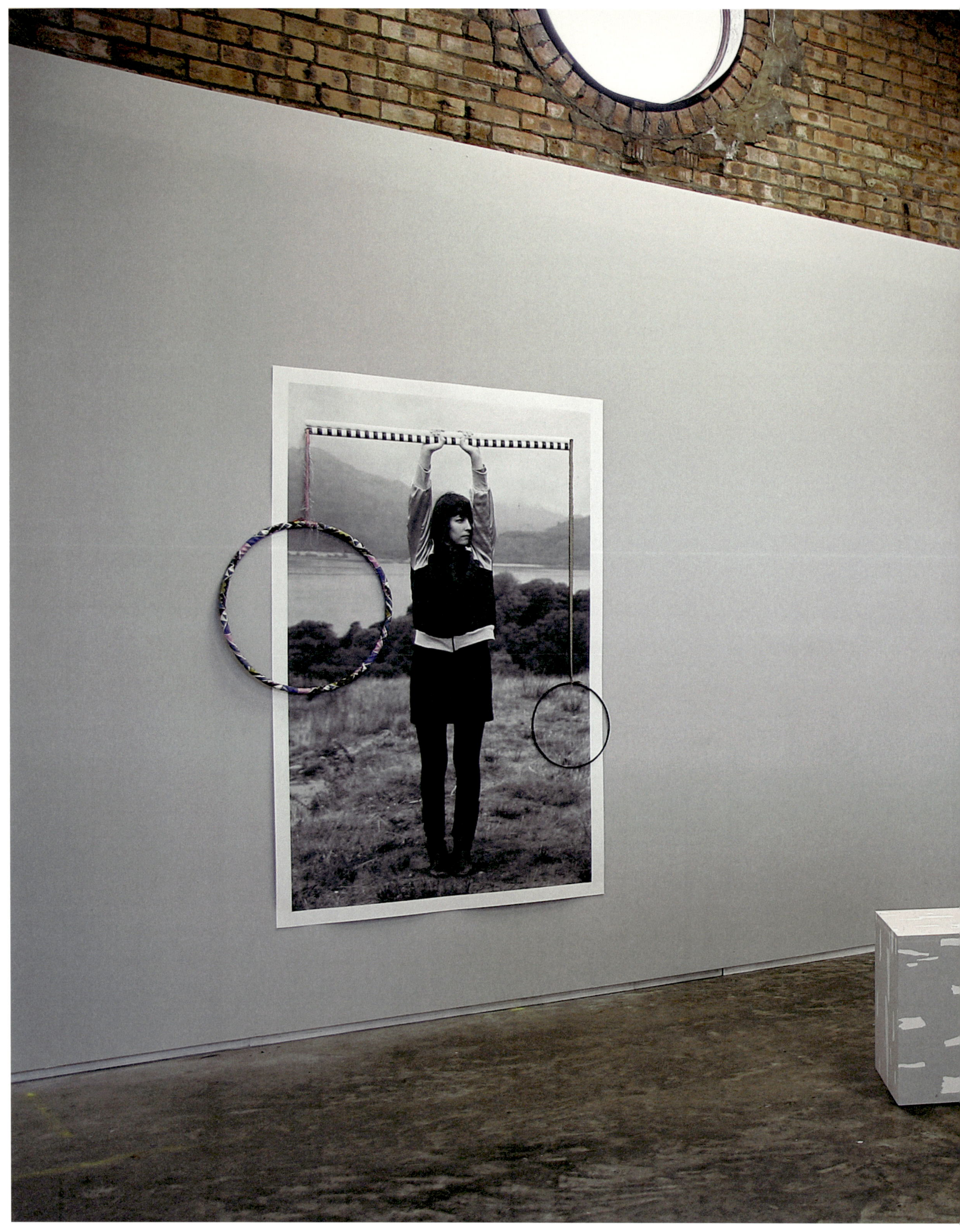

 T (balance), 2009, *E: Brick on a bench*, 2009, und / and *V*, 2009, Installationsansicht / Installation view *Ciara Phillips*, Washington Garcia Gallery, Glasgow 2009

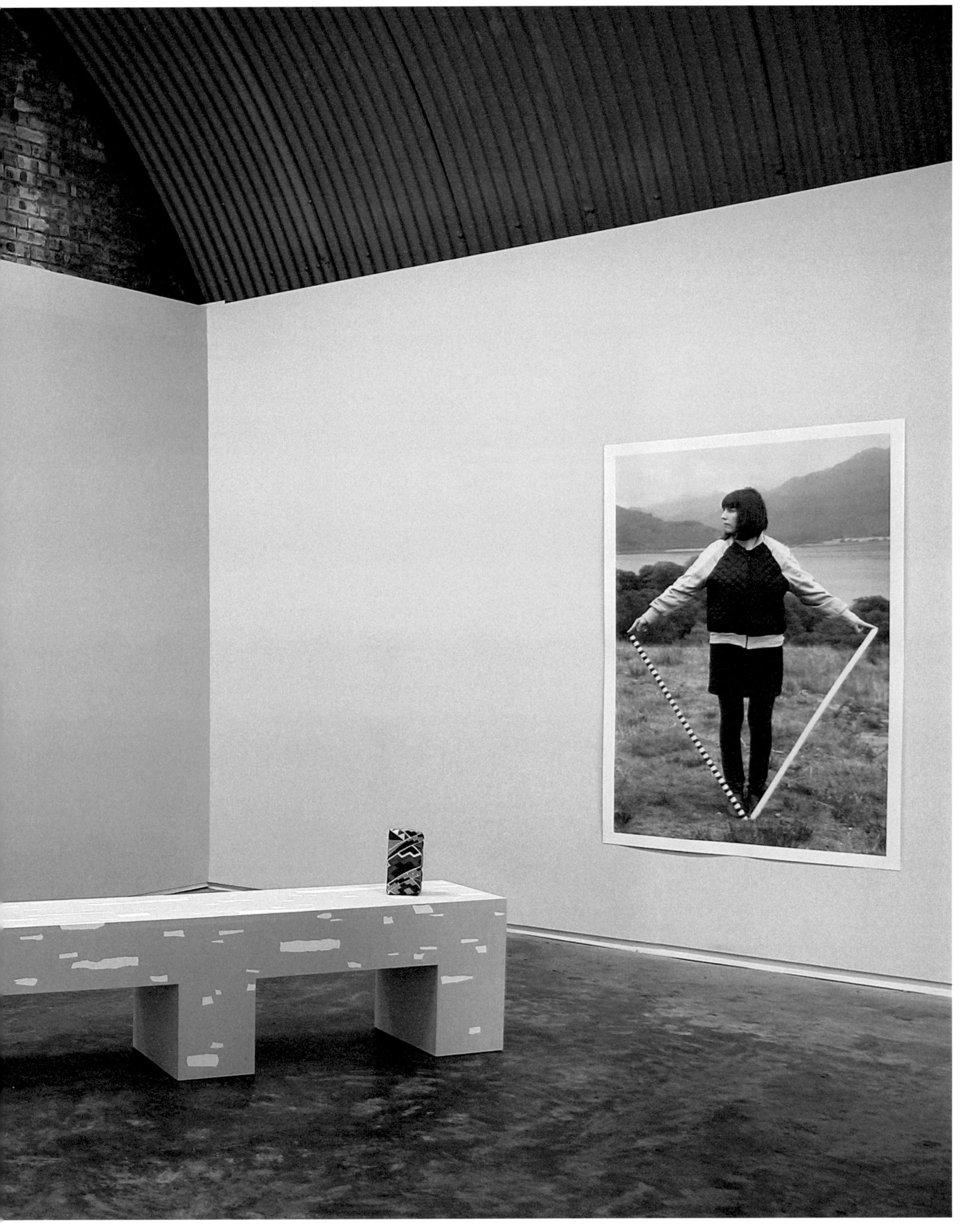

Ciara Phillips

Ciara Phillips

Lassen Sie uns über Produktion reden. Substantiv und Verb – „Produktion" und „produzieren" – zählen zu jenen Begriffen, die Lektoren gelegentlich aus dem Manuskript eines Kunstkritikers zu streichen versuchen, weil sie diese für überstrapazierte Modebegriffe halten. Es gibt jedoch Fälle, in denen ein Autor dieser Streichung Widerstand leisten sollte: wenn die Worte nützlich sind, wenn sie sich als anschaulich erweisen und etwas von der Arbeit der Künstlerin und ihren Arbeitsmethoden vermitteln. Ein Text über Ciara Phillips ist so ein Fall. „Künstlerische Produktion" deutet an, dass das Endergebnis von Phillips' Tätigkeit wesentlich von den Mitteln der Herstellung geprägt ist und aus ihnen hervorgeht. Der Begriff legt nahe, dass das Kunstobjekt, selbst wenn es im Ausstellungsraum sich selbst überlassen ist, dem Publikum dennoch die Nuancen seiner Entstehungsgeschichte verraten wird. Die künstlerische Tätigkeit wird sichtbar gemacht. Das Verb wird zum Substantiv.

Phillips' Siebdrucke sind formalistische Experimente. Abstrakte Striche, Muster und gefleckte Landschaften aus Tusche stehen in Spannung zu klar definierten, symbolisch suggestiven Formen, figürlichen Motiven oder gelegentlich auch Fotografien. Ein mehr als ein Meter hoher Druck auf Papier aus der Serie *Slippery Under Pressure* (2012) zum Beispiel scheint eine Urne darzustellen. Die flache Form dieses mutmaßlichen Gefäßes ist umgeben von einem großflächigen, vielleicht modernistischen Muster aus blauen Rechtecken auf Grün. Das Grün jedoch wiederholt sich in der facettenreichen Farbpalette und Textur der Urne und suggeriert so ein flüchtiges Objekt, das sowohl von seinem Hintergrund gebildet wird als auch im Unterschied zu ihm existiert. Wie für Phillips' Werk typisch, zelebriert diese Darstellung zum einen die Flächigkeit des Drucks und spielt zugleich mit den Möglichkeiten von Tiefe und Perspektive, die ein Betrachter darin entdecken kann. Diese vielfältigen und mehrschichtigen Zeichen fordern dazu auf, die künstlerischen Arbeitsphasen und Momente des Experimentierens, die in die Produktion des Werks eingeflossen sind, nachzuvollziehen, um die dem Bild eigene Dichotomie besser zu verstehen.

Wenn *Slippery Under Pressure* die Quintessenz von Phillips' Spagat zwischen Figuration und Abstraktion darstellt, dann ist *The Treatment Must Be Appropriate To The Material* (2013) ein Musterbeispiel für das spielerisch-gestische Extrem der Künstlerin. Das aus zwei Siebdrucken in Schwarz-Weiß bestehende Werk zeigt ungestüme, genüsslich chaotische und formal ungezähmte Zeichensetzungen. Diese kraftvollen Spuren, die Bewegung und Aktion andeuten, spiegeln Phillips' Arbeiten auf Zeitungspapier wider: typischerweise einzelne, ausgerichtete Tuschelavierungen von beträchtlicher Größe, deren Papier bis an den Rand des Druckmotivs beschnitten ist. Die Verwendung solcher Zeichensetzungen durch die Künstlerin steigert das Bewusstsein des Betrachters für die physische Aktion, die ihrem Medium anhaftet, und ist vielleicht auch ein parodistischer Wink an die performative, wenngleich malerische Geschichte der Abstraktion.

Indem sie die Aufmerksamkeit des Betrachters auf die physische Aktion der Werkproduktion und die intuitiven Entscheidungen lenkt, die diese steuern (die Künstlerin macht keine vorbereitenden Pläne, und ein Werk wird nicht durch irgendein dogmatisches Schema herbeigeführt), spielt Phillips mit der Geschichte der Druckkunst und initiiert einen subtilen Vorwurf gegen Ruskins Ablehnung der „schändlichen Mechanisierung" von Reproduktionstechniken in der Kunst. Durch die Mittel der Herstellung entsteht eine werkimmanente Distanz, über die hinweg Phillips' schöpferische Stimme dennoch durchdringt.

Let's talk about practice. 'Practice' – as both a noun and a verb – is one of those words that editors sometimes attempt to scrap from an art critic's copy, accusing it of being voguish and overused. There are times, however, when the writer should put up some resistance to its dismissal from a text. When it is useful, when the word proves descriptive and conveys something of the artist's work and working methods. Writing about Ciara Phillips would be one of these occasions. 'Practice' suggests that the end result of Phillips' work as an artist is integrally informed and wrapped up in the means of its production. It suggests that the art object, even when left to its own devices in the gallery, will nonetheless let slip to its audience the nuances of narrative behind its realisation. The artist's practice rendered visible. The verb made noun.

Phillips' screenprints are experiments in formalism, with abstract strokes, patterns and mottled landscapes of ink sitting in tension with clearly defined, symbolically suggestive shapes; figurative motifs; or, occasionally, photographic images. A print of over a metre in height and on paper from the *Slippery Under Pressure* (2012) series, for example, seems to depict an urn. Surrounding the flat shape of this apparent receptacle is a broadly repeated, perhaps modernist, pattern of blue rectangles on green. The green resurfaces within the multifarious palette and texture of the urn, however, suggesting a vapourish object that is both made up of its background and distinct from it. As is characteristic of Phillips' work, it is a scene that is both a celebration of the print's flatness and, simultaneously, intoxicated with the possibilities of depth and perspective that the viewer can mine the composition for. These varied, layered markings request one to trace the stages of the artist's labour and moments of experimentation that went into the work's production, in order to better understand the dichotomy inherent within the image.

If *Slippery Under Pressure* (2012) represents the apotheosis of Phillips' stretch between figuration and abstraction, *The Treatment Must Be Appropriate To The Material* (2013) is an example of the artist at her most playfully gestural. The edition of two screenprints, monochromatic black and white, sees a wild fashion of mark-making, delightfully messy and untamed by form. These broad markings, suggestive of movement and action, echo Phillips' work on newsprint: characteristically single, sizable, directional washes of ink, the paper cut down to the silhouette of the print marking. The artist's use of such mark-making heightens the viewer's awareness of the physical action inherent in her medium; also, perhaps, a burlesquing nod towards the performative, albeit painterly, history of abstraction.

In directing the viewer's attention towards the physical action of the work's production and the intuitive decision-making that leads this (the artist makes no preparatory plans and a work isn't catalysed by any dogmatic conceptual schema), the artist is toying with the history of printmaking and instigating a subtle rebuke to Ruskin's dismissal of the "vile mechanisation" of reproductive technologies in art. A distance is invoked in the works by the means of their production, yet nonetheless Phillips' authorial voice echoes through.

The artist is present in her more figurative work too. Accompanying a screenprint on cotton – a line of parallel large white circles on a murky blue-purple background – in the 2013 diptych *Autotypy / And more* is a photographic image, screenprinted on paper. In this second plate of the pairing, a woman, her back to the viewer, holds one of the editions of *The Treatment Must Be Appropriate To The Material* (2013). It's a neat, self-referential trick, affirming that, for

Auch in ihren eher figurativen Werken ist die Künstlerin präsent. Im Diptychon *Autotypy / And more* (2013) stellt sie einem Siebdruck auf Baumwolle – einer Reihe großer, parallel angeordneter weißer Kreise auf undurchsichtigem blau-violettem Grund – einen Siebdruck auf Papier zur Seite, der die Vergrößerung einer Fotografie zeigt. Auf dieser zweiten Tafel des Bildpaares hält eine Frau in Rückenansicht einen der beiden Drucke von *The Treatment Must Be Appropriate To The Material* in die Höhe. Dieser geschickte selbstreferenzielle Kunstgriff bestätigt, dass sich die Lehren von Abstraktion und Figuration für Phillips nicht gegenseitig ausschließen. Ihre wiederholte Verwendung des Häkchenmotivs und des Zeichens „x" greift diesen Punkt erneut auf. Indem sie die Motive auf Plakate oder Stoffbanner druckt, fordert Phillips uns auf, sowohl von ihrer eigentlichen Gestalt als auch von dem symbolischen, bildlichen Wert Notiz zu nehmen, mit dem diese sonst ausdruckslosen Formen aufgeladen sind: Bestätigung, Ablehnung, ein Kuss, Zuneigung, Liebe.

Überwiegend pragmatische Gründe machen die Drucktechnik zu einem tendenziell sozialen und sogar gemeinschaftlichen Medium. Die Notwendigkeit zwingt Künstler dazu, sich zusammenzuschließen und die Ausrüstung oder Atelierressourcen zu teilen. Während dieser Aspekt in Phillips' künstlerischer Praxis wohl außerhalb ihrer Kontrolle liegt, sollte er gleichwohl als mitbestimmend für ihr Arbeitsergebnis verstanden werden. Häufig demonstriert Phillips diesen Vorgang des Produzierens durch die formale Inszenierung einer Ausstellung, in der sie den Gemeinschaftscharakter der Werkproduktion in den Vordergrund rückt. Während ihrer Ausstellung im Bristoler Stadtviertel Spike Island im Jahr 2012 teilte sie den Ausstellungsraum mit 70 Werken von Corita Kent. Die amerikanische Künstlerin und Pädagogin, die 1986 starb, bildet für Phillips einen der wichtigsten Bezugspunkte. In einem Nebenraum der Galerie richtete Phillips ein Atelier mit Druckwerkstatt ein und entwickelte gemeinsam mit Gastkünstlern und -designern eine Publikation nach dem Vorbild des *Irregular Bulletin*, der Hauszeitschrift des Immaculate Heart College in Los Angeles, zu der Zeit, als Kent dort unterrichtete. Zusammenarbeit steht auch bei Phillips' Projekten mit der Ateliergemeinschaft Poster Club im Vordergrund, die sie mit anderen Druckkünstlern in Glasgow gegründet hat. 2011 erstellte die Gruppe ihre Arbeiten an Ort und Stelle im Ausstellungsraum Eastside Project in Birmingham und reagierte dabei unmittelbar auf den Ort und seine Besucher. In Analogie zu einem der historischen Verwendungszwecke von Siebdrucken – als anonyme Werbeanzeigen oder Mitteilungen – wiederholt die Entindividualisierung der künstlerischen Praxis, auf die diese Projekte hindeuten, Phillips' Interesse an Ideen rund um die schöpferische Distanz im Produktionsprozess und ist damit ein weiterer Hinweis auf die Grauzone, in der die Künstlerin sich selbst positioniert – innerhalb und außerhalb der Produktion.

Phillips, the twin tenets of abstraction and figuration are not mutually exclusive. It's a point raised again through the artist's reoccurring use of the tick motif and the character 'x'. Printing them on posters or banners, Phillips asks us to take notice of both their intrinsic form and the symbolic, figurative value that these otherwise indistinctive shapes are loaded with: affirmation, refusal, a kiss, affection, love.

For largely pragmatic reasons, printmaking tends to be a social, and even collaborative, medium. Necessity will require artists to band together to share equipment or studio resources. While this aspect of Phillips' practice is arguably beyond her control, it should also be understood as one that nonetheless informs the output. Through the formal staging of an exhibition Phillips often demonstrates this process of making, foregrounding the communal nature of the work's production. In her 2012 show at Spike Island, Bristol, Phillips shared the gallery space with seventy works by Corita Kent. Kent, who died in 1986, was an American artist and educator and is a mainstay reference point for Phillips. In a side room, Phillips set up a studio and printing workshop, partnering with visiting artists and designers to develop a publication based on *Irregular Bulletin*, the in-house journal of the Immaculate Heart College during Kent's time teaching there. Collaboration is also at the forefront of Phillips' works with Poster Club, a print studio collective the artist established in Glasgow with a bevy of peers. In 2011 the group created work in situ at Eastside Projects, Birmingham, reacting to the space and its visitors. Inviting parallels to one historic purpose of screenprints, as anonymous advertisements or notices, the de-individualisation of practice to which these projects infer reiterates Phillips' interest in ideas surrounding authorial distance and the processes of production, a further allusion to the slippage in which the artist places herself in, and out, of the practice.

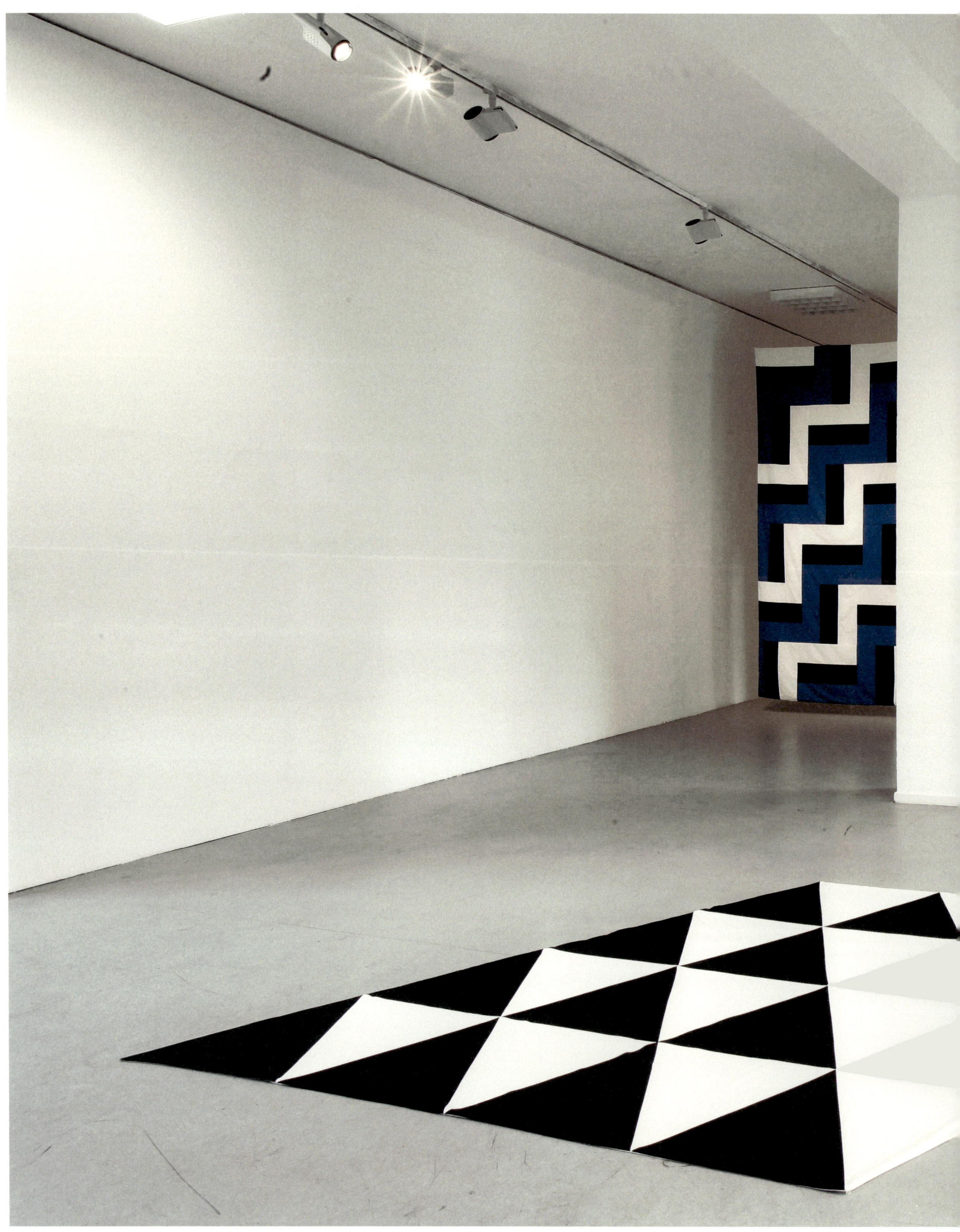

 Optimism and its signs, Atelier am Eck, Düsseldorf 2010

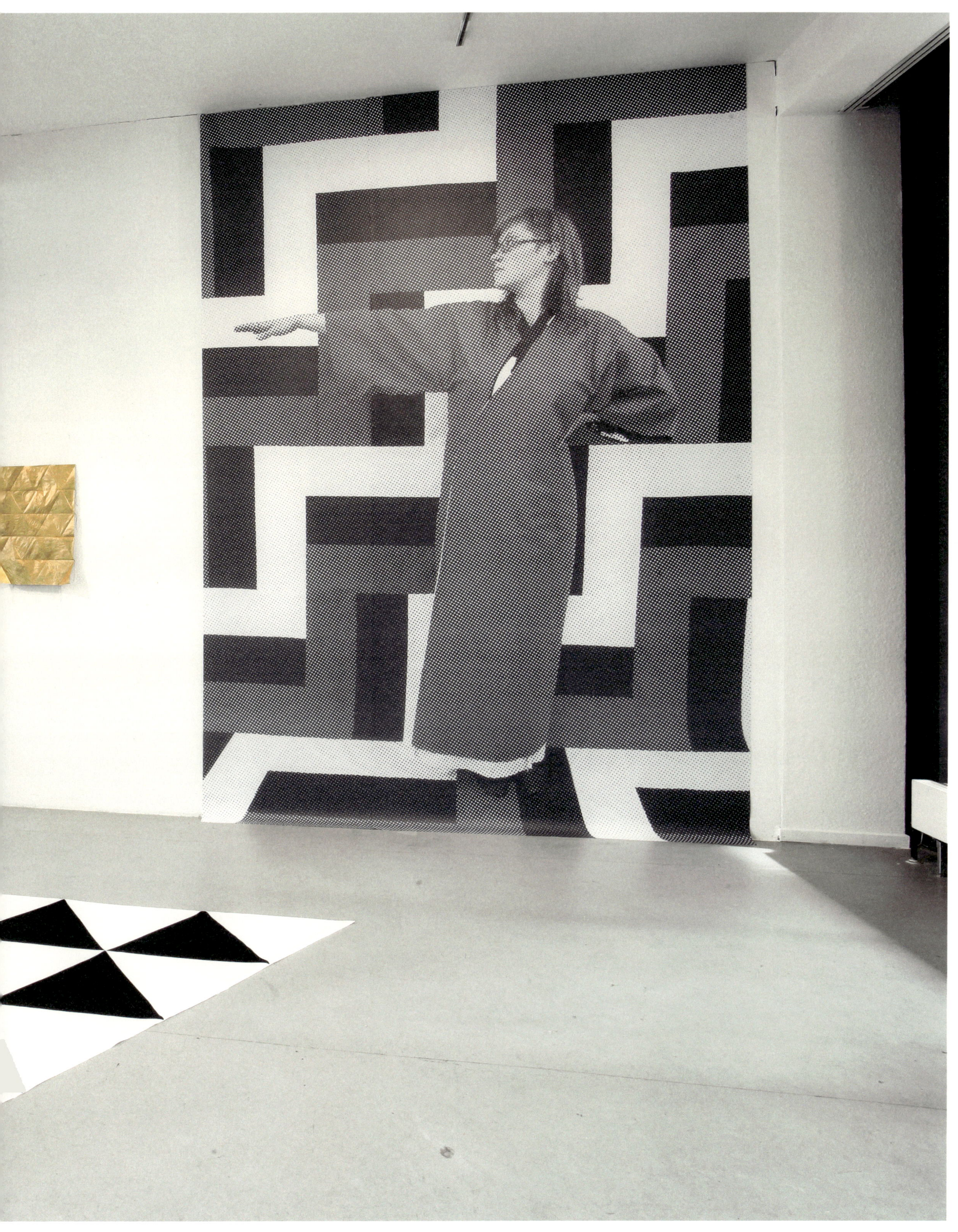

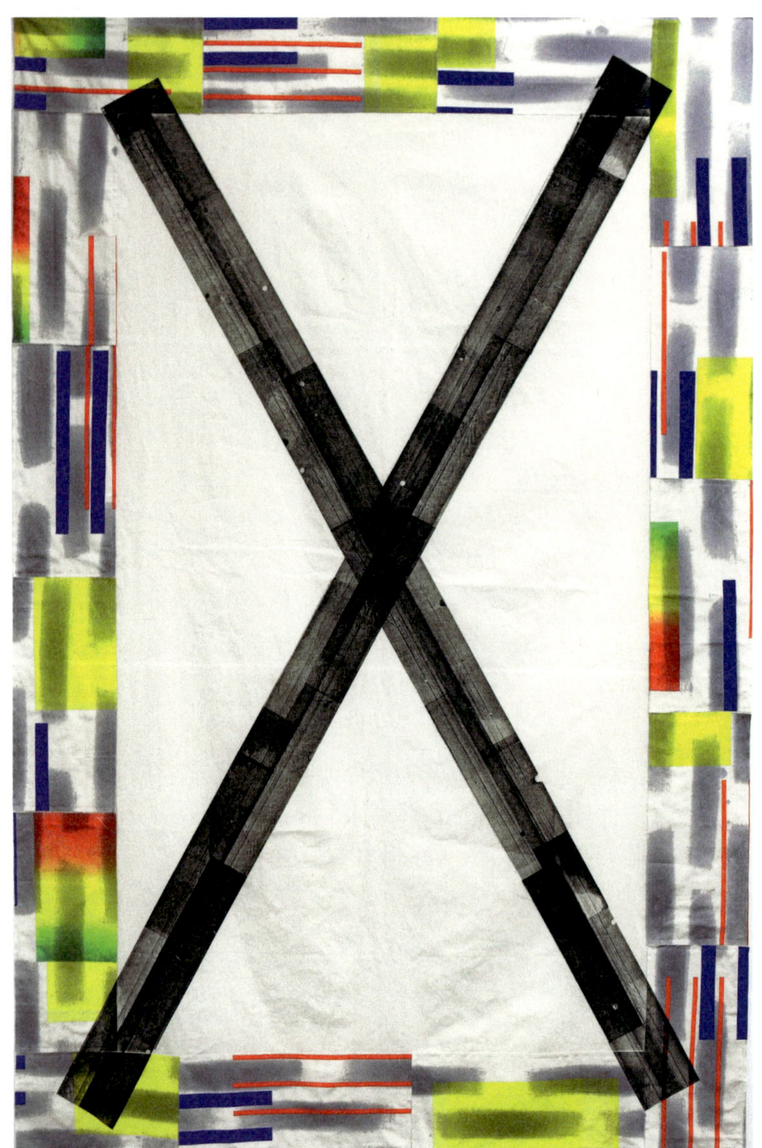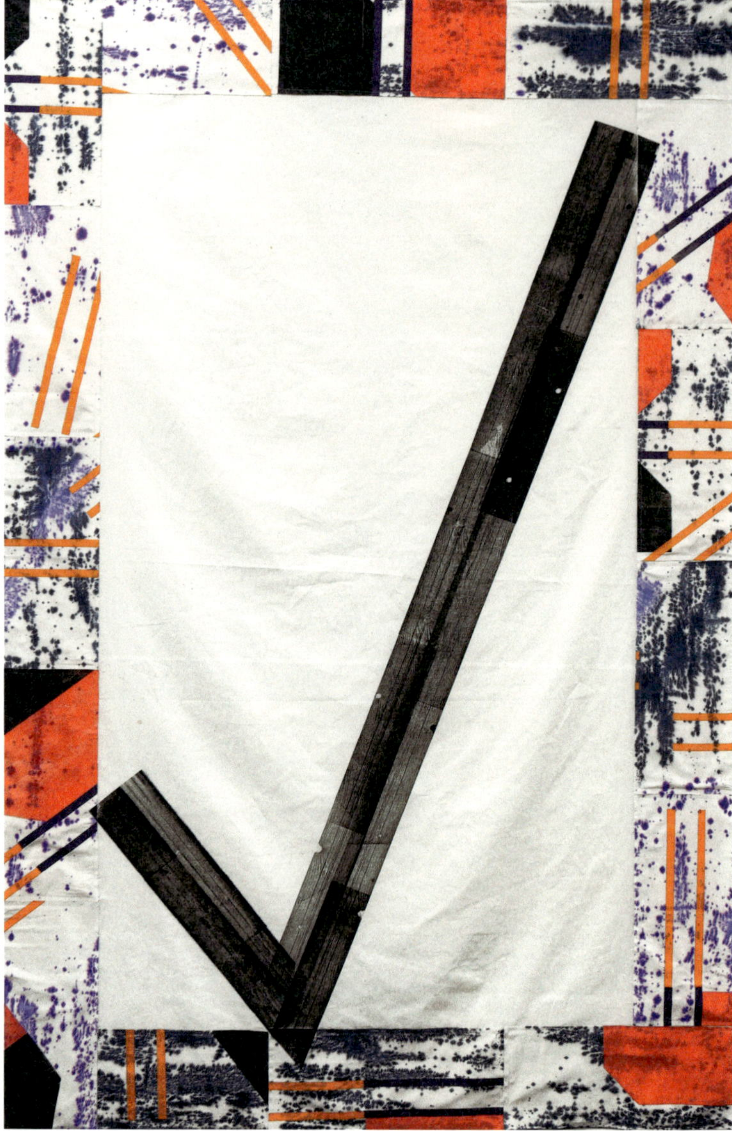

And other options, 2012 (links / left)
And other options, 2012 (rechts / right)

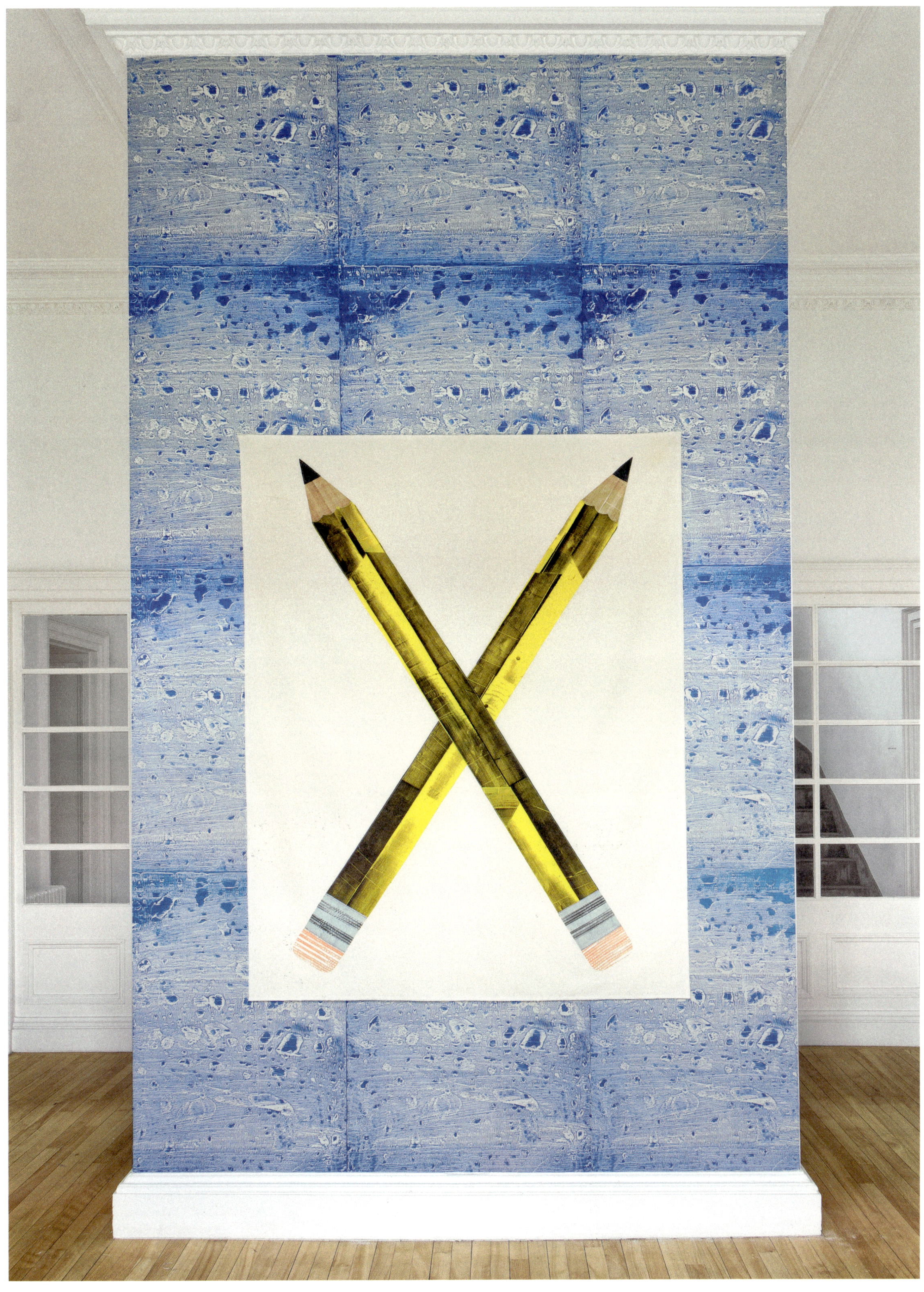

Pencil cross, 2013, Installationsansicht / Installation view *And more*, Inverleith House, Edinburgh 2013

Ciara Phillips

131

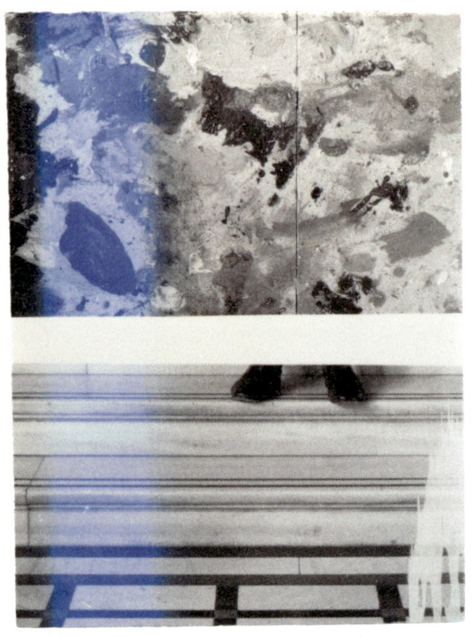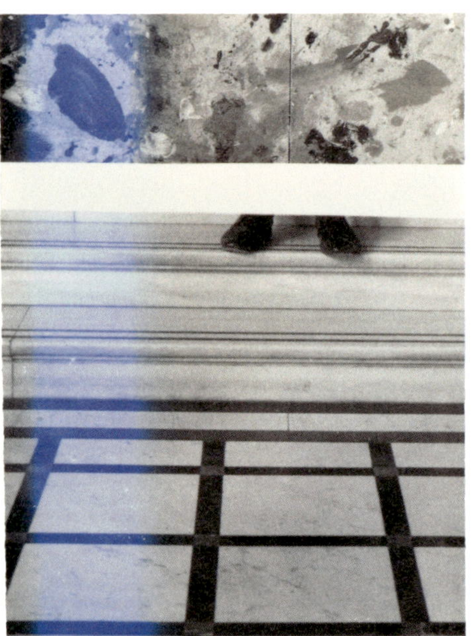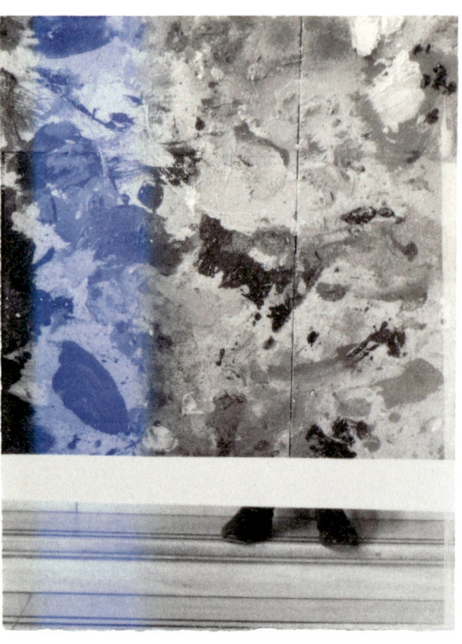

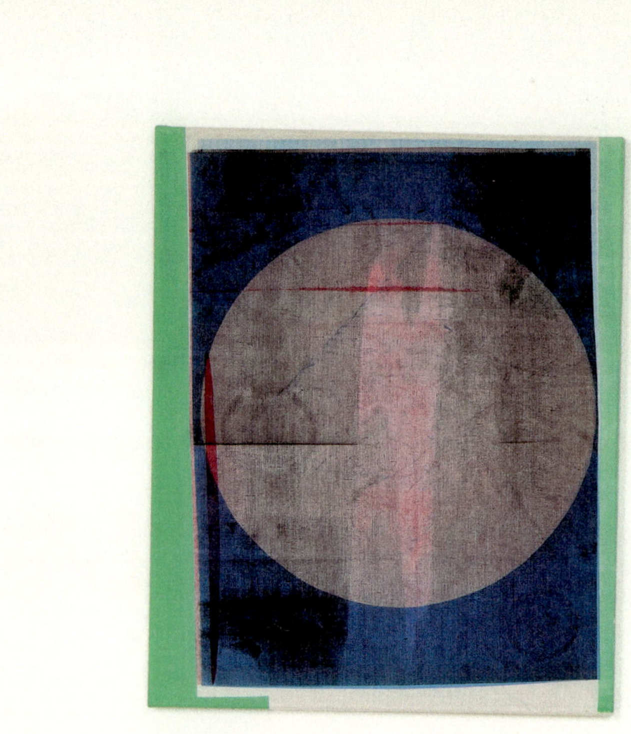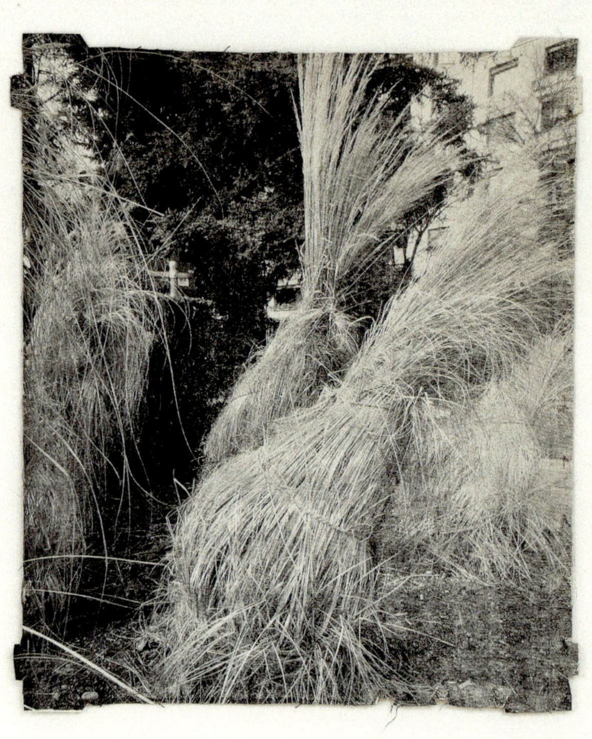

Century No. 14, 15, 16, 28, 63 (not quite always), 2013 (obere Reihe / upper row)
o, 2013, und / and *x*, 2013, Installationsansicht / Installation view *And more*, Inverleith House, Edinburgh 2013 (unten / bottom)

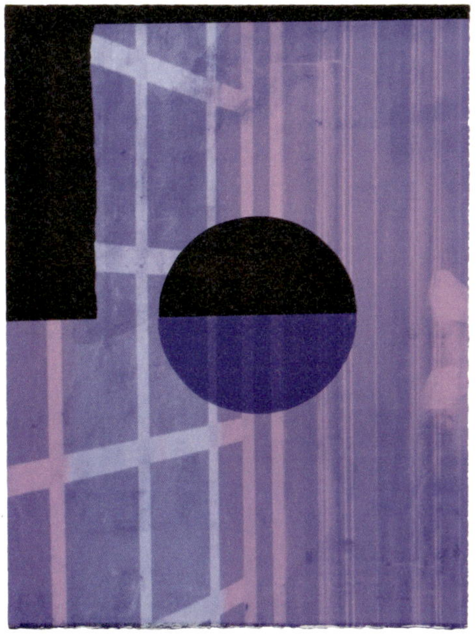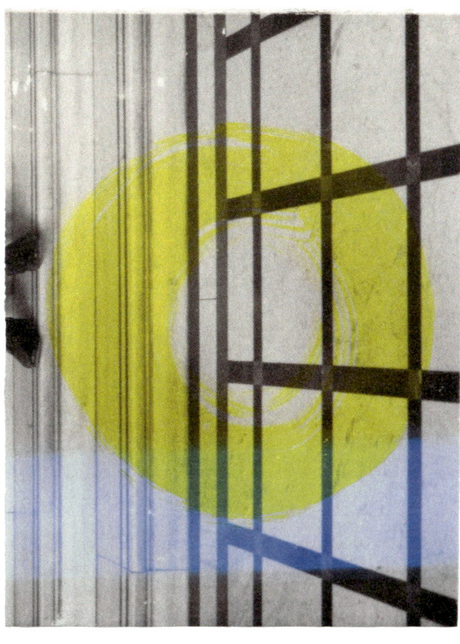

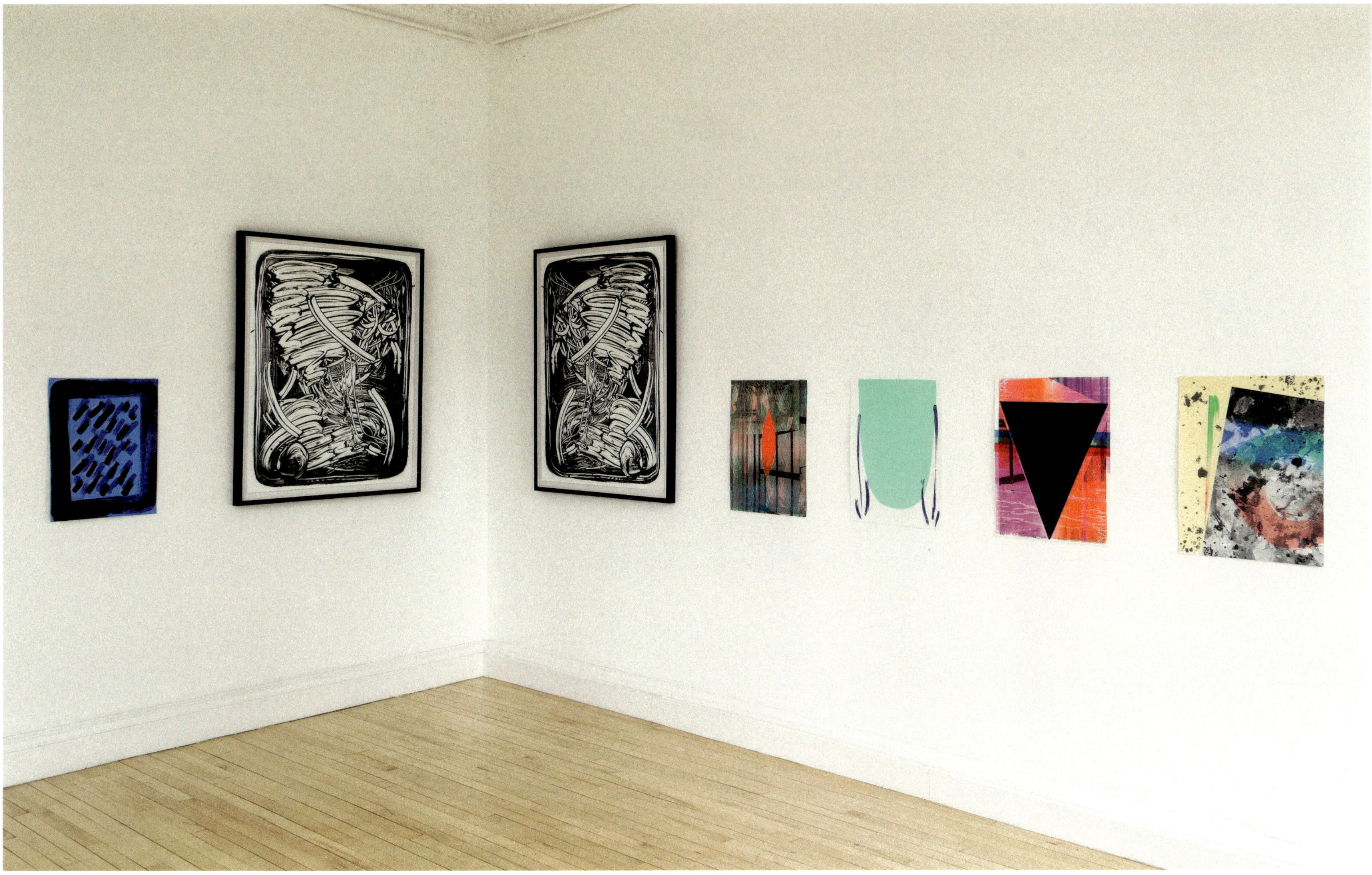

The treatment must be appropriate to the material, 2013, und / and *Century No. 17, 4, 18, 12*, 2013,
Installationsansicht / Installation view *And more*, Inverleith House, Edinburgh 2013 (unten / bottom)

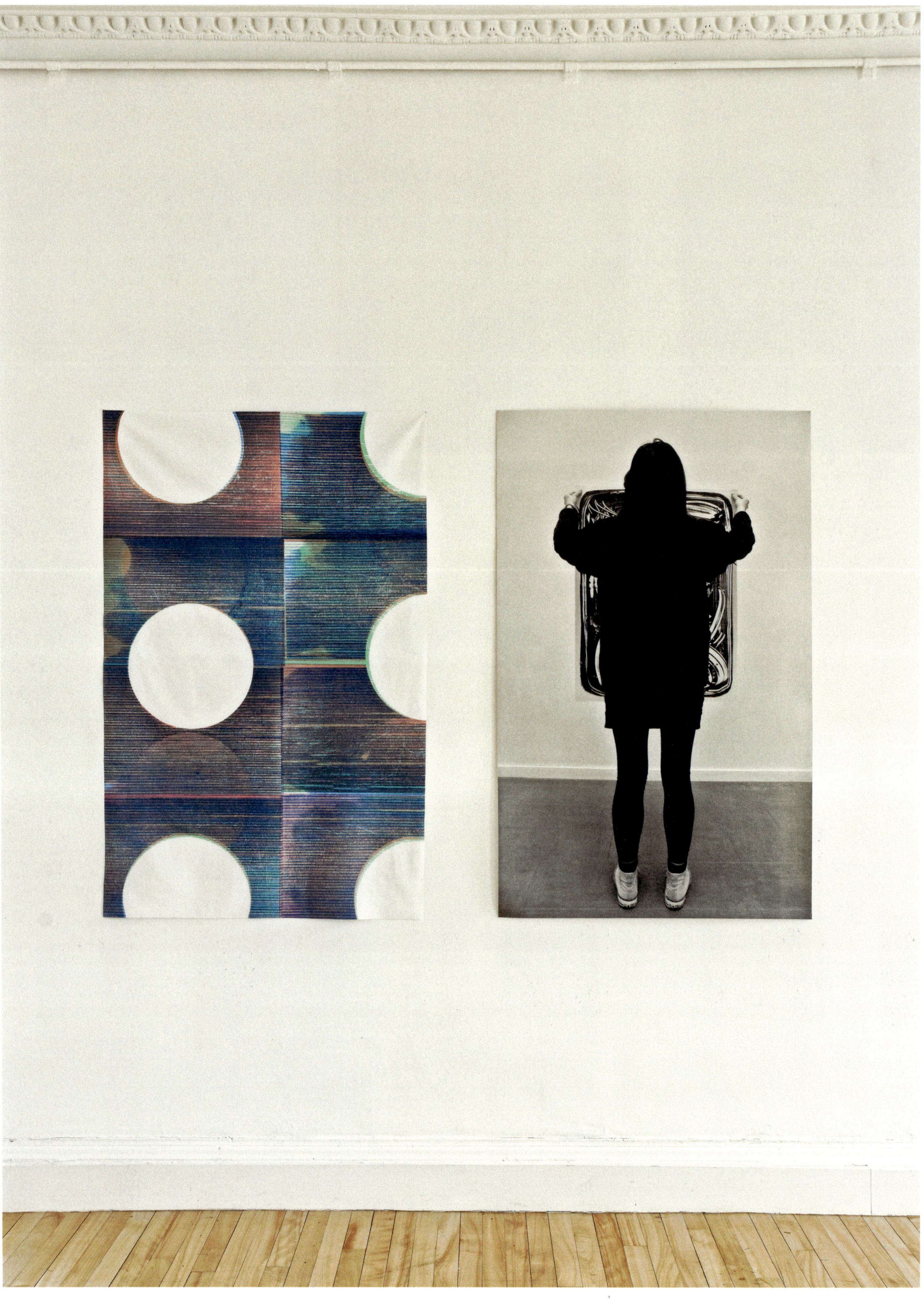

Autotypy / And more, 2013, Installationsansicht / Installation view *And more*, Inverleith House, Edinburgh 2013
Slippery under pressure, 2012, Installationsansicht / Installation view *And more*, Inverleith House, Edinburgh 2013 (S. / p. 135)

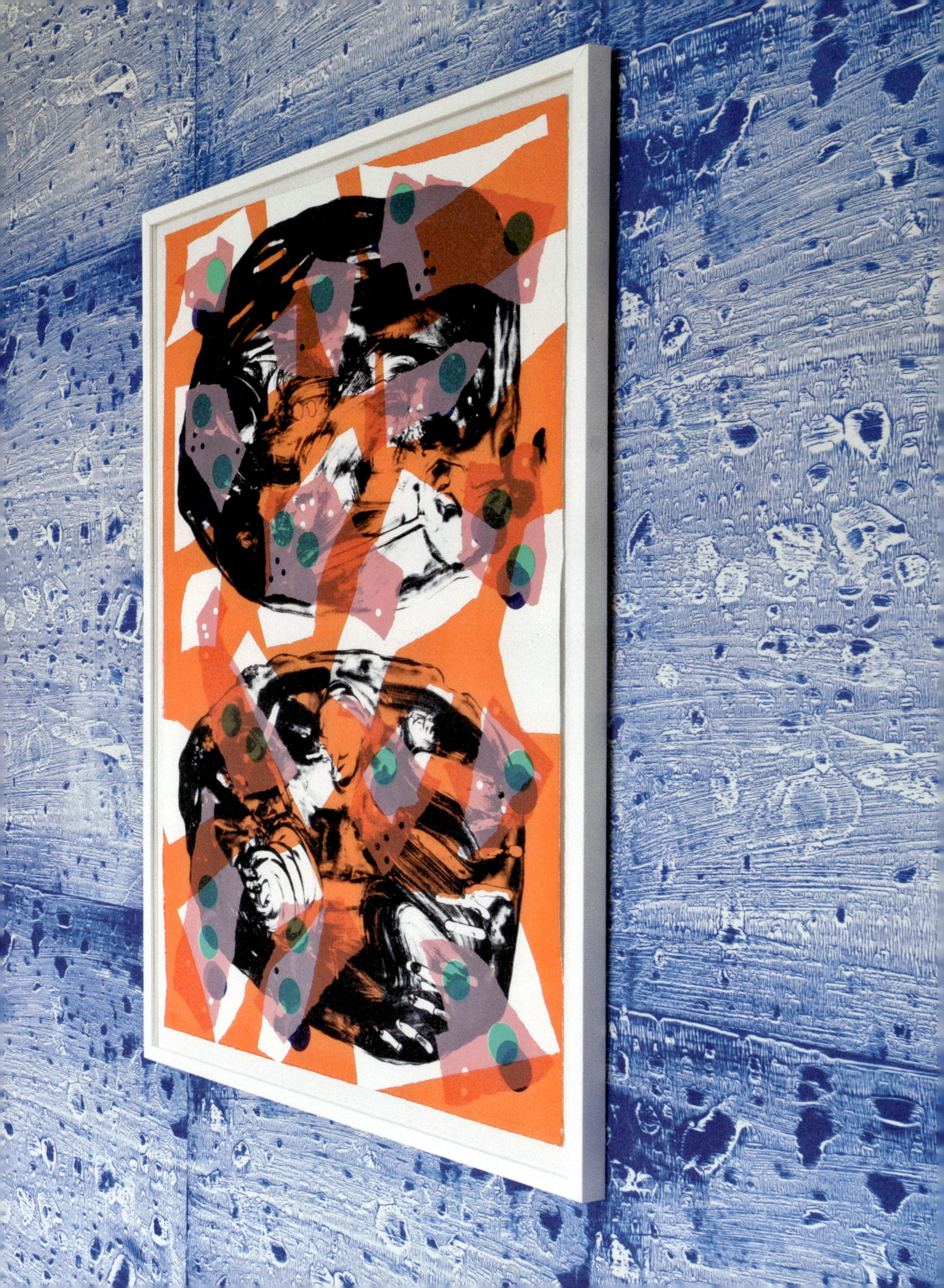

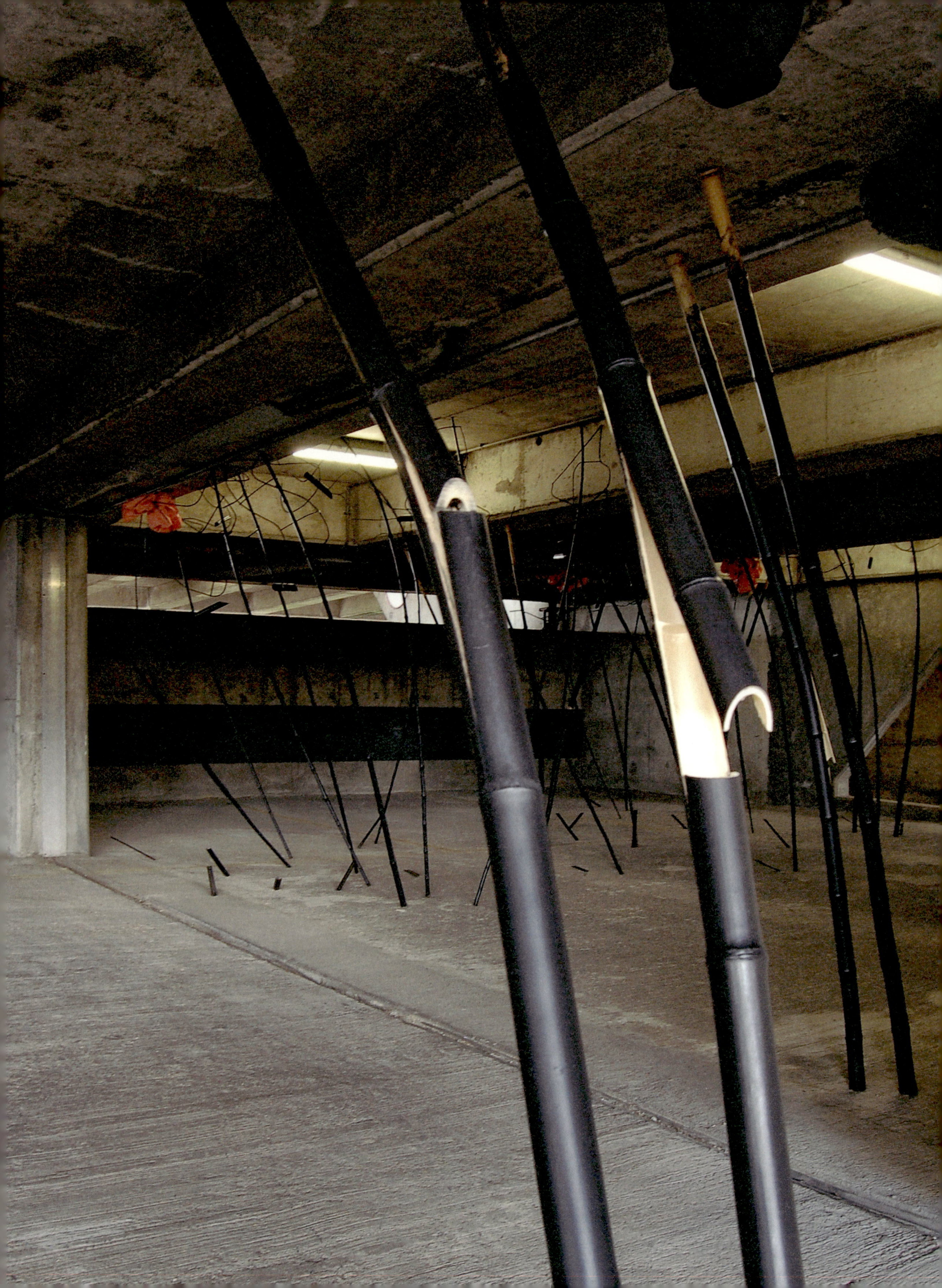

Mary Redmond

Biografie / Biography

Mary Redmond lebt und arbeitet / lives and works
in Glasgow, Schottland / Scotland
1973   geboren / born in Glasgow, Schottland / Scotland

Studium / Education

1990–1994   Bachelor of Fine Art, Glasgow School of Art, Glasgow
1996–1998   Master of Fine Art, Glasgow School of Art, Glasgow

Stipendien und Preise / Scholarships and Awards

2009   Paul Hamlyn Foundation, Visual Artist Award
2011   AIT Tokyo / Cove Park Exchange Residency

Ausgewählte Ausstellungen / Selected Exhibitions

„Mary Redmond", The Modern Institute, Glasgow (1999)
„Can 303s Heal?", Kiasma Museum of Contemporary Art,
Helsinki (2000)
„Here + Now: Scottish Art 1990–2001", Dundee Contemporary
Arts; Aberdeen Art Gallery (2001)
„Scott Myles, Mary Redmond, Stephen Sutcliffe", The Breeder,
Athen / Athens (2002)
„Mary Redmond", Alona Kagan Gallery, New York (2003)
„I Must Say That At First It Was Difficult Work",
Kunsthall Oslo (2010)
„Mary Redmond. The Floating World", Dundee Contemporary
Arts, Dundee (2010)
„Undone: Making and Unmaking in Contemporary Sculpture",
Henry Moore Institute, Leeds (2010)
„You, Me, Something Else", Gallery of Modern Art, Glasgow (2011)
„Bold Tendencies 2012", Peckham multi-storey car park,
London (2012)

Ausgewählte Publikationen / Selected Publications

„Here + Now: Scottish Art 1999–2001", Ausst.-Kat. / exh. cat.
Dundee Contemporary Arts, Dundee 2001
Sarah Lowndes, „Mary Redmond", in: *frieze*, Issue 72, 01/2003
„I feel mysterious today", Ausst.-Kat. / exh. cat. Palm Beach
Institute of Contemporary Art, New York 2004
„Undone: Making and Unmaking in Contemporary Sculpture",
Ausst.-Kat. / exh. cat. Henry Moore Institute, Leeds 2010

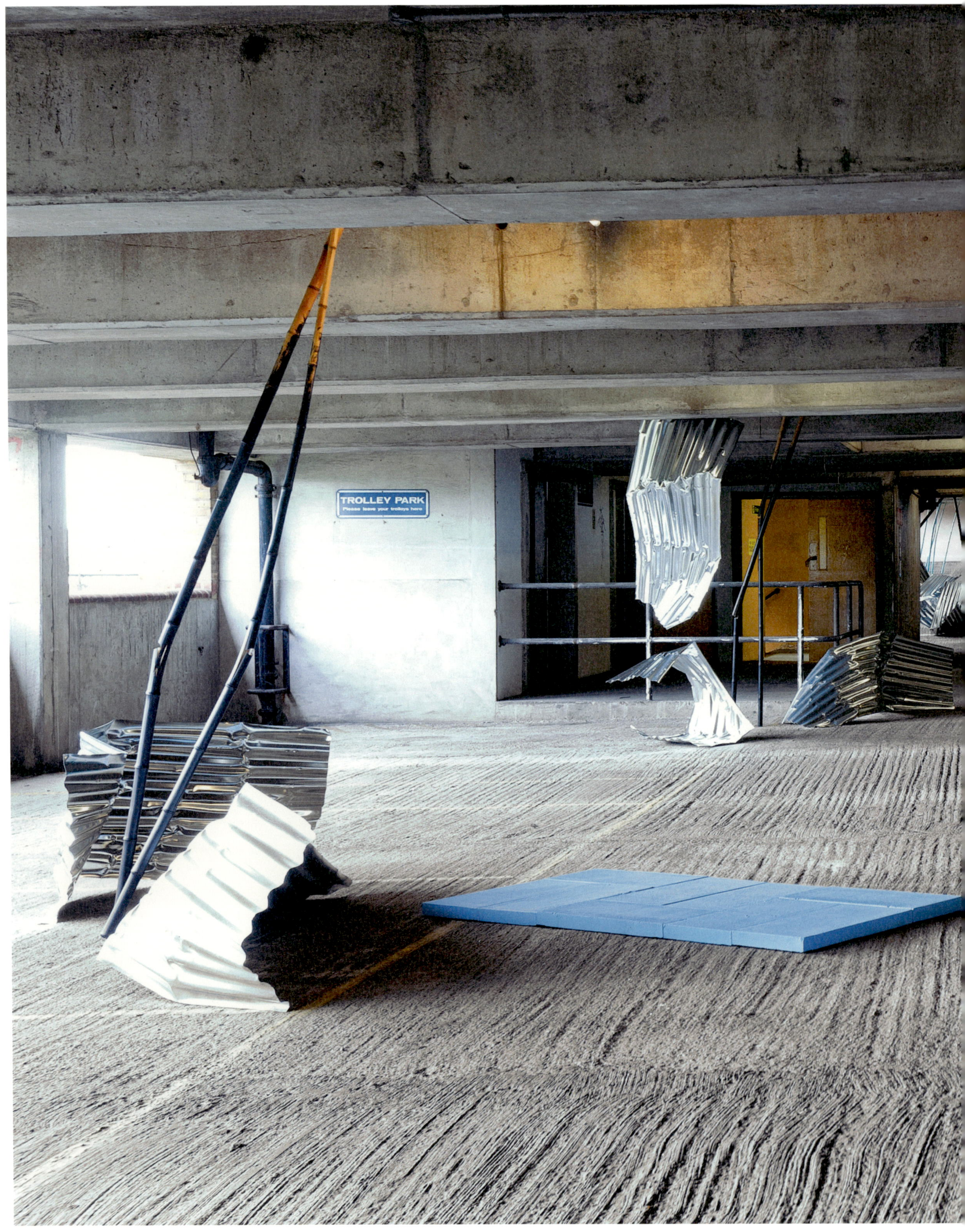

 Seven Split Overglide, 2012, Installationsansicht / Installation view *Bold Tendencies Sculpture Project 6*, Peckham multi-storey car park, London 2012

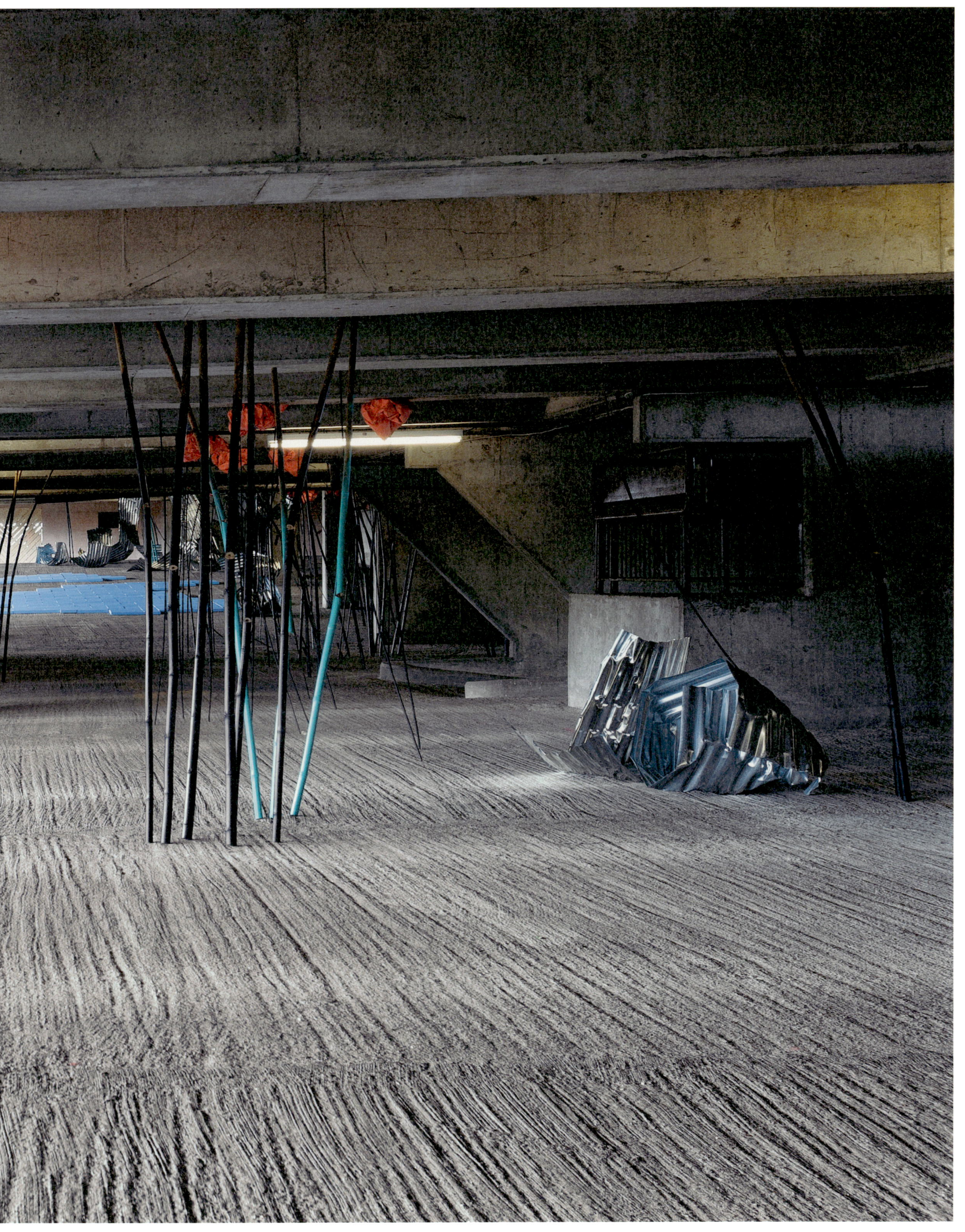

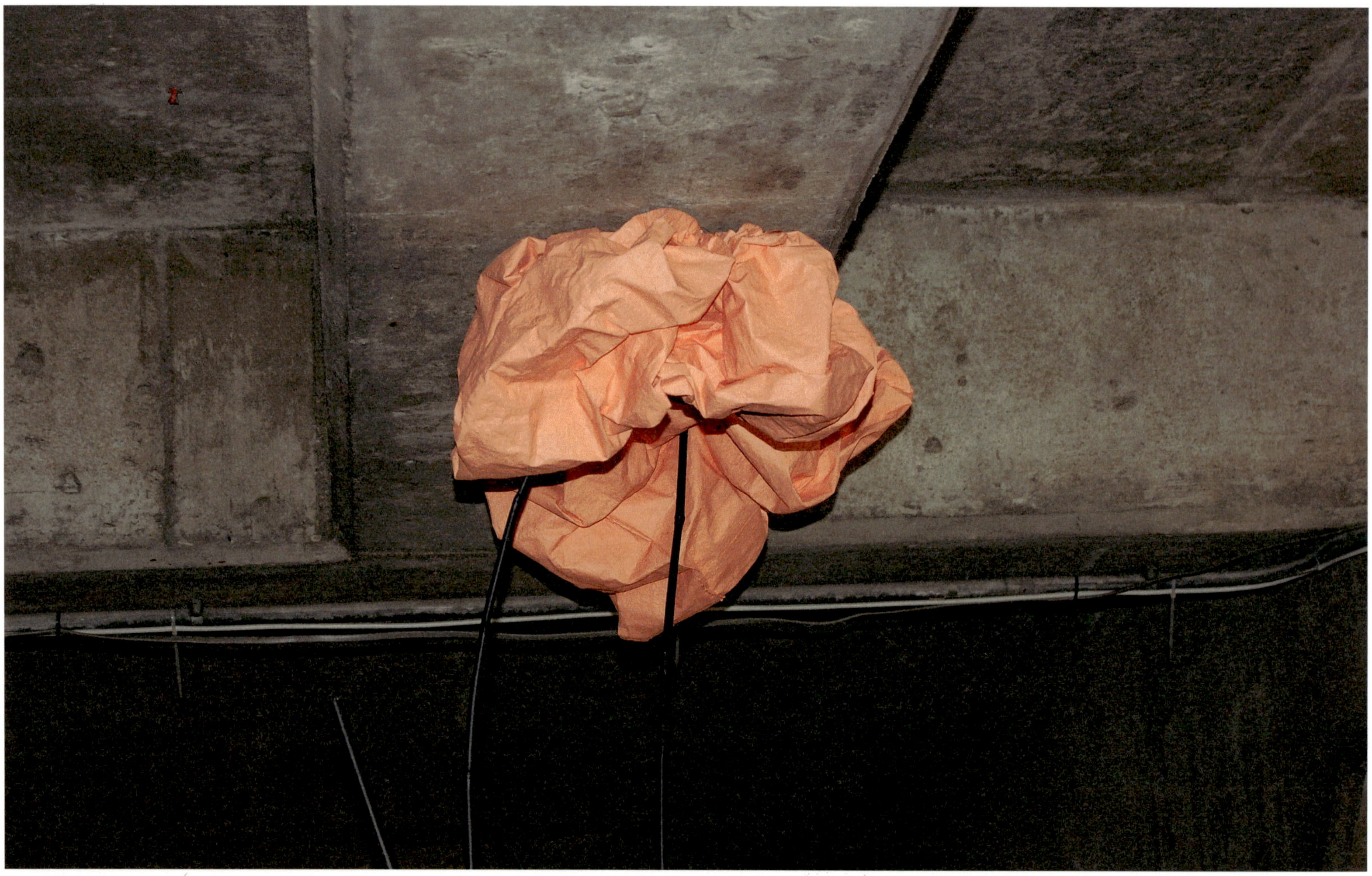

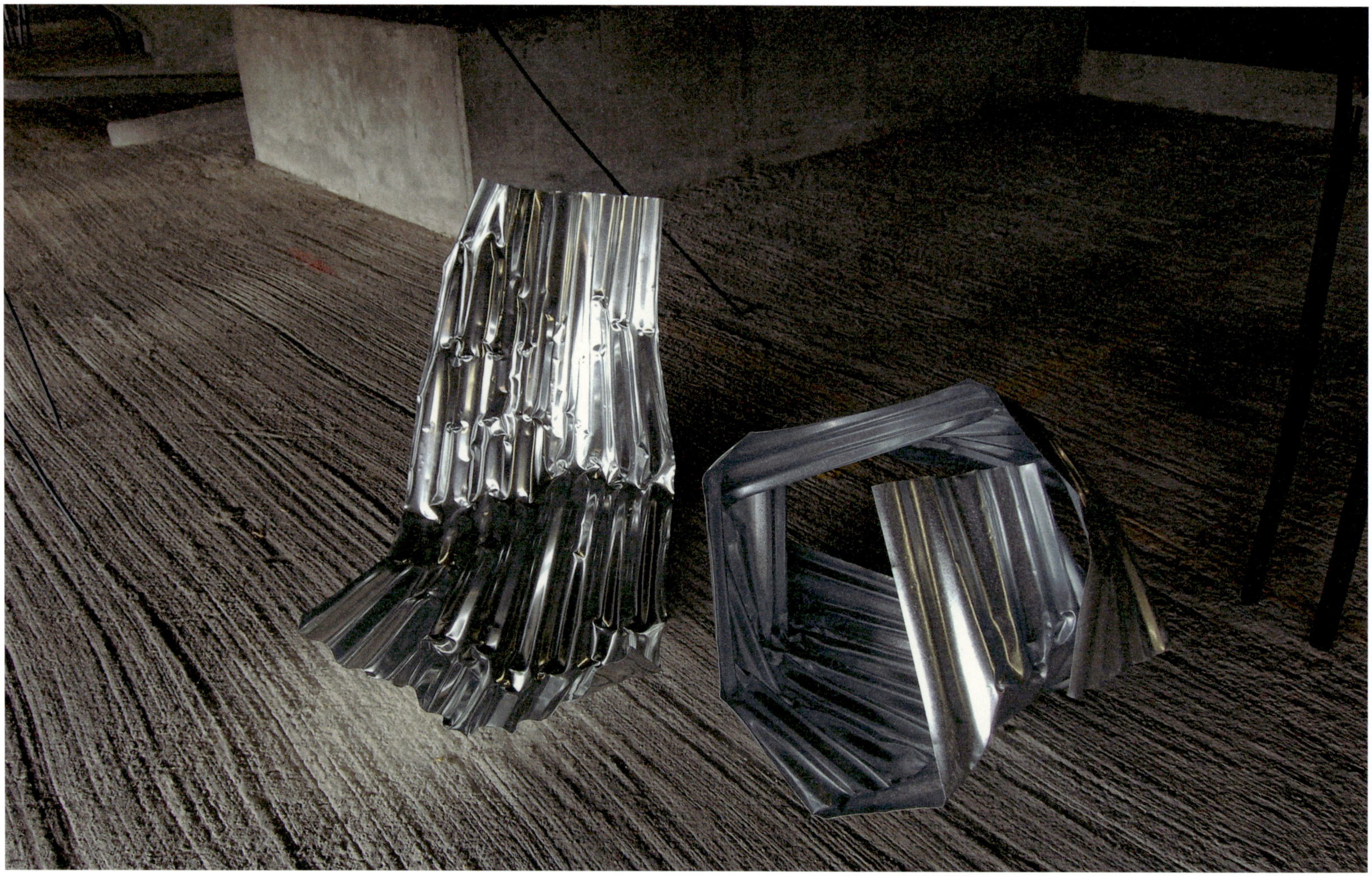

   Seven Split Overglide, 2012, Installationsansicht / Installation view *Bold Tendencies Sculpture Project 6*, Peckham multi-storey car park, London 2012

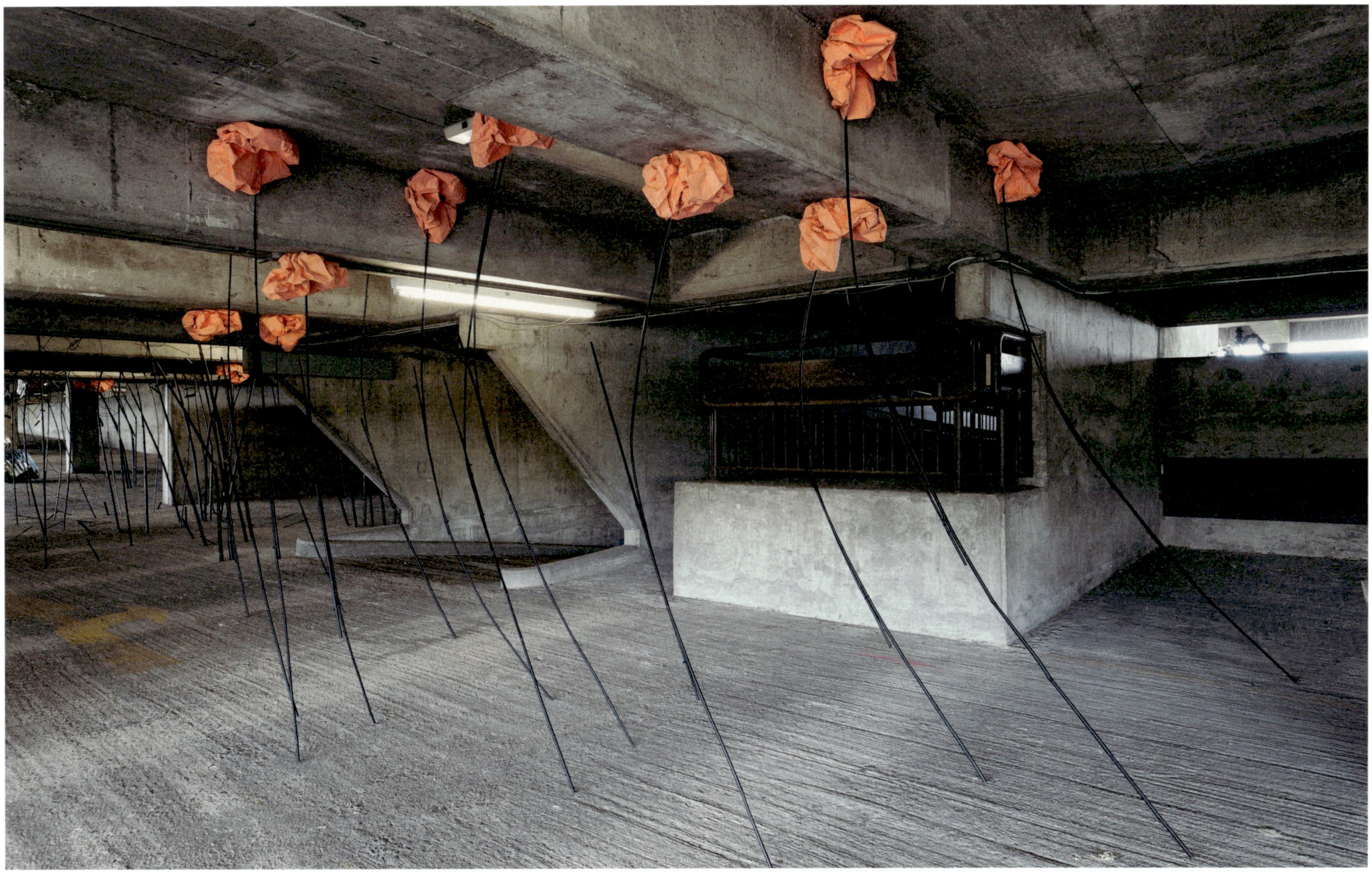

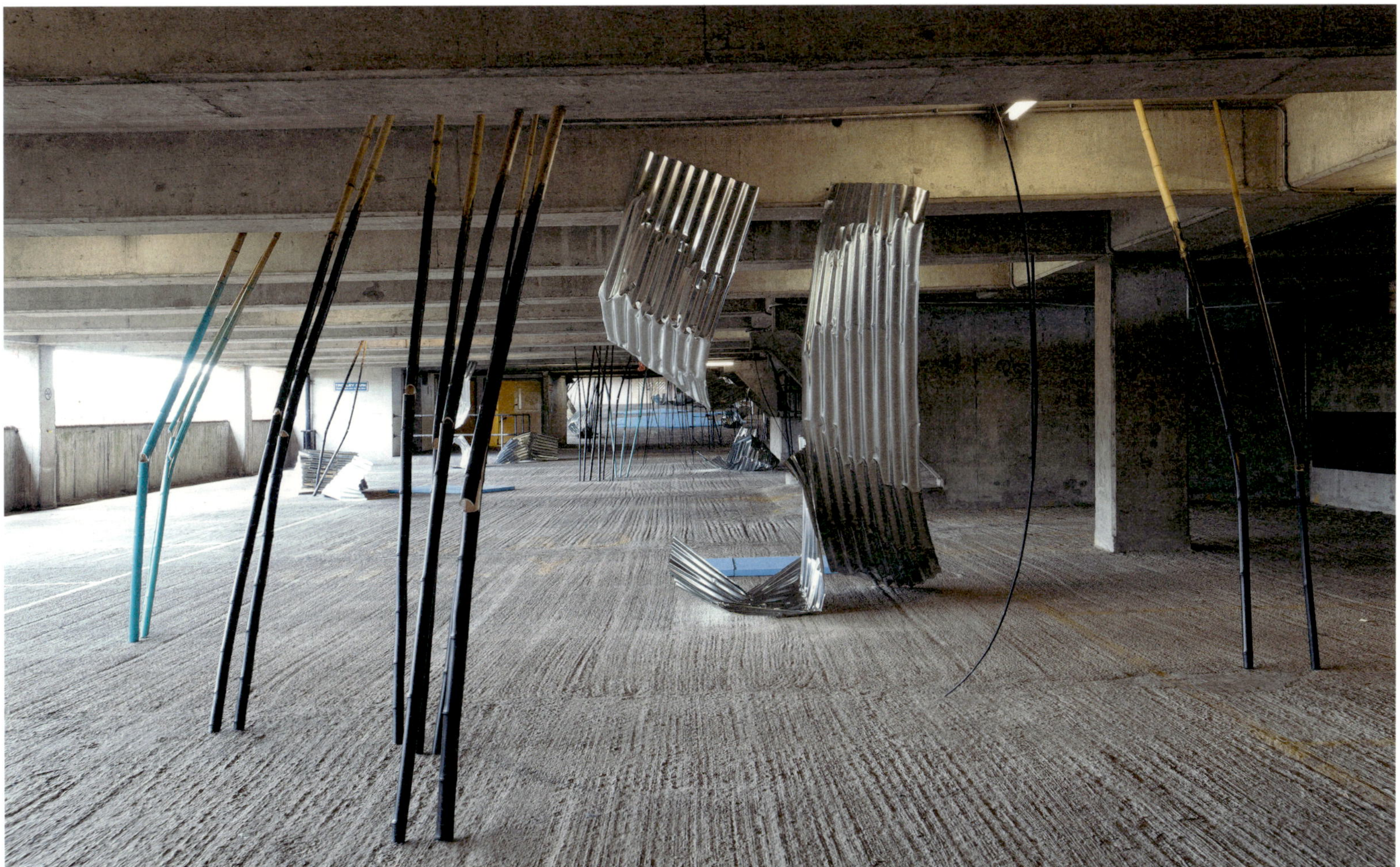

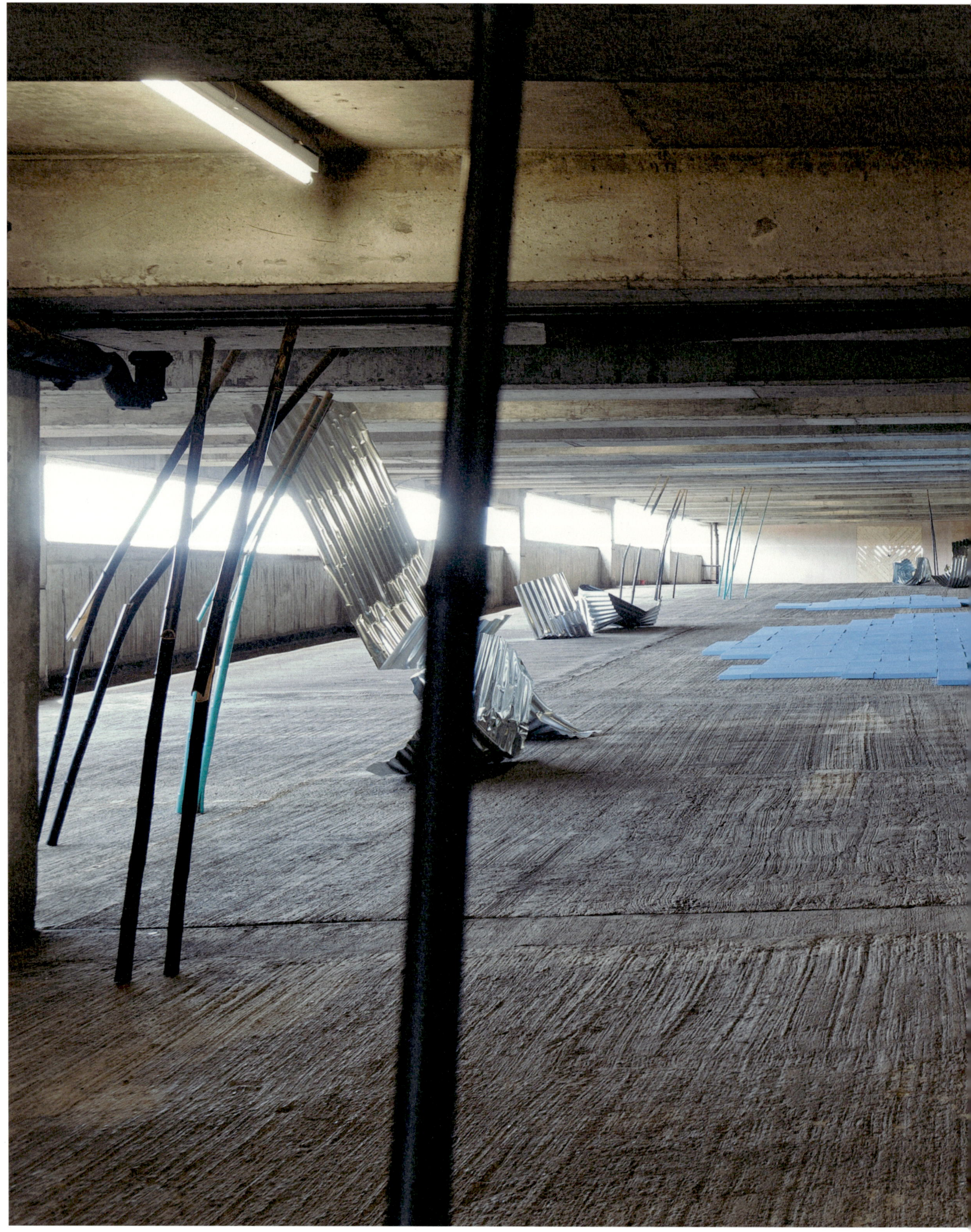

 Seven Split Overglide, 2012, Installationsansicht / Installation view *Bold Tendencies Sculpture Project 6*, Peckham multi-storey car park, London 2012

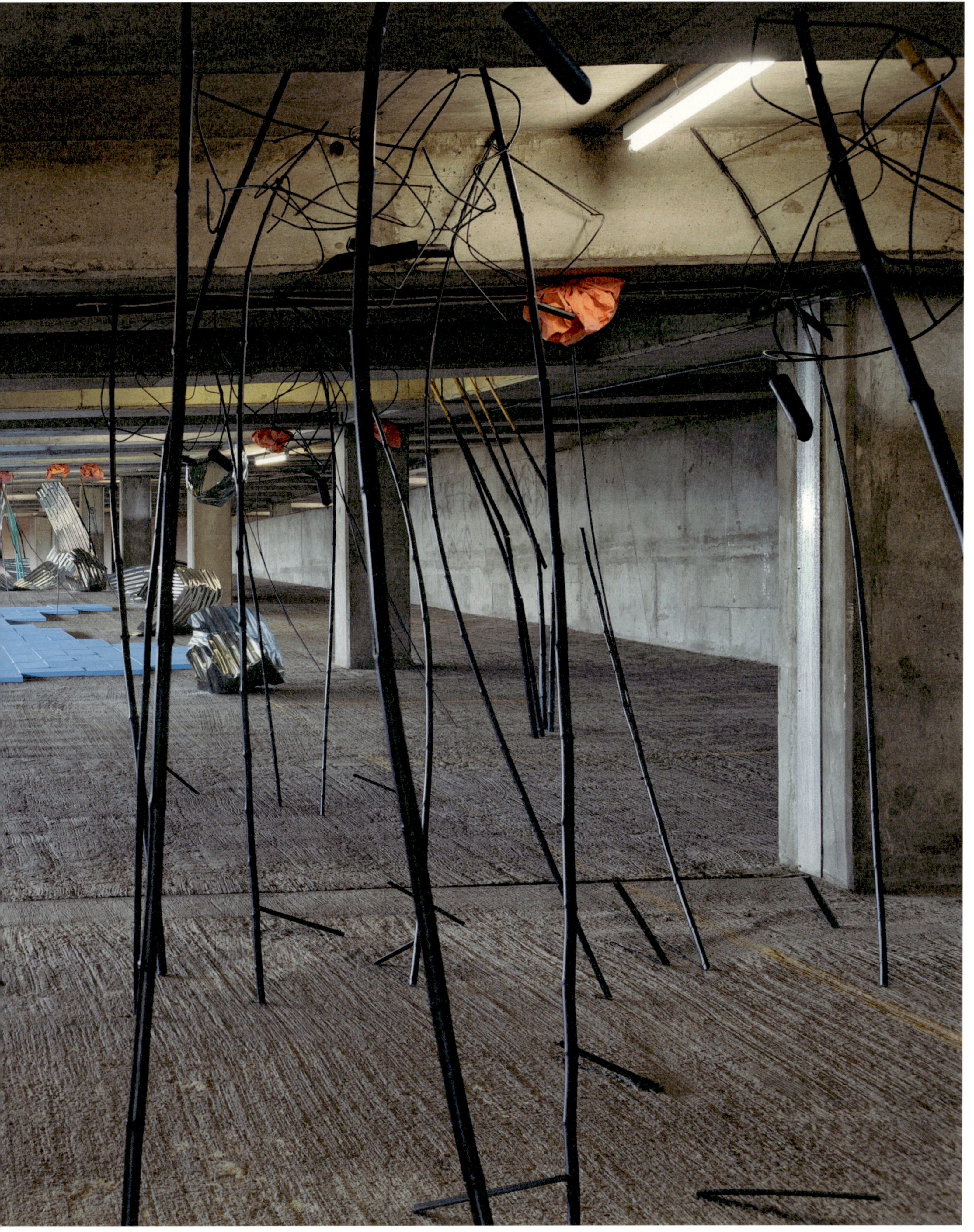

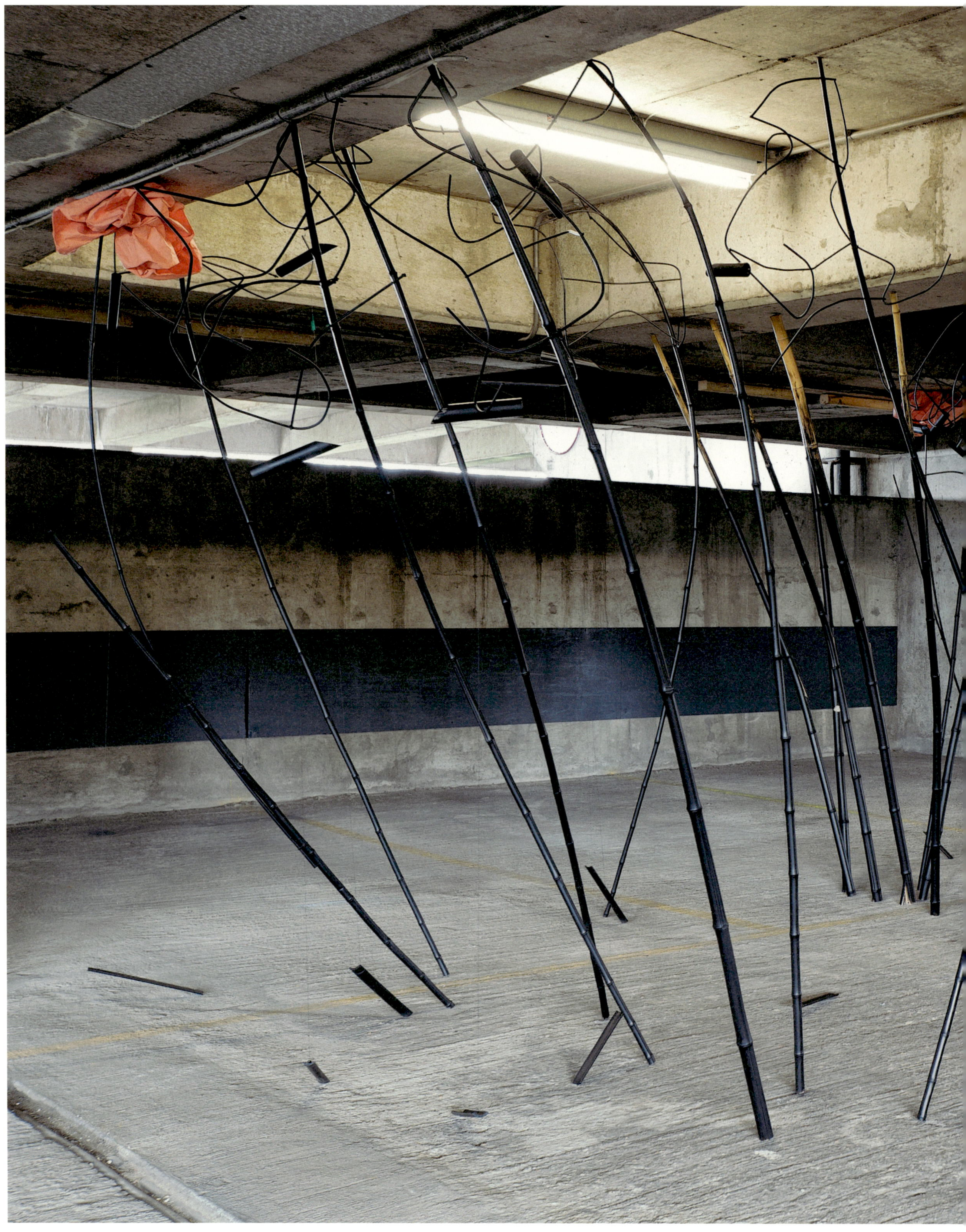

  Seven Split Overglide, 2012, Installationsansicht / Installation view *Bold Tendencies Sculpture Project 6*, Peckham multi-storey car park, London 2012

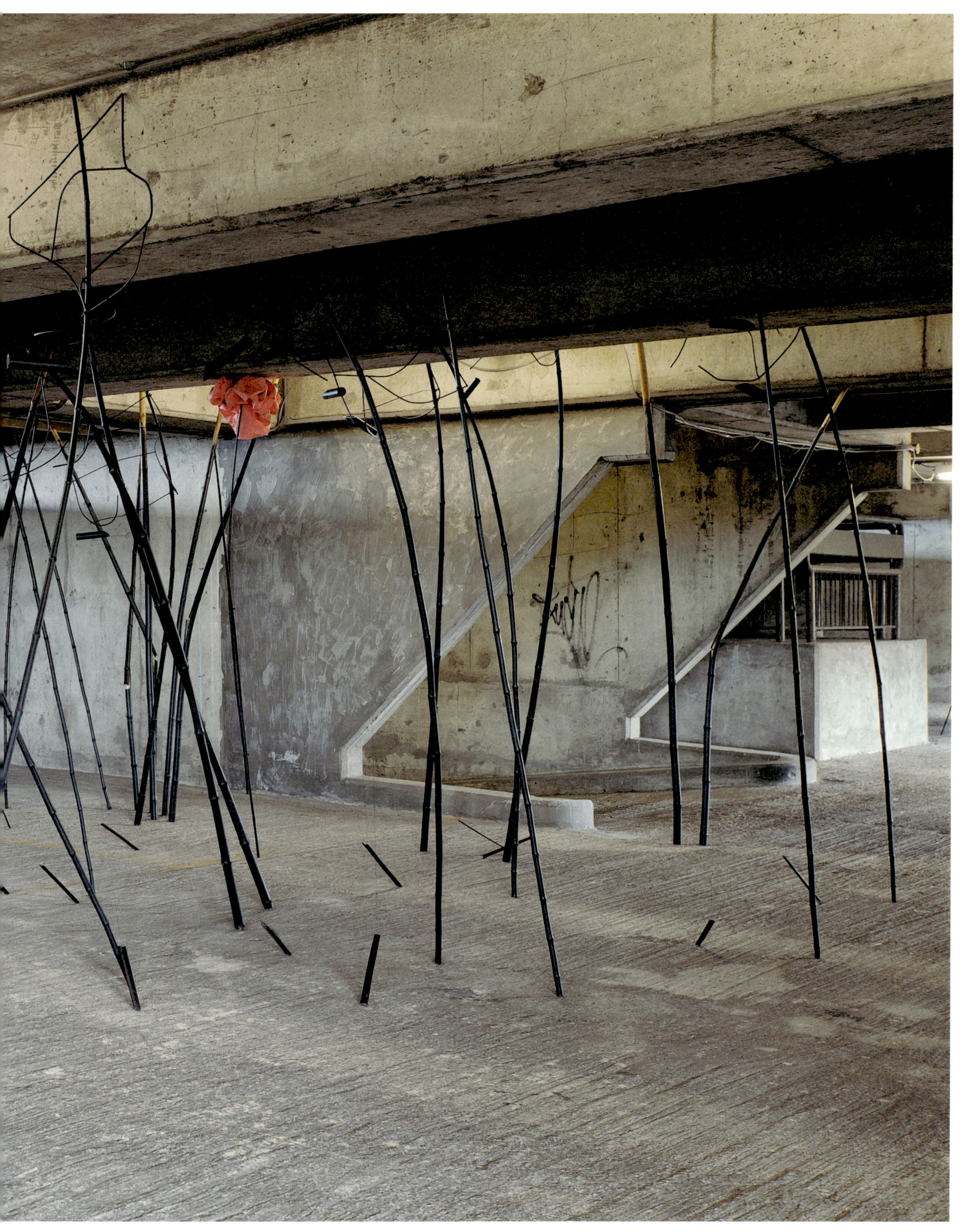

Mary Redmond

Für ihre Skulpturen kombiniert Mary Redmond gefundene und hergestellte Materialien sowohl organischen als auch industriellen Ursprungs. Manches, oft weggeworfene Dinge, findet sie in den Straßen von Glasgow, Dinge der Natur dagegen oft außerhalb der Stadtgrenzen. Wieder andere Materialien bezieht sie aus dem Ausland; für sie sind selbst banale Gegenstände wie Müllsäcke, die in anderen Ländern verwendet werden, aufregender als heimische Produkte. Mit all diesen Elementen entwirft Redmond eine besondere Poesie des Provisorischen, die nicht auf Langlebigkeit bedacht ist. Tatsächlich macht ihre Wahl alltäglicher, nichtkünstlerischer oder sogar minderwertiger Materialien es möglich, dass ihre Werke einfach zerlegt und wieder zusammengesetzt werden können – zu derselben Skulptur oder zu einem anderen, vollkommen neuen Werk: „Ich verstehe nicht, was für immer bedeutet", sagt sie.[1] Und erklärt: „Ich empfinde eine aufrichtige Zuneigung für Materialien, egal, ob gekauft oder gefunden – für deren Eigenschaften, deren Möglichkeiten, deren Vergangenheit und Zukunft, für die Geschichten, die in ihnen stecken, und die Zeit, die ich aufwende, um mit ihnen zu arbeiten."[2] Typische kleinere Werke von Redmond, wie *Che-Che Omo* und *Embroque* beziehen verschiedene Werkstoffe ein, darunter Perlen, Bast, eine Quaste, ein bemaltes Metallgitter, Stoff und Papier. Keines dieser Materialien wird von der Künstlerin eingesetzt als das, was es selbst ist, sondern sie verwandelt das Banale in etwas Fremdes, Schönes und Anziehendes. Doch Redmonds Repertoire umfasst auch großräumige Installationen, wie *5 Rows Over the Overglide* für die Gruppenausstellung *Red Marauder* im Glasgower Tramway, 2000, *Seven Split Overglide* für das Londoner Kunstprojekt *Bold Tendencies*, 2012, oder das ganz neue Environment für die aktuelle Ausstellung im Neuen Museum in Nürnberg.

Redmond lernte ich während meiner Vorbereitungen für die Gruppenausstellung *Undone* kennen, deren Schwerpunkt auf „handgemachten", in traditionellen oder sogar in Ad-hoc-Techniken gefertigten Skulpturen aus leicht erhältlichen Materialen lag. Damals schien es, als würden Skulpturen – zumindest wie in der Londoner Boulevardpresse dargestellt – vorrangig nach deren kostspieligen Materialien wie Diamanten oder Gold bewertet; der Materialwert schien wichtiger zu sein als das Werk selbst. Daher war es wohltuend und beruhigend, auf einer Schottlandreise einer Reihe von Künstlern zu begegnen, die „von den Möglichkeiten und Zielrichtungen der Bildhauerei wieder Gebrauch machten und die sich das Unmögliche konkreter Gegenstände zu eigen machten".[3] Durch Redmond verstand ich, was es heißt, als Bildhauer zu arbeiten und die physischen und visuellen Eigenschaften der Materialien zu verstehen.

Als Studentin an der Glasgow School of Art begann Redmond über die Grenzen des Atelierraums hinauszudenken und sich auf die Straße zu wagen, um dort nicht nur Materialien aufzuspüren, sondern auch Werke zu schaffen, Ausstellungsplätze dafür zu finden und – mit wenig oder keinem Geld – „die Einstellung eines Piraten" zu entwickeln.[4] Systematisch sammelt sie kunstferne Materialien und, um ein Werk zu schaffen, muss sie einfach nur „eine Sache mit einer anderen zusammentun, und schon wird eine weitere Sache daraus", wie sie selbst mit der ihr eigenen Untertreibung feststellt.[5]

Oft umgibt Redmonds Arbeiten eine Aura der Spontanität und Improvisation. Sie strahlen eine Art Unfertigkeit aus, können fragil und unbeständig erscheinen, so als würden sie jeden Moment auseinanderfallen. Doch obwohl Redmonds Installationen beiläufig aussehen, täuscht die Schlichtheit ihrer Bauweise geschickt darüber hinweg, dass ihnen in Wirklichkeit eine komplexe, bis ins Feinste

Mary Redmond makes sculpture by bringing together found and fabricated materials, both organic and industrial. She finds some materials on the streets of Glasgow, which are often things that have been thrown away, and some natural materials outside the city. Other materials she sources abroad; for her, even mundane items like the bin bags used in other countries are more interesting and exciting than those at home. With these materials, Redmond creates a particular poetry of the provisional, and she is not concerned about longevity. Indeed, her choice of ordinary, non-art or even low-grade materials allows her work to be easily disassembled and reassembled, in order to make the same sculpture or a different, entirely new work: "I don't understand what forever means,"[1] she states. And as she explains: "I have a sincere affection for the materials, whether bought or found – for their properties, their possibilities, their histories and futures, for the stories that are embedded within them and the time I spend making with them."[2] Typical smaller works by Redmond, such as *Che-Che Omo* and *Embroque*, comprise diverse materials including beads, raffia, a tassel, a painted metal grille, fabric and paper. None of these materials were used by her because of what they were per se, but rather because, by reconfiguring them, she turns the intrinsically mundane into something strange, beautiful and fetishistic. But Redmond also makes large-scale installations, such as *5 Rows Over the Overglide* for the group exhibition *Red Marauder* at Tramway, Glasgow in 2000 and, more recently, *Seven Split Overglide* for the 2012 exhibition *Bold Tendencies* in London, as well as the brand-new environment she made for the current exhibition at the Neues Museum in Nuremberg.

I first met Redmond whilst preparing a group exhibition called *Undone*, which focussed on sculpture that had been 'handmade' using readily available materials and traditional, if not ad hoc, techniques. At the time, it seemed as if sculpture was primarily valued – certainly amongst the London-based media – for costly materials such as diamonds and gold; the expense of the materials seemed more important than the work itself. On a trip to Scotland, it was therefore refreshing and reassuring to find a number of artists who "embraced the possibilities and speculations of sculpture, and who embraced the impossibilities of objective objects"[3]. I learned from Redmond something about what it means to be a sculptor, and began to understand the physical and visual properties of materials that attract her and the potential meanings these might have.

As a student at Glasgow School of Art, Redmond was encouraged to think beyond the confines of the studio space and to venture out onto the streets, not only to find materials but also to make work, find exhibition sites and – with little or no money – to develop "a piratical attitude"[4]. This encouraged her natural tendency to collect – with a magpie mentality – the items she uses in her sculpture. Her fascination with the material world of objects is one of obsession, involving a constant and systematic gathering of often non-traditional art materials. To make a work she simply has to "put one thing with another and it becomes another thing,"[5] she says, with characteristic understatement.

Redmond's work often has an air of spontaneity and improvisation, and also exudes a sense of provisionality. It can therefore appear fragile and unstable, as if at any moment it might unravel, collapse or simply fall away. But whilst her constructions and installations have a homespun appearance, the apparent simplicity of their fabrication is highly deceptive, and they actually have complex, finely balanced and tightly bound structures. This dichotomy between the made and unmade, the done and undone,

austarierte und fest verbundene Struktur zugrunde liegt. Diese Ambivalenz von Gemachtem und Nicht-Gemachtem kam in *Seven Split Overglide* deutlich zum Ausdruck. Mit dieser Installation für *Bold Tendencies*, eine jährlich stattfindende Ausstellung auf zwei Ebenen eines mehrstöckigen Parkhauses im Südlondoner Stadtteil Peckham, setzte Redmond viele ihrer künstlerischen Strategien um. Zunächst musste sie sich jedoch mit der Architektur selbst auseinandersetzen: Schwer, brutalistisch, hart und dominant, war diese den Wohntürmen im Glasgower Stadtteil Gorbals nicht unähnlich, in dem sie aufgewachsen ist.

Redmond produzierte *Seven Split Overglide* im Raum und für den Raum. Das Resultat fiel sowohl durch seine Zartheit als auch durch seine Raffinesse auf: Das Werk trat der massiven Architektur des Parkhauses entgegen, anstatt von ihr dominiert zu werden. Bevor sie dieses Werk schuf, hielt sich Redmond in Japan auf, und in seiner formalen Anlage – mit hellblauen Pools, mit Bambusstangen und pfirsichfarbenen Beuteln an der Spitze – vermittelt es Ruhe und Gelassenheit und erinnert an ästhetische Vorstellungen etwa eines Ikebana-Arrangements oder eines orientalischen Gartens.

Zudem hatte Redmond einen von ihr so bezeichneten „Traum des Architekten" im Sinn; darunter versteht sie eine romantische Vision à la Oskar Niemeyer, die, an exotischem Ort, den dunklen und bedrohlichen Anlagen, die Sir Basil Spence für das Gorbals ihrer Kindheit entworfen hatte, etwas entgegensetzt. Doch Redmonds „Pools" sind billige Betonplatten, die sie blau bemalt und arrangiert hat. Die perfekt ausbalancierten Bambusrohre bilden in Kombination mit Wellblechplatten eine Struktur, die so erscheint, als würde sie das schwere Gefüge der vorhandenen Überdachung abstützen. Die trügerische Wirkung und Unwahrscheinlichkeit dieser Anordnung erzeugt beim Betrachter ein Gefühl von Unsicherheit, Klaustrophobie und Anspannung. Tatsächlich war Redmond nur ein Jahr nach dem schweren Erdbeben vor der Küste der Stadt Sendai nach Japan gereist, als der Notstand im weitgehend zerstörten Kernkraftwerk von Fukushima noch immer ungelöst war.

Redmond arbeitet mit groben Skizzen, hauptsächlich aber vor Ort und instinktiv. Der große Maßstab stellt sie zwangsläufig vor weitere Herausforderungen. Die Gesamtinstallation, die sie entwirft, wird durch die Architektur, in der sie entsteht, vorgegeben, jedoch nicht begrenzt. Die Künstlerin berücksichtigt sehr unterschiedliche Sichtweisen auf das Werk sowie den Gang eines Besuchers durch ihr übergreifendes Environment. Während wir zwischen den Objekten hindurchgehen, entsteht der Eindruck eines Bühnenbildes, dessen seltsam unverbundene, fremdartige und doch vertraute Gegenstände nur durch uns zusammengeführt und in ein Gesamtbild gebracht werden können. Auf diesem Weg durch Redmonds Realität vermittelt sich ein performatives Element. Souverän in Stellung und vollkommen ausbalanciert, erhalten wir durch das Werk einen reizvolleren Eindruck unseres täglichen Daseins, doch zur gleichen Zeit wirkt es labil und droht, in jedem Moment zu kippen.

which Redmond explores, was writ large in *Seven Split Overglide*, her installation for *Bold Tendencies*, an annual exhibition arranged over two floors of a multi-storey car park in Peckham, South London. With this work, Redmond galvanised many of her main interests and preoccupations, but she had to first consider the intensity of the architecture itself: heavy, brutal, tough and dominating, it was not unlike the tower blocks in the Gorbals area of Glasgow, where she grew up.

Redmond made *Seven Split Overglide* in the space and for the space. The resultant work was remarkable both for its delicacy and refinement, and for the way it met the solid architecture of the car park head on, rather than being dominated by it. Before making this work Redmond had been in Japan, and the work has an affinity with a harmonious and formal arrangement such as an ikebana display or an Oriental garden, with limpid blue pools and bamboo canes topped by peach-coloured bags, redolent of calm and serenity. Moreover, Redmond had in mind what she refers to as a kind of "architect's dream", by which she means a Niemeyer-like romantic vision played out in exotic locations, in contrast to the dark and threatening spaces Sir Basil Spence designed for the Gorbals, which she knew from her childhood. But the 'pools' Redmond made are inexpensive concrete paving slabs she arranged and painted, while the perfectly balanced bamboo canes, combined with corrugated metal sheets and clothes racks, form a structure that actually appears to be supporting the great weight of the extant roof. The illusion and impossibility of this arrangement creates a sense of precariousness, claustrophobia and tension in the mind of the viewer. Indeed, when Redmond was in Japan, it was only a year after the major earthquake off the coast of Sendai, a time when the crisis at the nuclear plant in Fukushima was still unresolved.

Redmond uses rough sketches, but largely works instinctively on site. Working on a large scale inevitably throws up other challenges. The total environment Redmond makes is determined but not limited by the architecture that contains it. She also considers different viewpoints of the work and the viewer's pathway through the overall installation she has made. Walking amongst these objects, we have a sense of a stage set where oddly unrelated, alien yet familiar items are only united and activated by us. This instils in us a pervading sense of the performative as we make our way through Redmond's version of reality. Poised and perfectly balanced, it gives us a more attractive impression of our daily existence and yet at the same time it is unsettling – fragile, provisional and liable to change at any moment.

1   Stephen Feeke and Sophie Raikes, 'Undone: Making and Unmaking in Contemporary Sculpture', in Stephen Feeke, Lisa Le Feuvre and Sophie Raikes (eds.), *Undone: Making and Unmaking in Contemporary Sculpture*, exh. cat. (Leeds: Henry Moore Institute, 2010), p. 43.
2   Ibid., p. 41.
3   Ibid., p. 3.
4   Charlotte Higgins, 'Glasgow's Turner connection', *The Guardian*, 17 October 2011.
5   Feeke and Raikes, *Undone*, p. 41.

1   Stephen Feeke und Sophie Raikes, „Undone. Making and Unmaking in Contemporary Sculpture", in: Stephen Feeke, Lisa Le Feuvre und Sophie Raikes (Hrsg.), *Undone. Making and Unmaking in Contemporary Sculpture*, Ausst.-Kat. Henry Moore Institute Leeds 2010, S. 43.
2   Feeke und Raikes 2010, S. 41.
3   Feeke und Raikes 2010, S. 3.
4   Charlotte Higgins, „Glasgow's Turner Connection", in: *The Guardian*, 17. Oktober 2011.
5   Feeke und Raikes 2010, S. 41.

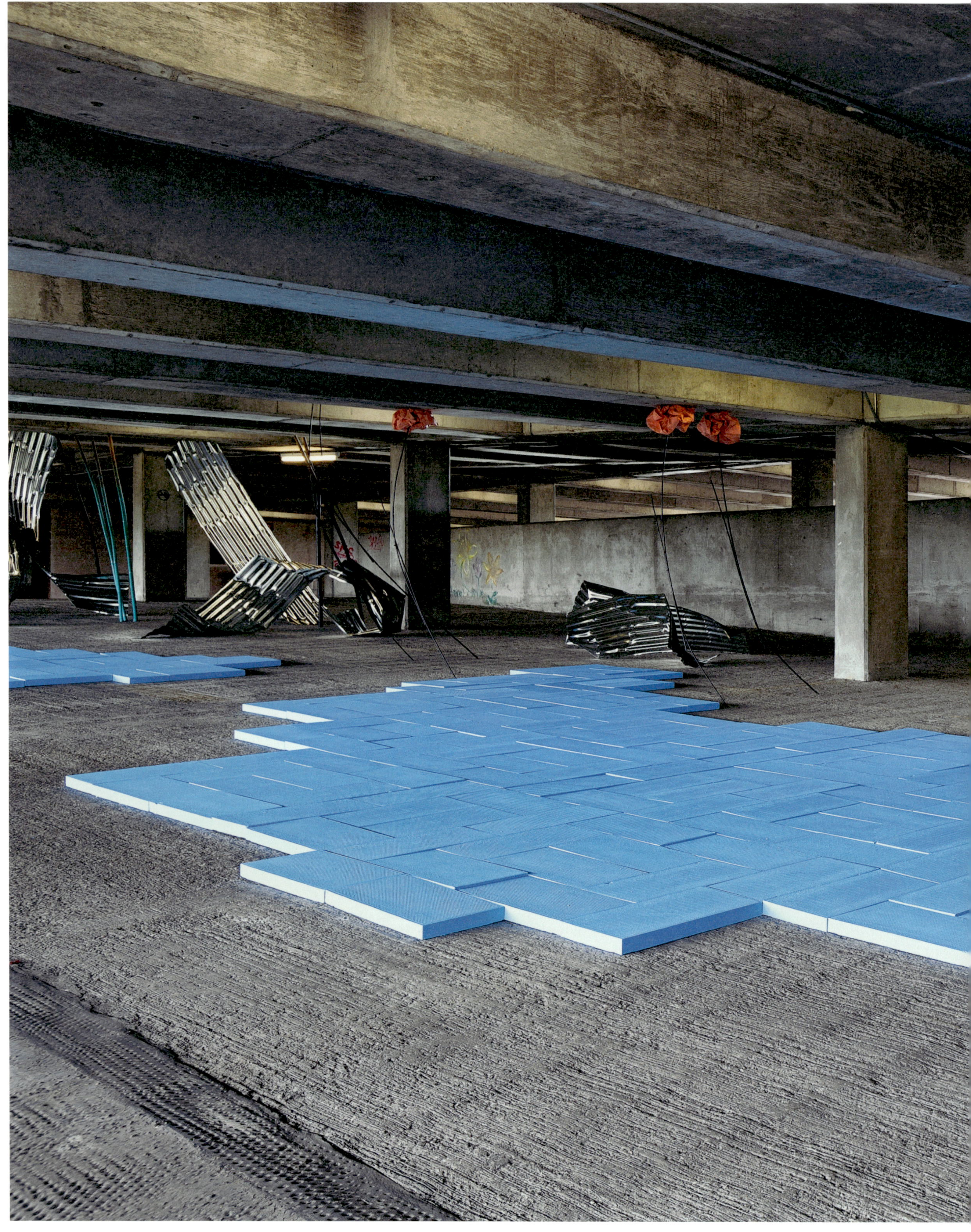

 Seven Split Overglide, 2012, Installationsansicht / Installation view *Bold Tendencies Sculpture Project 6*, Peckham multi-storey car park, London 2012

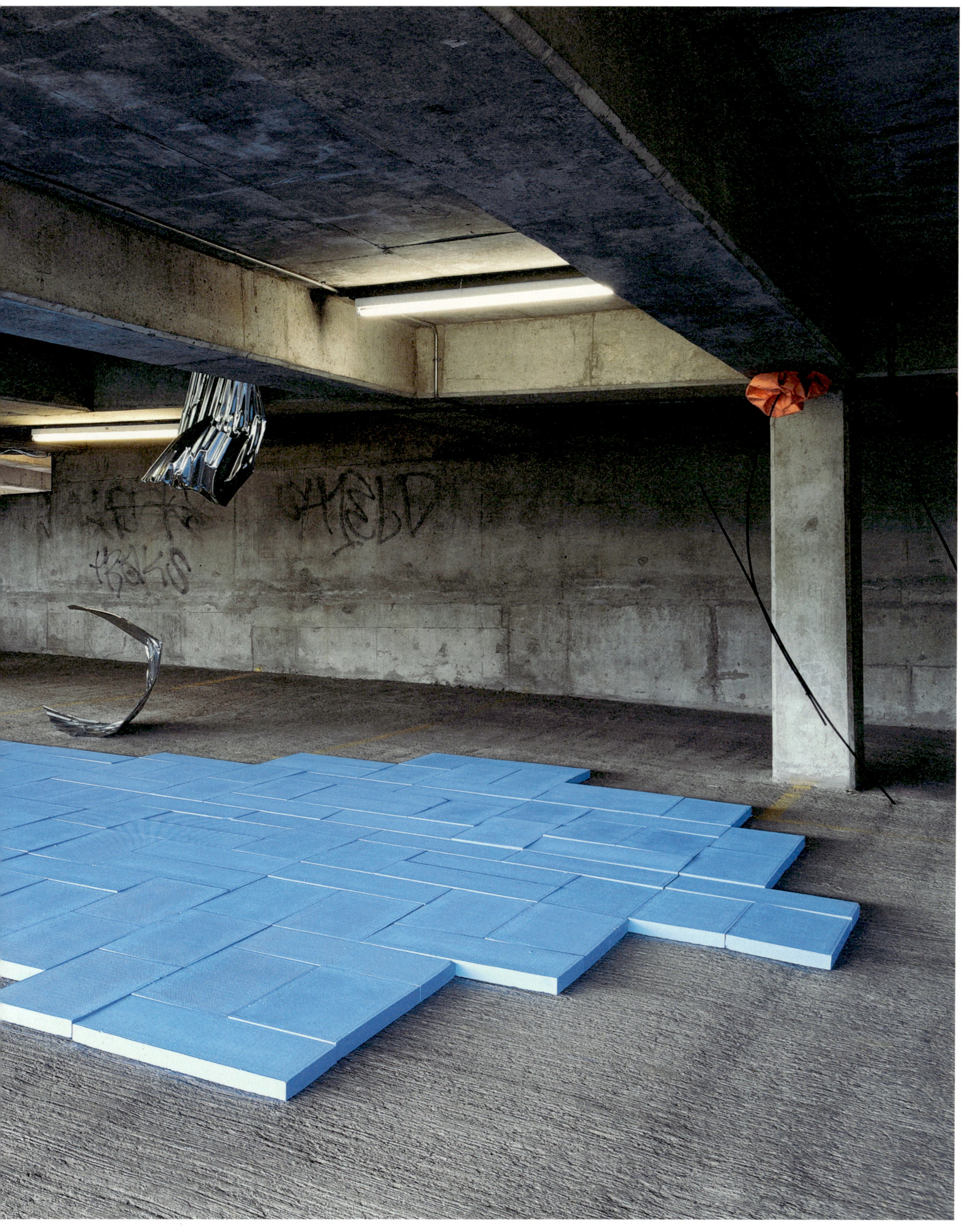

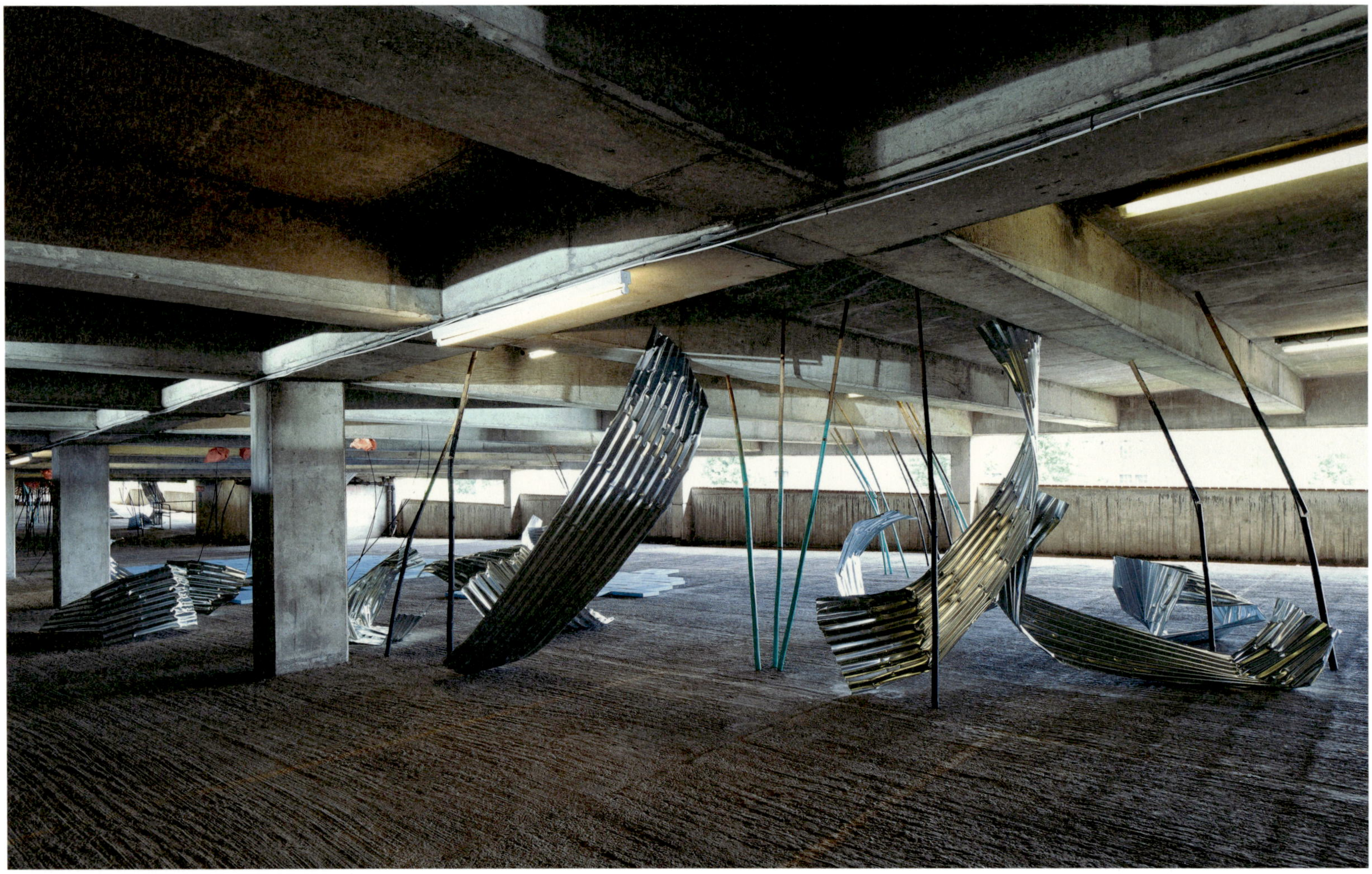

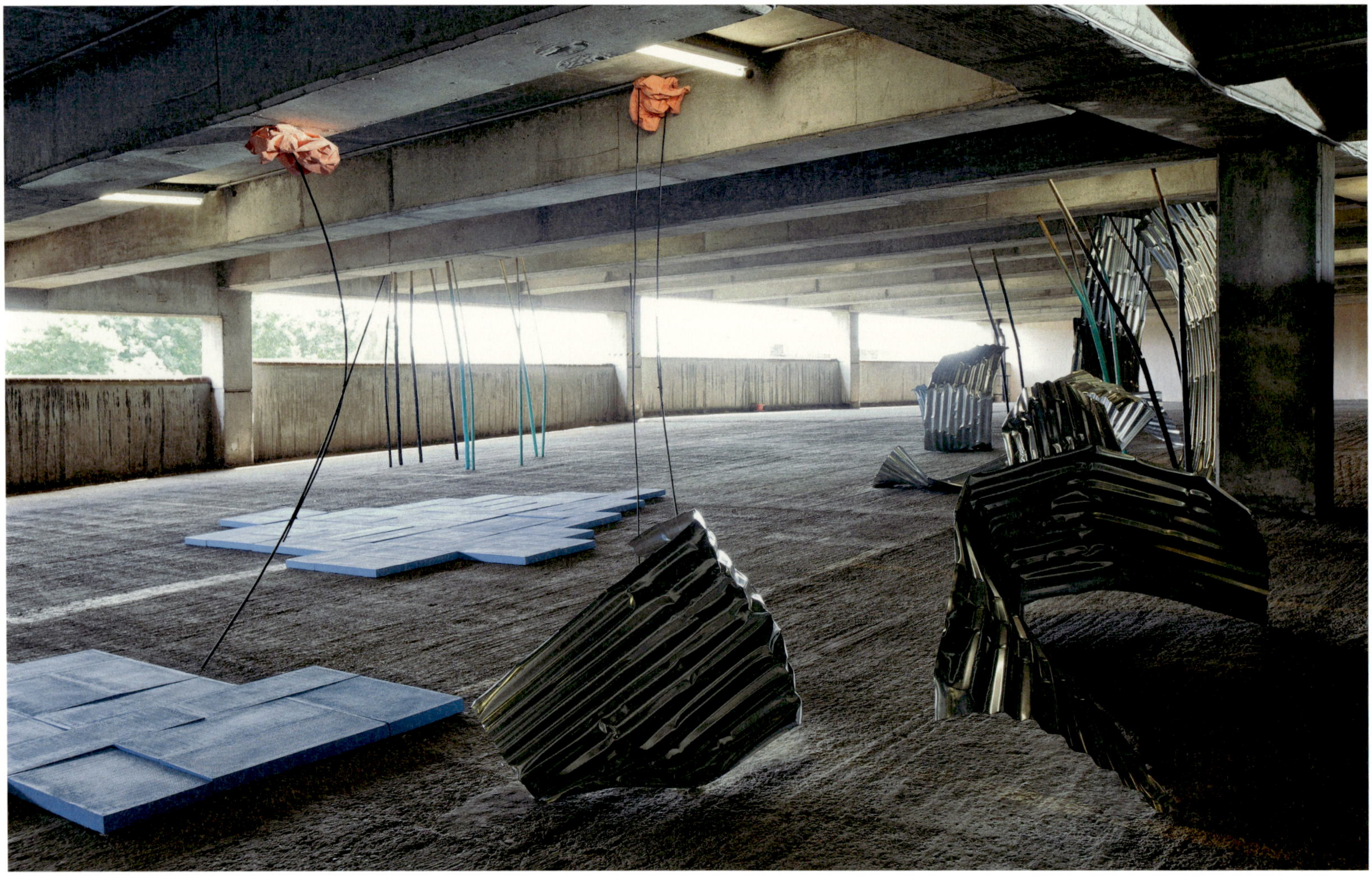

 Seven Split Overglide, 2012, Installationsansicht / Installation view *Bold Tendencies Sculpture Project 6*, Peckham multi-storey car park, London 2012

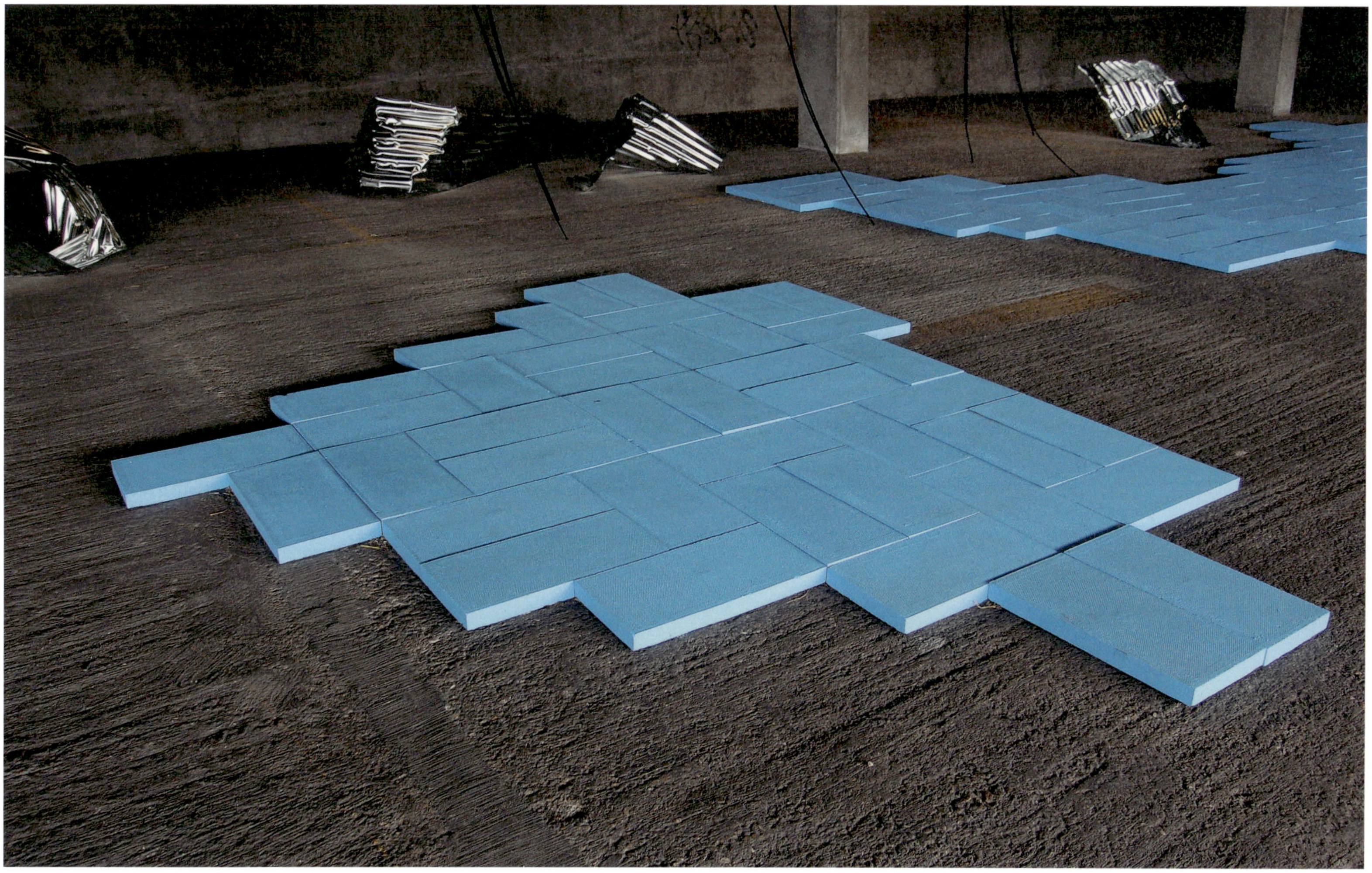

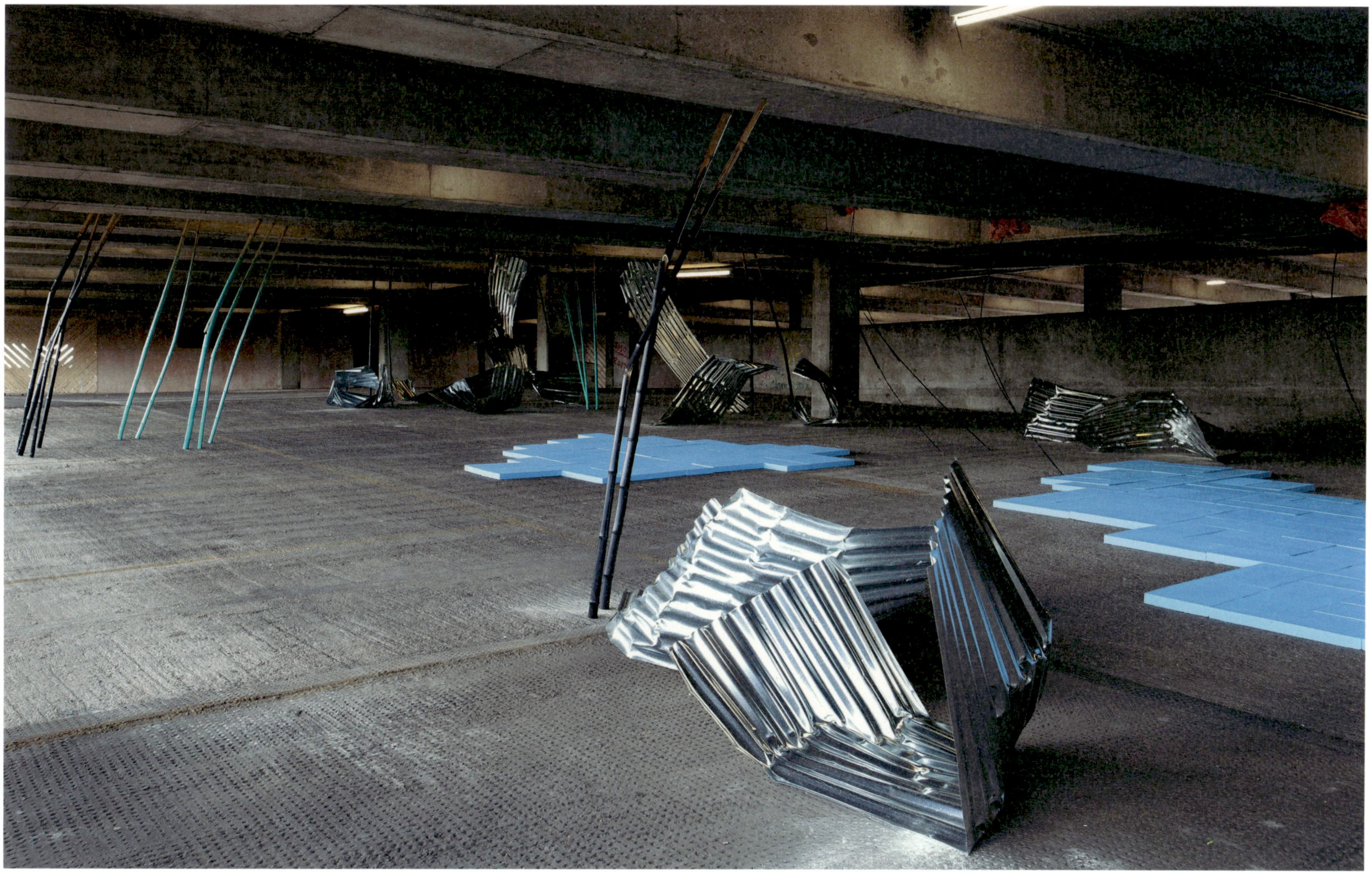

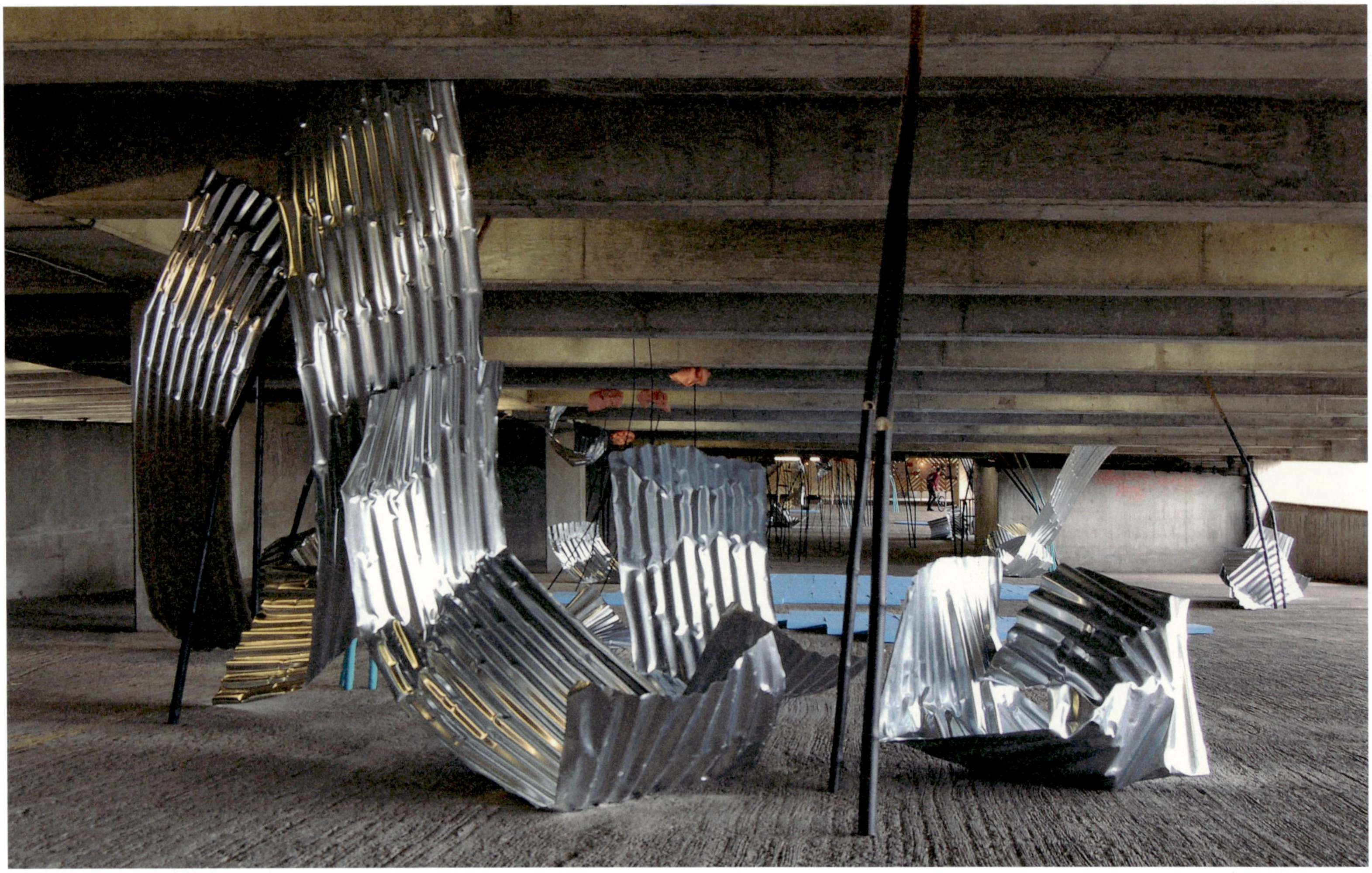

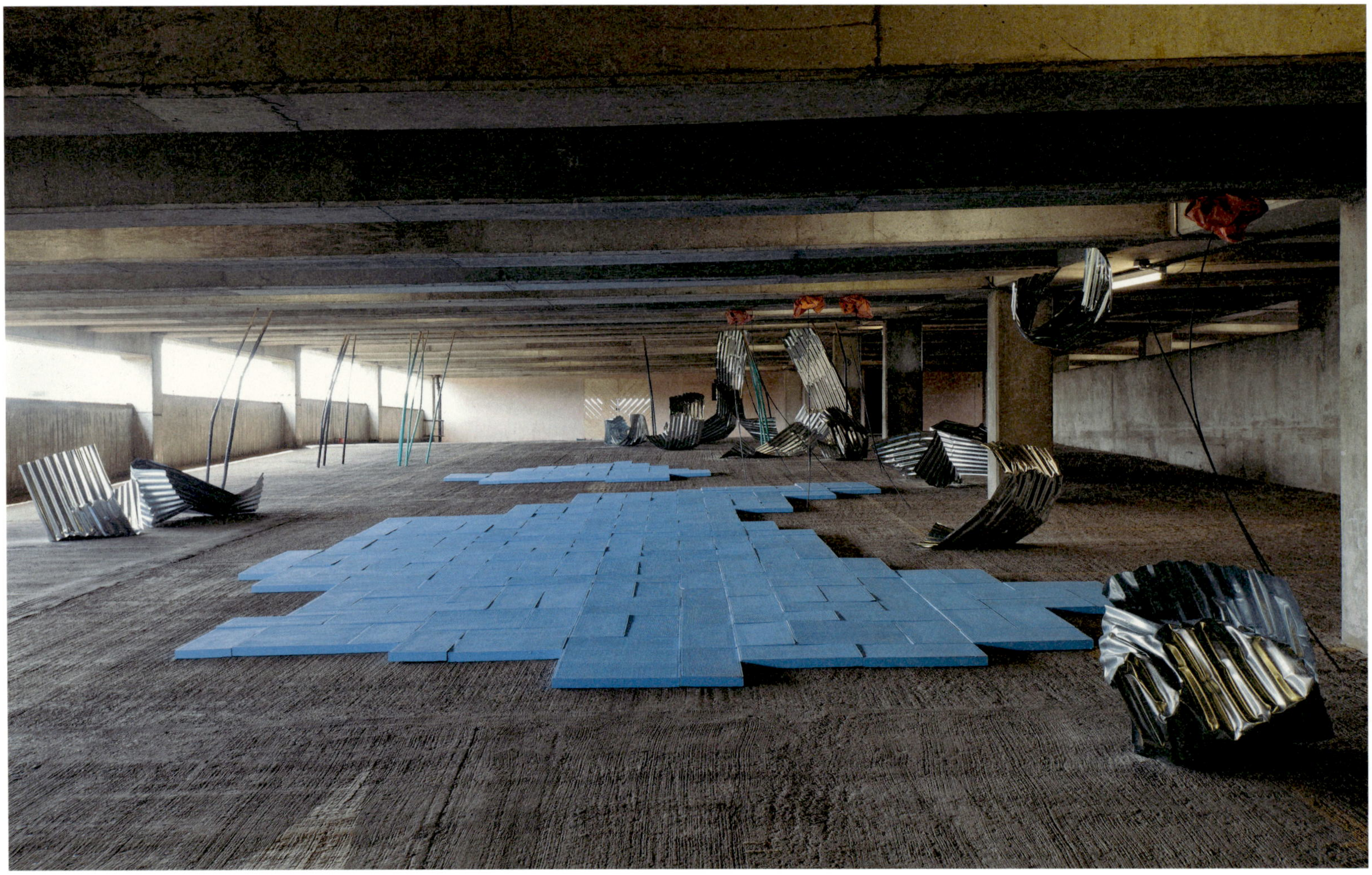

Seven Split Overglide, 2012, Installationsansicht / Installation view *Bold Tendencies Sculpture Project 6*, Peckham multi-storey car park, London 2012

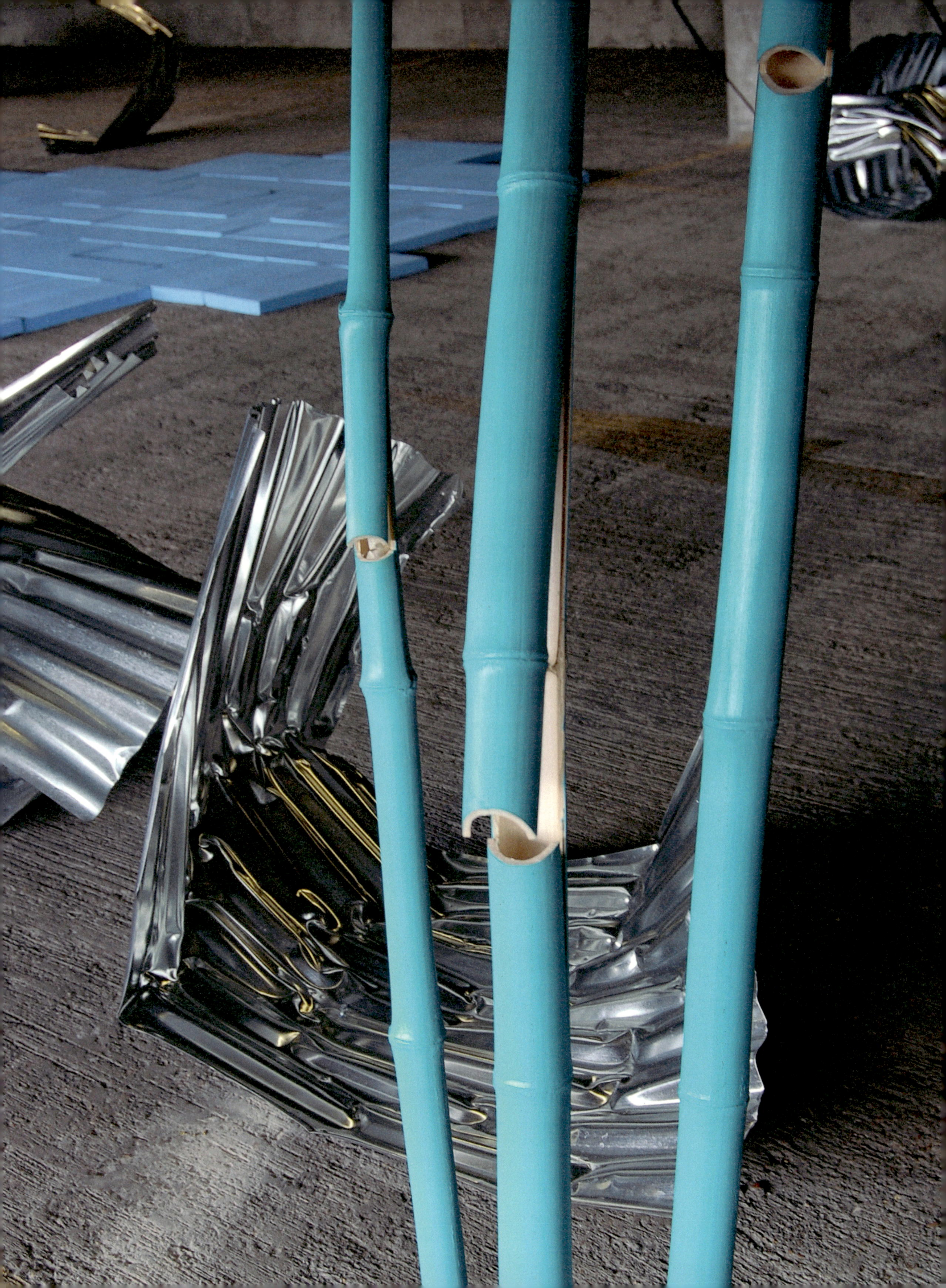

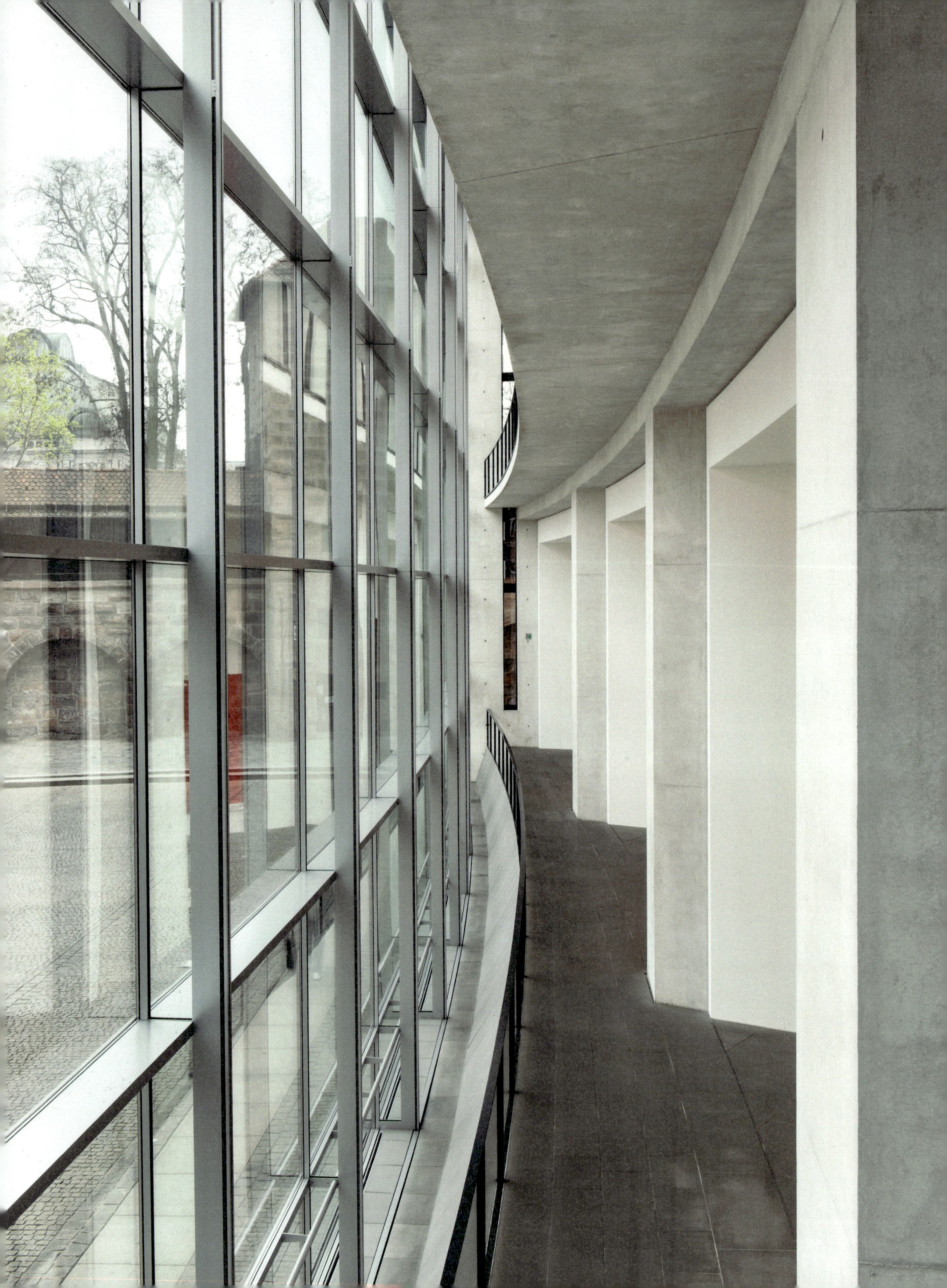

**Verzeichnis der ausgestellten Werke /
List of Exhibited Works**

Die Liste der ausgestellten Werke entspricht dem Stand zum Zeitpunkt der Drucklegung des Kataloges, noch vor der Einrichtung der Ausstellung. Änderungen sind daher möglich. / The list of exhibited works is correct at the time of publication but may change when the exhibition is installed.

Claire Barclay

Reason to push away, 2013

Mixed media Installation / Mixed media installation (pulverbeschichteter Stahl, Leinwand, Lycra, Samt, Feuerstein, Teer, maschinell bearbeitetes Aluminium, Spiegelfarbe auf Glas / Powder-coated steel, canvas, Lycra, velvet, flint, tar, machined aluminium, mirroring paint on glass)
Maße variabel / Dimensions variable
Courtesy of the artist and Stephen Friedman Gallery, London

This other trick, 2013

Siebdrucke, gerahmt / Screen prints, framed
Je / Each 42 × 59,4 cm
Courtesy of the artist and Stephen Friedman Gallery, London

Martin Boyce

Evaporated Pools, 2009

Krepppapier, mit Paraffin beschichtet /
Paraffin-coated crêpe paper
Maße variabel / Dimensions variable
Courtesy of the artist and The Modern Institute/
Toby Webster Ltd, Glasgow

*The Night Does Not Belong to Us,
It is Painted on the Air*, 2011

Sieben Laternen, Kette, lackierter Stahl, elektrische Bestandteile /
Seven lanterns, chain, painted steel, electrical components
Maße variabel / Dimensions variable
Courtesy of the artist and The Modern Institute/
Toby Webster Ltd, Glasgow

The Waves, 2011

Lackierter Stahl, Rost / Painted steel, rust
288 × 194 × 200 cm
Courtesy of the artist and The Modern Institute/
Toby Webster Ltd, Glasgow

Nick Evans

Coolie, 2013

Faserverstärkter Gips, bearbeitetes Messing, Leuchte /
Fibre-reinforced plaster, machined brass, light fitting
175 × 110 × 90 cm
Courtesy The Artist; Mary Mary, Glasgow

Fossil Table, 2013

Faserverstärkter Gips, Marmor /
Fibre-reinforced plaster, marble
80 × 70 × 72 cm
Courtesy The Artist; Mary Mary, Glasgow

4 Stools, 2013

Faserverstärkter Gips, Purpleheart-Holz /
Fibre-reinforced plaster, purpleheart wood
Je / Each 40 × 40 × 40 cm
Courtesy The Artist; Mary Mary, Glasgow

Hottentot Venus, 2013

Faserverstärkter Gips, mundgeblasene Glaskugeln, Leuchten /
Fibre-reinforced plaster, blown glass, light fittings
145 × 60 × 80 cm
Courtesy The Artist; Mary Mary, Glasgow

The Nightwatch, 2013

Faserverstärkter Gips, Schmiedeeisen, Glas, Leuchte /
Fibre-reinforced plaster, wrought iron, glass, light fitting
130 × 70 × 90 cm
Courtesy The Artist; Mary Mary, Glasgow

Nicolas Party

Decorative Pattern, 2013

Sprühfarbe auf Wand / Spray paint on wall
Maße variabel / Dimensions variable
Courtesy of the artist and The Modern Institute/
Toby Webster Ltd, Glasgow

Wall Drawing, 2013

Kohle auf Wand / Charcoal on wall
Maße variabel / Dimensions variable
Courtesy of the artist and The Modern Institute/
Toby Webster Ltd, Glasgow

Ciara Phillips

Things put together, 2013

Siebdrucke auf Papier / Screen prints on paper
Je / Each 101 × 68 cm
Courtesy of the artist and Kendall Koppe, Glasgow

Mary Redmond

Mango Street, 2013

Wellblech, Gerüstnetz, Seil aus Seegras, Isolierband, Kunststoffrohr, Baumwolle, Lack, Nylon, Plastiktüten /
Corrugated metal, scaffolding netting, seagrass rope, electrical tape, plastic pipe, cotton, paint, nylon, plastic bags
Maße variabel / Dimensions variable
Courtesy of the artist and The Modern Institute/
Toby Webster Ltd, Glasgow

Autoren / Authors

KITTY ANDERSON

Kitty Anderson studierte Bildende Kunst in London und absolvierte den Master of Arts in Curating Contemporary Art am Royal College of Art, London. Von 2004 bis 2007 war sie Associate Curator bei Frieze Projects, dem jährlichen Programm der Frieze Art Fair, London. 2008 wurde sie stellvertretende Galerieleiterin bei The Modern Institute, Glasgow. Seit 2009 ist sie Kuratorin bei The Common Guild, Glasgow. Darüber hinaus realisierte sie freiberuflich zahlreiche Projekte, so 2011 ein Gemeinschaftsprojekt mit den Künstlerinnen Anne-Marie Copestake, Kate Davis, Rachel Lowther und Lorna Macintyre sowie 2010 ein Projekt mit Claire Barclay für das Glasgow International Festival of Visual Art (gemeinsam mit der Kuratorin Siobhan Carroll). Sie schreibt für Magazine und Onlinepublikationen wie *Axis*, *PAR+RS* und *PILOT* und war Mitglied verschiedener Auswahlgremien, darunter The Arts Foundation Awards 2012 und 2013 und Durham Cathedral Artist in Residence programme.

Kitty Anderson studied fine art in London and undertook the Master of Arts in Curating Contemporary Art at the Royal College of Art, London. From 2004 to 2007 she was Associate Curator of Frieze Projects, the annual programme at Frieze Art Fair, London. In 2008 she joined The Modern Institute, Glasgow, as Associate Director. Since 2009 she has been Curator at The Common Guild, Glasgow. She has produced a number of freelance projects including a collaborative project with artists Anne-Marie Copestake, Kate Davis, Rachel Lowther and Lorna Macintyre in 2011, and a project with Claire Barclay for Glasgow International Festival of Visual Art in 2010 (with the curator Siobhan Carroll). She has contributed to printed and online publications including *Axis*, *PAR+RS* and *PILOT*, and various selection panels and advisory groups including The Arts Foundation Awards 2012 and 2013, and the Durham Cathedral Artist in Residence programme.

OLIVER BASCIANO

Der in London lebende Autor und Kritiker Oliver Basciano ist Managing Editor der Zeitschrift *ArtReview*. Er hat Artikel und Essays zu diversen Kunstzeitschriften sowie zu Künstlermonografien und Ausstellungskatalogen beigetragen. Basciano absolvierte den Master of Arts in Contemporary Art Theory am Goldsmiths College, University of London, und ist Trustee bei The Woodmill Studios and Gallery.

Oliver Basciano is a writer and critic based in London. He is Managing Editor of *ArtReview*. He has contributed articles and essays to various other art magazines, artists' monographs and exhibition catalogues. Basciano has a Master of Arts in Contemporary Art Theory from Goldsmiths College, University of London, and is a trustee at The Woodmill Studios and Gallery.

FIONA BRADLEY

Dr. Fiona Bradley studierte Kunstgeschichte an der Cambridge University und am Courtauld Institute of Art, London. Ihre berufliche Karriere begann sie an der Tate Gallery Liverpool, wo sie Ausstellungen, unter anderem mit Rachel Whiteread, Andreas Gursky, Paula Rego und Susan Hiller, konzipierte, sowie an der Hayward Gallery, London, wo sie Douglas Gordons große Einzelausstellung *what have I done* co-kuratierte. Seit 2003 ist sie Direktorin von The Fruitmarket Gallery in Edinburgh, dort kuratierte sie Ausstellungen und verfasste wichtige Publikationen mit schottischen als auch internationalen Künstlern, darunter Louise Bourgeois, Ellen Gallagher, Cai Guo-Qiang, Fred Sandback, Eva Hesse, Bill Bollinger, Callum Innes, Christine Borland, Tony Swain, Martin Creed, Claire Barclay, Lucy Skaer und Gabriel Orozco. 2007 gehörte sie der Jury des Turner Prize an und war 2011 als Kuratorin für den Beitrag Schottlands zur Biennale Venedig verantwortlich.

Dr Fiona Bradley read art history at Cambridge University and the Courtauld Institute of Art, London. She started her professional career at Tate Gallery Liverpool, where she made exhibitions with, among others, Rachel Whiteread, Andreas Gursky, Paula Rego and Susan Hiller, and at the Hayward Gallery, London, where she co-curated Douglas Gordon's major solo exhibition *what have I done*. She has been Director of The Fruitmarket Gallery in Edinburgh since 2003, where she has curated exhibitions and produced important publications with Scottish and international artists including Louise Bourgeois, Ellen Gallagher, Cai Guo-Qiang, Fred Sandback, Eva Hesse, Bill Bollinger, Callum Innes, Christine Borland, Tony Swain, Martin Creed, Claire Barclay, Lucy Skaer and Gabriel Orozco. She was a member of the Turner Prize jury in 2007, and in 2011 was the curator for Scotland's contribution to the Venice Biennale.

KATRINA BROWN

Dr. Katrina M. Brown ist Gründungsdirektorin von The Common Guild, einer in Glasgow ansässigen Non-Profit-Organisation für bildende Kunst mit einem internationalen Programm von Künstlerprojekten sowie Veranstaltungen und Ausstellungen. Brown übernahm die Leitung des Glasgow International Festival of Visual Art 2010 und 2012 mit Großprojekten von Susan Philipsz und Jeremy Deller. 2013 kuratierte The Common Guild den Beitrag Schottlands, *Scotland + Venice*, bei der 55. Biennale Venedig. Brown war Mitglied zahlreicher Gremien und Komitees, darunter Jury des Turner Prize 2011, Paul Hamlyn Foundation Awards for Artists; Comité Technique d'Achat, FRAC des Pays de la Loire (2005–2011); sie zählte zum Vorstand des IKT (International Association of Curators of Contemporary Art) und beriet die Arts Council Collection (2007–2009). Von 1997 bis Anfang 2007 war sie Kuratorin und stellvertretende Direktorin des 1999 eröffneten Kunstzentrums DCA – Dundee Contemporary Arts, wo sie neben großen Einzelausstellungen mit schottischen und internationalen Künstlern auch mehrere wichtige Gruppenausstellungen kuratierte.

Dr Katrina M. Brown is founding Director of The Common Guild, a not-for-profit visual arts organisation based in Glasgow, presenting an international programme of artists' projects, events and exhibitions. She was also responsible for the direction of the Glasgow International Festival of Visual Art in 2010 and 2012, including major public projects by Susan Philipsz and Jeremy Deller.

In 2013 The Common Guild curated the *Scotland + Venice* exhibition for the 55th Venice Biennale. Brown has served on numerous boards and committees, including the jury of the 2011 Turner Prize; the Paul Hamlyn Foundation Awards for Artists; the Comité Technique d'Achat, FRAC des Pays de la Loire (2005–2011); the Board of IKT (International Association of Curators of Contemporary Art) and the Arts Council Collection (2007–2009). From 1997 until early 2007 she was Curator and Deputy Director of Dundee Contemporary Arts, which opened in 1999, where she curated major solo projects with Scottish and international artists, as well as a number of significant group exhibitions.

STEPHEN FEEKE

Bis Dezember 2009 war Stephen Feeke Kurator am Henry Moore Institute, Leeds, wo er in allen Bereichen der Ausstellungskonzeption und des Projektmanagements tätig war. Dort erarbeitete er zahlreiche Ausstellungen zur Bildhauerei, darunter *Undone: Making and Unmaking in Contemporary Sculpture* und *Ice Age Sculpture*, und konzipierte vor allem Projekte im Dialog von zeitgenössischer und historischer Kunst. Zudem hat er viel dazu beigetragen, das Programm des Henry Moore Instituts geografisch auszuweiten. 2010 wurde er Kurator am New Art Centre, Roche Court in Wiltshire, wo er das Programm moderner und zeitgenössischer Kunst für die Galerie und den 15 Hektar großen Skulpturenpark verantwortet. Er hat darüber hinaus Ausstellungsprojekte kuratiert wie *Caro at Chatsworth* und *Bold Tendencies* und schreibt regelmäßig für *Museums Journal*.

Until December 2009, Stephen Feeke was Curator of Exhibitions at the Henry Moore Institute, Leeds, where he was involved in all aspects of exhibition making and project management. There he worked on a large number of diverse sculpture shows including *Undone: Making and Unmaking in Contemporary Sculpture* and *Ice Age Sculpture*, and developed a particular interest in the conceptual intersections between contemporary and historical art. He also did much to expand the geographical reach of the Institute's programme. In 2010 he became Curator at the New Art Centre, Roche Court in Wiltshire, where he directs a programme of modern and contemporary art for the Gallery and the 60-acre Sculpture Park. He has also curated exhibitions elsewhere, such as *Caro at Chatsworth* and *Bold Tendencies*, and contributes regularly to *Museums Journal*.

FIONA JARDINE

Fiona Jardine ist Autorin und Künstlerin. Sie studierte am Duncan of Jordanstone College of Art & Design, Dundee, an der Glasgow School of Art sowie an der University of Wolverhampton. Sie lebt in Glasgow und in den Scottish Borders, wo sie das Fach Contextual Studies für Studenten des Textil- sowie Modedesigns an der Heriot-Watt University lehrt.

Fiona Jardine is a writer and artist who was educated at Duncan of Jordanstone College of Art & Design, Dundee, Glasgow School of Art and the University of Wolverhampton. She lives in Glasgow and the Scottish Borders, where she teaches Contextual Studies to Textile Design and Fashion students at Heriot-Watt University.

MELITTA KLIEGE

Dr. Melitta Kliege, geboren 1962 in Düsseldorf, ist Kunsthistorikerin, Ausstellungsleiterin für Gegenwartskunst und Kuratorin am Neuen Museum in Nürnberg. Sie studierte Kunstgeschichte, Japanologie und Religionswissenschaften in Köln, Bonn und Berlin, und promovierte 1996 über Kunst der 1960er Jahre. Seit 1990 ist sie für zahlreiche Kunstinstitutionen im In- und Ausland tätig. Von 1996 bis 1998 kuratierte sie als wissenschaftliche Assistentin an der Hamburger Kunsthalle unter anderem *Bruce Nauman. Versuchsanordnungen.* Am Neuen Museum konzipierte sie u. a. eine Ausstellungsreihe zur jüngsten Kunstgeschichte sowie die Richard-Artschwager-Retrospektive. Zahlreiche Publikationen und Aufsätze zur zeitgenössischen Kunst, Lehraufträge an Kunsthochschulen und Berufung in Fachjurys zur zeitgenössischen Kunst.

Dr Melitta Kliege, born in 1962 in Düsseldorf, is an art historian, Head of Exhibitions for Contemporary Art and Curator at the Neues Museum – Staatliches Museum für Kunst and Design in Nuremberg. She read art history, Japanology and comparative religion at Cologne, Bonn and Berlin, and received her doctorate in 1996 for her thesis on art in the 1960s. Since 1990 Kliege has worked for a number of national and international art institutions. As an assistant curator at the Hamburger Kunsthalle from 1996 to 1998 she curated, among others, the exhibition *Bruce Nauman. Versuchsanordnungen*. At the Neues Museum she has devised a series of exhibitions on recent art developments and curated numerous solo and group exhibitions, including a major Richard Artschwager retrospective. She has published numerous books and articles on contemporary art, held teaching posts at art schools and served on juries and selection committees.

SARAH LOWNDES

Dr. Sarah Lowndes ist Autorin, Kuratorin und Dozentin an der Glasgow School of Art. Sie hat Artikel für *frieze*, *Art on Paper*, *Spike Art Quarterly* und *Afterall* verfasst sowie Texte zu Katalogen beigetragen, darunter *Richard Wright* (2009), *Robert Rauschenberg: Botanical Vaudeville* (2011) und *Dieter Roth: Diaries* (2012). Eine erweiterte zweite Ausgabe ihres Buches *Social Sculpture: The Rise of the Glasgow Art Scene* wurde 2010 von The Luath Press veröffentlicht. Zu den Projekten, die sie als Kuratorin betreute, zählen *Three Blows* (2008), *Votive* (2009), *Urlibido* (2010), *Dialogue of Hands* (2012), *Studio 58: Women Artists in Glasgow Since World War II* (2012) und *The Glasgow Weekend* (2013).

Dr Sarah Lowndes is a writer, curator and lecturer at Glasgow School of Art. She has contributed to *frieze*, *Art on Paper*, *Spike Art Quarterly* and *Afterall*, as well as to catalogues including *Richard Wright* (2009), *Robert Rauschenberg: Botanical Vaudeville* (2011) and *Dieter Roth: Diaries* (2012). An expanded second edition of her book *Social Sculpture: The Rise of the Glasgow Art Scene* was published by The Luath Press in 2010. Her curatorial projects include *Three Blows* (2008), *Votive* (2009), *Urlibido* (2010), *Dialogue of Hands* (2012), *Studio 58: Women Artists in Glasgow Since World War II* (2012) and *The Glasgow Weekend* (2013).

Der vorliegende Band erscheint anlässlich
der Ausstellung / The catalogue is published
on the occasion of the exhibition

**Funktion / Dysfunktion
Kunstzentrum Glasgow**

**Function / Dysfunction
Contemporary Art from Glasgow**

**Claire Barclay, Martin Boyce, Nick Evans, Nicolas
Party, Ciara Phillips und / and Mary Redmond**

18. Oktober 2013 bis 9. Februar 2014 /
18 October 2013 – 9 February 2014

Ausstellung / Exhibition

Ausstellung / Exhibition
Melitta Kliege

Registrar / Registrar
Susanne Teichmann

Ausstellungstechnik / Exhibition technicians
Werner Henne, Jutta Birle, Jürgen Schuster

Presse und Öffentlichkeitsarbeit / Press and PR
Eva Martin, Mario Rau

*Museumspädagogik /
Museum education programme*
Claudia Marquardt, Ulrike Rathjen

Restauratorische Betreuung / Conservation
Eva Pridöhl, Nürnberg

Dank / Acknowledgements

Kitty Anderson, Dr. Katrina Brown, Martina Buder,
Jenny Brownrigg, Amanda Catto, Dr. Paul Fischer,
Kate Gray, Christine Horber, Florence Ingleby,
Petra Kittler, Kendall Koppe, Ernst Georg Kühle,
Prof. Dr. Julia Lehner, Lena Mozer, Christina
Plewinski, Dr. Elke Ritt, Hannah Robinson,
Dr. Norbert Schürgers, Dr. Matthias Strobel,
Maike Teubner, Jacqueline Todd, Toby Webster,
Dr. Dirk Wintzer

Katalog / Catalogue

Herausgeber / Editor
Neues Museum – Staatliches Museum für Kunst
und Design in Nürnberg

*Konzeption und Redaktion des Kataloges /
Catalogue concept and editing*
Melitta Kliege

Redaktionsassistenz / Editorial assistance
Maike Teubner

Lektorat / Copy editing
Martina Buder (Deutsch / German)
Jacqueline Todd (Englisch / English)

*Übersetzungen aus dem Deutschen /
Translations from German*
Jacqueline Todd, Berlin (Kliege, Vorwort / Preface,
Grußworte / Forewords)

*Übersetzungen aus dem Englischen /
Translations from English*
Kurt Rehkopf, Hamburg (Anderson, Basciano,
Bradley, Brown, Feeke, Lowndes)
Sylvia Zirden, Berlin (Jardine)

Grafische Gestaltung / Design
Kühle und Mozer, Köln

Gesamtherstellung / Production
DZA Druckerei zu Altenburg GmbH, Altenburg

ISBN 978-3-86984-481-7

All rights reserved

Printed in Germany

Dieser Katalog enthält ein Einlegeheft mit den
Abbildungen der Installationen von Claire Barclay,
Martin Boyce, Nick Evans, Ciara Phillips, Nicolas
Party und Mary Redmond, die zur Ausstellung
Funktion / Dysfunktion im Neuen Museum in
Nürnberg entstanden sind.

The catalogue includes an insert with
photographs of the installations created by
Claire Barclay, Martin Boyce, Nick Evans,
Ciara Phillips, Nicolas Party and Mary Redmond
for the exhibition *Function / Dysfunction* at the
Neues Museum in Nuremberg.

© 2013 Neues Museum in Nürnberg,
Verlag für moderne Kunst und die Autoren

© für die abgebildeten Werke bei / for the
reproductions of works by:

Claire Barclay

Martin Boyce; Courtesy of the Artist and The
Modern Institute/Toby Webster Ltd, Glasgow;
Courtesy of the Artist, Johnen Galerie, Berlin and
The Modern Institute/Toby Webster Ltd, Glasgow
(S. / p. 71 oben / top, unten rechts / bottom right);
Courtesy of the Artist, Glasgow, Galerie Eva
Presenhuber, Zurich and The Modern Institute/
Toby Webster Ltd, Glasgow (S. / pp. 68 unten /
bottom, 79 unten / bottom)

Nick Evans

Nicolas Party; Courtesy of the Artist and The
Modern Institute/Toby Webster Ltd, Glasgow;
Courtesy Debbie and Mitchell Rechler (S. / p. 113
Mitte / middle), Courtesy of the Artist, Galerie
Gregor Staiger, Zurich and The Modern Institute/
Toby Webster Ltd, Glasgow (S. / pp. 102, 112 oben
links / top left); Courtesy of the Artist, The Modern
Institute/Toby Webster Ltd, Glasgow and Salon 94,
New York (S. / pp. 106 zweite Reihe rechts / second
row right, 107)

Ciara Phillips

Mary Redmond; Courtesy of the Artist and
The Modern Institute/Toby Webster Ltd, Glasgow

Tobias Rehberger

Wiebke Siem

Ross Sinclair

Simon Starling

© VG Bild-Kunst, Bonn 2013, für die abgebildeten
Werke von / for the reproductions of works by
Richard Artschwager, Joseph Beuys, Marcel
Broodthaers, Florian Slotawa

Umschlagvorderseite / Front cover
Martin Boyce, *Evaporated Pools*, 2009, Installa-
tionsansicht / Installation view *the spirit level*,
Barbara Gladstone Gallery, New York 2012

Umschlagrückseite / Back cover
Claire Barclay, *Caught In Corners*, 2009,
Installationsansicht / Installation view,
The Fruitmarket Gallery, Edinburgh 2009

Frontispiz / Frontispiece
Ciara Phillips, *East Stairwell, Laura*, 2011

S. / p. 4
Nicolas Party, *Decorative pattern Number 1
(+Still life)*, 2010 (Detail), Installationsansicht /
Installation view *Kiss of death*, The Glue Factory,
Glasgow International Festival, Glasgow 2010

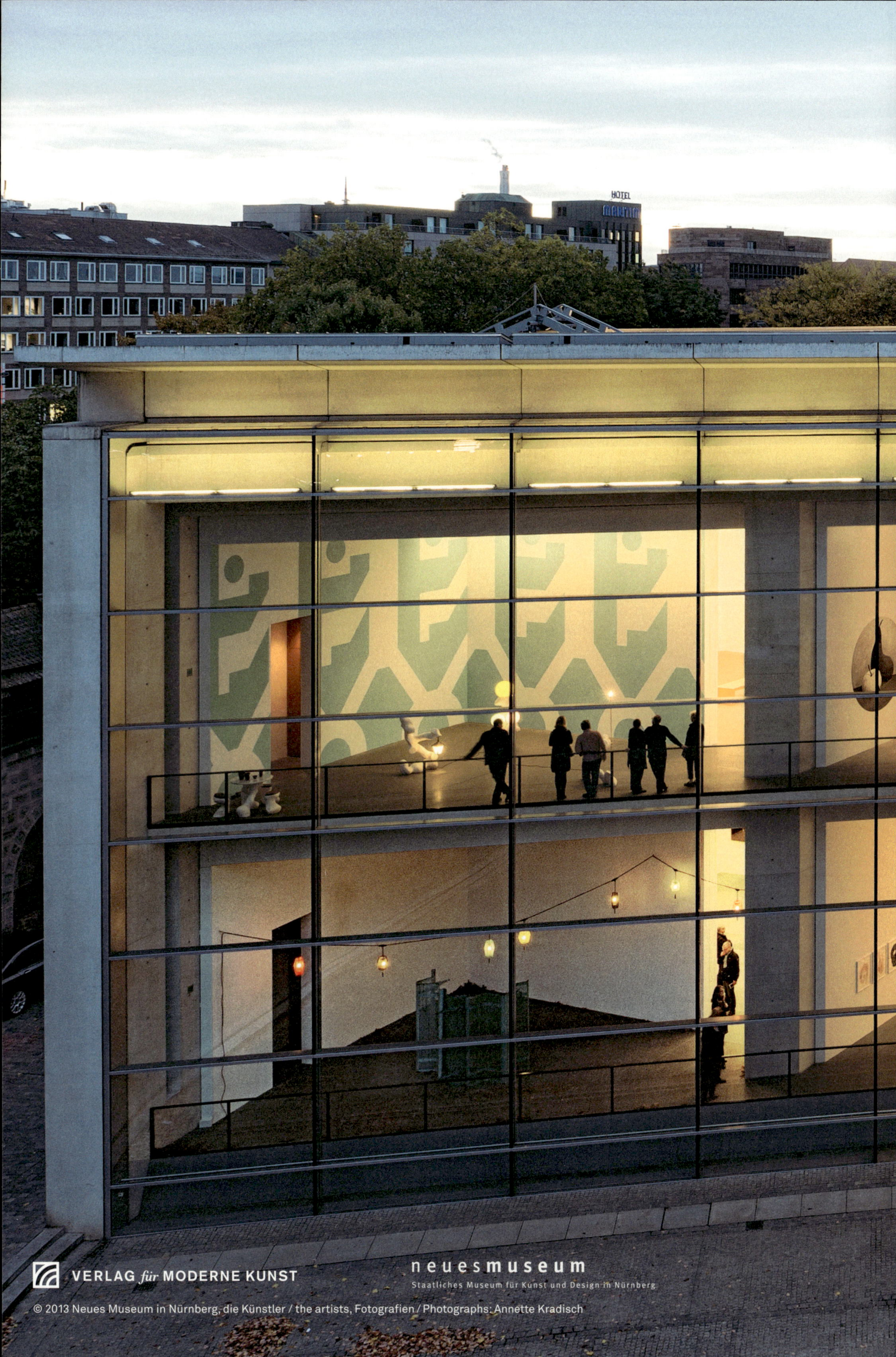

© 2013 Neues Museum in Nürnberg, die Künstler / the artists, Fotografien / Photographs: Annette Kradisch

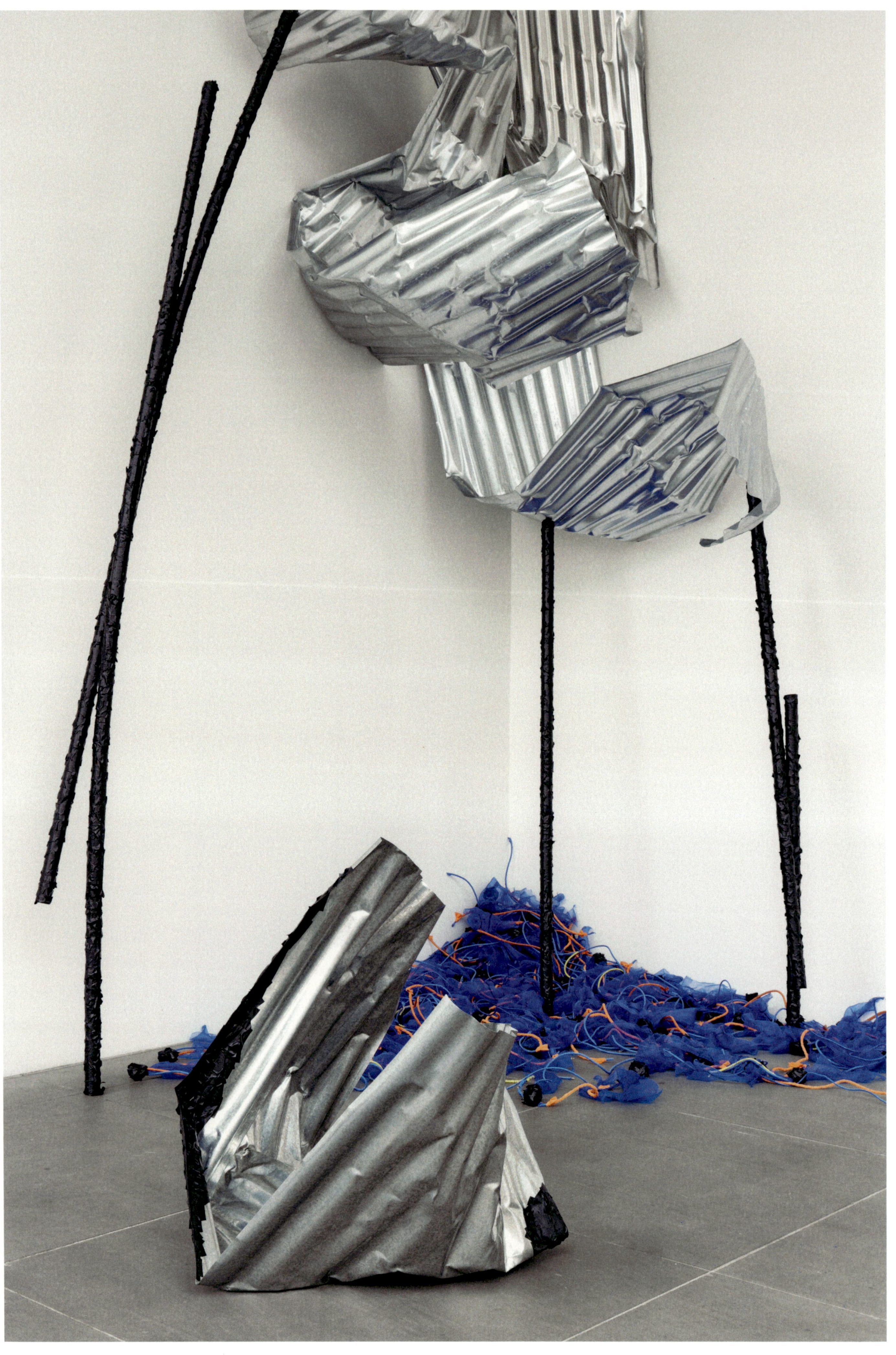

Mary Redmond

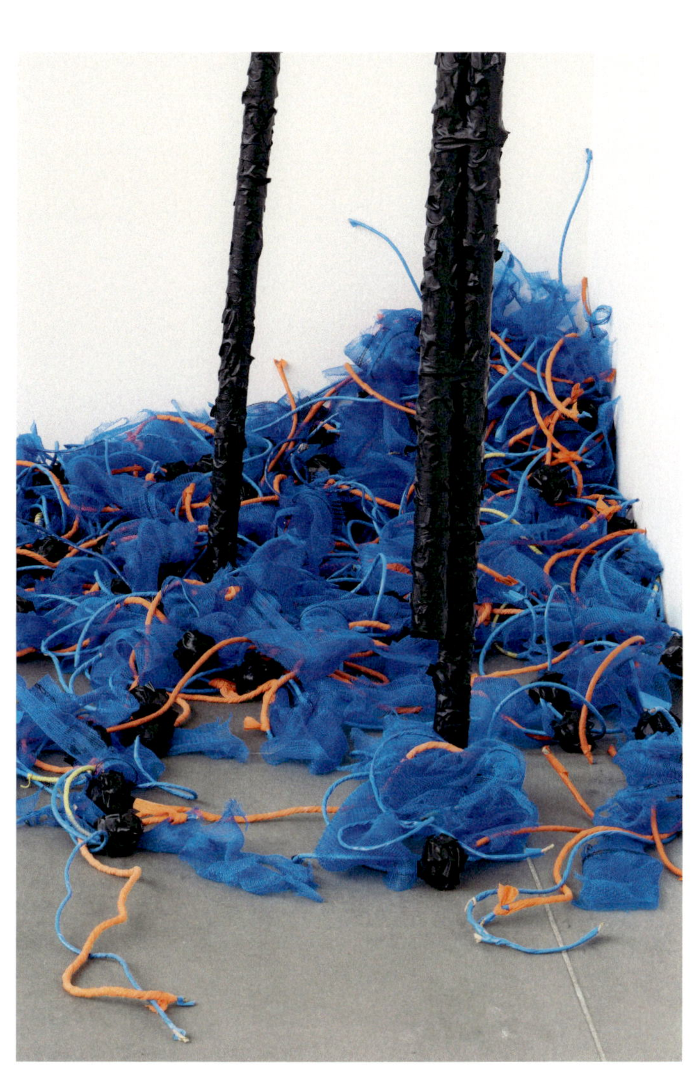
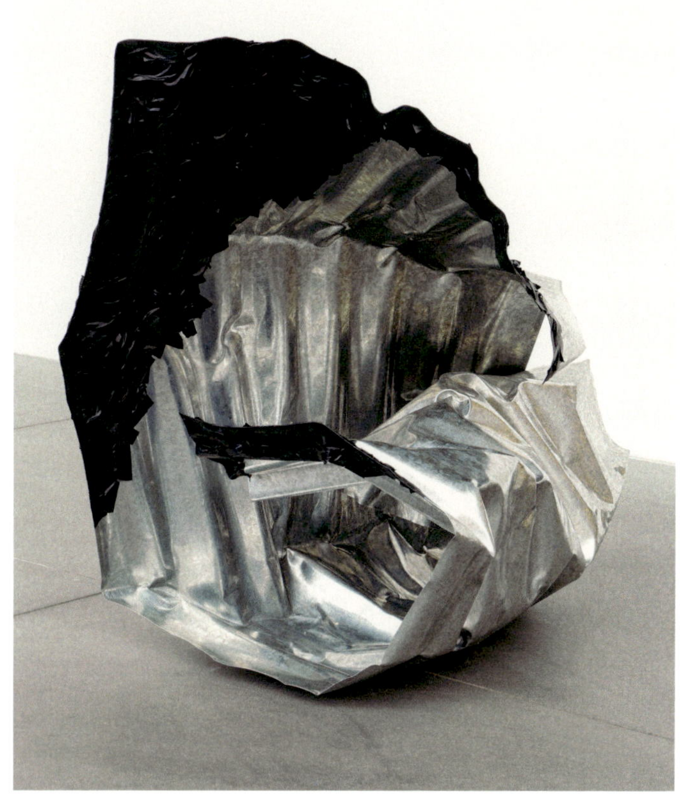

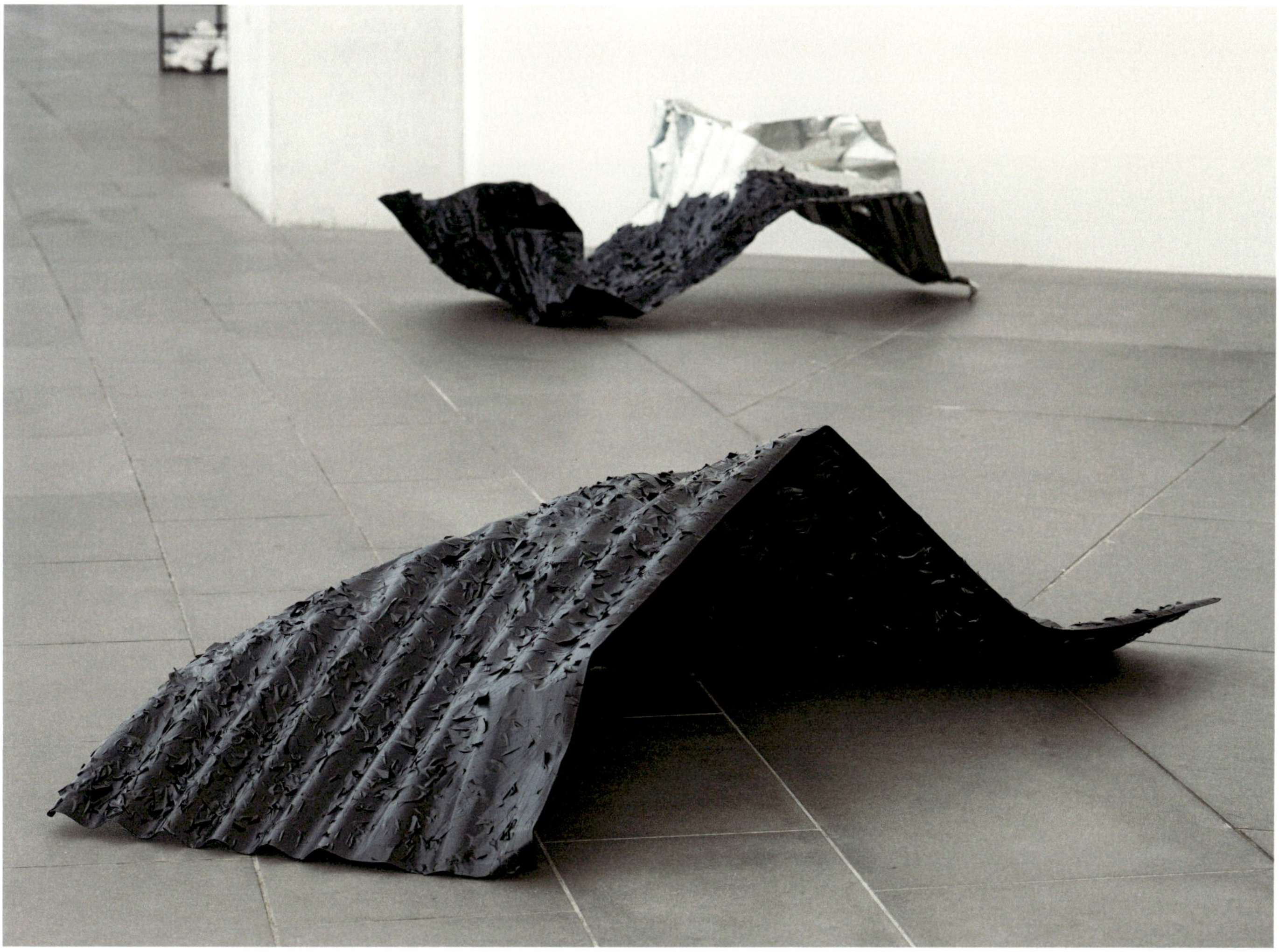

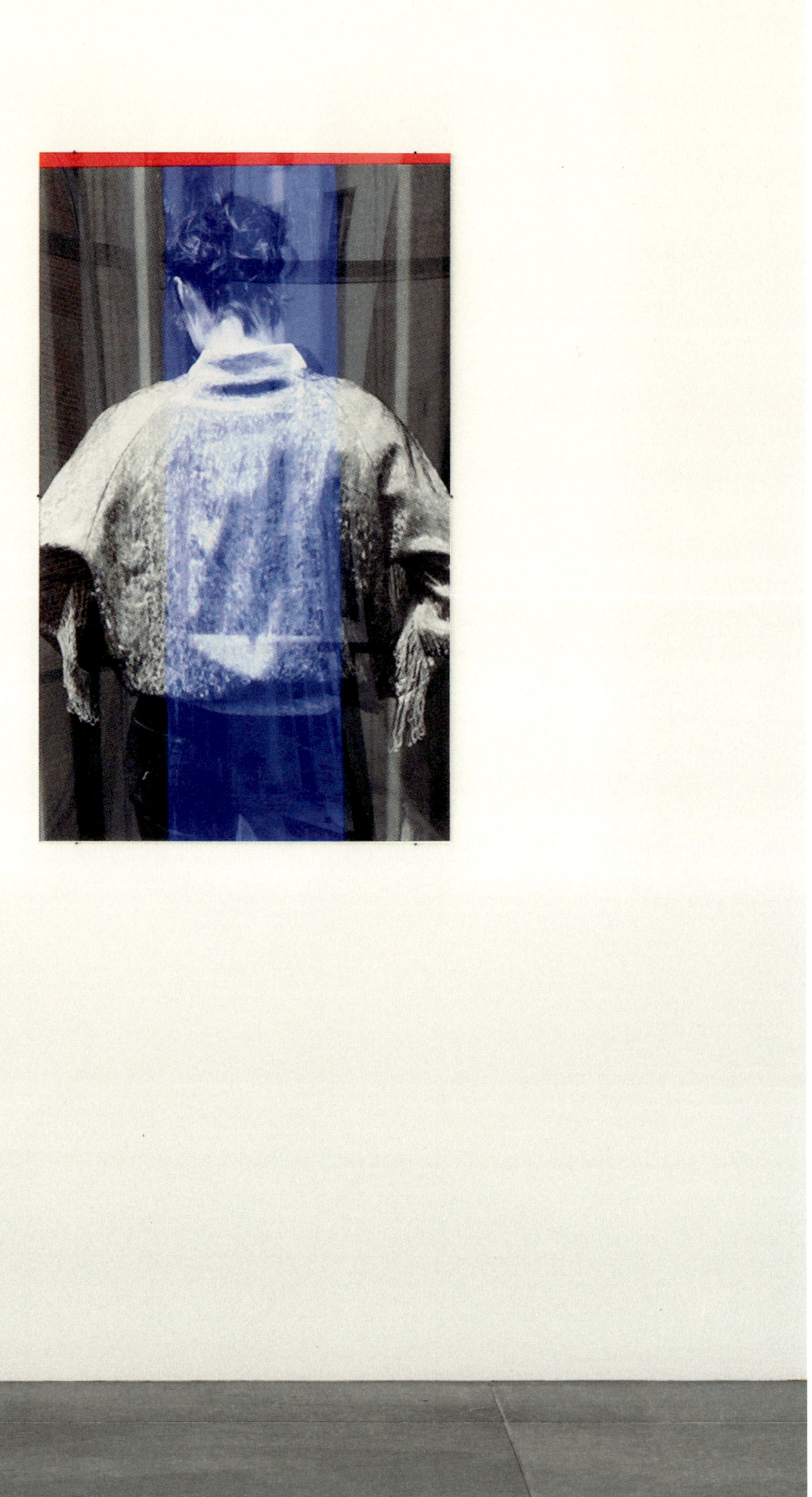

Ciara Phillips

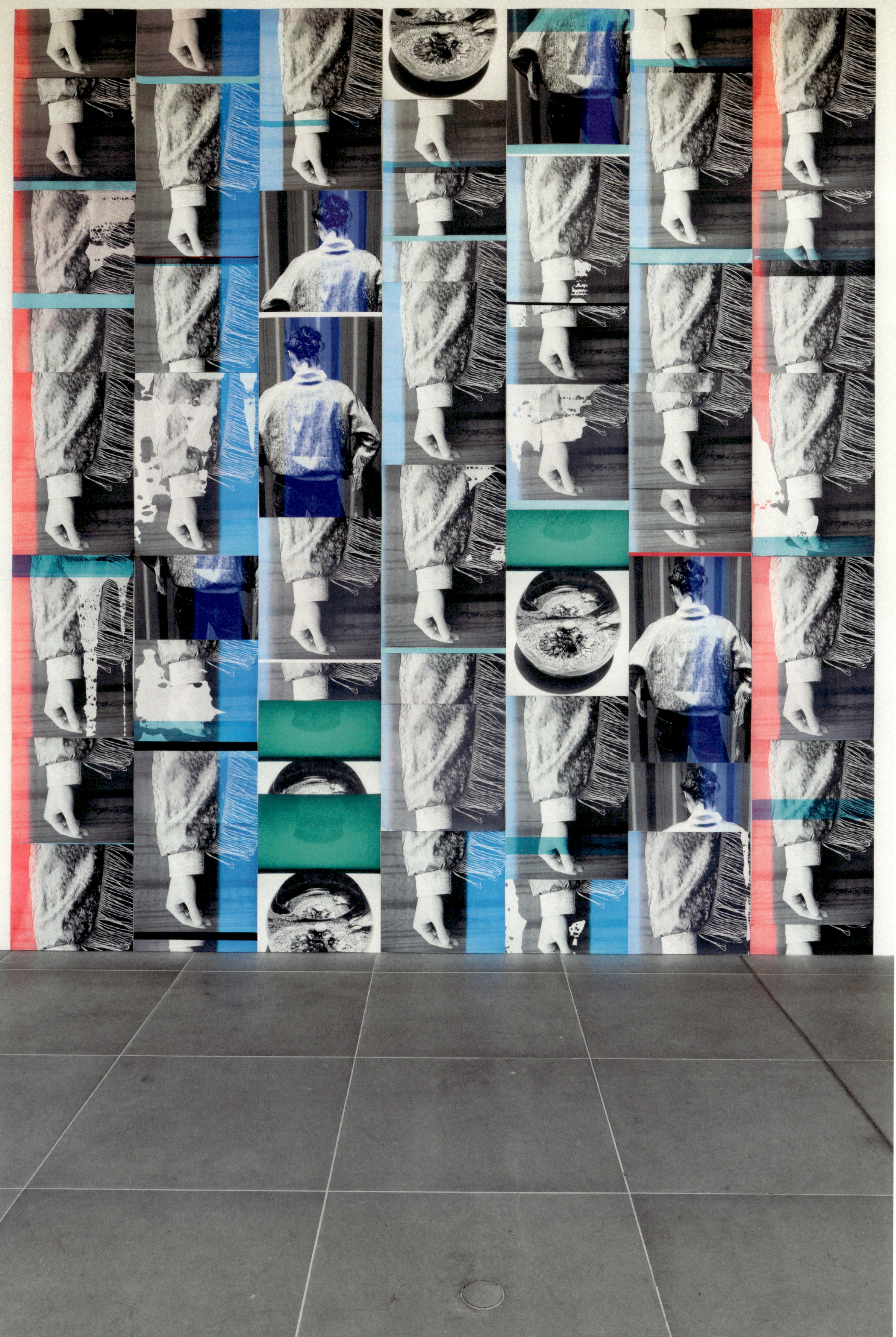

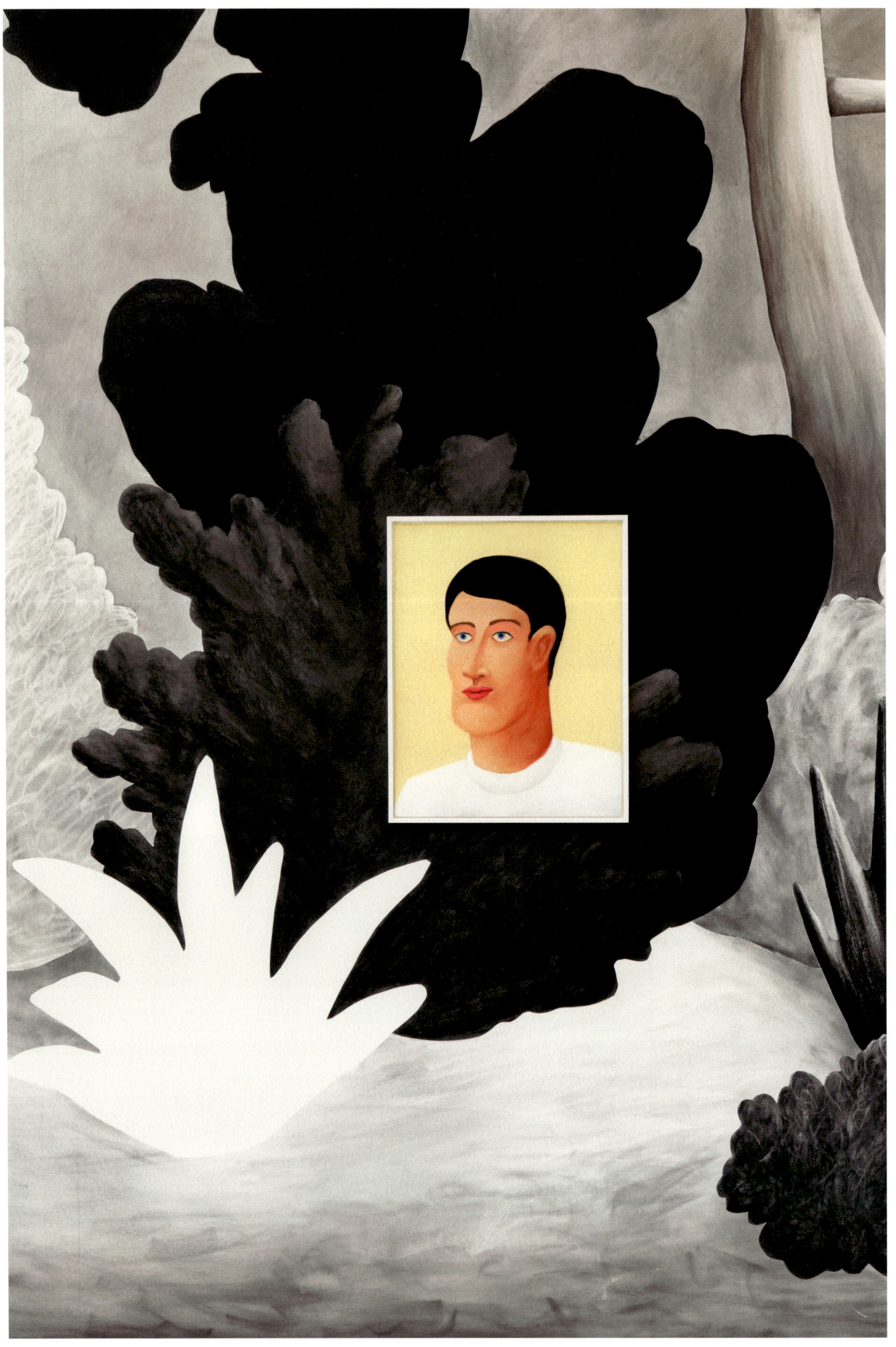

Nicolas Party

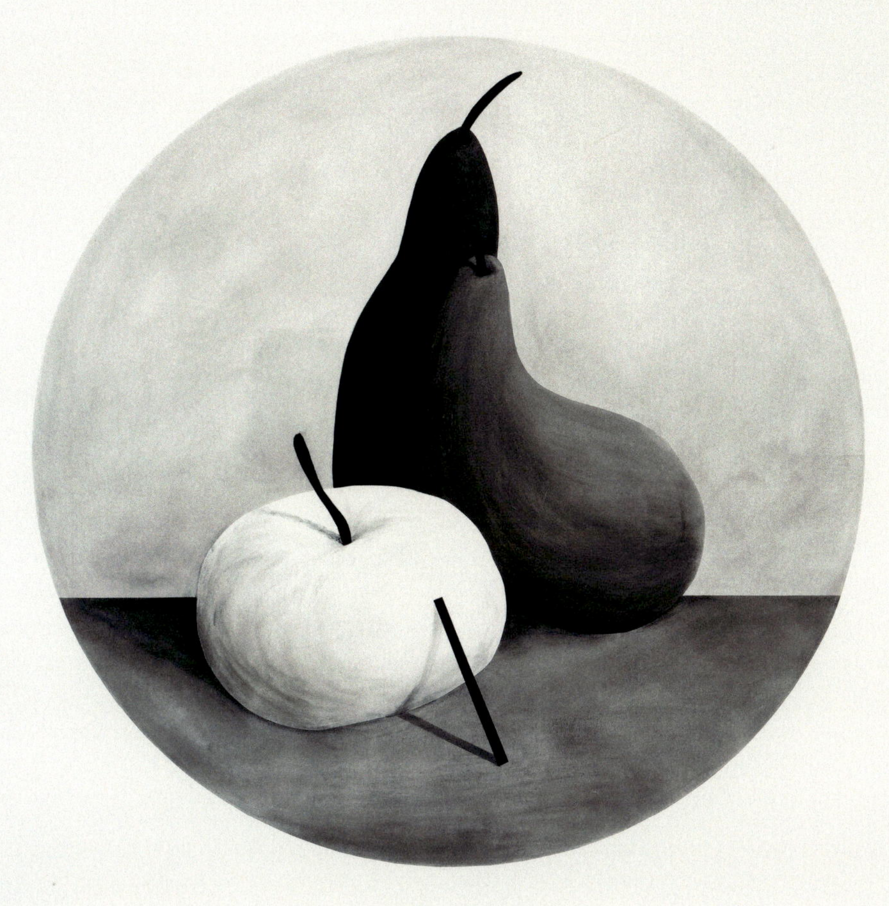

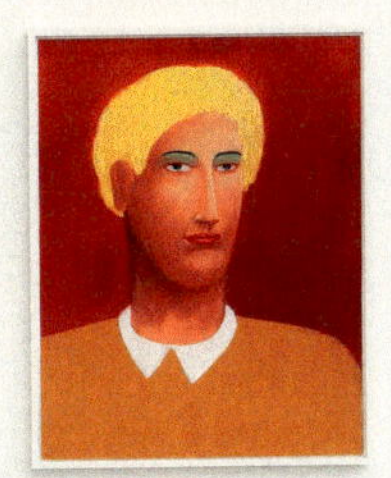

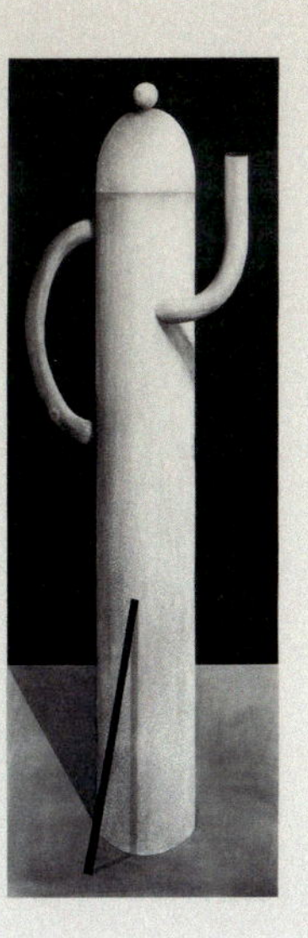

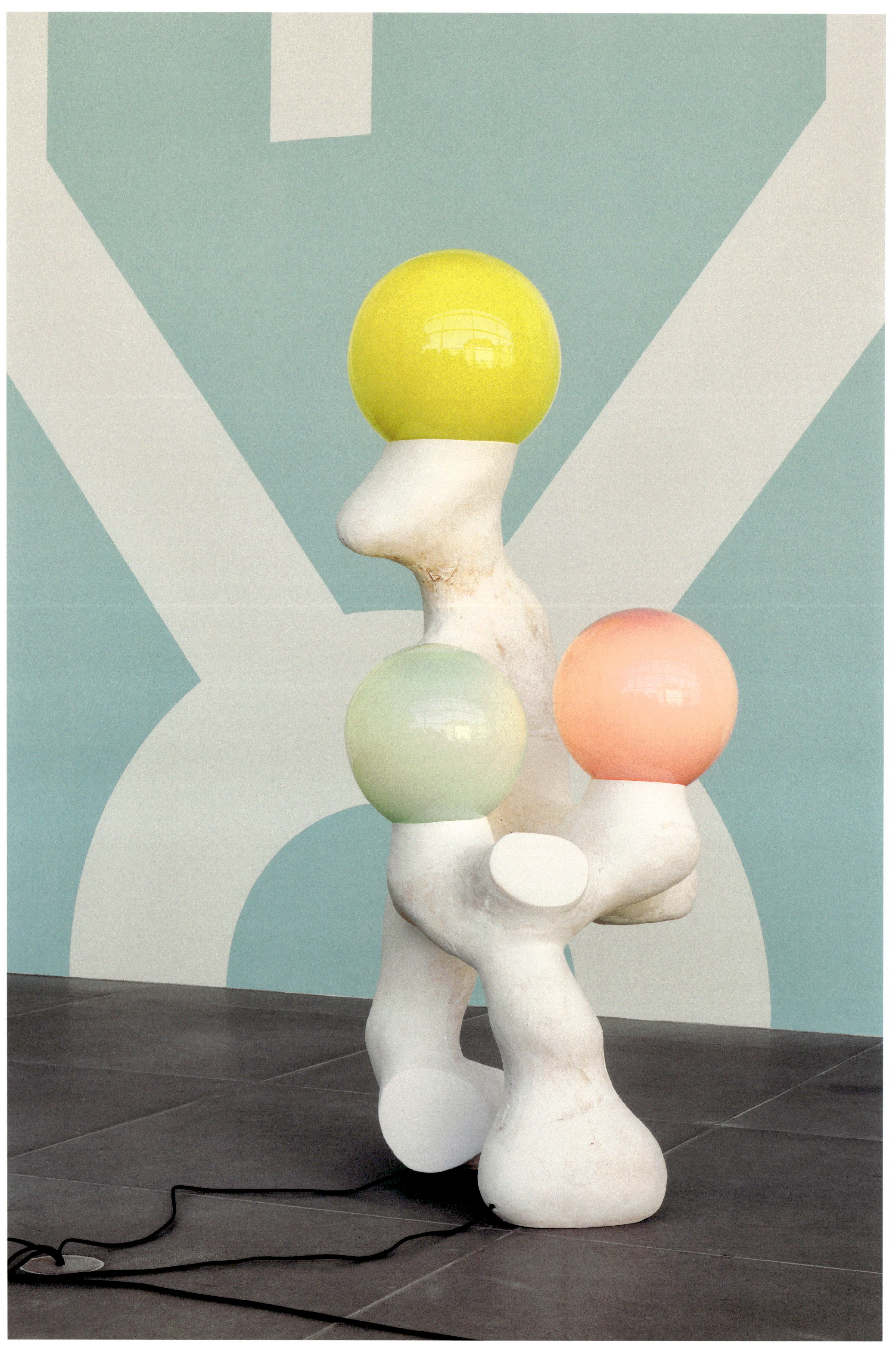

Nick Evans

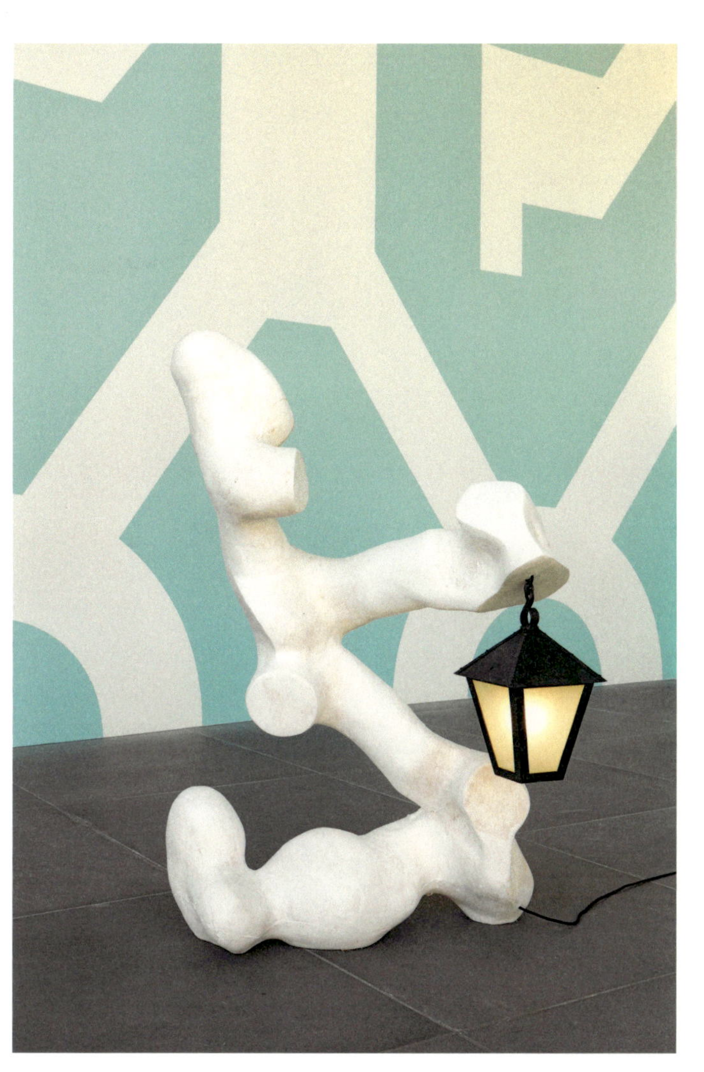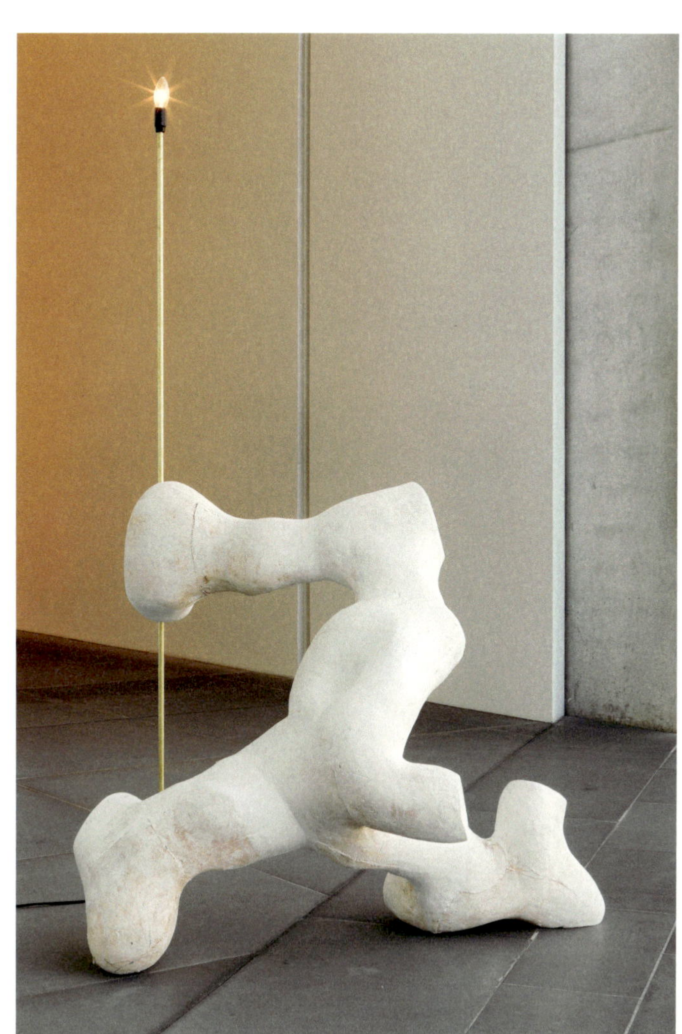

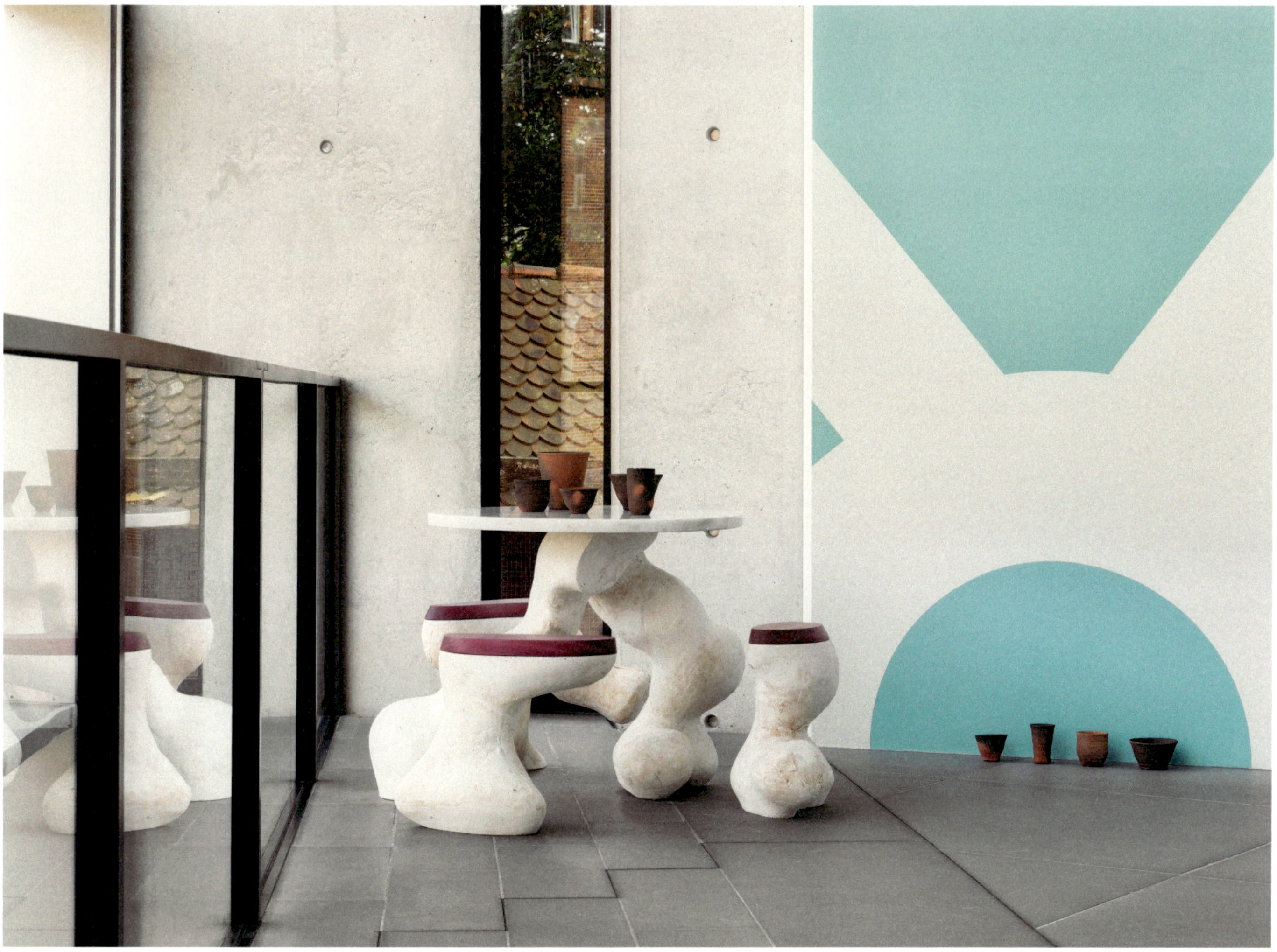

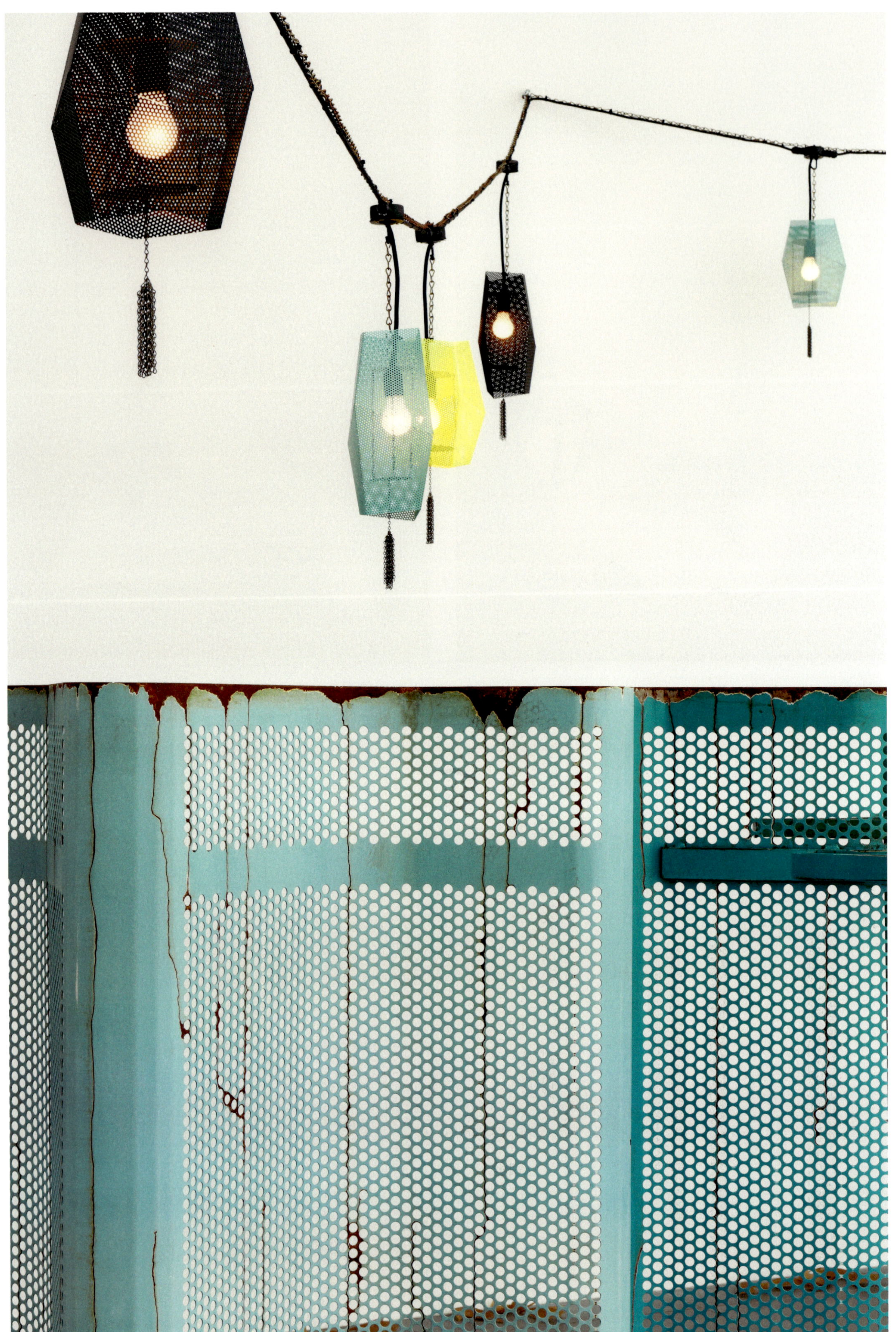

Martin Boyce

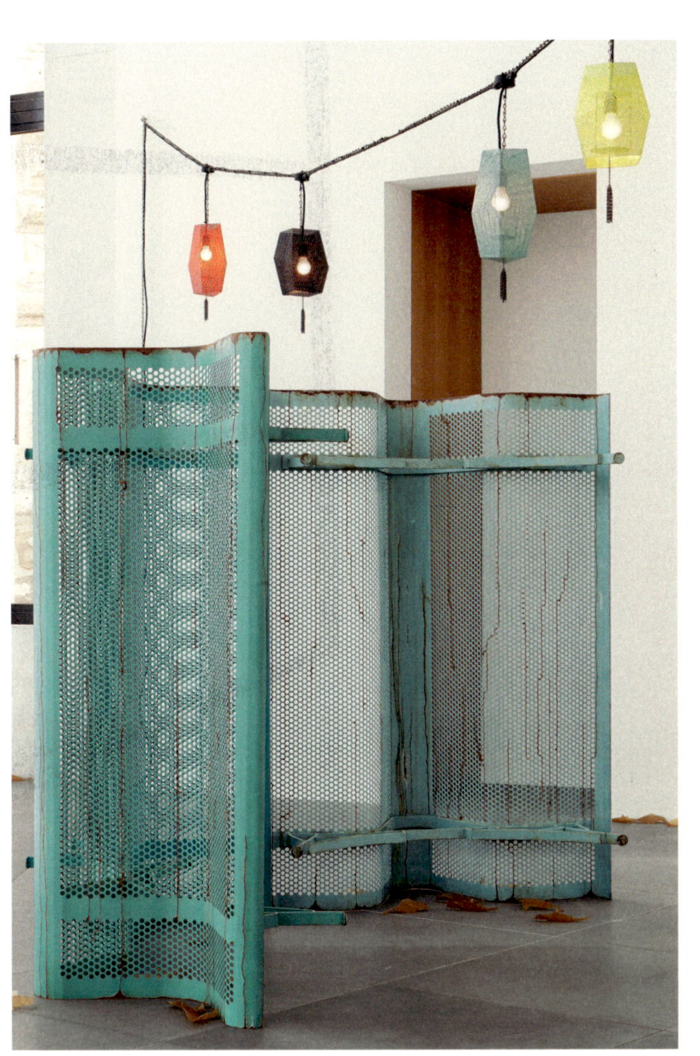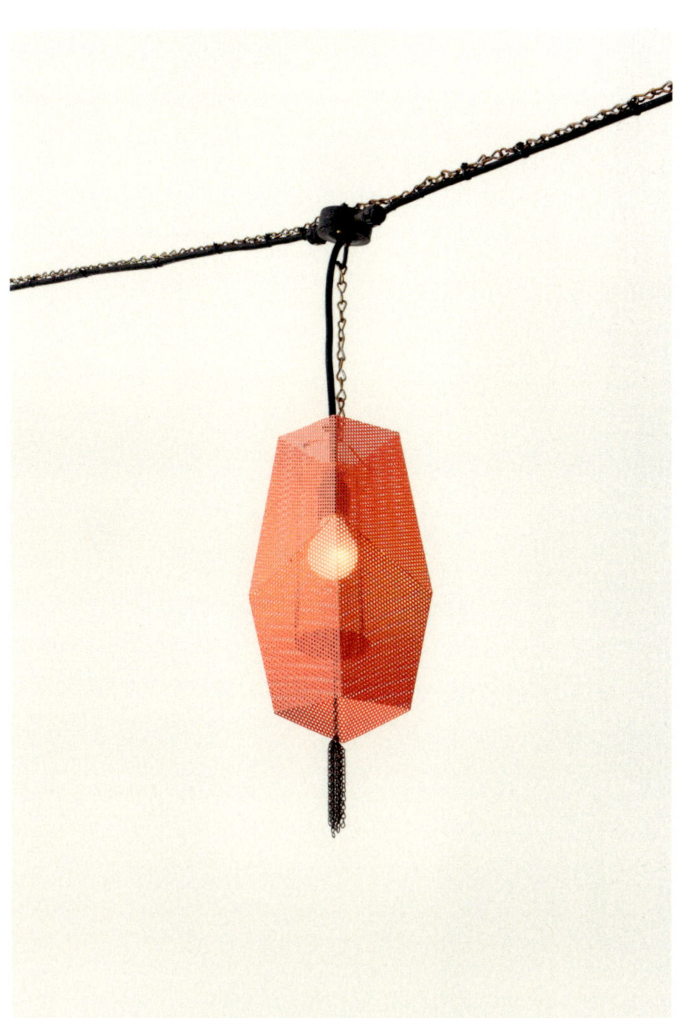

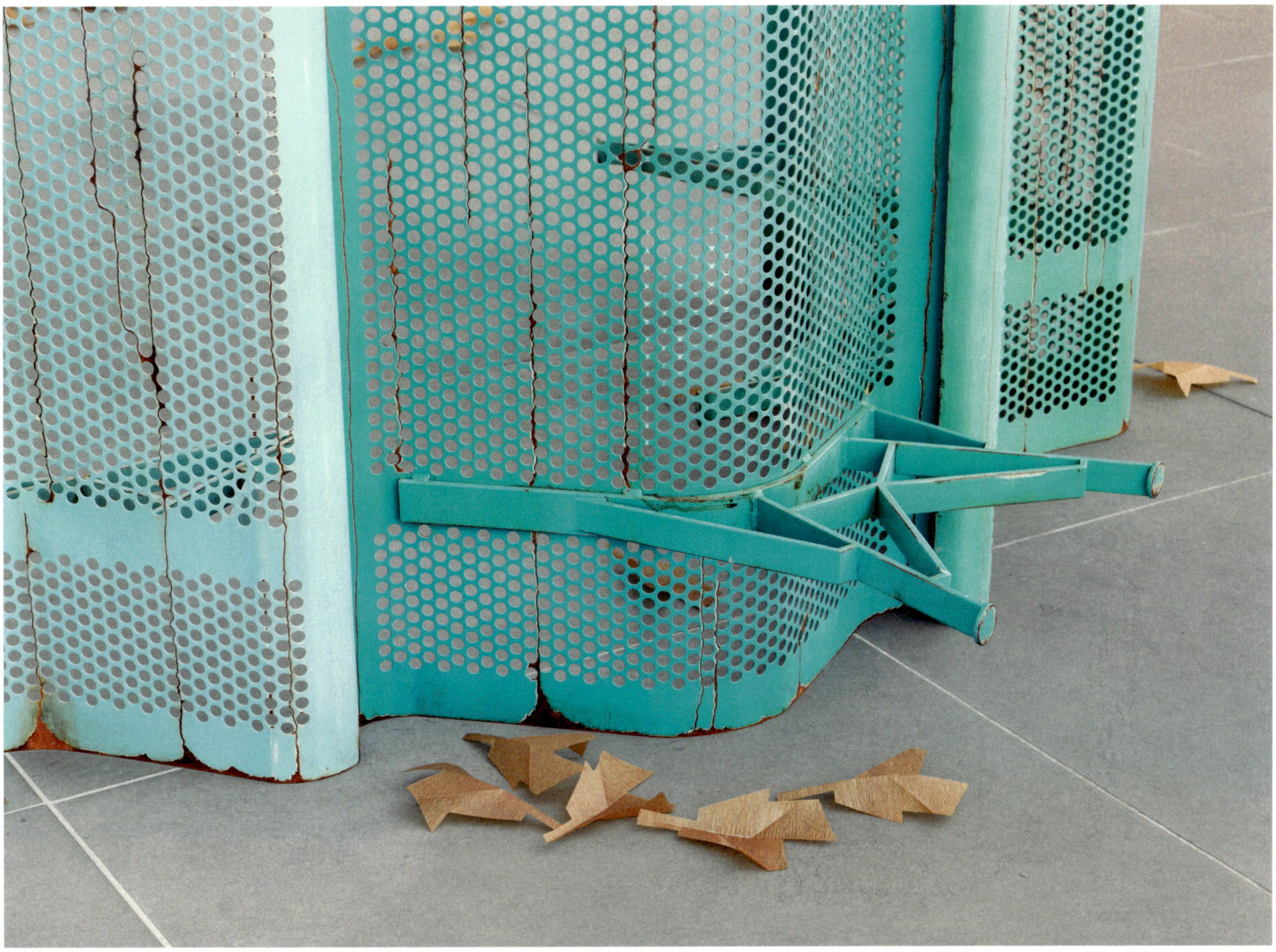

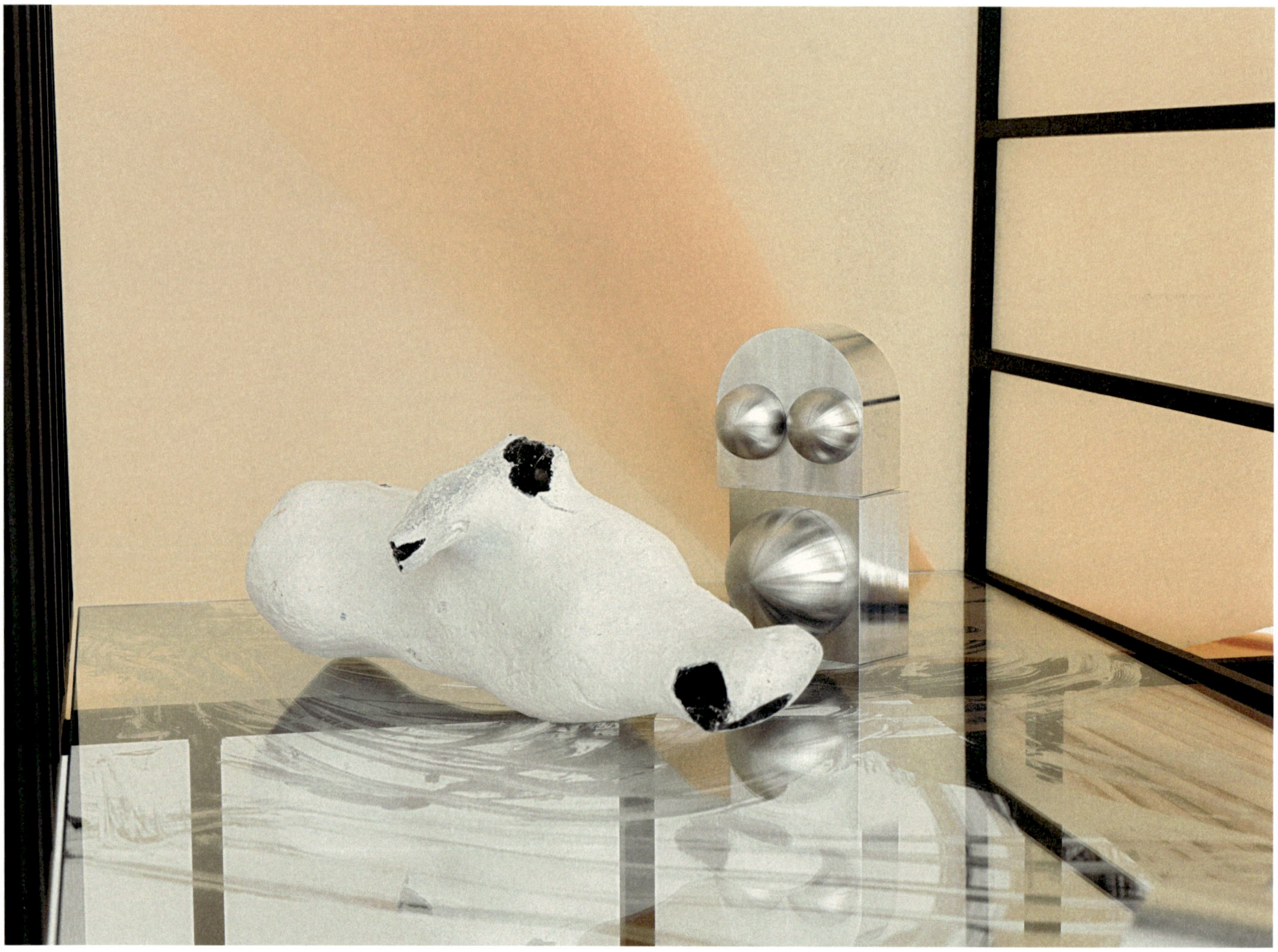

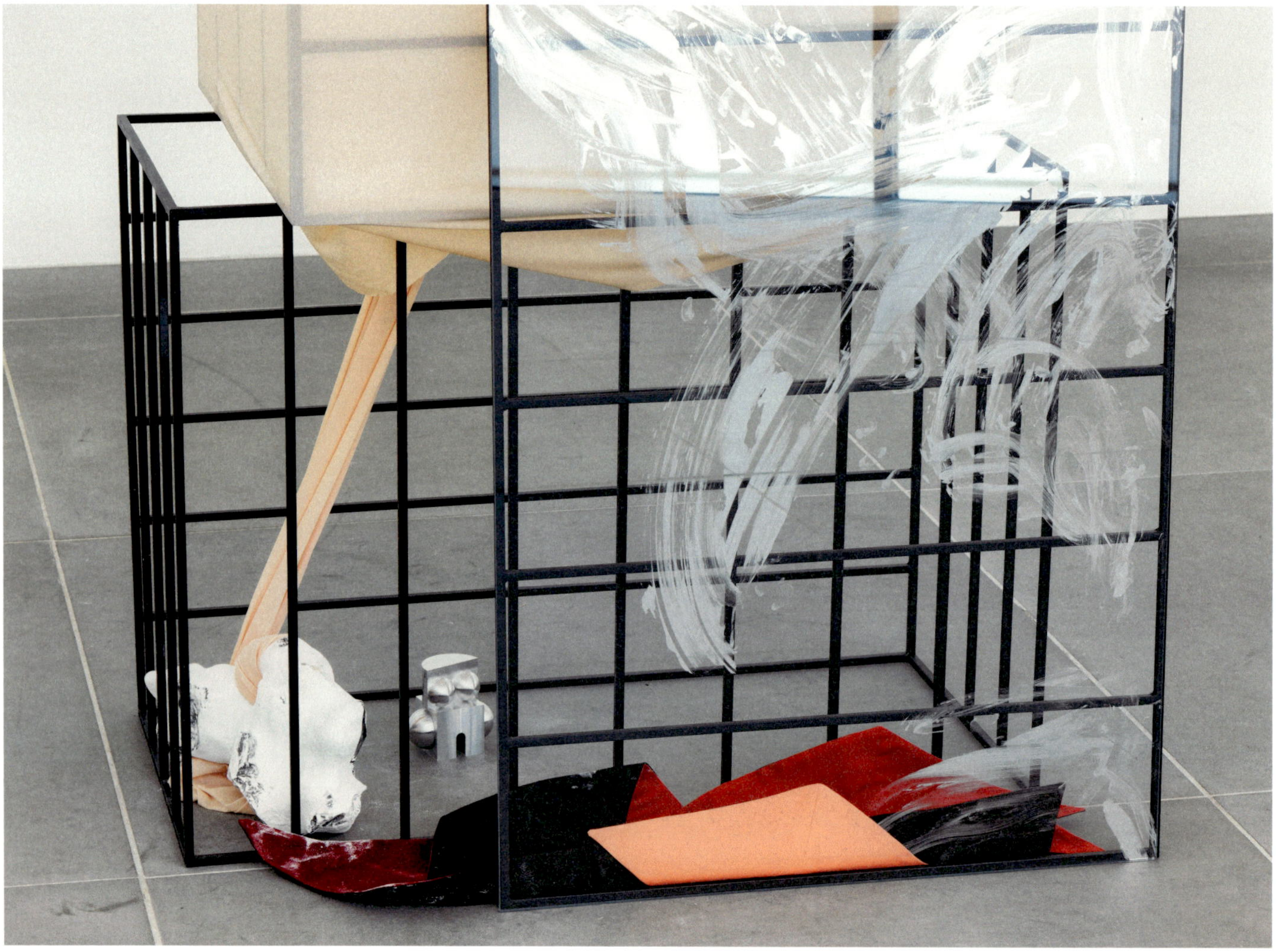

Claire Barclay

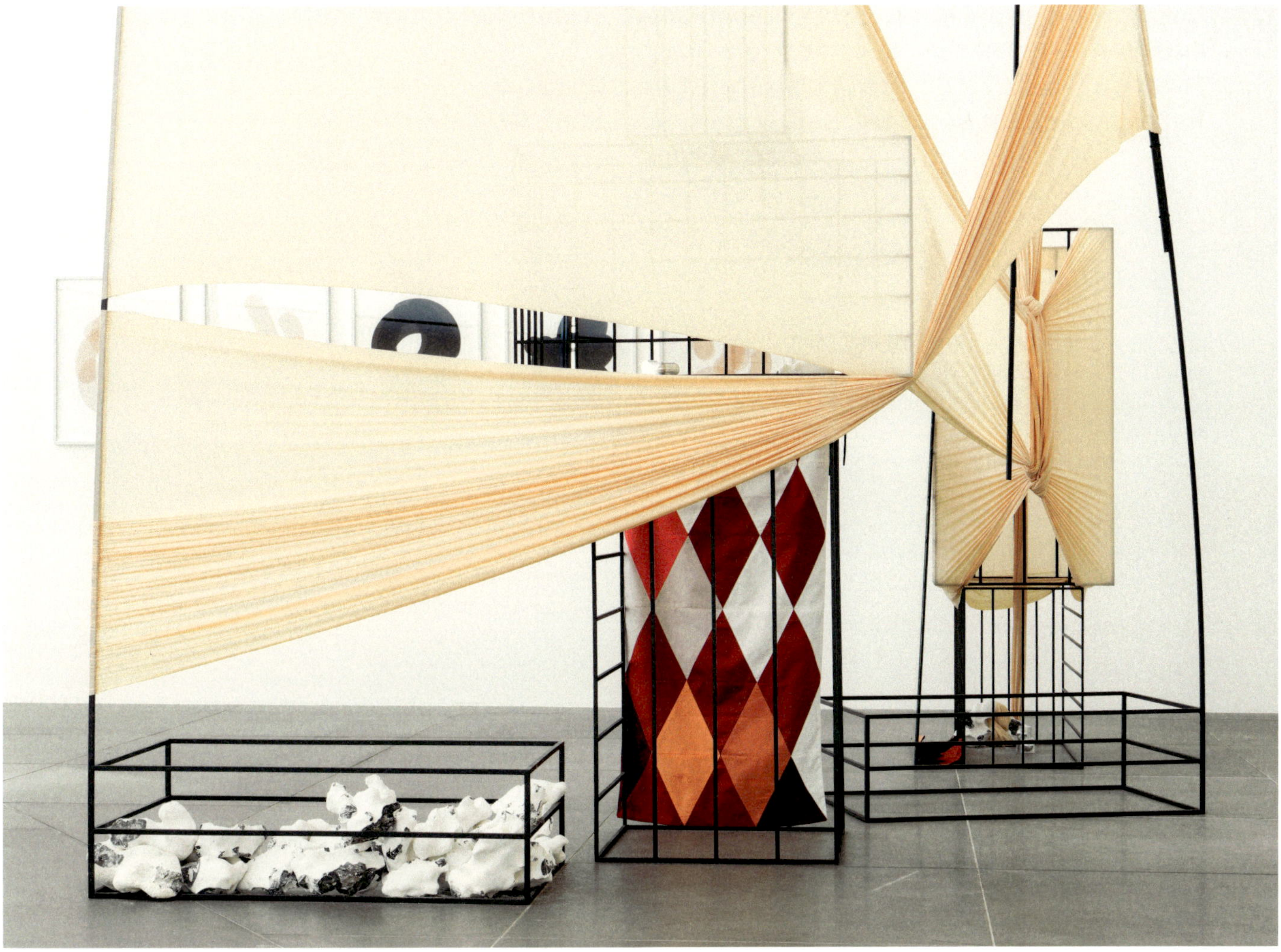

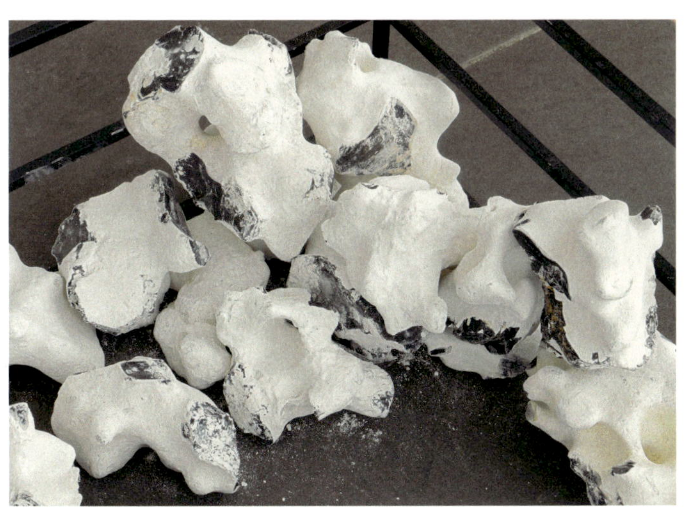

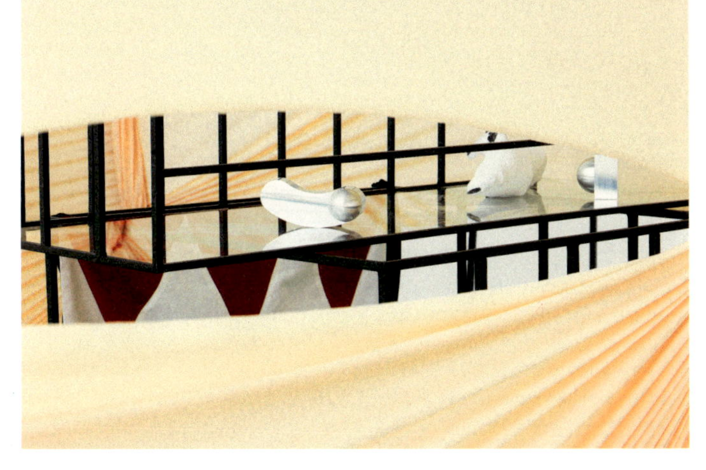

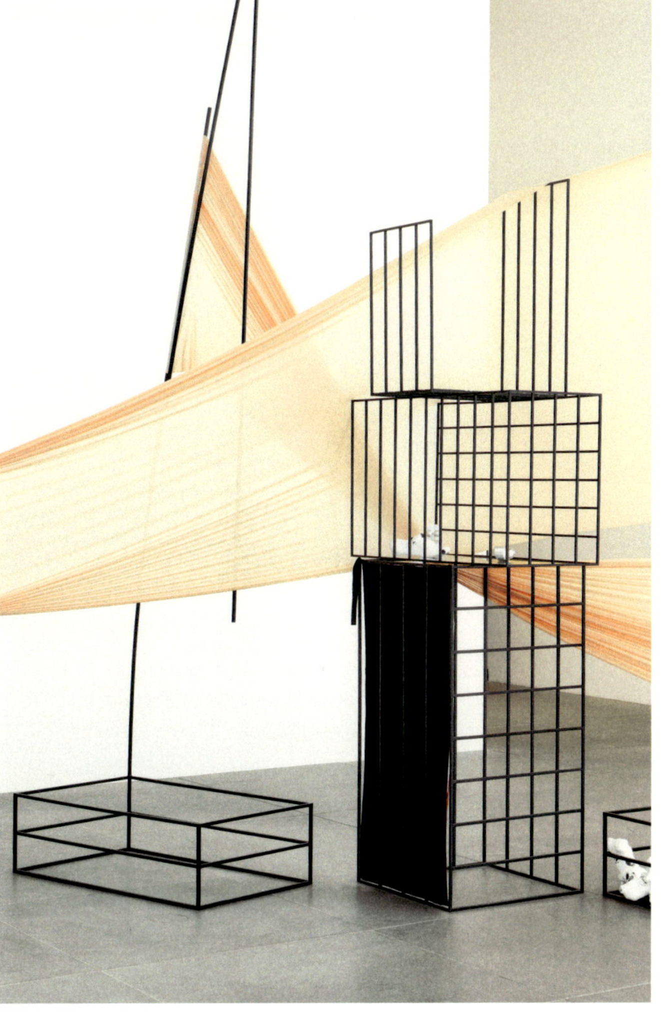

Claire Barclay

Unbound, 2013

Lackierter Stahl, Lycra, Feuerstein, maschinell
bearbeitetes Aluminium, Spiegelfarbe auf Glas,
genähter Baumwollstoff / Painted steel, Lycra, flint,
machined aluminium, mirroring paint on glass,
sewn cotton
ca. 400 × 275 × 360 cm

This other trick, 2013

Siebdrucke, gerahmt / Screen prints, framed
je / each 59,4 × 42 cm

Courtesy of the artist and Stephen Friedman Gallery, London

Martin Boyce

Evaporated Pools, 2009

Krepppapier, mit Paraffin beschichtet /
Paraffin-coated crêpe paper
je / each ca. 22 × 13 × 2 cm

*The Night Does Not Belong to Us,
It is Painted on the Air*, 2011

Sieben Laternen, Kette, lackierter Stahl, elektrische
Bestandteile / Seven lanterns, chain, painted steel,
electrical components
Laternen / Lanterns je / each ca. 50 × 30 × 30 cm
Kette / Chain ca. 1100 cm Länge / Length

The Waves, 2011

Lackierter Stahl, Rost / Painted steel, rust
288 × 194 × 200 cm

Courtesy of the artist and The Modern Institute/
Toby Webster Ltd, Glasgow

Nick Evans

Guardian with Light, 2013

Faserverstärkter Gips, bearbeitetes Messing, Leuchte /
Fibre-reinforced plaster, machined brass, light fitting
175 × 110 × 90 cm

Venus, 2013

Faserverstärkter Gips, mundgeblasene Glaskugeln,
Leuchten / Fibre-reinforced plaster, blown glass,
light fittings
145 × 60 × 80 cm

The Nightwatch, 2013

Faserverstärkter Gips, Schmiedeeisen, Glas, Leuchte /
Fibre-reinforced plaster, wrought iron, glass, light fitting
130 × 70 × 90 cm

Pacifying Giants, 2013

Wandfarbe / Wall paint
545 × 1528 cm

Nick Evans mit / with Alistair Dearie

The Picnic, 2013

Faserverstärkter Gips, Marmor, Purpleheart-Holz,
Terracotta / Fibre-reinforced plaster, marble,
purpleheart wood, terracotta
ca. 80 × 100 × 100 cm

Courtesy of the artist and Mary Mary, Glasgow

Nicolas Party

Decorative Landscape, 2013

Kohle auf Wand / Charcoal on wall
546 × 315 cm

Portraits, 2013

Pastell auf Papier / Pastel on paper
je / each 67,5 × 52,5 cm

Still Life, 2013

Kohle auf Wand / Charcoal on wall
252 × 82,2 cm und / and Ø 225 cm

Courtesy of the artist and The Modern Institute/
Toby Webster Ltd, Glasgow

Ciara Phillips

Things put together, 2013

Siebdruck auf Papier / Screen print on paper
525 × 477 cm

Things put together (Sophia), 2013

Siebdruck auf Papier / Screen print on paper
112 × 68 cm

Courtesy of the artist and Kendall Koppe, Glasgow

Mary Redmond

Low-Grade Oscillator, 2013

Wellblech, Gerüstnetz, Seil aus Seegras, Isolierband,
Kunststoffrohr, Nylon, Plastiktüten / Corrugated metal,
scaffolding netting, seagrass rope, electrical tape,
plastic pipe, nylon, plastic bags
ca. 545 × 550 × 550 cm

Courtesy of the artist and The Modern Institute/
Toby Webster Ltd, Glasgow

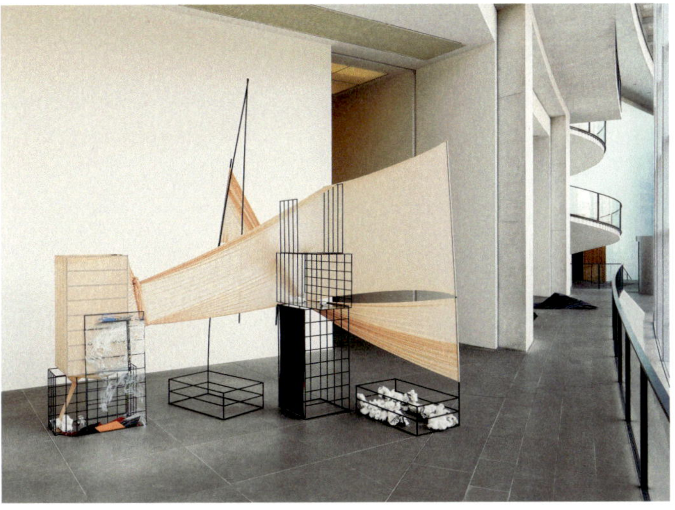

Claire Barclay

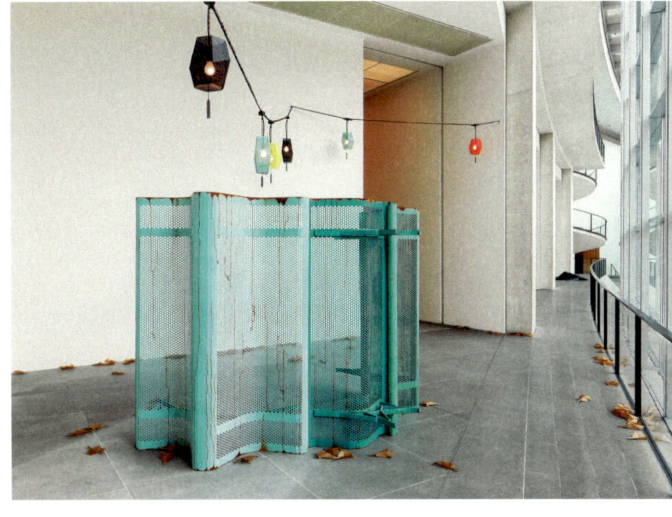

Martin Boyce

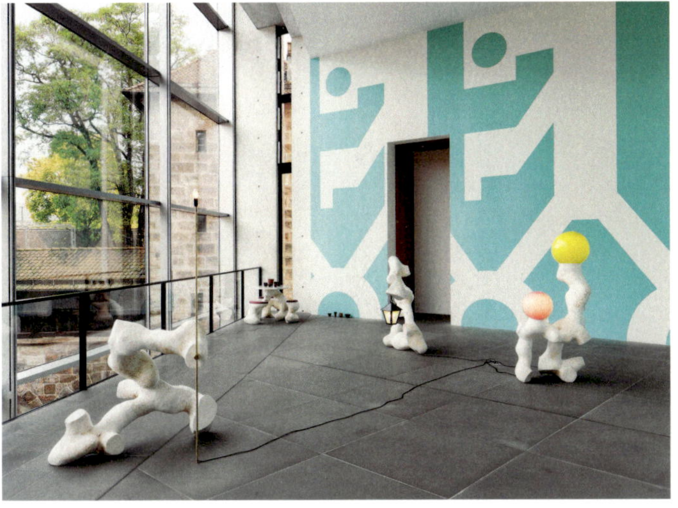

Nick Evans

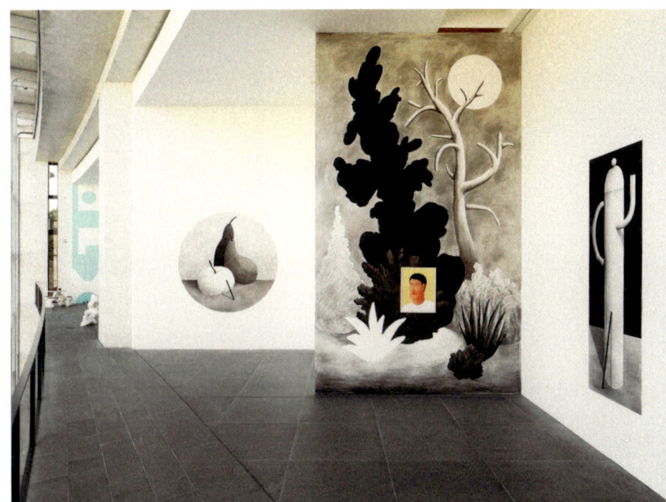

Nicolas Party

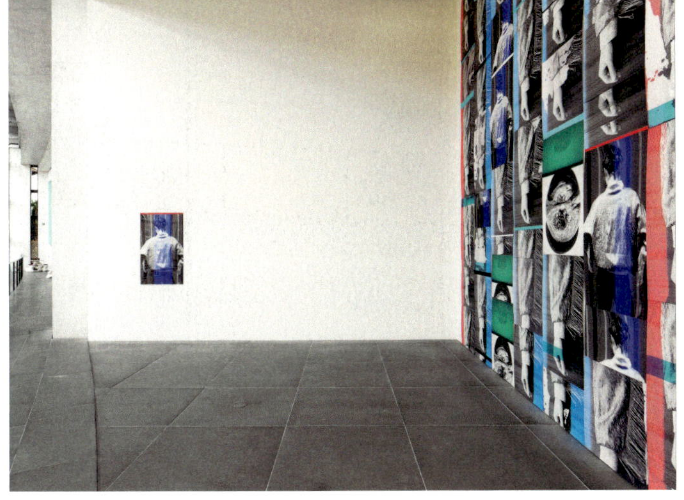

Ciara Phillips

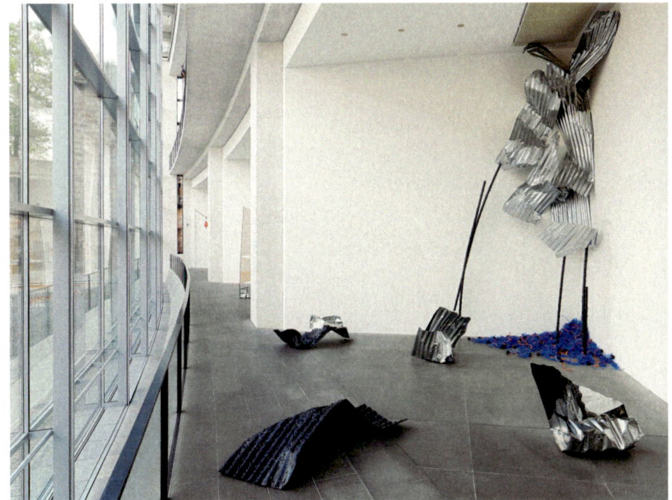

Mary Redmond

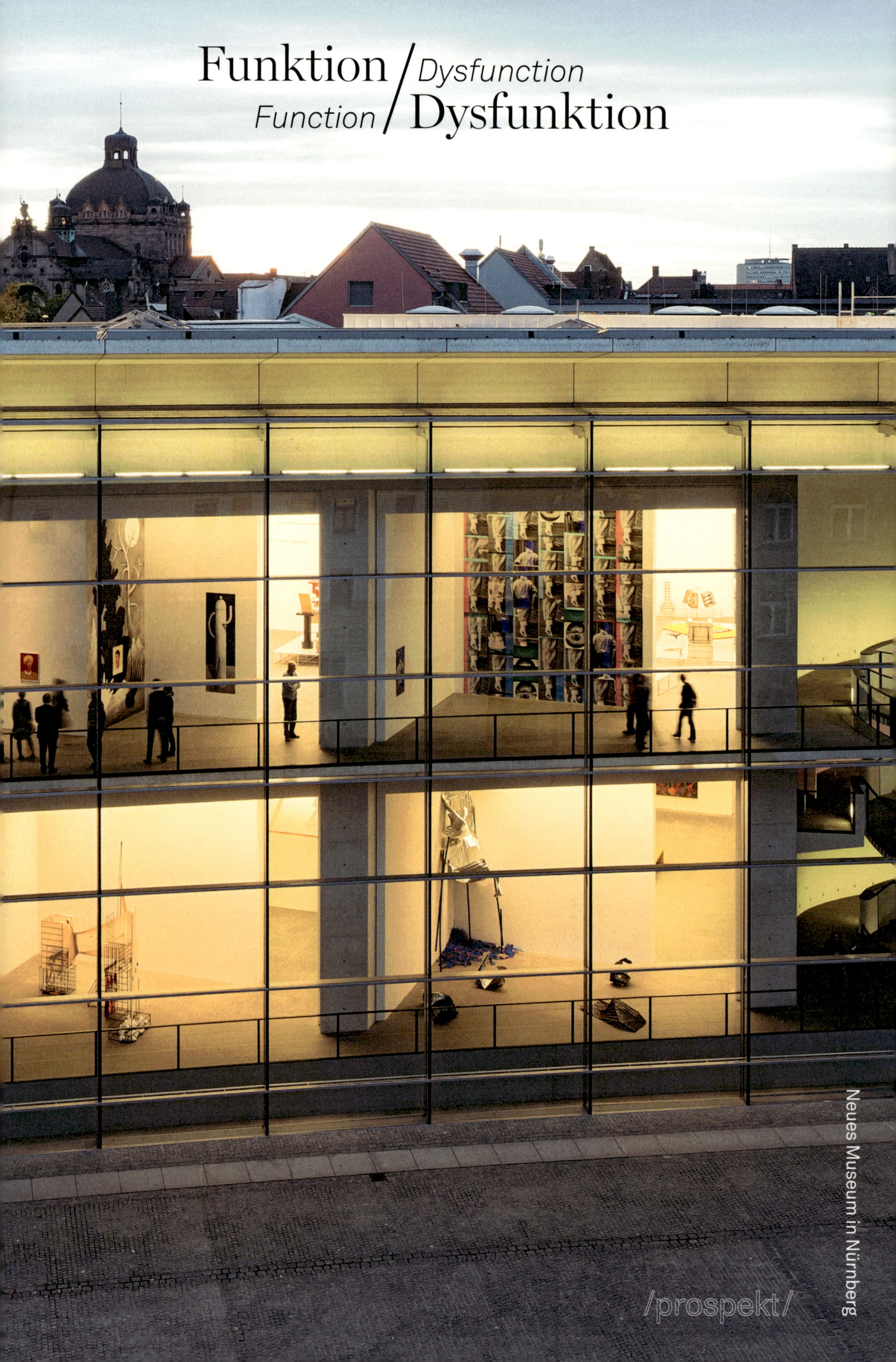

Funktion /Dysfunction
Function /Dysfunktion
Neues Museum in Nürnberg
/prospekt/